CHINA: The Other Communism

By the same author

VISA FOR POLAND

KHRUSHCHEV AND THE WEST

CHINA
The Other Communism

by K. S. KAROL

Photographs by MARC RIBOUD

Translated from the French by Tom Baistow

HILL AND WANG · New York

Designed by David J. Way

Manufactured in the United States of America
by American Book–Stratford Press, Inc.

Contents

Introduction

WHY I WENT TO CHINA

Before the war, at high school in Lodz, in Poland, I heard it said that the Chinese need only arm themselves with sticks to form an invincible army. The assertion was made by a geography teacher, Thadee Greyber. He was no racist and had no intention of instilling in us a fear of the "yellow peril." Quite the opposite; he was distressed to see the peaceful, hard-working, and poor Chinese allowing themselves to be beaten by the Japanese militarists, the allies of our enemies of the Berlin-Rome axis.

I do not know why or how Thadee Greyber had ended up in the respectable high school of a Polish provincial city. He had lived in France for a long time, spoke several languages, and taught geography, in which he had no interest whatsoever. He lived among his memories and loved to tell us about the world. In all his tales one felt a passionate antifascism, very rare in the conformist Poland of that period. The ideas he expressed in class could have gotten him into trouble, but his colleagues regarded him as an eccentric and did not take him seriously. Nor did his pupils. With scant respect, they called him "Uncle Greyber," and in his class they did anything that came into their heads. But Uncle Greyber never gave anyone bad grades; on the contrary, he rewarded all who listened open-mouthed to his tales. I was one of these, and I owe him a lot. It was he who made me want to see the wide world, who made me feel that everything that happened concerned me, and that, for example, the far-off Chinese were fighting the same battle as the European antifascists. Thanks to him I had a vague fellow-feeling for the Chinese, who had suffered so much and only asked to live in peace; indeed, those sticks with which Greyber would have liked to see the Chinese arm themselves would only be used to drive the foreigners out and nothing more.

Adolescent memories die hard. During my stay in China, each time I saw youngsters drilling with wooden guns I thought of Thadee Greyber and his ardent talks on the invincibility of China. Sometimes I even wondered what would have happened in the 1930's if the Chinese had been armed as my teacher had wished — if they might not have enabled fascism to be crushed sooner, and

2

if, by the same token, World War II might not have been avoided. In short, I was dreaming. My guides noticed this and worried about it, as they do not like to see their protégés get lost, even in the clouds. They were wrong; by raking up the past in this way I was beginning to understand why China did not appear at all menacing to me, despite her intention to be completely militarized.

If the rickshaw coolies have happily disappeared, many other Chinese "images" confirmed the ideas I had formed about this country when I was still at school: poor peasants bent double in the rice paddies, working with their bare hands; long files of men yoked to carts, pulling enormous loads; women hobbling along on their tiny bound feet; the teeming streets of overcrowded neighborhoods in the big cities. Today China is liberated, but the old China has not completely vanished. Traces of the aggression and exploitation to which she was subjected by the great industrial powers can still be found everywhere, but the country is visibly changing.

Those who have not seen the Chinese at work in vast gangs, building dams or roads just with their hands, cannot know what these people are capable of. Watching the Chinese undertake and finish gargantuan projects almost without tools, one does not know whether to applaud in admiration at their astonishing tenacity or to despair of a world that denies them proper equipment. For today the Chinese are conquering underdevelopment as my teacher imagined they would be able to win a war: with their hands, with sticks — and with their sheer numbers.

Admittedly, I arrived in China prejudiced in their favor. But it happens that I am familiar with most of the great industrial countries of the West, and the contrast between their prosperity and China's austerity and poverty is such that one asks with astonishment how a European or, even more incredible, a North American, who even if he is not rich lives comfortably, can be anti-Chinese and invoke the "yellow peril" to justify his hostility. Are the Westerners simply afraid that these poor ex-victims of the colonial powers are going to seize their wealth tomorrow? Does their bad conscience make them fear that one day the Chinese may demand redress for the misery and injustices to which their forefathers and fathers were subjected? Or are they simply blinded by an unthinking and primal anticommunism? There is no doubt that China has never had so many enemies as she has today, and yet she is still the victim of the established order of the world, an order which favors the already privileged countries.

But I do not seek to make you weep over China's misery. It is not the economic backwardness of China that is interesting, but the fact that she is now overcoming this by carrying out, at the cost of an enormous effort, an unprecedented experiment which, in view of her vast size and population, is inevitably bound to have consequences for the rest of the world. What I have just written may read like a slogan, but it is the truth; within a few decades a rural land of 650 million inhabitants, still virtually in the Middle Ages, will have transformed itself into an industrialized and modern country. It will suffer to achieve this transformation, and the mental attitudes of the Chinese of tomorrow will be shaped as much by their sufferings as by the traditions of their ancient civilization. It is therefore important to forget prejudices and to try to understand this incredible drive toward emancipation.

Given that, understanding means neither complete approval nor uncritical partisanship. I knew that I would see things in China that would repel or disturb me; this is not the first time I have found myself in a country that was "building socialism" — I am even a veteran in the building of socialism. At sixteen, driven by the war from my high school, from Lodz, and from Poland, I found myself plunged into the Soviet universe — a universe, I was assured, I would have to live in forever.

I was not unhappy about this, and I shed few tears for the colonels' Poland, wiped off the map in 1939. I was too young to be a member of the Communist Party, but I wholeheartedly supported it. In truth, I was even enraptured by it — so much so that I did not complain at the welcome my new Soviet fatherland gave me and all the other Poles who had fled the German occupation. A rather cold welcome, literally and figuratively: for me — and for many others — the road to Moscow passed through Siberia. This merely increased my happiness at reaching it. In Red Square, in front of the inscription in gold letters which proclaims the Soviets' solidarity with their "class brothers, prisoners of capitalism," I wept with joy and relief. This was shortly after the signing of the German-Soviet pact, however, and at that very moment, on the bridge over the Bug River, the U.S.S.R. was handing over German Communists to their Nazi executioners.

Five years later, toward the end of the war, I found myself in the same spot to meet the leaders of the Union of Polish Patriots, future cadres of the future Warsaw Communist administration, which had its headquarters in the Moskva Hotel. We spoke of our approaching return to Poland and of our intention to establish socialism there, of course, but without the misery and terror which had raged in the U.S.S.R. We discussed these "seditious" ideas while strolling around Red Square to avoid indiscreet ears and microphones. I no longer remember what slogan was then written on the walls of the GUM department store, which faces Lenin's mausoleum, and in any case I no longer had faith in slogans.

Returning to Poland in 1946, I asked myself too many disturbing questions about the U.S.S.R. to be able to throw myself completely into establishing the socialism of which she was the patron and to which I felt she would sooner or later apply her own methods. Chauvinism having already done too much harm in Poland, the idea of playing on the Polish nationalist sentiments to counterbalance the Soviet influence seemed to me a dangerous one. I felt ill at ease in the homeland I had returned to; perhaps I was destined to become an expatriate.

When I finally settled in France, I still believed in socialism. I did not dream, like many other refugees, of personal revenge; I did not wish my country's regime to collapse. Like many Western intellectuals, I continued to hope that communism would gradually become rational and international once more, that it would open its doors again to the search for truth, and that it would cease to be an article of faith. What I had seen during the seven years I spent in the Soviet Union proved to me, if there was any need of proof, that penury, dogmatism, and a country's intellectual withdrawal into itself did not mold model supermen capable of turning a great humanist ideal into reality. But perhaps these evils were inevitable in the first phase of the socialization of an underdeveloped country threatened from the outside, as the U.S.S.R. had been. And perhaps, once the most serious material difficulties had been overcome, the countries of Eastern Europe would resume their links with the universalist tradition and undertake the building of a society that was really collectivist.

When de-Stalinization began it was possible to hope that the Soviet bloc was taking this road. The old "religion" was seriously attacked; no one believed any longer that the highest leaders were the keepers of an absolute and unvarying truth which they protected against all criticism. Now everyone was going to be able to discuss things freely and rationally. Admittedly, ingrained habits in the various Communist countries and parties checked the movement, some religious souls bitterly defended the old faith that no one shared any more, and de-Stalinization gave rise to new contradictions in this world which had forgotten how a democracy really works. Liberty would come slowly, but the trend was irreversible; and we in Europe had the feeling that in spite of everything, the Eastern bloc was opening up. It was at this moment that the Chinese violently opposed the U.S.S.R.'s new policy. To be truthful, it was not unexpected.

Stalin had exploited the Soviet Union's proclaimed internationalism too cynically. No one believed it any more, and the idea of unconditional loyalty to the U.S.S.R. as the first socialist country and the leader of the world revolution was accepted only grudgingly. Each Communist country and party, without saying so openly, sought to recover its liberty of action and to protect its own interests more effectively. The Yugoslavs, and then the Poles and the Hungarians, all moved from veiled opposition to open conflict with Moscow before China did. But only China had the necessary weight and could hope to take the Soviet Union's place at the head of the international Communist movement.

From the time of her entry on the scene, therefore, China has played a key role in world politics. It has become impossible to ignore her and necessary to know her, not out of any sympathy for her or for any romantic reason, but because too many things depend on her.

"I have believed too long in the Soviet paradise to be able to believe now that another paradise even more remote and even more unknowable exists," Pierre Courtade, editorial writer and then Moscow correspondent of *L'Humanité,* told me shortly before his death. He had been a militant since the age of twenty and regarded membership in the Party as total commitment. I liked him and was his friend, but I pitied him for having to justify all the Party's decisions — even those which disturbed him deeply or, sometimes, dismayed him.

For my part, I never believed that China was a paradise, but I wanted to know what Chinese communism was like and to try to judge it on the spot and from the facts, without prejudice. As long as I had not *seen,* I felt I was not capable of holding opinions on the international policy of the Chinese, still less on their domestic policies. I have already said that I had a certain sympathy for this country and for its revolution, but I was in no sense unconditionally partisan, and in any case I had no special qualification which might make it easier for me to get an entry visa — which is not so easy.

A LUNCH IN ALGIERS

I secured this visa thanks entirely to a happy chain of circumstances. Thus the first Chinese person I was able to talk to about my book was Prime Minister Chou En-lai in person, on Christmas Day, 1963, during an official luncheon to which I had been invited almost by accident. To my great surprise, Chou En-lai was interested in my project and promised me his help. Six months later the Chinese Embassy in Paris told me my request was being considered, and six months after that I had my visa.

But the whole story goes further back. In 1962 my friend Marc Riboud, a photographer with the Magnum agency, suggested that I make a trip to China with him. Marc Riboud knows Asia well; he lived in India for a year; and in 1957 he had spent four months in China, had a great desire to go back there, and was the ideal companion for this kind of venture, which is much better undertaken by two people. So I agreed, and we had no difficulty finding publishers to finance us.

But to start with I had a personal difficulty to overcome. Although I have lived in Paris since 1950, I have not yet obtained my naturalization papers. I travel on the gray pass of a "Polish refugee," which immigration officers and policemen always look at with an astonishment tinged with distrust. For every trip, I have to apply for a visa, say why I want it, and above all convince the consuls concerned that I intend to return to France and not settle in their countries. Usually this involves nothing more than a loss of time, and, with the backing of the journals for which I work, I get my visa. I was not sure that the Chinese would be so easily satisfied.

Certainly, since I work for the *New Statesman,* I could have gone to the Chinese consul in London (at that time there was none in Paris), but I would have had to tell him: "I am a *New Statesman* journalist but I live in France on a Polish refugee pass after having been a Soviet citizen for seven years." I had a feeling that I would not be taken too seriously. And although I had written numerous articles on the Communist world, I told myself this would not make up for the hodgepodge of my national status. Moreover, the Chinese were then bitterly defending Stalin's Russia; they would therefore be particularly suspicious of someone who had left during the "good days" and had not spoken well of it — all the more so since, as we know, the Stalinists prefer rightists to those who criticize them from a socialist point of view.

Anticipating a certain refusal, I decided therefore to ask the advice of my friend Edgar Snow, author of a number of books on China; so, accompanied by Marc Riboud, I visited him at his home in Saint Cergue, Switzerland.

Edgar Snow, nonconformist American, has never been a Communist or even a fellow-traveler. He was simply in China at the height of her misfortunes and wanted to know who the "Red bandits" were and what they thought. In 1936 he sought them out in their remote hide-out in the Northwest and asked them why they were fighting. Mao Tse-tung answered him in person and even told him his life story. The other Communist chiefs could hardly do less, and Snow brought back from his trip a veritable "Who's Who" of Red China. He knows the country as no one else does. One needs only to open any serious book on China in order to see that they all owe something to Snow and that contemporary Sinologists and political analysts, no matter what country they are from, have borrowed abundantly from his works.

Snow told me that he could do nothing to enable me to secure a visa; too many journalists had already asked for his help, and in any case it would be of no use. Although without any intention of discouraging me, he told me that in his opinion I stood very little chance. Yet it was the single fact of knowing Snow which enabled me to get into China — and that brings me to a luncheon in Algiers.

In December, 1963, the Chinese government delegation, led by Chou En-lai, was making its first African tour. In Algiers the delegates were very effectively protected from the press; journalists were not allowed to see the Chinese except from a second-story balcony. Twenty attempts that I made to meet with Chou En-lai produced no results. I was on the point of returning to Paris when, to my great surprise, I received an invitation to a luncheon which Messrs. Bouteflika and Belkacem[1] were giving in honor of Chou En-lai at the university city on December 25. I had the good luck at

---

[1] M. Bouteflika is the Minister of Foreign Affairs and M. Cherif Belkacem was at that time the Minister of Education.

the table to find myself next to an interpreter and almost facing the Chinese premier.

Chou En-lai already knew his hosts and seemed very happy to see them again. At sixty-nine he did not have a gray hair in his head and looked younger than his years. Very aware of his charm, smiling, laughing, telling anecdotes, he was the life of the party. Toward the end of the meal, taking advantage of a lull in the conversation, I dropped Edgar Snow's name, wondering if Chou En-lai would react. He did. Turning his black eyes on me, he asked for news of our common friend. A moment later he leaned toward Bouteflika and asked him a question which I did not hear and to which Bouteflika replied rather loudly, "He is not an Algerian, but he is a friend of the Algerian revolution." As Chou En-lai apparently wanted to know more about me, Bouteflika added, "He is a journalist who is the friend of all revolutions."

This was the moment to bring up my biographical and national hodgepodge and to say that I wanted to visit China to write a book. Chou En-lai smiled, not in an unfriendly way, but plainly he had encountered many commentators on Communist affairs desirous of going to China. However, he handed me a paper and asked me to fill in my name and references. The title *New States-man* rang a bell. We talked about it for a minute and then I said that I had lived in the U.S.S.R. for a long time and studied there. This time Chou En-lai was clearly intrigued. "Where? When? How? Why?" He bombarded me with questions and I told him everything. "It was tough, the war in the Soviet Union?" he asked sympathetically. Then, without asking the question I feared, "Why did you leave the U.S.S.R.?" he talked to me about Poland, which he knows and likes, and concluded: "I am sure China will interest you very much."

For the sake of frankness I admitted that what I wanted to do above all was to make a comparison between the Chinese and Soviet experiments. "You shall write what you want to," replied Chou En-lai. Enough about my book. I told him that the Renault management found a forty-year-old memo about him in which he was already described as a dangerous agitator. Chou En-lai protested that he had never worked at the Renault factory and that it must have been a case of someone else with the same name, but he admitted that it was in Paris that he had become a Communist and drafted his first Marxist-Leninist journal. I then remembered that in addition to Snow, Chou En-lai and I shared another common

"friend," Prince Sihanouk of Cambodia, and I recounted what he
had told me one day: "All the students I send to Paris come back
to Pnompenh Communists. All those I send to Moscow come back
anti-Communists." This made a big hit; Chou En-lai translated it
for his compatriots. I said to myself later that having studied near
Moscow myself and not in Paris, perhaps I should not have
. . . but Chou En-lai did not draw any comparison and bade me a
very cordial good-by.

Three days later, as the Chinese delegation was leaving, there
was a great reception to which, this time, all the press was invited.
Chou En-lai was engulfed by the crowd, but because I wanted to
ask him how to go about getting my visa, I worked my way toward
him; I reached him, and he recognized me and said in his curious
French: *Comme ça va, Polonais?* which seemed to me to be a
good sign. For my visa he referred me to Madame Kung P'eng,
Deputy Minister of Foreign Affairs, who was with him in Algiers.
One year later I had my visa.

In Peking I had to see Madame Kung P'eng to secure an interview with Chou En-lai. To sound her out I asked if by any chance
the Prime Minister remembered our meeting in Algiers. "Of
course!" replied Madame Kung P'eng. "He was greatly intrigued by
you at that luncheon, and we spent a long time establishing who
you were exactly." This admission, free of all double talk, proved
that my dossier had been carefully examined, that they had nothing against me — neither my departure from the Soviet Union nor
my anti-Stalinist articles — and that the Chinese are less censorious
of one's past than I would have believed.

15,000 MILES IN FOUR MONTHS

We made this trip at our own expense and by prolonging it ran
no risk of abusing anyone's hospitality. Entering China at Canton,
we went to Peking by train; in other words, we took our time.
Before beginning our inquiry we wanted to see something of the
landscape and to familiarize ourselves, at least visually, with this
China where, from the moment one sets foot in it, one feels less at
home than in any other part of the world. Everything, even the
ways of eating, working, studying, enjoying oneself, seems different
from what we know.

In our luxurious sleeping car the only guide we had was Carl

Crow's book, which foreign tourists have been using since before World War I.

On arrival in Peking, having handed in at the Ministry of Foreign Affairs a list of what we wanted to see and the personalities we wanted to interview, we continued, Crow in hand, to see the sights like ordinary tourists. We met several adoptive citizens of Peking, Anglo-Saxons for the most part, who knew China well and helped us to draw up our itinerary.

We also toured the embassies and, with some diplomat friends, the best places for Chinese food. The winter was mild, the Hsin Chiao Hotel pleasant, our new connections interesting.

A few days later we were informed by a very official and very early telephone call that we could visit textile factory number three, as we had requested, and that our interpreter-guide awaited us in the lobby. We were hardly back from the factory when the telephone announced that we were expected at the Institute of Physical Culture and Sport and that, the following day, we could visit a suburban people's commune. We had started and we were not to stop; even the majority of our evenings were taken up, for we were constantly invited to entertainments organized for diplomats and foreign journalists. Moreover, it was on these occasions that we were able to get to know better the telephoning officials who were organizing our trips — and who, like us, seemed to prefer these impromptu and informal meetings to the rather stiff affairs in the Foreign Ministry salons.

Thus we had three very packed weeks in Peking, then Nanking, then Shanghai, whence the official "voice" recalled us urgently to Peking; Chou En-lai had agreed to the interview we had asked for. We waited three weeks for it, continuing our tours of interviews in Peking, and after seeing him, we returned to Shanghai for ten days. We immersed ourselves in this city where the craftsmen's workshops are cheek by jowl with the most modern factories; where the cadres of the new China were trained (and are still training); and where, more than anywhere else, are to be seen reminders of the whites who lived there shut away in their concessions.

From Shanghai a little twin-engined plane belonging to Civil Aviation of China took us, by short hops, to Wuhan, to Chungking, and finally to the heart of southwestern China, Kunming, capital of Yunnan province.

In the Southwest (sun, rice paddies, splendid landscapes) we discovered the China of national minorities: the Sanyis villages near Kunming and particularly around Nanning, center of the Kwangsi-Chuang autonomous region. Once oppressed by the Hans, these minorities hid away in the mountains, leading a miserable and primitive life there. The traces of this past are still visible everywhere. Our guides made no attempt to hide them from us, but they also made us visit the special institutes where they train the political, technical, and intellectual cadres who are responsible for ensuring the emancipation of these victims of the chauvinism of other days.

In Nanning, Kunming, and Kweilin — all southern cities — we were in that part of the country which would be most threatened in the event of the extension of the Vietnam war. Through these border regions pass all the railroad, highway, and air routes which link Hanoi to China and, indeed, to the whole Communist bloc. Here, in even the remotest villages the war came into all conversations, although life followed its normal course and the population seemed perfectly calm. At the airports we saw a few jets and some anti-aircraft guns, and nothing more. The only troop concentration we were able to see was at a road under construction on which masses of soldiers were working side by side with laborers and students.

Our "third China" was that of the human swarms in Changsha and Wuhan, two very old cities which are capitals, the one of Hunan province, the other of Hupeh. Great river ports on the banks of the Siang and the Yangtze (the Blue River), both have attracted part of the peasant population from the surrounding areas, which are periodically hit by the disastrous floods of these capricious rivers, and at all hours of the day their streets are packed like the approaches to a football stadium at the end of a game.

Mao Tse-tung was born in this region. We visited the village of his birth, Shao-shan, near Changsha, and the teachers' training school he attended, as well as the various lodgings from which he organized the peasants for the famous "autumn harvest uprising" of 1927. We did not make this pilgrimage merely to please our guides but also in order to get to know the background against which he grew up. And, too, we wanted to see what had become of this turbulent countryside where the masters of the old China had once found their work cut out for them. We saw it in a people's commune formed around Mao's old house, now a museum, which is a faithful reflection of the whole region.

It was in Wuhan, which comprises three towns (Hankow, Hanyang, and Wuchang), that Liu Shao-ch'i, Chairman of the Republic and until recently number two in the Chinese CP, won his fame. There he led the workers in a victorious assault on the British concession in 1927, and, for once, the foreigners accepted their defeat without too many reprisals.

The first thing you are shown in Wuhan is the bridge over the Blue River, this river which, until 1959, cut China in two: it could only be crossed by ferry, which slowed down all traffic terribly. On the great viaduct-bridge built by the new regime a special room has been set aside in which visitors are received and told about the prime importance of this "work of art."

Next we started out for the Northwest, where the Hwang Ho (Yellow River) flows. Here, in this mountainous land, the first Chinese state was born. The Yellow River actually is yellow, as are the mountains of loess: this is said to be the source of the legend that all Chinese are yellow — which is not the case.

Sian, center of Shensi province, was the capital of the ancient empire for eleven centuries, and it still contains many relics of the era, including a collection of magnificent Tang sculpture in its museum, which is without doubt the most beautiful in China. Today Sian has become a great industrial and university city. So during the week we spent in Sian we visited as many factories and institutes as historic monuments. We were also shown a prehistoric village discovered when the foundations were being dug for a factory.

But it was the next lap which we looked forward to with the greatest curiosity. From Sian we were going to Yenan, the holy place of Maoism, which from 1937 until 1947 was the capital of Red China. Yenan is 218 miles from Sian. No railroad, a very bad highway. To get there, there must be a dozen of you — that is to say, enough to fill a small special plane. We had the good luck to find a Canadian colleague, a couple of Chileans, and a family of Chinese from overseas who wanted to make the trip.

It was in the caves of Yenan, a strange troglodyte city, that the unshakable foundations of Maoist policy were laid. We spent more time there than we had expected (it was raining, and the Chinese pilots, very cautious, do not risk flying in this mountainous country when the clouds are low); then we returned to Peking for May 1.

After the huge fireworks display held in Tien An Men Square to round off the Labor Day celebrations, we left for the fifth lap of our tour: the three northeastern provinces, Liaoning, Kirin, and Heilungkiang, better known in the West under their old name, Manchuria.

In this enormous territory, more developed than the rest of China, the climate is barely milder than in Siberia. For 150 days of the year the temperature is below zero Centigrade (32° F.) and very often falls to –40° C. (–40° F.). But the subsoil is very rich — coal, iron, precious metals, and, today, oil — and Manchuria is an ideal center for industry. This was appreciated by the Japanese, who occupied it in 1931 and made it into Manchukuo, a puppet state which was in reality a colony.

Fourteen years of Japanese occupation obviously have left their mark. Certain cities, like Changchun, were almost entirely built by the Japanese in a style alien to the country. Others, like Harbin, had large populations of White Russians, who made this area their Far Eastern capital. All these cities are ugly and almost devoid of historical monuments.

During the war the Japanese industries were destroyed at the same time as Manchukuo, and almost all the big enterprises functioning today have been set up by the Communist regime. The most important factories, like the Anshan metallurgical combine or the Changchun truck factory, were built with the aid of the Soviet Union and, to a lesser degree, the people's democracies. But in July, 1960, all the Soviet technicians were recalled en masse by their government, which wanted to "punish" the Chinese for their political attitude. A hundred times, a thousand times we were told of this precipitate withdrawal — and not only to denounce the "crime of the Khrushchev revisionists." Rather it is because this is the first time in Manchuria's history that the Chinese alone are responsible for the running of all the factories. The policy of "relying on one's own strength" was particularly difficult to apply in Manchuria. Our guides did not conceal the fact that Russia's unilateral abrogation of the agreement had created serious problems here more than anywhere else, but they ended by declaring proudly that today everything was going well.

We returned to Peking in the middle of May with 15,600 miles of China in our legs and heads. We now had to put into some kind of order all that we had seen and heard, and also had to try to find the answers to questions we had been asking ourselves during our travels. I therefore spent a month interviewing people while Marc Riboud went on his own to Inner Mongolia.

During this month I met Mr. Wu Chen, Vice-Minister of Agriculture; Mr. Hu Cha, Director of Higher Education; Mr. Chen Chun, Deputy Editor of *Jenmin Jih Pao;* Madame Yung Kuang, Director of the Department of Women and Children; and Mr. Yuang Lung-kwei, well-known economist and Vice-Chairman of the Chinese Committee for International Trade. Marshal Ch'en Yi,[2] Vice-Premier and Minister of Foreign Affairs, agreed to reply in writing to my questions on the international situation. After which, in June, we left China.

BETWEEN STALIN AND MAO

We beat several records in China; to begin with, the record for length of stay. Journalists who are not permanently accredited rarely spend more than two months in Peking. We stayed there for two months and also spent another two in the provinces, which enabled us to set a new record for mileage covered in China. We traveled the length and breadth of the country, from Kunming and Nanning (which are on the border of Vietnam) to Harbin, which is near the Russian border; from Shanghai in the Southeast to Yenan in the Northwest.

And during our visit we were given a record number of interviews and visited a record number of factories, people's communes, schools, and universities. But, of course, our aim was not to beat records.

From my very first days in Peking the Chinese system struck me as having a curiously diverse character. The official jargon as well as the theoretical attitudes of the people I talked to, and the occasional portraits of Stalin one sees almost everywhere, reminded me of my youth in Soviet Russia. But otherwise I failed to fit the pieces of the Chinese puzzle into a Stalinist pattern. For example, the wage system has absolutely nothing in common with the former Soviet system. The type of hero projected for the admiration of the masses is also completely different. Many other things, too, provide evidence of radical differences, and I got the paradoxical impression that into the old Stalinist mold had been poured material Stalin would not have accepted at any price.

If we pressed our investigations as far as possible, it was essen-

---

[2] Since June 1, 1965, there have been no ranks in the Chinese Army. Titles are used in this book to indicate the holder's former rank or position.

tially because we wanted to resolve this contradiction between the Stalinist doctrinal orthodoxy of the Chinese and their "heretical" practice.

For us the Stalinist system formed a whole: a certain way of rapidly industrializing an underdeveloped country, a monolithic party which controlled everything, a religious sort of ideology intended to arouse the workers' ardor and to justify the ruthless repression of those who did not conform. All these elements produced a certain type of man and were so closely interwoven that it was difficult to say which had produced which — whether, for example, it was the process of industrialization and forced collectivization that gave birth to the Stalinist ideology, or whether, on the contrary, it was as a result of the ideology created by Stalin's control of the Party that industrialization and collectivization were imposed in such a brutal way. In reality, all these things happened: the means used were forced on the U.S.S.R. by the situation in which she found herself in 1927, and she could perhaps use no other means to attain her goal.

It was not the defenders of Stalinism who made this claim. Western analysts and historians, while attacking the Stalinist religion, showed that Stalin was as much the prisoner as he was the promoter of his system. Sorcerer's apprentice, he unleashed a chain reaction he was unable to control, and under the pressure of events, he was led to make decisions based on immediate circumstances, whose consequences he could not foresee.

Stalin did not coldly calculate that he would have to send 20 million citizens into forced-labor camps. Neither did he foresee that he would have to favor, in a manner fraught with consequences, the key workers and cadres. These measures were dictated by the necessities of socialization in a country which was not prepared for it either politically or economically and in which the ordinary people did not meekly accept orders from above.

To achieve his ends, Stalin no doubt knew that he would have to employ both the stick and the carrot, but he certainly did not foresee the extent to which repression would grow or the depths of corruption that a policy of favoritism would lead to in a period of scarcity. Enshrined in dogmas, his infallibility, his farsightedness, his "Marxist-Leninist" orthodoxy helped him to conceal Soviet reality from the world and to defuse all internal attempts at resistance. The Stalinist religion did not take care of everything, but it justified the witch hunt, inspired a healthy fear, and immunized believers against all outside influences. Reared in this climate, the Soviet acquired certain characteristics and a certain vision of the world which his language reflected.

What has happened in the people's democracies proves that this phenomenon is not specifically a Russian one. Erected empirically, the Russian system clothed itself in a doctrine, and in all the countries which have adopted this doctrine, we have seen the same type of man being created. Repression in Poland was perhaps less severe than in Hungary, but Stalinism was the same in both countries. Czechoslovakia was very much more advanced than Rumania, but both adopted the same type of administration. And even in the non-Communist countries the Communist parties, which had no political police at their disposal to enforce discipline, hardened themselves and adopted a strictly hierarchical organization. A certain intellectual attitude and a certain language that are specifically Stalinist have therefore come to appear in our eyes as indissolubly tied to a system.

From afar, reading official Chinese statements written in "Stalinese," so to speak, we expected to find Stalinism in China — all the more so because the Maoist leaders have refused to take part in the de-Stalinization movement and have remained attached to Stalin's precepts. Not, certainly for sentimental reasons; the Chinese CP has had plenty to complain about when it comes to Kremlin interference. But in order to become industrialized, underdeveloped China had to apply the formula which had succeeded in Russia. Mao, like Stalin, would have to resign himself to sacrificing several generations to achieve the industrialization without which socialization is impossible.

That is roughly what we had thought when we set out, but we were no less curious to see what the Chinese version of Stalinism was like. The Chinese CP had the reputation of being relatively flexible; its leaders were understood to be very well informed on what really took place in the U.S.S.R. and on what resulted from it. We supposed, therefore, that they would avoid some of the excesses caused partly by Stalin's lack of foresight. In short, we expected to find a perfected and, if one can use the word, "moderate" Stalinism.

What we did not know and what struck us from the start was that the Maoists absolutely reject the Soviet economic pattern. Undoubtedly they have retained from Stalinism a concept which fits their situation and which they feel acts as a spur on the masses.

They use the revolutionary language of the Stalinist period and launch appeals to the "class brothers who are the prisoners of capitalism." In addition, they have kept the idea that the Party must be monolithic and play an educational role. But the education dispensed by the Chinese CP — as we have already seen — differs radically from that dispensed by the Soviet CP.

The Chinese want to ensure the development of their country without recourse to physical coercion and without favoring the shock workers. There is no piecework in the factories, Stakhanovism is not extolled, and there are no labor camps.[3] The slogans do not proclaim the fundamental importance of heavy industry, which was the keystone of Soviet industrialization and was given absolute priority. Agriculture remains the basic factor, and apparently no one considers it merely a means of amassing capital for industrialization.

Already, although the market is far from saturated and, as a result, customers are not very demanding, the distribution organizations are responsible for checking the quality of merchandise. Everywhere technical cadres are being trained in large numbers, but they are compelled, despite the loss of time, to put in a stint of manual work in order to prevent them, at all cost, from regarding themselves as an elite as a result of their isolation from the masses. The same thing applies to the bureaucrats, inevitably numerous in a vast country bent on becoming centralized: any attempt to achieve a standard of living even marginally higher than that of the masses is penalized. In every sphere similar measures have been taken which testify to a concern for egalitarianism that never preoccupied the Soviet leaders to this degree.

Admittedly, a certain egalitarianism was practiced in Stalin's Russia; education and medical care, for example, were free. But if all had an equal chance at the start, those who "ran faster" were favored. The Chinese are determined that the whole nation must advance together by reducing to a minimum the inequalities which can appear in a poor country in the process of socialization; while the Soviets, on the contrary, chose to use them as incentives.

To achieve this egalitarianism, there must obviously be regu-

[3] Certainly it is known that "politically suspect" people are often sent to the communes for long periods. This involves many individual tragedies; but in spite of everything the method is much more humane than deportation to a forced-labor camp. After all, to be compelled to live like 80 per cent of the population is not comparable to living behind barbed wire and being excluded from society.

lating mechanisms: it is the Maoist theory which provides these by a kind of "code of good conduct" and a new scale of values adapted to the Chinese situation. Material advantages are never awarded to the elite; they are urged instead to help the backward and to perfect themselves by serving the people. As for the workers on the lower rungs of society, they are taught to put the collective welfare first and to rely solely on the advancement of the whole in order to achieve a richer life — richer morally to begin with, and then later, materially.

It is plain that such a system is even more "religious" than Stalinism was. To be a "good Communist" in China it is not enough to worship Mao or to trust the Party implicitly; one must at all times respect the moral rules and resist absolutely the slightest selfish or antisocial temptation. It seemed to me, however, that this Chinese puritanism was understandable and acceptable. One must not forget that China, a country self-conscious about her underdevelopment, still remembers only too well the ravages caused by the corruption, immorality, and selfishness which swept the country only seventeen years ago and whose effects are still visible.

This ideology can act as a regulator of the Chinese economy; it is not a dogmatism fabricated retrospectively to justify decisions already made. It was born of a long trial experienced by all the "faithful" and for that very reason is specifically Chinese and therefore not very exportable.

This constant anxiety of the Maoists to stick to the reality of their country's situation limits their pretensions as "theoreticians." They often pretend to be simple practitioners of Stalinism rather than admit that their economic system is radically different from that of Stalin's Russia. They are working in a society which is in the middle of transformation, which changes from day to day, and they must constantly adapt their system to the new demands of new situations. They prefer, therefore, to concentrate on a few basic principles concerning man's prime role in production, for example, or the absolute priority of the collective whole, without codifying their present administrative methods, which in their eyes are merely the means (adapted to circumstances) of arriving at Communism. They do not seem to be concerned, either, with the idea that development will be affected by the means employed any more than they are with the idea that the means can modify the end they seek to attain — the establishment of a communist society — for who knows exactly what a communist society should be like?

In fact, it is very probable that they are not unaware of the problem but that they prefer not to raise it, and that they are no longer intent on stressing the originality of their own experience, for fear of being accused of revisionism at the very moment they are bitterly accusing the Soviet Union of it. Paradoxically, since the outbreak of the crisis in the international Communist movement the Maoists have become more egalitarian and more "Chinese" than ever. They claim, nonetheless, to remain faithful to the Stalinist doctrine (which governed the Communist world until 1956) because this, they believe, is bound to ensure them the leadership of the socialist camp.

But to achieve their ends the Chinese are obviously being compelled to "split" Stalinism even more than their opponents have done. For the Maoists, as we have seen, there are two aspects of Stalinism. On the one hand are the "basic principles" which they consider sacred: the class struggle in the post-revolutionary period, which justifies the dictatorship of the proletariat and the monolithic nature of the Party, and the solidarity of the socialist camp in the face of the class enemy. On the other hand there are the particular forms that Stalinism took in the U.S.S.R.: the Party's relationship to the masses and the economic and administrative methods which Mao acknowledged to be "tainted with errors." In his view, therefore, each party must retain only the fundamental principles of Stalinism; moreover, he has reconfirmed these in his works by relating them to the special circumstances of his country. This is why, the Chinese say, Chairman Mao's "thought" enables all domestic problems, collective or individual, to be solved, while at the same time spreading the internationalist spirit which must consolidate the unity of revolutionaries throughout the world. Each country must have its own Mao who, within the immutable framework of Stalinist principles, would apply special solutions to the special problems of that country — economic development being, let us repeat, a special problem.

But can the Stalinist doctrine thus be "cut in two"? Is this way of doing things a useful simplification, or does it lead to insuperable contradictions? Already, in order to defend Stalin, the Chinese have not just been compelled to admit that he committed "certain practical errors" while at the same time retaining his "just principles." They also have been obliged more and more often to pick and choose these principles, keeping some and forgetting others. Sometimes they try to mitigate their difficulties by labeling as Stalinist, principles which never were so, for example, the pri-

ority of the human factor in production. They recall at every turn
that Stalin said, "Man is the most precious capital." But they are
deaf to reminders that Stalin also said, "The cadres decide everything," or that tractors are more useful than militants in the establishing of socialism. It is not passion they lack when defending
Stalin but, occasionally, assurance — even when they are talking
about "basic principles."

Furthermore, this adherence to Stalinist orthodoxy sometimes
restricts the Chinese capacity to analyze world events accurately.
This is particularly glaring when they talk of the upheaval in the
Soviet Union in recent years. They violently condemn the material-
incentives policy of Khrushchev and his successors. According to
them, this policy does not even succeed in concealing their real
aim of assuring the privileges of the *nouveaux riches* and restoring
capitalism. But they forget that Stalinism has always favored key
workers and imposed forced labor on rebels. At Stalin's death, a
recourse to terror being no longer possible for a variety of reasons,
his successors had no alternative but to support material incentives
more strongly than ever. They did so in a context that was politically and economically unchanged, since the monolithic Party was
still in power and the "basic principles" were still respected. In
order to explain the revisionist heresy the Chinese have therefore
been reduced to singling out a brief phrase from the 1961 program
of the Russian CP (eight years after Stalin's death) according to
which the U.S.S.R. has become a state "of the whole people" (and
therefore the dictatorship of the proletariat is no longer in force
there).

In fact, the recent history of the U.S.S.R. proves that when
certain mechanisms are removed from the Stalinist economic system, the whole system is qualitatively changed. The monolithic
nature of Soviet politics has become a brake on economic and
social development without even guaranteeing doctrinal orthodoxy
or the continuity of the quest for the Communist objective. This is
so obvious that it is impossible for us to believe that — even in
China — a hybrid Stalinism can be erected on economic bases
radically different from those Stalin wanted to establish.

Undeniably the Maoists, like all other Communists, have been
conditioned by thirty long years of Stalinism. It imposed on them
ways of thought, a language, methods of analysis and interpretation which they try to pass on to each new generation. But their
egalitarian economic policy gives a very special flavor to their

experience, as well as to the education they provide. And it is very likely that the new generation will be molded more by this aspect of Maoism than by Stalinist principles. In a country which favors political incentives, which calls for the voluntary participation of the workers, and which inculcates in them an egalitarian spirit, the population will sooner or later try to free itself from the rigid paternalism of the Party.

On the day that China catches up with her economic backwardness and is less threatened from outside, she will have to resolve the problems which face a developed society: the Chinese masses, as a result of the habits they are being made to assimilate today, will demand not more consumer goods, as happened in the U.S.S.R. after Stalin, but more democracy. Having chosen a different road to socialism from the Russian one, the Chinese will thus arrive at a different form of socialism.

At the present time the study of Chinese society and socialism is singularly complicated by the ambiguity of both the language and the concepts of the Chinese. We were constantly tempted to draw a parallel between the China of Mao and the Russia of Stalin — even if only because of the intensive personality cult. We had to ask the same questions a thousand times to get the Chinese to "confess" what they are really doing under cover of Stalinist orthodoxy. I did not get answers to all my questions, neither those bearing on the past nor those relating to the present, and I do not feel qualified to fill in these gaps with personal theories. I can only report what I saw and heard.

APPEARANCE AND REALITY

"From the top of the Kremlin tower one cannot see everything," say the Russians. In other words, there is a gulf between the leadership's view and the daily experience of ordinary citizens. During the seven years I spent in the Soviet Union I was able, unlike visiting foreigners, to confirm that this common-sense truth rests on solid foundations.

Like most of my Soviet comrades, I looked rather condescendingly on the rare foreigners we met at the university or in the streets of Rostov-on-Don, where I was a student for two years at the end of the war. Radiating fellow-feeling, they would shake hands warmly and look at us with a kind of jealousy; they envied us for being poorer than they (which was so obvious) and also for being so much more heroic and socialistic. We did nothing to disillusion them. On the contrary, when their approaching visit was announced, the more ragged among us went on leave so as not to spoil the effect. The others carefully avoided any show of pleasure or even surprise at the noticeable improvement in the dining-hall menu and allowed visitors to believe that we always ate as well as this.

The visits of prominent personalities from bourgeois countries brought us even more bonuses. The Russian people still remember the visit of the American Vice-President Henry Wallace. To honor him, "they" (among ourselves we always referred to the men in the Kremlin as "they" and "them") decided temporarily to suspend the practice of frisking workers as they left the factory gates. Workers in the food industry took such liberal advantage of the occasion to supply the black market with pork, meat, and other scarce products that there was a collapse of black-market prices in many parts of the country.

One saw few foreigners in Rostov, but unofficial news was spread throughout the Soviet Union via the grapevine. There was nothing counter-revolutionary about this. We approved of the officials' conduct toward foreigners; what they did was in defense of the socialist fatherland. And we did not dream of telling foreigners that in order to live we had to keep a sharp eye on a host of rather sordid matters: the arrival of rations, fluctuations on the black market, any relaxing or tightening of railroad controls, chances of going to the Ukraine or even to Moscow, where one could always find more goods. Very few foreigners knew about this double life of Soviet citizens and the effects it could have on their mentality and on the economic life of the country. Times have changed, and our friends in the U.S.S.R. and the Eastern European countries no longer have anything to hide from us, nor are they kept away from foreigners, as we were. Before going to China I knew that we would be like the visitors to the U.S.S.R. who were able to judge only from appearances because they never had the opportunity to sample the real life of the country. To begin with, we did not know one word of Chinese, and it was difficult to believe that the average Chinese would reveal the semi-illegal aspects of his life through the intermediary of an official guide. We had also been warned that it is difficult to make friends with any Chinese, and as Europeans are immediately identifiable, it is practically impossible for them to make any contact with the population behind their guides' backs. We had also been warned about the rigidity of interpreters who carry sectarianism to the point of refusing to translate questions they consider unorthodox.

We were lucky never to have an interpreter of this type. In each city we had different ones; those who talked like an official phonograph record were very rare. The great majority were frank and intelligent, worked in harmony with us, and went to great lengths to help us; and we practically never had a brush with them. When we spent rather a long time with them, they spoke freely to us of their lives, and there was one who even admitted that he had learned English by listening to the Voice of America. As for my interpreter in Peking, In Sun-lin, I have rarely met such a fine, perceptive, discreet man.

However, our good relationship with our guides was based on a tacit "nonaggression" pact. They did not try to indoctrinate us or to prevent us from mixing with "bad company" — in Peking I often went to see Russians and other foreigners. We, in return, avoided embarrassing them by asking for "impossible" things. Marc Riboud did not request permission to take photographs of an air exercise we watched in the provinces. I did not ask about any black market.

If there is a "double life" in China, therefore, we are unaware of it; but we did everything we could to find out what the ordinary citizen's life is like, and I believe I am able to assert that the Chinese do not practice what I shall euphemistically call the "wangling" that swept the U.S.S.R. during the war, that they are singularly, scrupulously honest — which is, at any rate, a sign.

The political enthusiasm of the masses seems to be sincere, but I shall not risk saying whether it really is. The intellectuals I met were all ardent Maoists, but I was unable to meet those who were having trouble with the regime. Some Party officials admitted to me that an opposition existed, but of its strength and aims I know only what they told me. I was told of the crises which have rocked the intelligentsia over the last twenty years, but I was not allowed to gather any direct evidence.

I was also told, but in an even more vague way, of opposition among the ranks of the workers and peasants. I do not therefore believe that there is absolute unanimity or that the whole Chinese population cares passionately about politics or, more accurately, about the ideology the government presents to them as politics; so I was not surprised to hear from the editor of a daily newspaper that its circulation rose especially during the table-tennis championships. Let me add that I thought I noticed that Chang Tse-tung, table-tennis champion of China, is clearly more popular than certain political chiefs.

China is too vast and too complex to be judged as a whole. I saw the countryside and the cities, and I have compiled a record which is not slanted by any thesis and which does not abstain from stating what struck me as good or bad, disturbing or reassuring.

This record, which is set out in Chapters Two, Three, and Four of the book, comprises reports and evidence on the various aspects of Chinese society sixteen years after the proclamation of the People's Republic. I have already said that this society did not represent a stable entity definitively molded, and that the Chinese leaders never ceased to concentrate on its transformation. We were often told during our stay that certain existing features were destined to disappear more or less rapidly, and we ourselves discerned jarring elements in the Maoist edifice which seemed to be doomed.

But all these changes and upheavals will of necessity develop out of the situation I observed during the sixteenth year of the Chinese revolution. By describing this as fully as possible, I hope to throw light on the internal dynamics of Chinese society and enable readers later to form an opinion on the changes that will undoubtedly come about.

THE ADVENT OF THE RED GUARDS

To be accurate, these changes began to take place in the spring of 1966 under conditions which have had few precedents in modern Communist history. "Plants grown in a hothouse have no chance to become hardy," said Mao Tse-tung in 1957 in order to explain the necessity of the ideological struggle and of criticism for the future of the Marxist doctrine in China. This was on the eve of the period known as the "hundred flowers," during which the Chinese were able to express their criticisms of the Communist regime. But the criticisms did not please Mao: they were mainly "right-wing" and allied to those which the intellectuals of other Communist countries directed at their governments in demands for rapid de-

Stalinization and liberalization. According to Mao Tse-tung, such demands were not constructive.

But he did not abandon the idea of instigating one day a re-examination of the existing system in China from a left-wing stand-point, which would lead to a radicalization and communization of the country. Such a movement would enable "the dust of the old society, which will not disappear of its own accord, to be swept away," according to one of the Communist Chairman's expressive metaphors.

The Marxist doctrine was not the only plant grown in the hot-house of the new China in the view of the Maoists. They questioned themselves on the state of morale of the new generation which had never known the misery of the civil war, or the famine and humilia-tion of the semicolonized China of the past. And Mao Tse-tung has said in every letter to Edgar Snow that the future of the Chinese revolution would remain uncertain as long as this generation had not given proof of its fighting spirit and devotion to the common cause.

The Chinese I met told me of their anxieties on this score and stressed particularly the precedent of the Soviet Union, which, according to them, was in the process of degenerating into a capital-ist country because the generation of revolutionaries had not been able to inculcate a fighting spirit into its successors. In Chinese eyes the economic and social structure of a country is not enough to guarantee its socialist future. The "revisionist" spirit flourishes today in the U.S.S.R. although industry has been nationalized for a long time and the land was collectivized. Why couldn't the same thing happen in China?

I often had difficulty in following these arguments, not only be-cause the "decadence" of the U.S.S.R. was not as obvious to me as it was to the Maoists, but particularly because I had discovered no sign of the revisionist spirit among the young Chinese. It was rather their political fervor — not to say fanaticism — which in the end disturbed me. More than once we noticed how difficult it was to discuss politics with these impassioned youngsters who were unable even to imagine the existence of a world different from their own and who accepted every statement of Maoist propaganda as gospel truth.

Talking with them, I searched in vain for a glimmer of the irony my contemporaries in Russia had allowed to emerge in the company of foreigners from time to time. But the young Chinese seemed to me to be much more isolated from the rest of the world, perhaps because for one thing their country had vastly different cultural traditions from the Judaeo-Christian civilization of the West. (The great majority of Chinese have no more knowledge of Jesus Christ than have most Westerners of Confucius.)

Then, one day in the spring of 1966, we learned that these zealous youngsters had begun to stick up posters with huge lettering (a sign of anger) within the precincts of Peking University. They were in protest "against the reactionary academic authorities" who, according to them, continued to defend the old culture and were guilty of many other sins against the proletarian regime. This was the signal which started off the "great cultural revolution" prepared — if the Chinese press is to be believed — by Chairman Mao Tse-tung himself. There was no question whatsoever of its being a local incident, limited to the precincts of Peking University. For if the rector and his assistants were able to poison the minds of the young with impunity for ten years, it is obvious that they were protected or at least tolerated by the Party officials of the capital. The Communist leaders of Peking were therefore taken to task by the young zealots, who demonstrated with drums and cymbals outside the offices of the city council. The Mayor of Peking, P'eng Chen, one of the top men of the regime, was not attacked by name, but he was discreetly dismissed from his Party post.

The disease did not rage in Peking alone. Every day the Hsinhua (New China) news agency revealed the existence of protest movements in other universities and in other cities. At first, all the cultural officials were attacked, with the exception of Lu Ting-i, an old companion of Mao Tse-tung's and Minister of Culture, who was simply replaced by T'ao Chu, another veteran of Maoism. Lu Ting-i's first deputy, Chou Yang, did not benefit from the same leniency despite his thirty years' service in the Party ranks: he was singled out as the principal culprit responsible for the cultural errors of the preceding years. It happens that I had a very long interview with this leader during my stay in Peking. I spent five hours with him at the International Club, where he outlined to me his concept of proletarian culture, which appeared to me to be as antirevisionist and orthodox as it is possible to be (the reader will find the text of this interview in Chapter Four). I admit, therefore, that on reading the accounts of the meetings at which "peasants, workers, and soldiers" vented their indignation with this implacable revisionist and enemy of Chairman Mao's thought,

I had some difficulty in understanding with what exactly they could reproach him. Subsequent events, however, have clarified the mystery a little.

This movement known as the "great cultural revolution" merely used the cultural problem as a pretext. Its real object was to launch a vast campaign of "left-wing" criticism, the mass movement to "sweep away the dust" which Mao Tse-tung had wanted for so long. Indeed, passions were unleashed in China and suddenly young zealots were seen everywhere, putting up angry posters, searching the apartments of suspects and even administration offices, submitting the provincial cadres of Party and government to real public interrogation.

Eventually, on August 1, 1966, the Central Committee met in Peking to examine the situation. Mao Tse-tung personally directed this session, and in the sixteen-point resolution which was adopted one can discern, if not his style, at least his postulates. The Central Committee, in fact, encouraged the young rebels and regarded the cultural revolution as a kind of vast national debate enabling the masses to test the orthodoxy and political fervor of the cadres and at the same time to educate themselves.

"Chairman Mao has always taught us that a revolution cannot be accomplished with much elegance and delicacy or with much kindness, friendliness, courtesy, moderation, and magnanimity. The masses must educate themselves in this great revolutionary movement and learn to make the distinction between what is just and what isn't, between the ways of acting correctly and incorrectly"[4] — thus proclaimed the Central Committee, while stressing that the debate must be conducted without violence. "The masses must declare what is just and correct what is wrong in order gradually to secure unanimity. . . . Study the facts, persuade by reasoning — this is what must be done in the debate. It is not permissible to use compulsion to overcome the minority which supports different views, because truth is occasionally on its side. Even if it has erroneous views, it is always allowed to defend itself and to keep its opinions. In a debate there must be recourse to reasoning and not to compulsion or coercion."

Then the Central Committee pointed out that the Party cadres divided themselves into several categories and that each must be

[4] The point in question is a catalogue of virtues advocated by Confucius and which, according to the Maoists, must not be observed, particularly during a period of revolution.

treated in a different way. The good cadres must be left in peace; the "relatively good" cadres must be criticized but not too rigorously; the cadres which had committed serious mistakes but were not composed of anti-Party and antisocialist right-wingers must be subjected to severe criticism without being persecuted. These had to be argued with as long as was necessary to convince them of their errors. Finally, a small number of anti-Party and antisocialist right-wingers must be expelled purely and simply.

These directives did not appear so very clear, but even less so was the problem of practical execution. Who would organize all these debates? Who would decide in the last resort which cadre must be expelled because it was anti-Party, and which should be pardoned despite errors committed? Admittedly the Central Committee resolution recommended the formation of "permanent cultural revolution committees" of the same kind as the Russian soviets of 1917, but the Russians had previously risen spontaneously and in China there was no czar to overthrow.

In fact, it was not soviets that were being formed in China in 1966 but another type of organization, copied from the Soviet model of the heroic period, the Red Guards. On August 18, 1966, Mao Tse-tung, surrounded by Lin Piao, Chou En-lai, and all the other top leaders, presided over a Peking rally in which a million people, mainly young, took part; from then on groups of students and schoolchildren wearing red arm bands began to appear in the streets of the capital. They set about renaming streets, closing expensive restaurants, the International Club, where I had often interviewed Chinese leaders — now considered too bourgeois — as well as many other establishments which "diverted the working people from their ideal." The Red Guards' imagination appeared to be limitless since they condemned barbers as well as street signs and announced that from henceforth traffic would cross on the red light and stop on the green, as the color red was incapable of braking movement.

But these gatherings of the Red Guards were hardly lighthearted affairs. Despite the directives of the Central Committee, the debates with suspects, "bourgeois" or "revisionist," were not always characterized by patience and respect for the minority point of view. Foreign news agencies, including Tass, every day reported excesses, and things went even worse in the provinces than in the capital. The Chinese press itself pointed out that in many areas the local officials resisted the Red Guards' pressure and sometimes even called on the workers and peasants to resist them. They declared that they derived their authority from the Central Committee and that those who opposed them were thus rebelling against the Communist Party.

Contrary to what one might logically have supposed, the Central Committee supported the Red Guards and not the Party cadres, as you can judge from this extract from the editorial in the *Jenmin Jih Pao* of August 23, 1966:

"It is an excellent thing that large masses of students should rise to make revolution and oppose these gentry. It is also excellent that they are publishing newspapers in bold type. And it is no less excellent that they are expressing their opinions broadly and frankly and engaging in the great debate. These revolutionary students have the right to parade and demonstrate in the streets, the right of assembly, of association, of speech, and of publication. They dare, by invoking the thought of Mao Tse-tung, to criticize the errors of the Party committee of their own branch or those of the Party committees of the higher echelons, which rightly helps to correct the leadership of these Party committees. As for those who are fundamentally headstrong and obstinately refuse to repent and to correct themselves, it is not a serious matter if they perish — in fact it is a good thing.

"The Red Guard, the Red Flag Combat Group, and other revolutionary organizations are legal organizations under the dictatorship of the proletariat. Their actions are revolutionary and legal. Whoever opposes them goes directly against the teaching of Chairman Mao and the decision of the Central Committee of the Party.

"The broad mass of workers, peasants, and soldiers is the main force of the great proletarian cultural revolution and the powerful supporter of the revolutionary students. We must stand fast at their sides and support their actions with the greatest fervor and the firmest revolutionary determination."

There was more to come. A few days later 500,000 Red Guards went to Peking to "compare their experiences with those of the capital's young revolutionaries," and once again Mao Tse-tung, Lin Piao, and Chou En-lai came to congratulate them on the services they had rendered to the revolution. "Don't let yourselves be annihilated!" cried Lin Piao, and he reminded them that the Liberation Army which he commands and which is also in the van of the cultural revolution would protect the Red Guards if necessary.

"You didn't see everything in China," people have sometimes

said to me in Paris. "The revisionists must be extremely strong
there if Mao is compelled to combat them with such radical
weapons." I do not believe, however, that the strange purge which
is taking place today in China is aimed at an organized faction of
supporters of the Soviet Union, "revisionists" comparable to the
Trotskyites of former days. I simply think that China is not a
country where it is easy to make a career in the Party machine
and where it is not enough to make orthodox professions of faith
to be considered a good Communist. The cadres I met in China
seemed to me to be devoted body and soul to Mao, and I did not
get the impression that they led a particularly luxurious life. But it
is a fact that I did not see everything and, above all, that our
criteria of privileges are not the same as those of the Chinese.

It seems to me that the Red Guards represent a new pressure of
egalitarianism and militancy, which in fact was already singularly
developed in 1965. Will this movement release new ideas for the
building of socialism, as Mao desires? One may doubt it, but this
possibility cannot be excluded, particularly if one admits that the
matter in question is a very special socialist venture being realized
in an underdeveloped country which is threatened from outside
and which needs a lot of inventiveness for it to be able to make
progress and defend itself.

Some Westerners wish to see in the present cultural revolution
a simple manifestation of neo-Stalinism because one type of terror
now reigns in China and because the cult of Mao is as fervent
there as was that of Stalin. One also recalls that by a strange coin-
cidence the purges in the U.S.S.R. were carried out in a particularly violent manner seventeen years after the revolution, following
the assassination of Kirov in Leningrad.

But the comparison is once more fallacious. In the U.S.S.R. the
purges were a police operation, conducted by the all-powerful
N.K.V.D. The suspects disappeared in silence, were exiled after
summary judgments delivered behind closed doors or without trial.
Later, when he had to conduct the war, Stalin resuscitated czarist
heroes, the Suvorovs and the Kutuzovs, he reopened the churches
and restored their golden epaulets to the officers; it cannot be said
that he ever relied on either mass movements or the revolutionary
spirit.

Mao behaves in a radically different way. It is the Red Guards
who, at his call, hunt down the revisionists, and their orders are to
"educate by persuasion," not to suppress or exile. Finally, far

from exhuming the Chinese Suvorovs, Mao renounces the heritage of the old China, he abolishes ranks and stripes in his army, he launches a great campaign against superstition and religion, and he extols more and more an egalitarianism Stalin never preached. Rather does the great cultural revolution mark a further rupture between Maoism and Stalinism. Whether one wishes it or not, the facts each day confirm that the concepts of Mao Tse-tung are very different from those of Stalin, and that his faith in the revolutionary spirit of the Chinese enables him to resort to methods the former Soviet dictator would never have dreamt of.

THE SPIRIT OF YENAN

These methods were not devised today: to understand their origin, it is better to study the history of Maoism rather than that of the U.S.S.R. All that I saw in China appeared to me in a different light as a result of discussions I had with Chinese leaders about China's recent past. To understand what the Chinese are doing, one must know where they came from. It is unimportant whether their views of past events are accurate or not. A faith can feed on disputable facts without losing either its dynamism or its power to attract. That is why the next chapter is a long one, "Their History as They See It Today."

Today all the commentators recall the spirit of Yenan and explain that Mao wants to transform China completely into a Spartan republic similar to the one he organized in northwestern China between 1937 and 1947. The Chinese Red republic therefore has its own myth, but to understand what it really was one must put it in its historic, economic, and social context. The reader will see that it was not through any taste for asceticism that the Chinese established their principal bases in the semidesert of the Northwest and that it was not only for doctrinal reasons that they opted for an egalitarianism rarely seen in modern times.

But if it is true that China is "Yenanizing" herself, it is because once more she must face the prospect of a prolonged armed struggle with an adversary who to begin with is a thousand times stronger than she. In 1937 it was Japan; today it is the United States.

Peking is 2,500 miles from Vietnam, but the frontier cities of

Kunming and Nanning are only a few minutes' flight from the bases of the American jet bombers. There is not even any need for a general like the one in *Doctor Strangelove* for a rain of bombs to flatten these two great Chinese cities: a pilot's error would be enough. Worse, in South Vietnam the Americans are building remarkably sophisticated and costly bases and military installations — they stock even nuclear weapons. Are these gigantic efforts being made solely to hold South Vietnam? May they not rather be preparing for the war against China?

One may ask oneself the question, and the Chinese do not fail to do so. In May, 1965, when the American expeditionary force in Vietnam still consisted of only 80,000 men, I had a private conversation in Peking with a very highly placed Chinese official who told me: "This is only the beginning. The Americans are going to bring in hundreds of thousands of troops, they are going to bomb Hanoi, they are going to try to invade North Vietnam, then they are going to bomb China, which is as close to Vietnam as lips to teeth. Then they will experience what the Japanese once experienced — they will have the whole world against them and they will never be able to sustain a prolonged war against us."

My high official did not want this war. He attached too much importance to American students' pacifist movements and quoted Walter Lippmann's articles and the speeches of Martin Luther King at every turn; but he was perfectly lucid about the mechanics of escalation, and events supported him. He explained to me that China must prepare herself for the worst and face the heaviest sacrifices. All this was told to me confidentially. If I mention it, however, it is because all that has happened in China in a year, including the astonishing advent of the Red Guards in the streets, is explained precisely by this conviction of the Chinese leaders that they must prepare themselves for a prolonged war with the United States.

It wasn't China who started the war in Vietnam, nor is she prolonging it by forbidding the North Vietnamese to negotiate. If the Americans wished tomorrow to sign agreements with the N.L.F. along the lines of the Evian pact between France and Algeria, Mao Tse-tung would not oppose it. More than a year before De Gaulle's speech at Pnompenh, Chou En-lai, in an interview which appears in this book,[5] drew a parallel between the solution of the

5 See Appendix E.

Algerian problem and that which he wanted for Vietnam. But Johnson does not invite the Vietnamese to any Evian conference. What he proposes to them is always a sort of "heroes' peace," an agreement which would reinforce the American position in the South and compel the N.L.F. alone to lay down their arms. It is natural that the Chinese should point out to the Vietnamese that negotiations of this kind would be a trap and tantamount to capitulation pure and simple.

If the Chinese were cynical opportunists, if they practiced a neo-Stalinist diplomacy and put their own interests above those of the Vietnamese, they would, on the contrary, put pressure on Hanoi and the N.L.F. in order to extinguish at any price the fire which threatens to set China ablaze. "Capitulate temporarily, sacrifice yourselves to ensure the safety of the Chinese revolution, guarantor of our common future," etc. That is the kind of language the Chinese would have used to the Vietnamese if they were neo-Stalinists. But demonstrably Mao neither shares Stalin's concept of "political realism" nor believes in the virtues of appeasement. Finding himself faced by an implacable enemy stronger than himself, he is getting ready to engage in a long war which will gradually reverse the balance of power, as was the case during the war against Japan.

The speeches made in Peking last August on the Red Army's anniversary repeated the orders of the day and the slogans of 1941 and 1942. Today, as formerly, the army must undertake not only the defense of the country but also a good share of its industrial and agricultural production; it must set an egalitarian example and become "an agitator and collective organizer." As during the Yenan days, it must teach all Chinese to be peasants, workers, soldiers, militiamen, and intellectuals at the same time. And it is not by chance that the head of this army, Lin Piao, has become the number two of the regime.

The program of the great cultural revolution also recalls that of Yenan in many instances. In the old China the word "culture" did not have the same meaning as in the West. In this country, which had practically no religion, the Confucian values justified the old order, enclosed the Chinese in family groups or in clans, without in any way stimulating either a social sense or national sentiment. To build up a unified and collectivist China, the Maoists had always foreseen the revolt against the old feudal culture and the old customs. Admittedly, during the Yenan period they were more cautious and dealt with their "cultural heritage" in a way today's

Red Guards no longer do. Perhaps at that time they wanted to lead the population into liberating itself from an obsolete past, while today they want to end the resistance which the past still exercises against them.

The only truly new element in the program is the Mao cult. In Yenan Mao was not yet an infallible saint: his authority was not contested, but he shared the glory with his closest companions, in particular Chu Teh, the famous commander of the 8th Route Army (on the Communist flags of those days Chu Teh's portrait appeared alongside Mao's); and in 1949, when they took power, the Maoists decided not to name either towns or factories after living leaders.

The Mao cult is therefore a rather recent development. It is practiced with a fervor that grows daily and represents the most offensive aspect of present-day China. Do the Maoists want to give a superabundance of confidence to the peasant masses, who will certainly need it in the terrible test that threatens them?

For the Maoists know that America's military power is very much greater than that of the old Japan, and that she is capable of inflicting dreadful devastation on China. In order for the struggle to be carried on in a country of immense size but limited communications, every people's commune, every peasant would have to be determined to resist. Only then—according to Mao—would China become "an armed ocean able to engulf any armed invasion."

In the West one can hardly believe that the Red Guards, with their brutality and their fanaticism, might be able to make any contribution to the Chinese defense potential. At first sight they constitute a divisive and disruptive factor for the whole country. The present purges have obviously divided even the highest levels of the Communist Party, for not all the leaders were agreed about the methods used in the great cultural revolution (which explains the changes in the CP hierarchy and the partial eclipse of Liu Shao-ch'i). Further, both Party and government machines have been disorganized and disoriented, and the economic life of the country has surely suffered (even if only temporarily). If one is to believe the Western news agencies, the majority of the population was dumbfounded and exasperated rather than enthused by the exploits of the unleashed Maoist youth.

But from a Peking point of view this "sweeping away the dust" operation nevertheless represents a factor of national unity, since it must demonstrate that in China the barriers between those who govern and those who are governed cannot exist and that no privileged minority would be tolerated there which could rise above the status decreed for all. The masses are called upon to check and supervise the conduct of everyone, and this continual social pressure ought to ensure unity and equality in both sacrifices and progress. This, at least, is what the promoters of the cultural revolution, whose principal inspirer is Mao Tse-tung, say and hope.

Must, therefore, everything the Maoists do be justified? Has the left in the West not already made the mistake of approving the excesses that took place in the Soviet Union in the name of the danger which menaced the first country of socialist revolution? This book is not an apologia for China, and at no time have I hidden the facts which offended me "in defense of the interests of People's China." I am convinced that the Chinese revolution has given dignity and hope to the Chinese, but I am nonetheless sure that every revolution needs criticism as man needs air to breathe: this was laid down in the formula employed by Rosa Luxemburg in her message to Lenin appealing for freedom of discussion in the U.S.S.R. and warning him against the inevitable arbitrariness of "His Majesty the Central Committee" which sets itself up as the supreme judge of what is good for the building of socialist society.

But in order to be able to criticize certain aspects of Chinese policy usefully one must start from the reality of the situation in which these are developing and not from prejudice and tendentious reports. But China has few friends in the West. We shall see in the last section of this book what her relations are with the outside world and more particularly with the socialist camp that was supposed to help and protect her. The Chinese certainly share responsibility for the split which has taken place, and they refuse to recognize in the policies of the others, particularly the Soviet Union's, the reflection of a situation that differs from their own, and which determines certain choices in the case of the Soviet Union. They prefer to conduct the debate with foreign Communists in religious terms, as if only one single orthodoxy could exist in the workers' movement, and that all those who deviate from this are heretics.

Unfortunately, the other Communists act in the same way and nourish their anti-Chinese emotions to the point of accepting the most improbable versions of Chinese events—the kind fed to them by the enemies of communism and the whole left, who seek to discredit China in order to preserve the world *status quo*. Today, therefore, it is permissible in the important newspapers of the West to write any fables about China without any attempt whatsoever to establish the truth. Hence the legends about the yellow peril, about Chinese megalomania, about the Maoists' superiority complex born of 4,000 years' history, etc.

"Know thyself, know thine enemy, and in a hundred battles thou shalt win a hundred victories," says an old Chinese proverb. It was not my intention to get to know China in order to help to defeat her. On the contrary, I wanted to show that she was not the enemy and that she could even one day, sooner than we think, become our ally in the battle for a more just and more humane world.

CHAPTER ONE:

Their History as They See It Today

China's 4,000 years of history are written on her face. Everywhere emperors' tombs, monuments, pagodas bear witness to an ancient civilization renowned for its refinement and its technical achievements. But one Chinese city alone, although it is the biggest, has virtually no history: Shanghai. No emperor lived there, no sage wrote his books there, no artist of the golden age ever painted it. This city owes its development — one must say it in a whisper to avoid offending Chinese susceptibilities — to a whim of the English; for the latter, after forcing the Treaty of Nanking (1842) on the Chinese, demanded that they be given a gateway to the north and, paradoxically, chose this sprawling market town on the Hwang Pu River, a tributary of the Yangtze, in southeastern China.

In spite of its unusual origins, the rise of Shanghai is the most significant and the most symbolic of modern China's history. Here, even more than in Canton and the other ports open to foreigners, came the clash between the new commercial civilization of the West and the old civilization of the East. It was in Shanghai that the Chinese saw their first railroad, their first modern factories, their first foundry.

The new production methods and trading system obviously favored the advancement of those Chinese who adopted them soonest. Founded to serve the needs of an agrarian society, the old Confucian hierarchy was no longer relevant in Shanghai, with its banks, its steamships, and its factories. Here the key to power was money — no longer success in the imperial examinations, which were based on the Confucian classics and which for centuries had produced a highly literate governing bureaucracy. While people still continued to respect them, the conventions which governed relations between the emperor and his subjects, and relations between the members of a family, were no longer suitable for the pursuit of wealth in tough competitive conditions. Even the most conscientious servants of the empire did not always decline the opportunities offered by dealings with the foreign devils. The "bales of cotton which the British merchants had bought at bayonet point" — to use Karl Marx's phrase — breached at one blow all the barriers Confucian China had thrown up to keep out barbarian influences.

This country had known many invasions, but it had always absorbed its conquerors. The Manchus imposed their dynasty on them in the seventeenth century; but in the final reckoning it was Manchuria that became Chinese, and not the other way around. The European invasion was of a different kind. The white men had no intention of setting up a new dynasty in Peking or of occupying all China. They simply demanded the right to trade profitably and considered it essential to ensure protection in order to be able to sell their goods (including opium) on their own terms and to buy cheaply those made on the spot. They even built their own factories to exploit the abundant manpower, which was unprotected by any law.

Against this new kind of conqueror, China's only defense was to beat the foreigners at their own game, that of production and trade. This time there was no longer any point in assimilating the invaders, but instead the modern economic techniques which were the source of their power.

How could this be achieved? The old China was in no state to undertake a struggle of this kind. Capitalism had no roots in the country, 90 per cent of it rural and split up into provinces and districts that were barely in touch with one another. The new middle class, emerging in Shanghai and other cities, was faced with the competition of large and experienced international companies: the more they strove to resist foreign inroads by imitating the foreigners and adopting their way of life, the more they cut themselves off from the real China. The literate bureaucracy, foundation of the Confucian system, allowed itself to be tempted by the profits of untrammeled trade, but it had no reforming bent. It thought only of preserving its privileges and of consolidating its hold on its feudal territories, thus creating centrifugal forces that led, step by step, to the virtual disintegration of imperial China.

To develop, capitalism needed a huge unified market, and therefore a centralized state; grafted onto China like a foreign body, it produced developments which ran counter to its aims. While it had the capacity to corrupt, it was neither able to create the energies needed for the adjustment to a new pattern of life nor to produce an influential industrialist class.

Certainly groups of intellectuals and technicians who were in no way inferior to their European colleagues emerged every year in

Shanghai or in Canton. But, hardly out of their towns, they found themselves in a world where recent upheavals served only to aggravate old evils. Bandits exactly like those described by Confucius in the fifth century B.C. roamed the country at will, even widening their field of activity thanks to modern transportation facilities: they no longer terrorized merely villages and townships, but whole provinces or districts. The more able among them even succeeded in moving into the foreigners' world or in recruiting virtual armies to become war lords.

Today in Shanghai, as one walks along the Bund — the waterfront of the Hwang Pu — among the buildings of the foreign banks and big businesses that have vanished (on whose walls one still finds the occasional name plate of a great international corporation such as Shell), or as one glimpses the roaring British lions in front of the town hall, it is easy to imagine the drama in which this generation of Chinese found themselves: they were brought up in the ethos of the conquerors, they went to the same universities and they read the same books, yet they remained powerless to organize their country on the Western model.

Nothing illustrates this dilemma better than the rise of Dr. Sun Yat-sen. Graduate of the medical university at Hong Kong, a great admirer of Lincoln, very familiar with the United States, he wanted China to become a republic on the American pattern. He even succeeded in founding a republican party[1] which helped to bring down the Manchu dynasty in 1911. But to make his victory a permanent one he needed to find somewhere in the country men who would form the backbone of a new administration. But such men did not exist. Instead the power vacuum at the center strengthened the hands of the old local rulers, and far from setting up a modern republic, the revolution of 1911 encouraged warlordism.

The only solution for Sun Yat-sen was to enlist the co-operation of the least dishonest and most nationalistic of the generals, but his attempts to bring this about failed. As soon as an army was mustered under the national and republican banner, its leaders, republican yesterday, changed in turn into war lords. The social structure of the old China still provided too many opportunities for authoritarian rule for the ambitious not to be won over. As for the

---

[1] In August of 1905, Sun Yat-sen organized in Tokyo a republican association, Tung Meng-hui (Sworn League), which was in 1912 rebaptized Kuomintang (Party of the People and of the Country).

enlightened elements who hoped for the creation of a middle-class society, they were too few in number to tip the scales.

Sun Yat-sen's plan to build a bourgeois republic without the bourgeoisie but with a military caste that was "patriotic" and "faithful to the constitution" miscarried woefully.

Desperate, Sun Yat-sen sought the support of the foreigners and even believed, for a moment, that only the occupation of China's major cities by Western troops would allow him to hold free elections. He bombarded the Western chancelleries with notes explaining how the whole world would benefit from helping China to emerge from chaos, but he failed to convince anyone.[2] In fact, the Westerners were his allies in name only. It is true that no statesman in Washington, Paris, or London would have publicly condemned his laudable intention of bringing liberty and justice to China. But neither was anyone in a hurry to see this great country unified again and capable of negotiating on an equal footing. Although they were to be condemned morally, the war lords were much easier to live with. They always needed arms and money, and they were ready to hire themselves out to the highest bidder. Each big nation thus had its own war lords and through this medium could even wage war on its rivals.

In view of the foreign occupation of China, it was logical that Dr. Sun Yat-sen's appeals had no effect. The nationalist leader was ready to guarantee the privileges which the Westerners had acquired, but the weakness and division of his country were a surer guarantee than his word, given in a moment of anguish, and which he could very well go back on.

Admittedly, at the time of World War I, the American President, Woodrow Wilson, was in the process of ending these unequal relations with China. His Fourteen Points on the establishment of democracy throughout the entire world gave rise to high hopes among enlightened Chinese. At Versailles, however, the victors decided not to implement these but simply to hand over the defeated Germany's former possessions to Japan. The chagrin of the Chinese was as great as their enthusiasm had been.

It was almost at the same moment that the sound of gunfire from the cruiser *Aurore* on the Neva brought them the news of the victorious revolution in Russia. For the first time a great European

---

[2] See the testimony of his widow, Soong Ch'ing-ling, to Edgar Snow in *Journey to the Beginning* (New York, Random House, 1958), p. 93.

country renounced the privileges acquired under the unjust treaties imposed on China, and even suggested a solution to her troubles. Moscow invited the Chinese to join the anti-imperialistic struggle and promised them an important place in the family of free nations. "By throwing off the foreign yoke you will help in the liberation of all peoples, including those of Europe and America," proclaimed the Bolshevik government, assigning the Chinese a world role for the first time.

The intellectuals were the first to answer this appeal. Even Dr. Sun Yat-sen, although he did not believe in the class struggle, supported it. But the pioneers of the new liberation movement were two of the most prominent professors in the country: Li Ta-chao and Ch'en Tu-hsiu. Both were Western in outlook and had long ago broken with traditional society.

Ch'en Tu-hsiu, after passing the imperial examinations, had created a resounding scandal by publicly insulting Confucius. Following stays in Tokyo and Paris, he founded in 1915 an avant-garde review with a French title, *La Jeunesse,*[3] and published a fierce editorial against traditional values. "Better that all our ancient culture should disappear than that our race perish by its inability to live in the modern world." This inflammatory issue had to be reprinted several times to meet the demand of students who rushed to get copies: 200,000 were sold in a few days.[4]

On May 4, 1919, the two professors gathered their students at the foreign legation district in Peking to protest against the Treaty of Versailles, and thus launched a vast popular movement which rapidly outgrew its student origins. They established contacts with Moscow and became the propagandists in China of the Russian Revolution. Li Ta-chao gathered round him in Peking a whole group of young idealists converted to Marxism, among them a young librarian from Hunan called Mao Tse-tung.

But the newborn workers' movement had to face the same problem as had, previously, the bourgeois modernists: how to change China? The answer seemed to be clear. In Shanghai and in the big port-cities there was already a working class, unorganized but large, who could count on the support of the radical intelligentsia,

[3] In Chinese it was called *New Youth,* the title under which it is usually quoted.
[4] According to the evidence in *Youth Movement in China,* p. 100, written by a student named Wang and quoted by Benjamin Schwartz in *Chinese Communism and the Rise of Mao* (Cambridge, Harvard University Press, 1951).

disillusioned by its experiences. Here, logically, the movement to unify and reform all China had to begin.

History shows that nothing came of it. The Chinese proletariats fought many a courageous battle in the cities, but they lost them all. Caught between their imperialist enemies and the medieval provinces, cut off themselves from the real China, the workers were no more successful than the middle classes in resolving the contradictions of this complex society or in planting the banner of the new China on the buildings of the foreign merchants. It was not the modern city of Shanghai which liberated China, but the revolutionary movement from the countryside which finally set Shanghai free a century after the start of her industrial rise. It is true that this movement was led by men faithful to the Marxist doctrine and convinced that they represented the workers imprisoned in the big cities, but this was not how Marx and Lenin had envisaged the historic role of the proletariat and its party. All their prophecies were thus overturned. Some even say that the logic of history was violated. Nonetheless, this experience of the Chinese Communists colors all their present thinking. These are the men who govern China today; in order to understand them I have tried to see their history as they see it, how they explain the extraordinary rise of their party.

Besides, this question interests not only China. It is astonishing that the Chinese revolution should have succeeded in an essentially peasant country, but there is nothing to show that the same thing will not happen elsewhere. Some — chiefly the Chinese — even think that the Chinese revolution will serve as a model for revolutions which will inevitably break out one day in the underdeveloped countries of Asia and Latin America. It is therefore essential to study the mechanics of it deeply. I also asked to be allowed to visit all the historic areas in order to try to "see," and to hear directly from the principal protagonists, how the events of the last thirty years took place. I often amazed university professors by talking more about the past than the present. But it is my view that the past is one of the major keys to the China of today.

I could not go everywhere. It is practically impossible, for instance, to retrace the route of the Long March, one of the finest pages in the Maoist epic. But in spite of that and the difficulties which often arise in discussions with men who do not always share our conception of historical truth, I have been able to reconstruct the main stages of this revolution, or rather to assemble the version which millions of Chinese learn today and which inevitably colors their political consciousness and vision of the world. I unearthed no new revelations capable of controverting the theories held by serious historians on the birth of Maoism. But I learned, by talking and looking, why the theories taught in present-day China are often considerably different.

THE TWELVE, THE SIX, AND THE QUESTION OF METHOD

In the former French Concession in Shanghai, in modest Wang Tse Street, the gates of No. 108 are painted black and well kept. No one lives in this house and no commemorative plaque marks it. To gain admission, one must make application and make an appointment. So one afternoon I presented myself, accompanied by my official escort (a representative of the Foreign Ministry and my interpreter). A man of about fifty, with the refined face of an intellectual, greeted us, watched by curious passers-by. "Welcome to this place, where the first congress of the Chinese Communist Party opened on July 1, 1921," Mr. Lin, who is playing host, says a trifle solemnly. "This house is being converted into a museum and the work is not yet finished, but everything you see is authentic or a faithful reproduction of the original."

I reply in the same manner: "I have visited several museums in your country. Everywhere this house is mentioned — that's why I have made a point of visiting it. To understand a political movement it is essential to know its history." Actually, I am thinking: "To understand a communist movement it is essential to know *how* it presents its history." But at the beginning of my pilgrimage to the fountainheads of Chinese communism I have no wish to say anything that might appear even mildly "polemical."

Mr. Lin takes me around the house, which is very much bigger than it looks from the outside; Chinese architecture has a knack of disguising space. From the start one is surprised by the comfort enjoyed by these secret delegates, who were twelve in number, like the Apostles. On the ground floor, a spacious meeting room furnished with seats and with a handsome large black table, and adorned with antique pottery; on the first floor, an equally large lounge, a kind of smoking room with very comfortable armchairs, a dining room giving onto another big room in which we have just sat down in front of six large portraits.

"Why did these twelve young men need such a comfortable place to meet?"

Mr. Lin smiles. "These men were young indeed, but they were tackling a task of historical importance. Lenin himself followed their discussions day after day, and in 1919 he said that the Communists of the Far East would have to solve problems never faced by the other parties. Besides, the French police never allowed the delegates to work peacefully here. They had to seek refuge on the shores of Lake Shaohsing, in Chekiang province, where they held their later meetings under cover of boating parties. They weren't simply young men who talked!"

Mr. Lin's assurance and the respectful silence of the others hint that he is no mere official who recites a piece learned by heart and does not dare answer questions that are not on the agenda. With broad strokes of the brush he paints a historical picture of the China of 1921 and winds up thus: "In 1920 the Communist Manifesto of Marx and Engels was translated into Chinese, and from that year Marxist circles were formed in Shanghai, in Peking, in Wuhan, in Canton, and in Tientsin. In Changsha it was Chairman Mao Tse-tung who founded the local circle. But for the circles to accomplish their task they had to have a national party. Each circle therefore sent two delegates to Shanghai in order that they might found the Chinese Communist Party. They represented fifty-seven permanent members, but already they could count on the support of many sympathizers among the working class."

"Who were these delegates?"

Mr. Lin rises and points to the six portraits, one by one: Mao Tse-tung, Chairman of the Communist Party of China; Tung Pi-wu, Vice-President of the Republic; Ch'en T'an-ch'iu, Ho Shu-heng, and Teng Yeng-ming, all three of whom died with glory in battle; and finally Wang Chin-wei, also a martyr of the revolution.

"But there were twelve of them. Where are the other six?"

Mr. Lin makes a gesture of mild irritation which says: "If you only let me get on with it, you won't need to ask pointless questions." And then he goes on: "Marxism was then a novelty. The twelve representatives of the Marxist circles weren't all battle-tried revolutionaries, and they didn't always have the clearest of ideas. Some wanted an oversimplified workers' movement. As a result, one of the delegates whose portrait is not here wanted to ban all intellectuals from party membership. His name would mean nothing to you, and we ourselves can hardly remember it. He ended up by forming a Trotskyite splinter-group which faded, like himself, into oblivion. On the other hand, one urged that the party should be a Marxist study group rather than a fighting organization. He ended up, a few years later, as personal secretary to Chiang Kai-shek. Only the six comrades you see before you represented the true Marxist core thanks to which a party of the Bolshevik type was founded, based on democratic centralism and meant to lead a mass movement."

I ask again: "Wasn't Ch'en Tu-hsiu one of the delegates?"

"At the time of the congress Ch'en Tu-hsiu was in Canton and unable to take part. Nevertheless he was elected Secretary-General of the Party. It was a mistake, of course, but one must remember that Ch'en Tu-hsiu was a radical democrat, very well known for his anti-imperialist sentiments. Unfortunately his fondness for pragmatic philosophy prevented him from becoming a true Marxist and, as a result, from analyzing the situation correctly. His right-wing and opportunist tendencies did a lot of harm to our party, but we don't deny that from 1921 to August, 1927, he was Secretary-General."

We come to Li Ta-chao: detained by other business in Peking, he also was unable to take part in the secret meeting in Wang Tse Street. But Mao Tse-tung's former preceptor is warmly saluted by Mr. Lin as a complete Marxist and a victim of the imperialists and reactionaries who treacherously killed him in 1927.[5] And Mr. Lin adds: "The scaffold on which he was hanged is in the Museum of the Revolution, and we shall always honor his memory."

One question, however, Mr. Lin leaves unanswered: he does not know if a representative of the Comintern took part in the congress. He readily admits that the comrades of the Third International helped the congress delegates, but seems unaware of the existence of a Dutch Communist, known under the pseudonym of Maring, who, according to trustworthy sources, was one of the organizers of the Shanghai meeting.[6a]

This is not the only gap in Mr. Lin's memory. It is certain

[5] Li Ta-chao was arrested on April 6, 1927, in Peking by soldiers of the war lord Chang Tso-lin, who, with the tacit approval of the Western diplomats broke into the legation quarter and invaded the Soviet Embassy. Nineteen other Chinese militants were executed at the same time as the celebrated professor.

[6a] Maring, whose real name was H. Sneevliet, later broke with the Comintern and founded a left-wing socialist party in Holland. He was executed by the Nazis during the Occupation.

that among the six men whose portraits are missing was Chang Kuo-t'ao,[6b] who was one of the leaders of the Party for the next fifteen years. But during the Long March, in 1935, he opposed Mao Tse-tung and broke away, taking with him the important army he commanded. Little is known about this clash, for the evidence is scarce and partly hearsay. However, Mao Tse-tung himself refers to it in several of his works, particularly in *On the Tactics of Fighting Japanese Imperialism.* He seems to have done everything to bring about a reconciliation with Chang Kuo-t'ao, and from 1936 to 1938 Chang once more became one of the leading directors of the Party, even becoming Vice-Chairman of the Red Republic of the Northwest. Only after 1938 did he finally break with Mao and, according to the latter, rejoin the Kuomintang's secret service.

The fact that a politician helps to create a new party is no guarantee of his future loyalty to it. The history of the European workers' movement abounds in turncoats who, after playing a more or less militant role in its ranks, ended up in the opposite camp: in France, Jacques Doriot was a Communist before he formed a fascist party, collaborated with the Germans, and donned the uniform of the Waffen SS. In Italy, Mussolini had been a socialist. And Sir Oswald Mosley, leader of the British fascists, had been one of the pillars of the Labor left wing. That some of the founders of the Chinese Communist Party should later have gone over to the right or even to the extreme right is not really all that surprising. But for us the fact that they may have "gone wrong" is no reason for failing to mention even their names when talking of historical events they took part in.

What was a revelation to me during these conversations about the birth of the Chinese Communist Party was the perfect naturalness — I would even say the clear conscience — with which the Maoists suppressed all reference to those who, by the Party's lights, had dishonored themselves. In their view, a politician who compromises himself by an act condemned by the Party automatically deletes himself from history and nullifies, *ipso facto,* all his previous merits. He becomes a "non-being," and his name is never again mentioned in public unless the Party considers it necessary to condemn him as a traitor and an enemy of the people. To Mr.

[6b] Chang Kuo-t'ao, who now lives in Hong Kong, is believed to be publishing his autobiography in the U.S. in the near future.

Lin and all the other Chinese I have had conversations with, this practice seems perfectly normal; and those who argue the point in the name of historical truth appear to them to be defending dubious characters.

In the specific case of the first congress of the Chinese CP, moreover, it is difficult for a Westerner to refute the Chinese official line in precise detail. Foreign historians know little about this event, even to the point that different historians are not agreed on the names of those who took part. According to Isaacs, for example,[7] Shao Li-tzu — future dignitary of the Kuomintang — was one of the twelve, but he is not named by Schwartz.[8] Others believe that Ch'en Tu-hsiu and Li Ta-chao took part in the congress, while Edmund Clubb declares they did not.[9] By all accounts the fact of someone's having taken part in the Shanghai meeting was not regarded at the time as of prime importance, and this title of honor was not emphasized then in the participants' biographies.

The relative obscurity which still enshrouds the event today could, if the Chinese adopted purely Stalinist methods, enable them to substitute six portraits of martyrs or "good Communists" for those of the militants who "went wrong." They could even declare that there were only six delegates without unduly shocking historians. Not so long ago Stalin made a practice of such substitutions and suppressions in the case of events which were much more widely known and more easily verifiable.

But the Maoists are loath, it seems, to resort to such flagrant frauds. Having laid down the principle that history does not have to be revealed in its entirety, they feel free to keep only what they consider essential without having to fill in too many of the blanks.

In Shanghai, in the house where the Chinese CP was born, one gets a good insight into this process of simplifying history. "There were twelve, but only six of them are interesting," they tell you, and the matter is settled. Unfortunately, when one comes to the confused history of the following years, it is not always possible to gauge the importance of such suppression or to discover the real reasons for certain silences.

[7] Isaacs, Harold, *The Tragedy of the Chinese Revolution* (Stanford, Stanford University Press, 1961), p. 58.

[8] Schwartz, Benjamin, *Chinese Communism and the Rise of Mao* (Cambridge, Harvard University Press, 1951), p. 217.

[9] Clubb, Edmund, *Twentieth Century China* (New York, Columbia University Press, 1963), p. 114.

WHAT USE IS AN INTERNATIONAL?

This practice of omission applies not only to individuals; certain institutions — the Comintern, for example — are pushed into the background in such a way that one has to search very carefully to find any trace of them in the exhibitions and museums whose purpose is to spread the present version of Chinese history — and there are plenty of these. Even in public gardens one frequently sees pavilions displaying photographs connected with an episode of the Maoist epic. The Museum of the Revolution, built in Peking's central square for the tenth anniversary of the liberation, is one of the biggest buildings in the city; and copies of practically every exhibit there are sent to all the provincial museums, which are visited by millions who go to learn their history.

Among the documents I saw everywhere, time and time again, were facsimiles of foreign Communist journals which, since before World War II, had glorified the exploits of the Chinese CP. But never did I see any Comintern publication. However, if one wanted evidence of the interest shown by foreign Communists in the struggle of their Chinese comrades, it was to be found in considerable quantity in the records of the Third International.

In fact the Communist International, founded by Lenin following the October Revolution, was not merely a co-ordinating body; its aim was to organize, throughout the world, directly and actively, the proletarian struggle. To belong to it, the Communist parties of the different countries (formed for the most part by breakaways from the main body of the socialist movement) had to accept twenty-one conditions, one of which bound them to carry out the decisions made by headquarters, which had the right to intervene in their internal affairs. The Comintern leadership even reserved the right to appoint the men they considered the most able to run member parties. Thus every Communist party, big or small, agreed to sacrifice part of its independence for the common good.[10]

[10] Given this centralized structure of the international Communist movement, all the decisions made at that period by the different Communist parties, including the CCP, can be attributed to the Comintern. And one can take into consideration the fact that until 1935 at least, the Chinese Communist leaders consulted Moscow very regularly, even on decisions of detail. Only in exceptional circumstances, when communication with the Comintern was impossible, were they sometimes forced to act independently.

In 1920, in Moscow, Lenin declared from the platform of the second congress of the Comintern that this rule did not bring foreign parties under the dictate of the victorious Russian Bolshevik party, but, on the contrary, that that party undertook to help its less powerful fellows.

Its guiding principle was as follows: "The interests of the proletarian struggle within a country must be subordinated to the interests of the struggle at the international level, and the nation which has defeated the bourgeoisie within its boundaries must resolve to make the greatest sacrifices for the overthrow of international capitalism."[11]

The Communist strategy was therefore worked out collectively and aimed at exploiting to the full every revolutionary situation, wherever it might occur. And now, after the succession of defeats in Europe, China became in the Comintern's eyes the nerve center of the anti-imperialist struggle and was duly accorded complete priority.

The Marxist classics had not dealt in depth with the Far Eastern problem, but they had nonetheless sensed the importance which the awakening of China or India could have in the political transformation of the world. "The capitalist conquest of China," wrote Engels in 1895, "will speed up the overthrow of capitalism in Europe and in America." And Marx before him had written: "The coming rising of the European peoples will depend more on what happens in the Heavenly Empire than on any other event."[12]

These prophecies, often recalled by Comintern speakers, suddenly began to come true. In the 1920's, indeed, China was shaken by a series of violent blows. Until 1918 no union had ever been formed, but now workers' organizations sprouted like mushrooms after a shower. Strikes broke out everywhere, even in foreign-owned concerns, despite the threatening presence of European and Japanese war fleets. And it was in Hong Kong itself, island fortress of Britain, most firmly rooted of all the European powers, that

---

Several Western historians have tried to establish more accurately to what degree even secondary decisions were dictated by Moscow; but as the Comintern archives are not open for foreign research, they are often obliged to make do with rather slight clues or to venture unverifiable guesses.

[11] See Lenin, "Preliminary Scheme of Theses on the National and Colonial Question," in *Communist International,* June–July, 1920.

[12] These quotations are taken from a report by Zinoviev drawn up on April 15, 1927, for the attention of the next plenary session of the Executive Committee of the Third International.

the first great trial of strength between the Chinese workers and their foreign bosses took place.

On January 12, 1922, the dockers and seamen stopped work and demanded at one swoop both a 30 per cent raise and union rights. At their head was a young sailor, Su Chao-cheng, who was later to become one of the great figures of the Chinese trade union movement.[13] Caught short by the boldness and scope of the movement, the British reacted at first with threats. But the Chinese, whom they had until then regarded as docile, had a second surprise in store: rather than start work again under the old conditions, they trekked out of the city. In Canton, Sun Yat-sen (who in 1920, with the help of General Ch'en Chiung-ming, had been successful in forming a new government) welcomed them with open arms. All over China, as far away as the distant Northeast, demonstrations of support were organized, quite spontaneously, and collections were made in aid of the strikers. Totally unprepared for a reaction of such magnitude, the British ended up by giving in; and on March 8 the strike came to an end with the complete victory of the seamen and dockers. A month later, in Moscow, Lenin announced with touching optimism: "China has already entered the revolutionary struggle in the international movement for world revolution."[14] On the first of May the founding congress of the All-China Federation of Labor opened in an atmosphere of triumph.

The Hong Kong strike was not inspired by the Kuomintang, although Dr. Sun Yat-sen had taken a political risk in supporting it. Present-day Chinese historians claim that the young Communist Party played a formative role in the strike as well as in the creation of the Federation of Labor, and all over China photographs of these events are displayed, extolling the merits of the valiant comrades of the 1920's. But if one studies the biographies of the principal architects of the Hong Kong victory, this claim appears to be highly dubious. Su Chao-cheng, chairman of the strike committee, joined the CP only in 1925,[15] and his deputy, Li Wei-ming, who became chairman of the Federation of Labor, did not join

[13] See his biography in Wales, Nym, *The Chinese Labor Movement* (New York, John Day Co., 1945), p. 208.

[14] Lenin, *Works* (Moscow, Foreign Languages Publishing House), Vol. 18, p. 74.

[15] Su Chao-cheng in 1926 became chairman of the Chinese Trade Unions. In 1927 he was Minister of Labor in the left-wing Kuomintang government in Wuhan. He died two years later in Shanghai at the age of forty-one.

until 1926.[16] Further, no one who was an important member of the Party at that time played a major part in the strike.

The question of knowing who was in at the beginning of the mass movement is not a purely academic one. It was the subject of a Comintern debate which, a few years later, was to turn into a decisive trial of strength between the Stalinists, who were in the majority in the Russian CP (and therefore in the Comintern), and the opposition minority grouped around Trotsky.[17] For Stalin, champion of the "socialism in a single country" line, the essential point was to find allies to defend the U.S.S.R. against an eventual anti-Communist crusade by the Western powers. Patently the anti-imperialistic struggle of the Chinese was weakening the mortal enemies of "the foremost socialist fortress in the world," and Stalin was determined to support the main anti-imperialist group, whoever they might be. He hardly believed in the chances of a Communist revolution in China, and evoking in rather high-handed fashion the precedent of the 1905 revolution in Russia, he declared that China would first have to go through a capitalist phase of development under the bourgeoisie. The Kuomintang seemed to him to be perfectly fitted for this historical middle-class task, and so he asked the Chinese Communists to give it their unconditional support.[18]

More of an idealist, more convinced of the possibility, if not the imminence, of world revolution, Trotsky believed it was the Communist International's first duty to bring about Communist revolutions whatever the cost. He inferred from his theory of permanent revolution that the Chinese bourgeoisie's term of power would be as brief as Kerensky's had been in Russia. According to him, the two phases of the revolution — bourgeois and prole-tarian — had to be brought together to the point where they "tele-

[16] Li Wei-ming, first chairman of the Federation of Labor, died in 1927.

[17] The most impartial account of the part played by the Chinese affair in the duel between the Stalinists and the Trotskyites is provided by Deutscher, Isaac, *The Prophet Unarmed: Trotsky, 1921–1929* (London, Oxford University Press, 1959), pp. 316ff. Deutscher, well-known biographer of Stalin and Trotsky, whose personal records he had the privilege of studying, avoids glorifying the insight of either of the protagonists of the historic Moscow debate of 1927. He reveals the merits of Trotsky and also certain of his weaknesses. Contradicting Trotskyite historians, Deutscher shows particularly that if Trotsky was basically right, his reaction to Stalin's Chinese policy was tardy enough, since he did not publicly launch his great attack until 1927.

[18] According to Moscow, the Kuomintang, reorganized by Sun Yat-sen, became the "bloc of the four classes": bourgeoisie, petty bourgeoisie, workers, and peasants.

scoped." Trotsky did not forbid foreign Communists to conclude alliances with other parties — and therefore was not opposed to the Chinese CP's collaboration with the Kuomintang — but he advised them not to sacrifice their objectives and principles to such alliances. Now, however, under pressure from Stalin, already master of the Comintern, the Chinese Communists were virtually forced to subordinate themselves completely to their Kuomintang partners.

The first contacts between the Bolshevik government and Dr. Sun Yat-sen had been made in the days of Lenin, who used to correspond with the Chinese Nationalist leader.[19] But it was only at the beginning of 1923, when Sun Yat-sen's star was on the wane once again, that a pact could be reached. A friend of Trotsky's, Adolf Abramovitch Joffe,[20] went to carry out the negotiations in Shanghai, where Sun Yat-sen had gone, exiled temporarily by the disloyal General Ch'en Chiung-ming. The Kuomintang leader eagerly accepted the Soviet Union's help in reorganizing his party and approved the plans for collaboration with the U.S.S.R. and the Communists. The latter were apparently much less enthusiastic about the idea of forming a united front with the Nationalists — and under their direction — and, according to Chen Tu-hsiu, the Comintern had to enforce discipline to bring this about. A representative of the Russian CP, Michael Borodin,[21] arrived in China soon after as a special adviser attached to the Kuomintang. It was he who drew up the basic rules of the reorganized Kuomintang along lines similar to those of the Bolshevik Party. The new Kuomintang held its first congress in Canton in January, 1924, and the Communists, notably Mao Tse-tung, took part.

Sun Yat-sen had enough authority over his Nationalist supporters to get them to accept, without too much trouble, his new political orientation. It seems that he was not too exacting with the Communists, who, according to the principle in effect at the time, could defend their ideas and exercise their influence while fighting under the blue banner of the Kuomintang. It is perhaps for this reason that many Party veterans consider, without saying so, that

[19] See Pischel, Enrica Collotti, *Le origini ideologiche della rivoluzione cinese* (Turin, Einaudi, 1959), p. 121.

[20] Adolf Joffe, one of the most brilliant Soviet diplomats, negotiator of the Brest-Litovsk peace pact, killed himself in November, 1927, in protest against the exclusion of the Trotskyites from the Russian Communist Party.

[21] Michael Borodin lived in the U.S. for fifteen years and only returned to Russia after the October Revolution. Following the failure of his mission to China, he was relegated to an unimportant post.

the Sun Yat-sen–Joffe pact yielded the greatest rewards for the extreme left. Dr. Sun Yat-sen sincerely believed that the overriding demands of the national struggle would be strong enough to stave off class war in China. He even wrote that in his country there were no rich and poor, but only the poor and the very poor. According to him, the property-owning classes of China were so tightly controlled and so humiliated by foreign capitalists that their wealth was purely relative, was constantly threatened, and gave them no political privileges, for these were already monopolized by foreigners. In his view, there was one sole objective for all Chinese: anti-imperialism.

This was a dangerous illusion. The richest Chinese, or, if one wishes, the least poor, were very attached to their property and their privileges, however modest they might be. They were by no means ready to sacrifice them on the altar of national unity, and although content to see the workers in the ranks of the Kuomintang, they were not keen on strikes and mass demonstrations. In 1925 their fears began to grow; the "anti-imperialist" movement had assumed such proportions that the Canton middle classes felt they were already living in a Soviet republic.

On May 30, 1925, barely two months after Sun Yat-sen's death, the British fired on a crowd of demonstrators on the Nanking Lu in Shanghai, killing a dozen Chinese workers and students. The next day the city was paralyzed by a general strike. Even domestic servants left the foreign concessions. The European colony suffered a bad attack of nerves. At Hankow and Canton their defense forces stepped up action against the Chinese demonstrators. On June 11, British sailors killed eight and wounded twelve at Hankow. On June 23, British and French soldiers killed 52 and wounded 117 at Canton.

The Chinese workers replied to this massacre with wholesale strikes, and the whole population with a total boycott of British goods. Hong Kong was once again brought to a standstill. At Canton the unions organized armed strike pickets to enforce observance of the anti-British boycott. More than 2,000 guns were distributed to the workers, who converted the gambling houses into dormitories for the strikers. Pickets searched vehicles and people on foot to prevent any Chinese from taking food supplies to the Anglo-French island of Shameen, which is in the very heart of Canton. A special tribunal, set up by the strike committee, meted out arbitrary justice to those who did not observe the boycott. The workers were not officially in power in Canton, but to see their armed representatives in action one could misunderstand — and the wealthy Chinese did misunderstand.

The middle classes felt themselves overwhelmed, and so they looked for a strong man, someone who would be able first of all to restore order and then to change the balance of power within the Kuomintang, which leaned dangerously to the extreme left. They found their man in the person of General Chiang Kai-shek,[22] who knew how to show his displeasure occasionally at the scheming of the extremists. At Sun Yat-sen's death Chiang was not the next in succession, but circumstances favored him: Liao Chung-k'ai, the most left-wing member of the dead leader's entourage, was mysteriously murdered in August, 1925; and two other Kuomintang leaders who were implicated in the affair, Hu Han-min and Hsu Chung-chi, were asked to leave Canton. At one blow Chiang became number two in the Party — behind the faint-hearted Wang Ching-wei — as well as already being number one in the Nationalist army.

On March 20, 1926, while the strike was going on in Hong Kong and the anti-British boycott was still in effect in Canton, Chiang

[22] Chiang Kai-shek's biography, as related by Harold Isaacs in *Tragedy of the Chinese Revolution* (pp. 81–82), makes interesting reading: "Scion of a moderately well-to-do Chekiang merchant family, Chiang Kai-shek was at military school in Tokyo when the first revolution took place in 1911. He hurried back to Shanghai where he joined the staff of a general named Ch'en Ch'i-mei. Under Ch'en's patronage, Chiang met Sun Yat-sen. He also came into contact with Yü Ya-ch'ing, then already a powerful compradore, and Chang Ching-chiang, a millionaire banker and dealer in bean curd and curios. Chiang also associated with Huang Ching-yung, one of Shanghai's notorious underworld leaders, and is generally believed to have become a member at this time of the most powerful secret society in Shanghai, known as the Green Circle. . . ." The fleshpots of Shanghai apparently suited his taste, and for a time we find him operating as a petty broker on the Shanghai stock exchange. Either through cupidity or ignorance — the records are not clear on this point — he was soon penniless and on the streets. "Chang Ching-chiang and his other sponsors bailed him out of a difficult situation. They made good some questionable losses, lined his pockets, and shipped him off to Canton to link his fortunes with those of Sun Yat-sen. Few investments have ever paid greater dividends. . . .

"In Canton, Chiang Kai-shek joined Sun Yat-sen's military staff. After Sun made contact with the Soviet government, he sent Chiang to Moscow to study Red Army methods. Chiang left China in July 1923 and remained in Russia for six months. . . . On his return to Canton at the end of the year, Chiang became the dark-haired darling of Borodin and the Russian military advisers. In May 1924 they set up the Whampoa Military Academy. Chiang Kai-shek, the only military man who had been to Russia and studied Russian military methods at first hand, and what is more, a man who made himself sound reliably radical, was the logical choice for director."

Kai-shek suddenly began to make mass arrests among the Communists, not sparing even the Russian advisers. The pretext chosen for this operation was frivolous; the consequences were grave. Wang Ching-wei considered it wise to take several months' leave in Europe, and the Communists gave in without too much protest. Chiang became master of the situation and could dictate conditions to revolutionary Canton. They were Draconian for the Communists. The strong man of the Kuomintang insisted that they supply him with a list of their members[23] and that they promise not to recruit any longer from among the members of his own party. He then settled the legal dispute with the British in an agreement reached in the absence of any representative of the strike committee; and this time the Hong Kong strike, which had lasted fifteen months, won nothing for the workers.

Present-day Chinese historians accuse Ch'en Tu-hsiu, the leader of the CP, of not having foreseen the political overthrow of the Nationalist bourgeoisie and of not having recognized Chiang Kai-shek's personal ambitions, even after his strong-arm action in the spring of 1926. However, Ch'en Tu-hsiu in a letter to the militants in 1929, after his exclusion from the Party, gave a very different version of his role at the time and explained that he was compelled constantly to act under pressure from the Comintern.[24] The disturbing news from Canton did not change the Comintern's attitude toward the Kuomintang. It was even admitted to the bosom of the Communist International as a "sympathetic party"; and its representative, "Comrade" Shao Li-tzu, took part in December, 1926, in the work of the seventh plenary session, which, at Stalin's re-

[23] According to the current figures, the Chinese CP at the beginning of 1927 numbered 57,957 members, 53.8 per cent of them workers. But in his report to the Comintern, Zinoviev claimed that the Party had 15,000 adherents. (See his memorandum drawn up on April 15, 1927, for the attention of the plenary session of the Executive Committee of the Third International.)

[24] "Ch'en Tu-hsiu was straightforward, soft, and lacked self-confidence," wrote Deutscher in *The Prophet Unarmed* (p. 318); "and these qualities made him a tragic figure. At every stage he frankly stated his objections to Moscow's policy; but he did not stick to them. When overruled, he submitted to the Comintern's authority; and against his better knowledge carried out Moscow's policy." Convinced after the coup of March 20, 1926, that Chiang Kai-shek was preparing to fight the Communist Party, Ch'en Tu-hsiu asked the Soviet advisers in Canton to divert from the arms deliveries to Chiang Kai-shek at least 5,000 rifles, which would allow the Communists to arm the rebelling peasants of Kwangtung. His request was refused. (See Deutscher, *The Prophet Unarmed,* p. 321.)

quest, condemned the Trotskyites for their criticism of Chiang Kai-shek and of the policy of the four-class bloc in China!

Chiang was thus able to break up the Communist organizations and unions in his country without any protests from his allies in Moscow. Stalin was apparently not unaware of the right-wing tendencies of the Nationalist general, but in his opinion they were compensated for by his determination to fight imperialism. By unifying China, Chiang was unleashing — always according to Stalin — a revolutionary process *sui generis*. His actions, therefore, were not to be opposed by the extreme left; and the U.S.S.R. was to give all possible help to the Nationalist army, which, under the supreme command of Chiang Kai-shek, was marching toward the North to free China of the war lords before liberating it from the imperialists.

It was in the spring of 1927, in Shanghai, that this policy reaped its most disastrous results. It caused tens of thousands of deaths, not among the war lords or among the imperialists, but among the Chinese workers. On March 21 the Shanghai workers succeeded in driving out the demoralized troops of the war lord Sun Ch'uan-fang. They wanted to ease the task facing Generalissimo Chiang Kai-shek's Nationalist army, which was marching on the city.[25a] The

----

[25a] Edgar Snow in his *Red Star Over China* (London, Gollancz, 1937), pp. 60–61, describes Chou En-lai's role and how the rebellion of March 21 was carried out. "Chou En-lai was ordered to prepare an insurrection and help the Nationalist Army seize Shanghai. A youth of twenty-eight, with no formal military training, little experience with the working class (from which, as son of a big bourgeois family, he had been isolated), with no guidebook to show him how to make an insurrection, and none to advise him (the chief Russian advisers being with Chiang Kai-shek), Chou arrived in Shanghai equipped only with a revolutionary determination and a strong theoretical knowledge of Marxism.

"Within three months the Communist Party had organized 600,000 workers, and was able to call a general strike. The response was unanimous, and a terrifying experience to the smug populace of this greatest stronghold of foreign imperialism in China. But the insurrection failed to materialize. Unarmed and untrained, the workers did not know how to go about 'seizing the city.' They had to learn empirically the necessity of an armed nucleus of workers. And the militarists accommodated them.

"Underestimating the significance of the first and then of a second strike, the old northern warlords merely cut off a number of heads, but failed to halt the labour movement. Chou En-lai and the famous Shanghai labour leaders, Chao Shi-yen, Ku Shun-chang, and Lo Yi-ming, now succeeded in organizing 50,000 pickets, and in the French concession secured premises where military training was secretly given to 2,000 cadres. With mausers smuggled into the city, an 'iron band' of 300 marksmen was trained, and this was the only armed force these Shanghai workers had.

"On March 21, 1927, the Communists called a general strike which closed

news of this victory fired the enthusiasm of Communists all over the world. In Paris, Semard, Monmousseau, and Cachin lauded it during a big meeting at the end of which they sent the following telegram to Chiang Kai-shek: "The working class of Paris salutes the Chinese Revolutionary Army's entry into Shanghai. Fifty-six years after the Paris Commune and ten years after that of Russia, the Chinese Commune marks a new step toward world revolution." The next day *Die Rote Fahne,* journal of the German CP, and the French Communist *L'Humanité* published pictures of Chiang Kai-shek on the front page, and *Pravda* was also enthusiastic.

But the "liberator" had more interests in common with the property-owners of Shanghai than with the armed workers.[25b] He wasted no time in making the point; and April 12, 1927, is solemnly commemorated as a St. Bartholomew's Day Massacre of the workers, cold-bloodedly carried out by Chiang Kai-shek with the help not only of his army but also of gangsters hastily recruited from the city's underworld.[26] This tragic day has inspired a whole literature, beginning with André Malraux's *Man's Fate.* Coinciding, within a few days, with the opening of the meeting of the executive branch of the Comintern in Moscow, the massacre put Stalin in an embarrassing position. He was tough enough and clever enough, however, to prove that his policy was the right one, despite the distressing episode in Shanghai, which — according to him — discredited Chiang in his own party and sounded the death knell of his career.

Actually, on April 17, 1927, the Kuomintang government, sitting in Wuhan, did condemn Chiang Kai-shek for his treachery in

---

all the industries of Shanghai, and put 600,000 workers, organized and militant for the first time in their lives, behind the barricades of revolution. They seized first the police stations, next the arsenal, then the garrison, and after that, victory. Five thousand workers were armed, six battalions of revolutionary troops created, and a 'citizens' Government' was proclaimed. "It was the most remarkable *coup d'état* in modern Chinese history."

[25b] Chiang Kai-shek's *volte face* was certainly precipitated by the strong reaction of the Western powers whose warships shelled Nanking on March 24, 1927, to protect their nationals. This was certainly interpreted by Chiang Kai-shek as a warning to break with the Communists if he wanted to win Western friendship.

[26] It is noteworthy that the two sons of Ch'en Tu-hsiu, Secretary-General of the CP — Ch'en Chao-nien and Ch'en Yen-nien — were among the thousands of victims of this bloody day. Photographs and personal belongings of Chen Yen-nien, the better known of the two, are on display in the Great Museum of the Revolution in Peking.

Shanghai. But Chiang already wielded the real power. All attempts to oppose him by weak politicians like Wang Ching-wei[27] or by Nationalist war lords like the "Christian General" Feng Yü-hsiang[28a] were doomed to failure and collapsed. Less than three months after the Shanghai incident all these Nationalist "brother-enemies" had rallied under Chiang's anti-Communist banner. The Communists had already been wiped out in Shanghai and in Wuhan by the time the order to resist was at last received. Renouncing their ambition to unify the country and make it independent, the bourgeoisie gave in to the foreigners, who supported Chiang Kai-shek, defender of their interests. But in return they were freed from the fear of the proletarian threat which had haunted them as long as the alliance of the "four anti-imperialist classes" had lasted.

In view of the severity of such a defeat, one might think that the Chinese Communists, victorious today, would have studied its history in minute detail. This would have allowed them to explain more fully to the younger generation the confusing documents of the fierce repression of 1927 and to throw more light on a major event in the history of the workers' movement.[28b] This revolution that failed did not concern only China; it brought into question the principles of the International and its relations with national parties, and one can draw lessons from its history that today would still interest all revolutionary movements. But no. The Chinese have little inclination to rummage about in their past, and they maintain an extraordinary secrecy about the events of 1927. In Shanghai the Nanking Lu is always called the Nanking Lu, and not, for example, "The Avenue of the Shooting of May 30, 1925." No monument has been put up to the martyrs of April 12, 1927. True, in the big national museums, some documents recall the

---

[27] Wang Ching-wei ended his career as a Chinese quisling. In 1937 he formed a puppet government under the Japanese. He died in November, 1944, in occupied Nanking.

[28a] Feng Yü-hsiang, a convert to Christianity, flirted with Moscow for a time as a self-styled "former worker." In 1930, three years after joining Chiang Kai-shek, he declared war on him, but failed to beat him and once again became one of his ministers. In 1947 he again became a dissenter, in New York, and sought Russian support. He died on October 5, 1948, in a mysterious fire in the Soviet ship that was taking him to Europe.

[28b] Paradoxically, the Russians published in the summer of 1966 two political biographies, one of Borodin, the other of Marshal Blücher, glorifying their role in China in the 1920's and showing how "ungrateful" the Chinese are to the Soviet CP, which helped them so much in the past.

defeat, but they have been selected only to demonstrate the misdeeds of the "right-wing deviationists" in the heart of the former Chinese CP leadership and to condemn the chief sinner, Ch'en Tu-hsiu, first Secretary-General of the Party.

Yet no one accused him in my hearing of treason or of premeditated sabotage. No one treated him as an "enemy of the people," no one stressed the fact that after his expulsion from the Party in 1929 he became a Trotskyite.[29] The charge against Ch'en Tu-hsiu is more subtle than that; it denounces above all his inability to analyze correctly the social relationships within the Kuomintang and in the country generally. He was simply a "bad Marxist," and that was enough for him to lead his party to disaster. "For the strength of the Communists resides in their scientific doctrine, and those who know how to interpret it correctly are sure of victory," said one of my guides conclusively, looking respectfully at Mao Tse-tung's portrait.

The official procedure governing visits in China is, nevertheless, conducive to arguments. Leaving a factory or museum, just before the last cup of tea, the Chinese always declare that they need criticism and advice; and they insist, in the name of friendship between peoples, that one should offer some. Emboldened by such encouragement, I always said everywhere that I regarded as incomplete the history of the "first Chinese revolution" they teach today and then went on to reveal the facts I have cited above on the role of the Comintern and of Stalin.

I was always heard out very politely, and no one seemed to dream of protesting against the crime of lese majesty I was committing in questioning the "great Stalin," under whose portrait our discussions frequently took place. Some of my guides seemed surprised by my "theories," as if they were hearing them for the first time, remaining incredulous, hesitating to give a verdict, and quickly ending the conversation with the formal ritual: "Our party has already said that Stalin committed certain errors, but his merits cannot be ignored as the modern revisionists would wish."

Others, on the contrary, took up the challenge and defended tooth and nail the line that Ch'en Tu-hsiu alone was responsible.

[29] Arrested by Chiang Kai-shek's police in 1932, Ch'en Tu-hsiu was tried semipublicly and took advantage of his trial to make a fierce attack on the Kuomintang regime. He was condemned to thirteen years' hard labor and died in May, 1942, at the age of sixty-three.

"Our party," they said, "at this period was already powerful enough for its leaders to decide alone what policy should be followed. We are still grateful to Comrade Stalin and to the foreign parties for having helped us in our struggle, and we refuse to hold them responsible for the errors of our right-wing deviationists."

The idea that the Comintern could have had the right and the means to impose its will on the Chinese Communists appears totally improbable to them today. In the opinion of China's present-day historians it is not worth examining.

Only a very high figure in the regime, in a private conversation, expressed his scepticism about the whole conception of the Communist International, but he over-rode criticisms with generalizations about the usefulness of organizations of this kind: "In this matter historical experience is conclusive. To begin with, there was the First International,[30] which we all honor as the pioneer of the workers' movement, although it did not know how to bring about a revolution. Then there was the Second International,[31] numerically stronger and apparently better organized. But during its term no revolution took place, and it was only after it broke up, during World War I, that the great October Revolution in Russia occurred. Later there was the Third International.[32] There again, no sign of any revolution; but after its dissolution in 1943 a whole series of revolutions followed, among them the Chinese revolution, and more recently still, that in Cuba."

These comments, made privately, do not add up, it is true, to a biting criticism of the directives which the Comintern gave to the Chinese CP during the 1920's. Perhaps they presage that the Chinese CP will end up by applying itself to a much deeper examination of this period; it is too soon to know. Meanwhile the "right-wing and opportunist deviation of Ch'en Tu-hsiu" is the only explanation given to young Chinese for the tragedy of the "first Chinese revolutionary war." For them the Comintern is a "non-being" like those other "non-beings," the six founders of the Communist Party whose portraits are not on show in the house at No. 108 Wang Tse Street.

[30] The First International, founded in London on September 28, 1864, ceased activities after the Congress of Philadelphia, 1876.

[31] The Second International emerged from the congress held in Paris on July 14, 1889.

[32] The Third International was founded in Moscow in March, 1919, and dissolved on May 15, 1943.

VILLAGE OF THE MAOS

At Canton, capital of the Chinese left during the 1920's, a strange five-story pagoda stands on a hill overhanging the city; it is the Museum of the Peasant Revolutionary Movements. We visited it on the day of the Spring Festival, as the New Year is now called.[33] It is no longer a religious festival, but it is still a holiday. Everywhere the daily routine stops, as on May Day or October 1.[34] The city is literally inundated with flowers, and the pagoda-museum is invaded by crowds in their Sunday best, among them soldiers, intellectuals, and members of neighboring people's communes who have come to town with their flowers.

To get through these history-lovers one must use one's elbows. Our guide and one of his friends (a student of history, who has joined us, no doubt, to perfect his English) appeal to their fellow-countrymen to give us priority, but they do not wield enough authority to get the crowd to comply. Fortunately they both know the place so well they are able to describe in detail all the exhibits and documents we cannot get near.

From the balcony of the pagoda, on which we take refuge from the crush, we look out over the festive city and mark the spots where the great workers' battles of 1922 to 1927 took place. There is the Pearl River, which runs through the city. British and French gunboats used to patrol all around the Island of Shameen, Anglo-French territory which the Chinese could not enter. But each May Day hundreds of thousands of enthusiastic demonstrators, joined by peasants from the outskirts, marched along the embankment of this same river, out of bravado, chanting their hatred of imperialism.

Recalling this with our guides, we come to the heart of the problem. Why is this museum, where workers' manifestoes and strike photographs are displayed by the hundreds, called "Museum of the Peasant Revolutionary Movements"? "Because," reply my guides, "Chairman Mao, who was the member responsible for the rural sector on the Joint Control Committee of the Kuomintang and the Communist Party from 1924, set up a Peasant Institute in

[33] In 1965 this festival was celebrated on February 1.

[34] October 1, anniversary of the proclamation in 1949 of the People's Republic.

Canton where he regularly gave lectures and where the rural revolutionary cadres of Kwangtung and Hunan and other provinces
were formed. Some of these courses were afterwards published and
are displayed here. Everyone can thus note that Chairman Mao
was the first to understand that in China revolution could not
succeed without the massive and active support of the peasantry."

According to my guides, the other Party leaders, intellectuals
like Ch'en Tu-hsiu, kept their distance from the wretched population of the countryside. True, they knew their misery and their
grievances, but they secretly harbored a vague contempt for these
illiterates who did not speak their scholars' language and who, in
their opinion, were incapable of understanding what the revolution was really about. As a result they were always nonplussed in
the sterile discussions with the bourgeois Nationalists and relied
above all on united action with them.

"Chairman Mao," continue my guides, "tried to explain to
them that the revolution in the countryside was under way without
their knowledge and that the real problem for the Party was no
longer how to awaken the peasantry but how to take over control of
an irresistible, already-primed movement. In the spring of 1927 he
presented his report on the situation in Hunan province, describing
in detail the upheavals already caused by the peasant unions, but
the Party's Secretary-General refused to publish it. Today that
report occupies the place of honor in this museum, and it is one of
our Chairman's most admired pieces of writing."

To enable me to understand the situation in the countryside at
that period, my guide and his friend tell me a story, true or legendary, which everyone here knows by heart.

"Since the latter half of the last century the poor peasants of
China had been in a state of near-revolt. They had lost all confidence in the Manchu dynasty, which did not know either how to
resist the foreigners or how to improve the country's lot in the
slightest. When a Kwangsi schoolmaster, Hung Hsiu-ch'üan, stood
up to the Manchus, the peasants rushed to swell his army as mountain torrents swell a river. Wherever it passed, whole villages rallied to its ranks and chased the mandarins and their troops. Thus it
was that Hung Hsiu-ch'üan was able to cross China victoriously,
almost from one end to the other, and establish in Nanking the
capital of the Heavenly Kingdom of Great Peace, Taiping. Un-
happily, he committed certain political and strategic errors and did
not succeed in seizing Peking. After ten years of glorious battles

the men of Taiping were overcome by the Manchu forces and their Anglo-American mercenaries. But the victors were so afraid of the vanquished men of Taiping that after the capture of Nanking they decided to slaughter them to the last man. In a few days they killed more than a hundred thousand and threw their bodies into the Yangtze. The river became so jammed with them that it was impossible to cross. But the peasants who watched this multitude of martyrs floating slowly toward the sea said: 'They are not dead. They are going away to recover their strength, and then they will return.' "[35]

The spirit of revolt spread abroad by the people of Taiping was not crushed, therefore, by the imperial repression; it simply waited for another opportunity to show itself openly. The fall of the Manchus, the war-lordism, the corruption encouraged by the foreigners gradually undermined this agricultural society which had had its day. The peasants no longer believed in the old customs and rites and no longer expected salvation to come from their rulers. In Kwangtung province, as soon as the Kuomintang established itself there, peasant groups formed and resisted all attempts of the southern war lords to dislodge them. And when the national

[35] The *Times* of London published on July 17, 1964, a long article, "The World's Greatest Civil War," commemorating the hundredth anniversary of the capture of Nanking by the imperial troops, which confirms the incredible extent of the repression. Here are some extracts from it: "On July 19, 1864, the end came. Advised by the English engineer Gordon, 40,000 lbs. of explosive had been laid under the northeast corner of the walls of Nanking. When the smoke and dust cleared a gap of 40 yards let the imperial troops rush through to crush the starving inhabitants. The king's palace and the other palaces in the city, as the memorial sent to Peking reported: All burst into flame simultaneously . . . several hundred female attendants in the palace hanged themselves in the front garden while the number of rebels that were drowned in the city moat exceeded 2,000. We searched the city and in three days killed over 100,000 men . . . not one of the rebels surrendered themselves when the city was taken but in many cases destroyed themselves and passed away without repentance."

Further on, the writer of the article reports the impressions of English travelers like Lord Elgin, who was reminded of Pompei: "We walked along deserted streets between roofs of houses . . . heaps of rubbish blocked the thoroughfares, but they obstructed nobody . . . we almost felt refreshed by a foul odour which greeted our nostrils and warned us that we approached an inhabited street . . . the population was formerly estimated at about 500,000; it does not now contain above 500."

It is usually estimated that there were 20 to 30 million victims in this civil war which the *Times* considers the most destructive in all history. It was frequently the subject of debate in the British Parliament because the British government, which had promised to support the imperial forces, was bitterly criticized by Cobden, Bright, and many others.

revolutionary army in turn launched its campaign to conquer the North, whole villages rallied to it as they had done to the Taiping forces three quarters of a century before. Thanks to this active support, the expedition to the North, which left Canton in July, 1926, was able to make good time and reach Wuhan, on the banks of the Yangtze, in September of the same year.

My guides interrupt their story to lead me, despite the crush, into a room in which are displayed the weapons of the peasant rebels of Hunan and Hupeh: pikes and bill-hooks tied onto poles. They are the same arms that were used in the European revolts of the middle ages — but in the same room are posted the manifestoes of the different peasant unions, which refer not only to their demands but also to the struggle against imperialism and even to world revolution. During this epic period there were few photographers in the country districts of southern China; so the painters of today are commissioned to recall the battles in paintings which, indeed, illustrate page by page Mao Tse-tung's famous report on the Hunan peasant unions. One sees, for example, the peasants taking their revenge on the landlords and driving them through the villages at the point of their primitive weapons.

Elsewhere huge graphs show the membership of the peasant unions in the provinces occupied by Mao's National Liberation Army; if they are to be believed, millions of people took part in the movement. But, add my guides, these men had precise demands. They wanted radical agrarian reform and effective political power. However, the Kuomintang government, transferred from Canton to Wuhan, turned a deaf ear to their claims. Only Comrade Mao Tse-tung supported the peasant revolt and explained that even its supposed excesses served the national revolution. Apparently my guides do not know that the Wuhan government's Minister of Agriculture was a Communist, T'an P'ing-shan.[36] And even if they did know, their opinions would not change: be that as it may, at that time no one except Mao understood the peasantry.

I went in search of the rest of the history of the peasant war of

36 T'an P'ing-shan was one of the Chinese CP's most deferential followers of the Comintern line. He presented a violently anti-Trotskyite report at the seventh plenary session of the International Executive in December, 1926. But he was the prisoner of the Wuhan government, and gradually, to Trotsky's great satisfaction, he drew away from and finally broke with the CP and tried to form his own party. Nevertheless in 1948, on the eve of their victory, he became reconciled with his old comrades, and as a leader of the "revolutionary Kuomintang," became Vice-President of the People's Consultative Conference. He died in Peking in 1956.

the 1920's in the very spot in which it had taken place, in Hunan province, which lies between Canton and the Yangtze and which is regarded as one of the most beautiful provinces in China. According to an old Hunan saying, it is made up of three-tenths mountain, six-tenths water, and one-tenth valley. Geographically this may not be quite accurate, but it describes well enough the landscape dotted with lakes both large and small, traversed by rivers, and embossed with green hills.

In Hunan lies Shao-shan, the village where Mao Tse-tung was born. It comprises 600 houses scattered among hillocks on a wide expanse strewn with rice paddies and little ponds. The hotel, newly built in the main street, is already too small to take all the visitors who come to see the place where, in 1893, Mao Tse-tung first saw the light of day. For their benefit a museum has also been built in the heart of the village, full of photographs and objects connected with the life of Shao-shan's most famous son.

Seventy per cent of the villagers are called Mao. The other names are those of outsiders who married Mao girls. I am assured that at one time Shao-shan was peopled exclusively by Maos, all more or less related, and who comprised a very close-knit clan. The Ancestors' Temple, a large white edifice with two towers, belongs to the Mao community. Today one still enters it as if it were a shrine, but after climbing the few steps of a short stairway, one finds oneself not before an altar but in a meeting room furnished with a wide table and some rustic benches. The representatives of the people's commune meet here to discuss production and politics. In the old days the heads of families met around this same table and discussed the questions of harvest and mutual aid over a meal. The "wise men" then advised them of the sacrifices necessary to obtain good weather and a good crop from the heavenly protectors of the village. At these meetings ancestor worship and the tackling of practical problems were closely linked to the needs of each season.

It seems, however, that the solidarity of the clan, symbolized by the community temple, was not proof against the call of competition in the last century. Mao Tse-tung's father, Mao Jen-sheng, grew rich on grain speculation, and, one is told, he was so unwilling to help his neighbors that his son, already inspired by the collectivist idea, was always at loggerheads with him. And one stormy day, the story goes, Mao helped a poor peasant to gather in his crop in spite of threats from his father, who demanded that he work on his own land.

The Mao family owned twenty-one *mou* of land (about three acres), but to judge from the comfort of their house, consisting of four rooms and a little central court, it was enough to provide a living for five people.[37] Mao Tse-tung had a room of his own. He was sent to a private school in the village, then to the academy at Changsha, an expense which proves beyond a doubt that his father had some other source of income than his land. It is explained to us, moreover, that he wanted his son to be very well educated so that he could manage his business competently.

In the spring of 1965 we visited a house very similar to that of the Maos; in it lived fourteen people, including a leader of the women's brigade. In the old days, however, the vast majority of villagers lived in much worse conditions, and "solvent" peasants like Mao's father were extremely rare. Their privileged situation enabled them to exploit the poorest, who were continually threatened by famine and forced to mortgage their crops in return for immediate help. An unlucky peasant, unable to meet his payments, was taken to court, his land was confiscated, and his family was reduced to beggary because political and juridical power was entirely in the hands of the wealthy, who could even afford the luxury of recruiting their own local "law force."

It was to fight this arbitrary rule that the poor peasants, encouraged by propagandists from Canton, organized their famous unions in 1926. Mr. Mao Tun-ya, present chairman of the people's commune, was only a young boy at the time, but he has a very clear recollection of the period. Tall, thin, wearing a very well-cared-for working overall, and with more the air of a worker than of a peasant, he talks with great confidence. He welcomes me in the Ancestors' Temple, rather dark even in daylight, and explains that we are on the very spot where Chairman Mao Tse-tung held a large and memorable meeting in January, 1927.

"I remember it as if it was yesterday. That meeting was a red-letter day in the history of our village. The Chairman spent the first three days listening to the officials of the peasants' union and questioning all its members. He took notes for his report but said

[37] At Shao-shan I was told that Mao's family consisted of five people: his parents: Mao Tse-tung; and his two younger brothers, Mao Tse-ming (1895–1943) and Mao Tse-tan (1905–1935), both of whom were killed in battle. However, Professor Jerome Ch'en, in his recently published *Mao and the Chinese Revolution* (London, Oxford University Press, 1965), p. 19, asserts that Mao also had a sister, Mao Tse-hung. But there is no trace of her either in the house of Chairman Mao's birth or in the special museum recently opened in his native village of Shao-shan.

nothing. Then he summoned us to the Temple at last to give us his opinion and advice, asking us to bring our womenfolk to the meeting. Until then only men had been allowed in the Ancestors' Temple. The matter was discussed over a big meal. The women were scared to put a foot in the temple, and only a few accepted the Chairman's invitation. Those who did come stayed shyly at the door or hid in dark corners. But the Chairman made them come nearer and insisted that they be given a place in the front row. He began his talk by explaining to us that we were the victims of our old customs and that we were all equal, poor and rich, men and women. He even told us about his mother, whom our elders knew well, and who had more sense of justice than many men. He said again that it was not by chance that the poor peasants were the first to organize the union, since they were the most interested in seeing things changed. Even if they were less well educated than some of the well-to-do, they understood the country's needs and the meaning of its present struggle better. Don't listen to the so-called wise men, he repeated, because they are no wiser than you. After his speech all the wealthy villagers were scared. As for me, the day after, I joined the peasant youth movement. We didn't have any weapons, but the rich, now afraid of us, no longer dared to collect debts or to touch anyone. Some of them even fled from the village."

"But where did Chairman Mao's authority come from? Didn't he leave Shao-shan practically for good fifteen years earlier?" My question dumbfounds Mr. Mao Tun-ya.

"What? But everyone here knew him well and knew that he understood our problems. Besides, he came back to the village in 1925 to organize a Communist cell, which he stayed in touch with. And then one had only to spend five minutes with him to see that he had a special talent. Outwardly he was just like us and he spoke like us, but anyone could soon sense that he understood things that were beyond us. The moment he arrived in the village everyone ran to him for advice, even some of the rich ones, but he had ears only for the poor."

Mr. Mao Tun-ya's other memories seem to have been colored by his recent political education, the history of his village, and the experiences he has lived through. Thus he criticized the "opportunist and right-wing" leadership of the CP, which had held back the peasant movement and prevented the confiscation of the landlords' estates in the name of its alliance with the Kuomintang.

After their final betrayal by the latter, the revolutionary peasants were forced to defend themselves, weapons in hand, to avoid the same fate as that of the revolutionaries of the cities. An armed uprising took place in Hunan in the autumn of 1927, but the Kuomintang army succeeded in putting it down. Mao Tse-tung, who directed the struggle in the more important centers, did not return to his village, although the repression there was particularly severe. Mr. Mao Tun-ya and his deputy cited the names of different Maos who were shot or forced to flee. However, he ended on an optimistic note:

"Despite their victory that time, the rich never felt safe in our village. Things could never again be the way they had been before. People no longer had any faith in the elders and no longer bowed uncomplainingly to injustice. They simply waited for their chance of revenge. Chairman Mao Tse-tung's family's lands were seized, but it proved impossible to resell them; nobody was willing to buy that farm. Eventually it had to be let to a poor oaf who had a fit every time he saw an airplane because he thought it was Chairman Mao arriving. . . ."

Several years after the suppression of the "autumn harvest rebellion" in Hunan, which earned him severe censure and even temporarily excluded him from the CP Central Committee, Mao Tse-tung declared to Edgar Snow: "Whoever wins the peasants will win China. Whoever solves the land question will win the peasants."[38] His faith in the revolutionary potential of the country people was plain from the start of his political activity, and it is probable that it sprang from his intimate knowledge of the peasant world, a knowledge which intellectuals like Ch'en Tu-hsiu lacked. But how was one to find out if the young Communist Party could already, in 1926, win over the peasantry by satisfying their demands? All one hears about the peasant unions confirms the spontaneous character of the movement, but also illustrates its primitive aspects. The movement was difficult to set up. Could a revolutionary structure be built on a loose and unpredictable base? Even if one forgets the Marxist belief in the irreplaceable historic role of the urban proletariat, one can wonder to what degree the Party was able to provide enough cadres to convert the peasant unions into "country soviets," and how it would be able to control and defend them. The history of the first armed struggles in the coun-

[38] Snow, Edgar, *Journey to the Beginning,* p. 173.

tryside seems to prove that the right-wing errors of Ch'en Tu-hsiu were not the only things that held back the Communist conquest of the peasantry.

The Chinese historians of today answer these comments with quotations borrowed from the works of Mao Tse-tung, such as "A Single Spark Can Start a Prairie Fire" or "Why Can China's Red Political Power Exist?" Mao, in fact, explains in his writings why the Chinese Communists had to resort to an armed struggle and how the absence of a centralized state favored the establishment of Red bases in vast stretches of the country. But he developed these theses *after* the outbreak of what is now called "the Second Revolutionary Civil War," and not during the crisis years of 1926 to 1927. Then, after the Kuomintang's turnabout, the armed struggle was no longer a matter of free choice for the Communists — it was forced on them by Chiang Kai-shek, who planned to destroy them all, in town and country alike. The Communists were forced to fight back where they could, and in fact it was easier to do this in the chaotic rural areas than in the urban centers. Mao Tse-tung's two pamphlets explain this very well, but after the event.

Paradoxically, no one in China is able to show clearly at which point the Party decided definitively to give the order for the armed struggle. We are told that on August 1, 1927, the Red troops, under Yeh T'ing, Ho Lung, and Lin Piao, officers of the Northern Expedition, rose against Chiang Kai-shek and occupied Nanchang, capital of Kiangsi province. This date has been celebrated ever since as the birthday of the Chinese Red Army, and the troops wear a badge with the numbers 8–1 to commemorate it. But did Yeh T'ing and Ho Lung alone launch this battle against the Kuomintang? Was it a spontaneous movement or a movement started by the Party, which today claims paternity? Was this action also inspired by the Comintern?[39a]

On this point Agnes Smedley, an American journalist who devoted a large part of her life to pleading the Chinese cause and who is buried in Peking among the heroes of the Revolution, collected the evidence of Chu Teh, future Commander in Chief of the Communist forces. According to his account, a secret conference of Communists from every part of the country was held on July 18, 1927, in a little village in the north of Kiangsi. It was attended

---

[39a] Many Western historians believe that the Nanchang uprising was organized by Basso Lominadze, the representative of the Comintern in China at that time.

by Chou En-lai, who had just escaped death in Shanghai and who was known as the "iron man"; Su Chao-cheng, chairman of the Federation of Labor; T'an P'ing-shan, who had just resigned as Minister of Agriculture; the current Marshal, Liu Po-ch'eng, who was almost executed in Szechwan; and, of course, Generals Yeh T'ing, Ho Lung, and a few others. Mao Tse-tung, Li Li-san, and Chang Kuo-t'ao were also present, but Chu Teh did not know them well and paid little attention to them. It was he who was given the task, at the beginning of the conference, of working out the campaign plan and who, ten days later, commanded the troops which captured Nanchang.[39b]

One would think that a meeting of such importance, which led up to the historic date of August 1, 1927, would be mentioned in all the handbooks and recalled in every Chinese museum. It is not; and Agnes Smedley's book has not been translated into Chinese. Although reasons for this "discretion" obviously exist, I was unable to find out what they are.

In any event, after the dismissal of Ch'en Tu-hsiu on August 7, 1927, supreme power in the Party was entrusted to another intellectual, Ch'ü Ch'iu-pai, and not to one of the participants in the hypothetical meeting in Kiangsi. Little is said today about this second Secretary-General of the CCP. I believe, however, that I rediscovered his tracks in an area which is not regarded as one of the high points in the Party's history.

AN EMINENT MARXIST LITERARY CRITIC AND
THE "ADVENTURISTS OF THE LEFT"

Few men are as venerated in China as Lu Hsün, the great progressive novelist of the 1930's. He is often compared with Gorki, for his writings and his career indeed resemble those of the Russian Bolsheviks' fellow-traveler. Neither was a party member, but both lent their prestige and their talent to the extreme left's struggle. They were among the first to introduce proletarian themes into the literature of their countries. They were even similar physically: both were tall and thin and had heavy mustaches, and both were tubercular.

Today Lu Hsün's works enjoy impressive sales, and in Shanghai a large museum is dedicated to his memory. It stands in a park.

[39b] Smedley, Agnes, *The Great Road* (New York, Monthly Review Press, 1956), p. 199.

There one finds documents dealing with the ups and downs of Lu Hsün's life from the days of his medical studies in Tokyo to his secret activities in Shanghai during Chiang Kai-shek's "white terror." Foreign translations of his novels and articles by Western critics praising his work are also widely displayed. These latter have not been chosen because of their political orthodoxy; for instance, Claude Roy's articles on Lu Hsün[40] are prominently featured, although Roy left the French Communist Party some years ago.

On leaving the museum, we went — its director and my permanent guide — to the former Japanese quarter where, at No. 9 Shanyin Street, the great writer lived until his death in 1936. His house, tall rather than wide, comprises four rooms on three floors and is very modestly furnished. Lu Hsün, who was sought by the police, never lived there under his real name, but it was not this camouflage that protected him. His security was guaranteed by numerous admirers and in particular by a Japanese bookseller who was very well informed on police activities and always warned Lu Hsün in good time.

But Lu Hsün had very close ties with a Marxist literary critic, also wanted by the police but who could not escape their traps. He was called Ch'ü Ch'iu-pai, and he was killed by the Kuomintang at Tingcheu, in Fukien province, in 1935. Lu Hsün, continued the director, never recovered from this. He dedicated the rest of his life to compiling the posthumous works of his brother-in-arms and died of tuberculosis before he could finish the task.

The name Ch'ü Ch'iu-pai had a familiar ring about it. I asked my guides to tell me a little more about him.

"He was an eminent Marxist literary critic," replied the museum director, "and he collaborated so closely with Lu Hsün that in their later works, which they both published under pseudonyms, it is almost impossible to tell what is the work of one and what of the other."

"But wasn't Ch'ü Ch'iu-pai an important member of the Communist Party?"

"Certainly," answered the director without hesitation, "he was a militant member of the Party almost from the day it was founded, and he is regarded as one of the principal architects of the cultural renaissance in China."

"Wasn't he at one time Secretary-General of the Party?"

[40] Roy, Claude, *Clefs pour la Chine* (Paris, Gallimard, 1953).

The question seemed to create a certain confusion among my guides, who, before replying, debated for several minutes among themselves.

"It seems that he was," one of them said at last, "but he is above all respected and celebrated as a Marxist intellectual and a martyr of the Chinese workers' movement."

I asked for more details — in vain. My guides talked about the literature but not the history of the Party.

Without inferring anything from their attitude, but intrigued, I made further inquiries about Ch'ü Ch'iu-pai, to whom had fallen the particularly thankless task of leading the Communist movement following the defeat of 1927. I soon understood why my guides had given me only partial answers. All over China, Ch'ü Ch'iu-pai is represented in the same way: great Marxist critic, architect of the cultural renaissance, active member of the Party since its foundation, victim of the white terror of 1935.

But who, then, had led the Party after the departure of Ch'en Tu-hsiu? A note inserted in the works of Mao Tse-tung and most certainly drafted by him answers this question: "After the defeat of the revolution in 1927, a left-wing adventurist tendency developed in the heart of the Party. Viewing the Chinese revolution as a *permanent revolution,* the adventurist comrades refused to proceed to an orderly retreat, and supported by a small group of Party members, tried all over the country to start a series of local rebellions, which had no chance of success."

Although he is not named, it is clear that this note refers to Ch'ü Ch'iu-pai. Indeed, the phrase "what Marx called a permanent revolution" appears in one of his reports to the Central Committee in November, 1927.[41a]

This omission is plainly loaded with political significance: Ch'ü Ch'iu-pai played too important a role in the Party's life for him to be demoted to the rank of literary critic — even a Marxist literary critic — without a very powerful reason. What is this reason? It is difficult to say with certainty.

The period when Ch'ü Ch'iu-pai ruled the Party was short but

41a "The Chinese revolution," said Ch'ü Ch'iu-pai, "is protracted in nature and yet it is uninterrupted. It thus bears the nature of what Marx called a permanent revolution." Ch'ü Ch'iu-pai obviously referred to Marx to avoid the charge of Trotskyism, the theory of the permanent revolution being linked with Trotsky's name. This precaution was not enough to save him. See Schwartz, Benjamin, *Chinese Communism and the Rise of Mao,* pp. 104–105.

also one of the most tragic in the history of the CCP. Betrayed by their former allies — the Kuomintang — criticized by the Comintern (Stalin pretended that his directives had not been dialectically interpreted by the Chinese), compelled to resist to Chiang Kai-shek's counter-revolution, the Communists were in total disarray. Ch'ü Ch'iu-pai succeeded Che'n Tu-hsiu not only because he was the best-known and ablest leader but also because he represented apparently the left wing of the Party, which for a long time had been criticizing the conciliatory line. And Mao Tse-tung, since their meeting in 1924 at the founding congress of the reorganized Kuomintang, seemed to have shared the same views as Ch'ü Ch'iu-pai and worked closely with him.[41b]

But these theories, applied in particularly difficult circumstances, did not work out. The capture of Nanchang, celebrated today as a great victory (as we have seen above), was in fact only a short-lived success, if not a partial defeat. The new Red Army tried, indeed, to stir up similar risings in the other areas controlled by Chiang Kai-shek, but in vain. It took Swatow, which it was able to hold for only a week before it had to beat a retreat and was dispersed. Chiang Kai-shek's Nationalist army was not infiltrated from within, as some had predicted, and it did not break up. Chu Teh, followed by a few sparse units, had to seek refuge in the mountains of Kiangsi.

As we have seen, the "autumn harvest uprising" in Hunan, another feat of arms made much of today, did not bring the anticipated success. Mao Tse-tung could turn the peasant unions into "country soviets," but the movement was only a drop in the bucket. The other provinces did not budge, and the Hunan revolt, left to itself, hung fire. Mao could only, as a last resort, gather around him his most loyal supporters and set out for less accessible country. It was not until May, 1928, that he met up again with Chu Teh, on Ching-kan-shan Mountain, where he established with him his first fixed base, from which they hoped to fan out.

During this time the repression went on rigorously in the cities, where the Kuomintang was organizing "yellow" unions and consolidating its power. Ch'ü Ch'iu-pai was therefore forced to call on the workers to resist, whatever the cost. It is likely, however,

---

[41b] Stuart Schram in his *Mao Tse-tung* (London, Penguin Books, 1966) explains that Mao Tse-tung was in fact on the right wing of the Party and his opposition to Ch'en Tu-hsiu was on different grounds from that of Ch'ü Ch'iu-pai. But there is considerable evidence that Mao and Ch'ü Ch'iu-pai were friends.

that he believed in the success of his comrades in the provinces and relied on them to relieve the cities from the pressure of Chiang Kai-shek's forces. In his reports to the Central Committee he declares that he wants to co-ordinate the armed struggle of town and country, which doubtless explains why he led the workers to the barricades. Unfortunately there was nothing to co-ordinate. The provincial risings had collapsed; and when the Canton workers seized the city in December, 1927, they could not hope for help from any quarter. The setting up of their "commune" was no more than a gesture of despair, and the commune was obliterated in blood in the space of three days.[42]

The Canton Commune is not looked upon today as an error, nor is it one of the historic facts enshrouded in silence. This revolutionary spasm of the people is glorified, and it is even explained that it was necessary to show the whole country the Communist determination to fight everywhere, in the cities as well as in the countryside. Therefore Ch'ü Ch'iu-pai cannot be blamed for the Canton Commune, and at the same time it is difficult to hold him responsible for the other setbacks of 1927 without tarnishing the reputations of those who glory in having taken part in them. And finally, it is not easy to see what obvious error of Marxist political analysis he could be reproached with having committed during this series of catastrophes.

Suffice it to say that at the beginning of 1928 the Chinese CP was completely demoralized, disorganized, and almost without future. Someone had to be held responsible for this disastrous state of affairs, and it could be neither Stalin nor the Comintern. The dismissal of Ch'ü Ch'iu-pai at the sixth congress of the CCP in July, 1928, is therefore easily explained. Replaced by Hsiang Chung-fa, a trade unionist (the first worker to take over the CP secretariat), Ch'ü Ch'iu-pai was given the job of representing his party in the Comintern. The fact that he was trusted with such an important task and that in 1930, once again, he almost became

[42] Most Western historians assert that the Canton revolt took place at the express request of Stalin, who needed a Chinese victory (even a short-lived one) to coincide with the opening of the fifteenth congress of the U.S.S.R. CP, in the course of which Trotsky and his supporters were expelled from the Party. This view was first put forward by Trotsky himself in *Problems of the Chinese Revolution,* pp. 291–292, and has been developed by his friends, such as Victor Serge. It rests on the considerable amount of evidence concerning the fundamental role played in the rebellion by the Comintern's special envoys, like Heinz Neumann (who was executed by Stalin ten years later).

Secretary-General of the Chinese CP proves that he was by no means dismissed because of a violent disagreement on policy. Nothing in his history, therefore, either justifies or explains why he should have been confined to the literary realm.

Nevertheless, it was at this period that the Chinese Communists had to make a fresh start and choose a favorable path. Ensconced in their mountain base of Ching-kan-shan, Mao and Chu Teh proposed a gradual conquest of the country areas that, once realized, would lead in the long run to the encirclement of the cities, which would fall into their hands like ripe fruit. One determined one's policy according to whether one approved of this strategy.

It is probable that it had no appeal for Ch'ü Ch'iu-pai. True, he became Minister of Education in the Maoist government of the Kiangsi Republic of Soviets, but during the Long March he retired to Shanghai to take up a purely cultural struggle at Lu Hsün's side. Perhaps he did not believe that the Maoist plan would succeed, perhaps his health did not allow him to take part in so trying a venture, perhaps he was too attached to city life. He certainly did nothing which might merit his being treated as a "deviationist" or a "bad Marxist" like his predecessor. So it was simply decided that he should be handed down to posterity in his character of Marxist literary critic, friend of Lu Hsün and victim of the Kuomintang.[43]

A "MONSTROUSLY ABSURD" LINE

"The most remarkable aspect of Chairman Mao's dialectic is his ability to turn bad things into good things." This was confided to me in a low voice by a professor of history at the University of Changsha, the city in which the Chairman lived for many years and which was the scene of decisive events in his career. We were going to visit the little house he lived in during 1921, "Clear Water Pond," and we were talking about the trouble that had faced another inhabitant of Hunan, Li Li-san (who also came from Changsha).

"Mao Tse-tung therefore understood," continued the professor,

[43] In 1957 the Peking People's Press published the four volumes of the works of Ch'ü Ch'iu-pai. His *History of the Chinese Revolution* does not appear in these, however, although Western historians know of its existence thanks to old microfilms. Note also that Ch'ü Ch'iu-pai was only twenty-seven when he was Secretary-General of the CP and that he was shot at the age of thirty-six.

"that the main reason for the failure of the 1927 peasant rising lay in the fragmentation of the country, in its division into provinces that were virtually independent because they were governed by war lords who imposed a variety of strong regimes on them. This lack of unity was undoubtedly a bad and even a very bad thing, but Chiang Kai-shek, who sought the allegiance — theoretical at least — of the provincial squires, never dreamed of remedying it. Chairman Mao himself decided to use this lack of unity for the benefit of the revolution and thus to make a good thing of it. It is simple, he declared: as one moves out farther from the center of the province, local power becomes weaker, until in the frontier zones between provinces, it is practically nonexistent. It is there, therefore, that the Communists can establish their bases.

"His tactics were put into practice with remarkable success. In 1928 the Communists had only one base, on the border of Kiangsi and Hunan, near the mountain of Ching-kan-shan. By 1930 there were already ten similar bases in different frontier regions between provinces. Chairman Mao's conception was quite original and very well suited to the completely special characteristics of China. Indeed, in other continents, and above all in Europe, it is the frontier zones which are the most heavily fortified and most difficult to assault. In China, on the contrary, it was there that the new regime could most easily establish itself. After a foothold had been gained in these areas, propaganda had to be stepped up in the heart of the provinces and positions patiently consolidated. Chairman Mao explained that the reinforcement of these positions obviously demanded the formation of Red armies everywhere, for in China the political struggle was closely linked to the armed struggle.

"Unfortunately, neither the Chairman's tactics nor his successes were correctly analyzed by the Party leaders in Shanghai. They were leftists and subjectivists. The rural bases were of no great interest to them because, mistaking their wishes for facts, they wanted the revolution immediately and throughout the whole country. When they learned that the Red armies were being formed, the Party leaders demanded that they abandon their bases, join together in a single force, and seize big cities like Changsha, Nanchang, and even Wuhan and Shanghai. Their ringleader was Li Li-san; and to evoke this adventurist affair, one talks of the 'Li Li-san line.' "

I hazarded the opinion that perhaps Li Li-san believed that it was the working class and not the peasantry that was the main driving force of the revolution.

"But the best militant workers were to be found precisely in the frontier zone bases," replied the professor without turning a hair. "You mustn't imagine that these bases were organized by peasants. Not at all. It was the proletarian cadres of the Party who established them, helped, it is true, by the poor peasants, whom they educated at the same time as they directed them. I haven't got the exact figures in my head, but I think the Red armies were made up at least 30 per cent of workers from the cities. Chairman Mao always said, conforming to Marxist-Leninist doctrine, that the peasant revolution could only succeed under the direction of the proletariat. There have, therefore, never been two conceptions of the revolution, one proletarian, with Li Li-san as its embodiment, and the other peasant, with Chairman Mao as its embodiment. The question was simply one of deciding how to bring about the revolution in China in practical terms. Li Li-san's proposition was subjectivist and did not take account of realities; that of Chairman Mao was, on the contrary, realistic and flowed from his deep knowledge of the specific character of our country. It constituted an enrichment of the Marxist-Leninist doctrine, while that of Li Li-san was merely a deviation."

As we talked we arrived at the Chairman's former house; it is a very modest affair with two rather damp rooms which give onto a pretty interior garden. Two portraits hanging there brought us back to the discussion of Li Li-san. One is that of the young Mao, extremely thin, with long black hair and a fiery and penetrating gaze which seems fixed on something in the far distance. The other is that of his wife, Yang K'ai-hui; she has a round, calm face that contrasts strikingly with her husband's visionary look.

The young woman who showed us around told us about Yang K'ai-hui. She was the daughter of Yang Ch'ang-chi, a professor at the Changsha teachers' training college for whom Mao Tse-tung had a deep respect. She was a student in Peking when she married Mao. A Communist, she fought at his side. In 1922 she gave birth to their only son, Mao An-ying, who was killed in Korea in 1950.[44] Yang K'ai-hui was not always able to be with her husband during his exhausting battles. She was living in Changsha in 1930 when

---

[44] According to Professor Jerome Ch'en (*Mao and the Chinese Revolution*) this son was not the only child, since Mao also had a daughter. But in his house in Changsha there is no indication of her existence.

she was arrested and executed during the white terror that followed the brief occupation of the city by the Communist army, an occupation ordered by Li Li-san — and that brings us back to him.

At the city's big museum, where I was hoping to learn more about these events, a surprise awaited me.

What happened during the summer of 1930 decided the future character and orientation of the Chinese Communist Party. After its defeats, it marked time in the cities. Cowed by reprisals, faced by growing economic difficulties, the workers no longer responded to the calls to revolt, nor did the unions succeed in making a fresh start. But the Communists retained an unshakable conviction that this was merely a question of temporary difficulties, of a "momentary ebb of the revolutionary tide" which would rise again at a time, perhaps not far off, when circumstances would be more favorable. To the Communist leadership of the time it was unthinkable that the working class, entrusted with the historic mission of building the new order, should migrate to the country. It was in the factories, in these places of work, in the name of the collectivist spirit born of their own condition, that they had to create the revolution. The cities were therefore the only Communist battlefield; the Party leaders could not accept a proposition which gave the key role to revolutionary bases set up in distant rural areas by a few courageous comrades.

The strong man of this policy within the CP was not its Secretary-General, the ex-worker Hsiang Chung-fa, but a French-trained intellectual, Li Li-san.[45] It was he who, in 1925, directed the massive protest against the shootings of May 30 and learned from experience how an unforeseeable occurrence can arouse the seemingly apathetic masses. On his return from the U.S.S.R., where he had spent three years, he was put in charge of organization and controlled, in effect, the whole Party machine. He reluctantly admitted the existence of the provincial bases, which, isolated by their remoteness, enjoyed unparalleled autonomy in a party founded on democratic centralism. Li Li-san decided therefore to use the military potential amassed in these unorthodox bases to assault the cities and to hasten, as in 1925, the awakening of the proletariat.

---

[45] A Hunanese like Mao, Li Li-san met his future rival in Changsha long before the birth of the Chinese CP. But Mao explained to Edgar Snow (see *Red Star Over China*) that they never liked each other.

In June, 1930, Li Li-san summoned all the Red Army chiefs to a village in Kiangsi and put before them his plan for a general offensive in the center of the country. The Communist forces were to be concentrated in two armies, commanded respectively by Chu Teh and P'eng Teh-huai. To the first, Li Li-san entrusted the task of occupying Nanchang; and the objective of the second was to be Changsha. After these surprise attacks the two Red commanders were to link up on the Yangtze, encircling Wuhan, the Chicago of China.

The attackers' task was to be made easier, in principle, by the existence of another theater of war in the North, where the "Christian General" Feng Yü-hsiang was in revolt against Chiang Kai-shek. Li Li-san's directives were accompanied by a political analysis of the general crisis of capitalism, which had been brought on by the great depression and which was going to lead irrevocably to world revolution. Mao Tse-tung, political commissar of Chu Teh's army, was hardly convinced by these arguments; but like the military chiefs, he had no power to contest the authority of the strong man of the Central Committee; the dice were therefore cast.

At Nanchang, Chu Teh's army met with unexpected resistance and failed to take the city. But P'eng Teh-huai's army succeeded in dislodging the Hunanese war lord Ho Chien from Changsha. On July 29, 1930, Li Li-san proclaimed the government of the Soviets of China in this, the first great city to be freed by the Communist armies. "When the revolutionary tide rises," he declared optimistically, "it will take only three days to raise 90 million men." But only 3,000 workers attended a meeting to celebrate the victory. "The co-ordination of the Red Army's attack and the struggle of the masses in Changsha was not really brought about," ruled the Central Committee a month later. Even if military success could have been assured and exploited, which it was not, the apathy of the "sovietized" city completely invalidated all Li Li-san's "urbanist" theories. Here was the evidence that it was not the white terror alone that had paralyzed the Chinese working class: even in Changsha, where the workers could demonstrate freely, they hung back; and in the other cities Li Li-san's Republic did not evoke one gesture of solidarity.

Meanwhile the war lord Ho Chien had gone to ask the foreign powers for help; and now American, British, and Japanese gunboats began to shell the city from the Siang River. Even this direct intervention by the imperialist powers left the city unmoved.

On August 5 P'eng Teh-huai's army was forced to evacuate Chang-sha, where the reprisals that followed cost the lives of 5,000 Reds and "suspects," including Mao Tse-tung's young wife.

Caught up in the train of events he had set in motion, Li Li-san could not content himself with beating a retreat. He ordered Chu Teh to abandon the siege of Nanchang and to go to the aid of Peng Teh-huai and then, with him, to recapture Changsha. The battle on the outskirts of the city lasted with increasing violence until September 13, 1930. On that day Mao Tse-tung and Chu Teh made the most difficult and the most dangerous decision of their careers — they refused to obey the Central Committee of the Party and on their own initiative ordered a general retreat toward Kiangsi. Peng Teh-huai approved their decision, but a large number of Party members protested, harshly condemning their action. In Shanghai they were bitterly attacked by Ch'en Tu-hsiu, who, although he had been expelled from the Party, retained great prestige in the eyes of the extreme left; he even declared that their army, composed of the lumpen-proletariat and the outcasts of every class, was unworthy of representing the true revolution. By daring to face this trial of strength with the leader of the Central Committee, Mao and Chu risked expulsion from the Party — the Communists found it difficult to pardon the refusal to obey orders from the top. Mao and Chu, unlike the war lords, could not deploy their armies as they thought best. Without the Party's authority behind them, their campaign had neither meaning nor future. But, they had no choice, Chu Teh explained later to Agnes Smedley: "any other decision would have resulted in the destruction of 'the living heart of the revolution.' "[46]

However, the tremendous risk that Mao and Chu dared to take finally paid off: their troops followed them without a thought for the Party chiefs' censure; this was the proof that they were both more popular and more heeded than Li Li-san and his fellow-members of the Central Committee. On the outskirts of Changsha they virtually received the vote of those who were ready to fight under the Red banner of the revolution. The Central Committee, cut off from its working-class foundations, as events had clearly shown, and having no power to oppose them, realized that if it

[46] Smedley, Agnes, *The Great Road,* p. 279. It was in this book that I found the only detailed account of the military operations in the summer of 1930. Harold Isaacs (*The Tragedy of the Chinese Revolution,* p. 330) gives the essential information on the political situation in Changsha.

broke with Mao and Chu, it would risk becoming an impotent splinter-group of clandestine conspirators. It was therefore Li Li-san, and not Mao, who was condemned, who was forced to resign, and who vanished from the political scene. The official leaders in Shanghai kept their titles, but *de facto* power in the Party already started to shift toward the Maoists. Mao's basic decision to fight the campaign in the chaotic hinterland of a dismembered China was slowly but surely gaining ground among the Communists. It was logical, then, that Mao should end up by taking over the leadership of the Party.

I did not expect to find any revealing documents in the Changsha museum. The present-day didacticism of historical exhibits seems to make it difficult for them to account for events as troubled and as complex. But I did expect that the capture of the city, the foreign intervention, and the repression might be described and illustrated in detail. However, this is not the case. Admittedly, by looking thoroughly through the mass of photographs and documents covering the battles and reprisals of the period, one could find some which recalled the capture of Changsha. But my guides only showed them to me when I asked why the event had gone unrecorded.

This surprising circumspection does not prevent the "Li Li-san line" from being condemned harshly and systematically. No one accuses the former leader of treason and sabotage. As was Ch'en Tu-hsiu, he is cited as a "negative" example, a living illustration of the Marxist guide who took the wrong path. But Li Li-san is also one of the rare discredited Communist leaders who twenty-five years later was able to put his version of events before the Party congress (in 1956). Imagine Trotsky or Bukharin making a speech before the elite of the Soviet Communist Party in justification of their actions during the epic days; such an address would shake fabric and conscience, even if delivered in a moderate and conciliatory tone. But Li Li-san was never of the same mettle as these two men and his case was never so strong as theirs. Listen to him talking to his comrades:

"As is generally known, I was responsible for the mistakes of the Second 'Leftist' Opportunist Line, otherwise known as the Li-san Line, and took an active part in carrying out the First 'Leftist' Opportunist Line. At its Sixth National Congress the Party in no uncertain terms repudiated the mistakes of the First 'Leftist' Opportunist Line and pointed out that the chief danger in the Party came from putschism, military adventurism and commandism. Why was it that shortly after the Sixth National Congress I again made these mistakes? And why did these mistakes of mine assume even greater and more serious proportions? The most important reason was that although I had nominally admitted the mistakes of putschism, I did not go into their ideological roots. I merely repudiated certain obvious manifestations of my mistakes, but failed to use, and did not know how to use, the Marxist-Leninist stand, viewpoint and method to make a penetrating analysis of their essential nature and ideological roots. . . . And at the same time, my subjectivist, unrealistic and self-opinionated ideas expressed themselves in more and more frantic ways.

"Such unbridled subjectivism expressed itself politically in letting oneself be swayed by the passions of the moment, taking wishful thinking for reality, issuing arbitrary orders at will, doing things without either modesty or prudence, or with regard to consequences. Such a blind, impetuous and desperate way of doing things ignored the actual situation and conditions facing us. In cities where the White Terror was strongly entrenched, instead of taking pains to carry on hard work among the masses and build up the revolutionary forces bit by bit, the opposite was done: strikes and demonstrations were frequently called and uprisings repeatedly organized. In the rural areas, instead of going all out to set the peasant masses in motion to wage a revolutionary struggle for land reform, to develop guerilla warfare and gradually build up revolutionary bases, the revolutionary armed forces, young and numerically small at that time, were ordered again and again to storm the major cities. Then, instead of turning back after having been repeatedly and badly battered and knocked about, desperate and headstrong attempts were made to carry on the struggle to the bitter end. As a result, the revolutionary forces suffered serious losses. . . .

"In organizational matters, such violent subjectivism took the form of an excessive sectarianism. As the result, one could hardly keep a cool head and listen to the opinions of others. Comrades putting forward different views would be accused unwarrantedly of opportunism or misguided compromise; they would be discriminated against and vilified. And so an extremely abnormal situation arose in the Party and even led to the death of a number of splendid cadres. I would cite the example of the death of Comrade Yun Tai-ying which I always recall with remorse. Comrade Yun Tai-ying was working in the Propaganda Department of the Central Committee. Because he had on several occasions opposed adventurism in our way of doing things, he was accused of misguided compromise, removed from his position in the Party Centre, and given the post of secretary of the Party Committee of the Eastern District in Shanghai. Comrade Yun Tai-ying was one of the comrades the enemy was looking for. He was not well acquainted with the conditions in the Eastern District of Shanghai and, moreover, his eye-sight was very poor. One day he was challenged by the police in a general search in the streets and was thrown into jail. A renegade informed against him and he was done to death. . . .

". . . I shall not go into all the many, many instances during the period of ascendency of the Li-san Line of doing things which in effect damaged the revolution. Nor shall I dwell on the various absurd 'views' and 'theories,' associated with the Li-san Line. These are already well known to many comrades. . . ."[47]

If history had not confirmed Mao's theories in the revolt against him, Li Li-san perhaps would have been able to analyze his political concepts of that time more accurately. It is not for us to criticize him for rallying to the victor, or for the astonishing tone of his free confession. The Chinese, as we shall see later, practice criticism and self-criticism in a way that leaves us speechless.

For them, when former adversaries are today in perfect agreement on what was good and what was not good, a discussion that delves into the events is neither necessary nor useful. The battle of Changsha in 1930 was decisive for the Chinese Communists, but it cost them dearly in human lives and led to many painful schisms. So that the dead and all these unpleasant memories may lie undisturbed, they gloss over the details and confine themselves to teaching the young Chinese about the outcome of this clash of policies.

---

[47] After his eclipse in January, 1931, Li Li-san submitted to the leadership of Wang Ming, who, according to his own words, "tyrannized him like a woman tyrannizes her daughter-in-law." Until 1945 he filled secondary posts in Moscow. It was there that he learned, to his great surprise, of his election to the Central Committee by the seventh congress of the Party. After his return to China, he held important positions in Manchuria and then at the headquarters of the Chinese Federation of Trade Unions; he was even Minister of Labor in the first government of the People's China. At the time of the eighth congress of the Party, however, he was only assistant director of the Central Committee's industrial and communications section. His speech is published in the second volume of the *8th National Congress of the CCP* (Peking, Foreign Languages Press, 1956), pp. 249–251.

THE "REAL POWER FACTION"[48]

The Maoists enjoyed their first triumph on November 7, 1931. On that day, in a little market town called Juichin in Kiangsi province, the Chinese Soviet Republic was proclaimed, and Mao Tse-tung became Chairman. The army which had followed him in the retreat from Changsha had recaptured and reinforced the rural bases dear to Mao's heart. Scattered throughout the frontier zones of several southeastern provinces, these bases, it is estimated, already occupied nearly one sixth of the national territory and were stoutly defended by a full-strength Red Army.[49] It is not known exactly what the population of the Communist districts — termed "stable" areas — was at that time, but it must have been considerable, to judge from the admissions of the Nationalist press in its references to the ineffectiveness of the "mopping-up" operations carried out by Chiang Kai-shek's powerful forces.

It is still not easy to understand how these bases, separated by vast "white" areas, were able to communicate with each other, especially when one considers the poorness of Chinese transport facilities; but they did communicate, and so effectively that they even deemed it necessary to draw together more tightly by adopting common direction and legislation. The first All-China Congress of the Soviets was convened for this purpose, and it was this gathering which, symbolically, chose the fourteenth anniversary of the Bolshevik Revolution on which to announce the birth of its younger Chinese counterpart.

In today's museums there is no lack of documents concerning this memorable day. They testify that Mao Tse-tung was the inspirer, the organizer, and the head of the second Communist republic in history. It is Mao, quite young, with long black hair and tightly knitted brows, who occupies the place of honor among the commemorative photographs. It is his signature which appears at the foot of the Constitution of Soviet China, drawn up no doubt by him and adopted unanimously by the Congress of Juichin.

[48] A phrase coined by Benjamin Schwartz in his *Chinese Communism and the Rise of Mao.*

[49] An enormous diagram at the entrance to the room dedicated to the second Revolutionary Civil War in the Museum of the Revolution in Peking illustrates the extraordinary growth of the Chinese Red Army: 1928—10,000 men; 1929—22,000; 1930—62,000; 1931—145,000; 1932—170,000; 1933—300,000.

Always by his side is his smiling, almost laughing, military alter ego, Chu Teh, Commander in Chief of the Red Army. For Mao, although strategist and theoretician of the guerilla war, never wore a uniform and never held rank. On the contrary, he embodied the supremacy of the civil power over the military, a supremacy which is a fundamental principle for the Communists. But he had such a perfect understanding with Chu Teh that at that time they were regarded as two men from the same mold, and people referred equally to the Mao-Chu regime or the Chu-Mao regime.

Mao and his team did not want merely to organize and defend the Red bases. To satisfy oneself on this point it is enough to read the constitution promulgated at Juichin, which amounts to an appeal and a promise to the whole country, and is very much more than a series of immediately applicable laws. Although he knew that his authority did not extend to any important city and was not recognized by any foreign power, Mao nevertheless established labor legislation for major industry, limiting the working day to eight hours (six for those between the ages of sixteen and eighteen), and granting all workers an unbroken weekly rest period of at least forty-two hours. The People's Commissariat, which dealt with labor questions, was required to fix minimum wages every six months and to ratify collective contracts, which were not allowed to exceed a period of one year.[50]

In an appendix Mao also defined his policy toward foreign firms: "In order to assure China's full independence everything at present in the hands of the imperialists (concessions, customs administration, banks, railways, companies engaged in freighting, mining, and manufacturing) will be nationalized. Foreign industrialists will, however, be able to continue production on the condition that they sign concessionary contracts and strictly observe the Soviet government's laws."

As for enterprises owned by Chinese capitalists, they would not be immediately nationalized, but would be placed under the control of committees drawn from firms and unions. Only the factories of counter-revolutionaries guilty of sabotage would be confiscated

[50] Article 21 even foresaw the eight holidays of the year: January 1; January 21, anniversary of the death of Lenin; February 7, anniversary of the shooting of the Peking-Hankow railroad workers by the military; March 18, anniversary of the Paris Commune; May 1, International Labor Day; May 30, anniversary of the events of 1925 in Shanghai; November 7, anniversary of the Russian Revolution and of the formation of the Chinese Soviet Republic; December 11, anniversary of the Canton rebellion.

and converted into co-operatives or turned over to organs of the Soviet state, which would combat "with all its energy" speculation and agreements aimed at establishing price monopolies. Red soldiers, workers, and the poor of town and country would be completely exempt from the tax, which was to be paid by the bourgeoisie alone. The law would free both workers and the exploited classes from all outstanding debts.

But the only laws which could actually be applied at that moment were obviously those which concerned land reform and the "regulation relating to the privileges of the Red Army of the workers and peasants." Landlords' estates were to be confiscated purely and simply, while the land of rich peasants was to be redistributed, but not completely. The latter were allowed to retain enough land for the upkeep of their families. Army combatants were given priority in the allocation of confiscated land, and the rest of the community — especially the political cadres — had to help soldiers' families in their absence. The law even laid down that the cadres must contribute two days' work per week on soldiers' farms.

Finally, in another resolution involving the Red Army: ". . . The Congress urges the workers' organizations of nonsovietized regions to send revolutionary workers regularly to join the ranks of the Red Army. It is only by raising the percentage of industrial and agricultural workers serving in our ranks, by activating the work of the political sections and of the militants of the Party, and by strengthening the organizations of the Party and the Communist youth movement in the Red Army that proletarian leadership can be made secure."

This announcement of its program to the country should logically have been signed by the top leaders of the Party, who proposed to carry it out. One would assume as well that after the eclipse of Li Li-san and the tragic death of Secretary-General Hsiang Chung-fa (killed in Shanghai by Kuomintang police on June 21, 1931) power at the heart of the CP would have gone almost automatically to Mao Tse-tung, its most influential and popular leader. But the internal mechanism of the Communist world, always controlled by the Comintern, did not appear to obey the laws of logic.

At the Hotel Lux in Moscow, where the elite of the International were in session, Mao Tse-tung carried no weight. True, his name and his career were known to them, as is shown by the fact that *Imprecorr* (the Comintern's official bulletin) had, by mistake, on March 20, 1930, published the news of his death from tuberculosis, together with a eulogistic obituary notice.[51] But Mao had probably had no contacts with the Comintern and therefore could not count on its help to secure his promotion in the leading councils of the Chinese CP. Stalin had never met him. He had never read Mao's writings, and this ignorance was apparently mutual: if one is to believe Ch'en Po-ta, it was not until 1937 that Mao began to study Stalin's works.[52]

The Comintern delegates dealing with the Chinese CP, like Mif or Losovsky, therefore worked to advance the careers of the men they knew better and who offered a stronger guarantee of orthodoxy. With their support a group known as the "twenty-eight Bolsheviks" and composed of Moscow-trained militants took the destiny of the Chinese Central Committee in hand in 1931. Two of these stood out: Wang Ming (Ch'en Shao-yü) and Po Ku (Ch'in Pang-hsien). It was this pair who officially held power and who, in principle, decided policy.

There is nothing to confirm that the Congress of Juichin was organized without their knowledge or against them, but it is established that neither Wang Ming nor Po Ku was entrusted with any post in the new Maoist republic. They were not even given honorific titles, which their rank in the Party should have warranted if not rendered obligatory. Foreign historians have come to the conclusion that all did not go very well between Mao and the leaders who had the Comintern's blessing. They have even dubbed the men of Juichin "the real power faction."

The Chinese of today reject absolutely the idea that there was a conflict, open or latent, between the underground group in Shanghai and the organizers of the Soviet Republic of Juichin; and they state: "There was never any faction in our party, and Comrade Mao Tse-tung would be the first to condemn those who organized one." Let us therefore banish this term, unacceptable to "monolithic" Communists, and restrict ourselves to remarking that from November 7, 1931, Mao Tse-tung wielded the real power over a sixth of China's territory, that he had under his command an army of 145,000 men which was soon to double its strength, but that in the Party hierarchy he ranked only number six or seven.

My Chinese companions may not explain very clearly the rea-

[51] See *Imprecorr*, Vol. 10, No. 14 (March, 1930), Moscow.
[52] See Ch'en Po-ta, *Stalin and the Chinese Revolution* (Peking, 1953).

ons for this curious situation, but they readily admit that it was
detrimental to the young Maoist republic and to the Party; for
Vang Ming and Po Ku were mediocre Marxists whose political
directives were as badly adapted to the realities of the country as
those of their unhappy predecessors. Once more the Communists
paid a heavy price for "the errors of the third left-wing deviation
of the Chinese CP leadership."

In fact, two months before the Juichin proclamation, an event of
prime significance in the evolution of the country occurred — the
apanese invaded Manchuria. Chiang Kai-shek refused to confront
them in open country and even to declare war on them. He
ordered the war lord of the Northeast to abandon his territory,
no doubt in the hope that this sacrifice of a region would appease
the Japanese appetite. He was too preoccupied with the success of
the Reds in the rear to be able to consider a war against Asia's
greatest military power. His orders were therefore: "Mopping-up
first, resistance afterwards."

But this "mopping-up" was not easily carried out at the moment
when the Japanese, encouraged by Chiang Kai-shek's faint-heart-
edness, decided to attack Shanghai. It was January 28, 1932. Gen-
ral Ts'ai T'ing-k'ai's Nationalist 19th Army held them off coura-
geously for more than a month, and China was stirred by their
eroism.[53] The Kuomintang government's policy of always giving
priority to the campaign against the Communist bases became
more unpopular each day and disturbed even the Western
powers. Thus the League of Nations' commission of inquiry was
compelled to criticize Chiang Kai-shek almost openly:

"During the summer of 1932 the Nanking government decided
n large-scale military operations to crush completely the Red
rebellion. Operations began. They were to be accompanied by a
complete social and economic reorganization of the recaptured territories. However, no appreciable results were achieved."[54]

This progressive isolation of Chiang Kai-shek raised the hopes
f the Communists, who were supporters of the war against the
apanese. But the Wang Ming–Po Ku leadership was unable to

[53] According to Evans F. Carlson, *The Chinese Army* (New York, Institute of Pacific Relations, 1940), p. 18, General Tsai Ting-kai had received
from Nanking the order to abandon the city without a fight, but the Japa-
ese attacked at the moment he was withdrawing and compelled him to join
attle. See also Snow, Edgar, *Far Eastern Front* (New York, 1933), p. 221.
[54] This extract from the Lytton Report was provided for me in Peking
ithout details of the date of its publication.

grasp the situation. Their sectarianism was such that they refuse to negotiate with the 19th Army chiefs in Fukien who mutinie against the defeatist policy of the Nanking government. Treatin all non-Communists as suspects, the Party leaders accused th rebels of social democrat leanings and allowed Chiang Kai-shek t wipe out the 19th Army in a battle which it fought single-handed

The shortsighted policy of the "deviationists of the leadership manifested itself still more clearly in 1934 during Chiang Kai shek's fifth offensive against the Juichin republic. Failing to under stand that the Nationalist generalissimo, advised by prominen German strategists like Von Seeckt, was throwing enormous force into the battle, the leadership ordained a static defense and im posed a series of murderous battles on the Red Army.[55] To avoi defeat, Mao Tse-tung then made his historic decision[56] to aban don the southern provinces, and after a series of maneuvers t baffle the enemy, succeeded in breaking out of the encirclemen with the bulk of his troops to lead them on the Long Marcl toward the Northwest. In October, 1934, after almost three years existence, the Maoist republic of the Southeast transformed itsel

[55] The present version of the crimes of the "third deviation of the left" does not appear to coincide completely with the explanation of the same events given by Mao Tse-tung to Edgar Snow in 1936. At that time Mac said: "In this period we made two important errors. The first was the failure to unite with Ts'ai T'ing-k'ai's army in 1933 during the Fukien Rebellion The second was the adoption of the erroneous strategy of simple defense abandoning our former tactics of maneuver. It was a serious mistake to mee the vastly superior Nanking forces in positional warfare, at which the Re Army was neither technically nor spiritually at its best. As a result of these mistakes and the new tactics and strategy of China's campaign, combined with the overwhelming numerical and technical superiority of the Kuomin tang forces, the Red Army was obliged, in 1934, to seek to change the con ditions of its existence in Kiangsi, which were rapidly becoming unfavorable Secondly, the national political situation influenced the decision to move the scene of main operations to the Northwest. . . . In January, 1934, the second All-China Soviet Congress of Soviets was convened in Juichin, the Soviet capital, and a survey of the achievements of the revolution took place. . . . Preparations soon afterwards were made for the Long March. It was begun in October, 1934, just a year after Chiang Kai-shek launched his last campaign — a year of almost constant fighting, struggle, and enor mous losses on both sides." See Snow, Edgar, *Red Star Over China*, pp. 179–180.

[56] According to Robert North in *Moscow and the Chinese Communists* (Stanford, Stanford University Press, 1951) Mao did not make this key decision until *after* he had referred it to Moscow. Besides, one might even wonder how Mao could have made the decision alone — as the present version has it — since he was not yet at that time the supreme leader of his party.

nto a kind of nomadic republic, traveling across the provinces of China. All the Central Committee leaders, who had been installed n Juichin since January, 1934, took part in the march, but no one ad any further contact with Moscow. Everything had to be de- ided on the spot, including the question of Party leadership.

Three months after the departure from Juichin, in the moun- ains of Kweichow province, this problem was settled once and for ll. On January 6, 1935, the enlarged Political Bureau met at 'sunyi and elected Mao Tse-tung to the chairmanship of the Communist Party of China, the post he still occupies. Last year China celebrated the thirtieth anniversary of this event with great omp. Extra-large commemorative stamps were issued: from a nountain summit Mao contemplates the road leading into the ature; by his side is Lin Piao, number two in the regime, studying lans of future battles; behind them several soldiers flourish red ags. These stamps have been enormously popular. In February, ve weeks after they had been first issued, I saw men and women ning up in Peking to buy them and setting them out reverently as ' they were family souvenirs.

It was pointless to ask my Chinese companions if, in their pinion, the geographical situation of Tsunyi, this township buried the mountains and with no means of communicating with a enter as remote as Moscow, could have had any influence what- ever on the outcome of the historic conference.[57] The Comin- rn being for them, as I have already said, a "non-being," my uestion would have appeared absurd or unnecessarily provoca- ve. Note all the same that Mao in a speech (not published in his omplete works) claimed that after 1935 the Comintern never tervened in the internal affairs of the Chinese Party.[58] Mao's ccession to supreme power in the CP, therefore, coincided with a iser attitude in the International, which no longer tried to direct nd advise its Chinese comrades.

After the Tsunyi conference, therefore, Mao Tse-tung took over ontrol and had his troops undertake the extraordinary and trium- hant Long March, at the end of which they arrived in the North- est, in Shensi province. Edgar Snow has starkly set out the log of

[57] This is the theory of, among others, John King Fairbank, *The United ates and China* (Cambridge, Harvard University Press, 1958), p. 234.
[58] This speech, made at Yenan on May 26, 1943, as a comment on the ssolution of the Third International, appears in the book by Stuart Gelder, *he Chinese Communists* (London, Gollancz, 1946), p. 169.

this prodigious feat of arms in his *Red Star Over China*. Let me quote from it: ". . . there was an average of almost a skirmish a day, somewhere on the line, while altogether fifteen whole days were devoted to major pitched battles. Out of a total of 368 days en route, 235 were consumed in marches by day, and eighteen in marches by night. Of the hundred days of halts — many of which were devoted to skirmishes — 56 days were spent in Northwestern Szechwan, leaving only 44 days of rest over a distance of about 5,000 miles, or an average of one halt for every 114 miles of marching. The mean daily stage covered was 71 *li,* or nearly 24 miles — a phenomenal pace for a great army and its transport to *average* over some of the most hazardous terrain on earth.

"Altogether the Reds crossed eighteen mountain ranges, five of which were perennially snow-capped, and they crossed 24 rivers. They passed through twelve different provinces, occupied 62 cities, and broke through enveloping armies of ten different provincial warlords, besides defeating, eluding, or outmanoeuvring the various forces of Central Government troops sent against them. They entered and successfully crossed six different aboriginal districts and penetrated areas through which no Chinese army had gone for scores of years."[59]

"The military history of the world contains no other example of an army traveling a similar distance on foot with such short stops on the way," asserted my guide at the Museum of the Revolution in Peking. He could have spent hours telling me all the details of this epic, for it has been sung and illustrated by the best writers and painters in the country. Every Chinese knows the story of the taking of the bridge over the Tatu River or that of the crossing of the haunted mountains which no one had ever dared approach before. These obstacles were overcome by Mao and his partisans and thanks to them, the Communist revolution in China was able to make a new start.

Casualties were heavy. The Maoist army was decimated. Only 30,000 men reached the end of the journey. But these survivors were of such mettle that nothing was too tough for them. During the Long March Mao built up the elite cadres of Communist China. They could have been trained in a school that was less hard and less bloody but none that would have developed better the sense of human fellowship and comradeship. The stability of the

[59] Snow, Edgar, *Red Star Over China*, p. 206.

Maoist team is ensured in large part by the memory of the terrible trials of the Long March.

One evening in Peking we were shown a color film of the life of a Red Army unit during the Long March. This film was made in the studio with careful fidelity to make up for the complete absence of any contemporary film record. It is as successful as a reconstruction twenty-five years after the event could be, and I found it very moving. No political leader appears in it. Even Mao's name is rarely mentioned. It is a paean to the glory of the simple combatants — those who fell and those who have kept Red China on the march.

FROM THE FOX'S HOLE TO THE BREACH IN THE PACT

From the seventh to the tenth century, under the Tang dynasty, Sian was one of the great cities of the world (two million inhabitants, it is said), and it enjoyed abounding prosperity thanks to the Silk Road linking China with the Middle East and Europe. The Tang emperors were known for their tolerance and their breadth of view. One of them sent Hsüan Tsang, a particularly gifted subject, to India to study Buddhism; and when he returned seventeen years later, built him a splendid pagoda, 260 feet high, known as the Great Pagoda of the Wild Geese. It was here that Hsüan Tsang, over a period of nineteen years, translated the texts he had brought back from his travels and which were to introduce Buddhism into China. Buddhism is not the only foreign religion that benefited from the imperial tolerance. The Nestorians, an early Christian heretical sect, and the Jews were also authorized to propagate their faiths. Monuments and magnificent sculptures testify to the high cultural level in Sian at this time.

But a grave anxiety gnawed at the peace-of-mind of Ming Huang, the great Tang emperor (712–756) — his beautiful favorite, Yang Kwei-fei, never smiled.[60a] Fifteen miles from the city, at Lintung, there was a lovely pool, the Huan Chin, at the foot of Li-san

[60a] The story of Ming Huang and Yang Kwei-fei was much more complex than my guides in Lintung gave me to understand. In fact, it is considered a classic and has inspired many theatrical and cinematic works even outside China. But my guides were obviously better versed in politics than in history.

Mountain, from which a hot sulphur spring gushed. There the emperor built the Palace of Floating Snow, so named because in springtime snow from the mountain came sliding into the waters of the pool. This imperial gift won no smile from the sad Yang Kwei-fei. To cheer her up, Ming Huang thought he would organize a fake attack on the palace by the citizens. Seeing the unhappy "rebels" being driven off by the imperial guard, the emperor's favorite at last broke into loud laughter. Since then the palace has been known as "the Palace of the Laugh Which Lost the Empire"; for, in fact, soon after this simulated assault, the people attacked the palace in earnest, and the guards, thinking this was another example of the emperor's humor, failed to resist as strongly as they normally would have. The emperor and his favorite paid with their heads for their dubious practical joke.

Today no one visits Lintung to admire its relics of the past (such as Yang Kwei-fei's bathing pool). The imperial palace and its outbuildings were ravaged and burned down a dozen times, and what has been put up in their place is not worth the journey. If you are taken to Lintung and if anyone there recounts the emperor's misadventure for you, it is to prepare you for the story of much more recent events which confirm that Lintung brings no happiness to its rulers of the day. It was, in fact, here, on the night of December 12, 1936, that Generalissimo Chiang Kai-shek was arrested by his "patriotic anti-Japanese" officers. After this episode, which everyone knows as the "Sian incident," Chiang had to bow to the popular will and accept the Maoist idea of a national front.

A year earlier the Communists had hoisted their flag in the Northwest, and the Nanking government had entrusted the task of "exterminating the Red hordes" to the young Marshal Chang Hsüeh-liang. This former war lord from Manchuria had never reconciled himself to the loss of his Japanese-occupied territories, and he dreamed of returning with his Tung Pei (Northeast) army to the land of his birth.[60b] His influence also extended to the troops

---

[60b] Chang Hsüeh-liang was the son of a typical figure of the China that was disappearing, Chang Tso-lin. Originally a simple bandit, the latter had organized a virtual army and become war lord of the Northeast. From 1911, he ruled as master of Manchuria and, with the support of other war lords, even aspired to the control of all China. Frequently his troops broke through the Great Wall in bids to occupy Peking. In 1925 they even reached Shanghai. Chang Tso-lin, although protected by the Japanese, clashed with them from time to time; many thought that the Japanese were behind the blowing-up of his private train by a mine in June, 1928. His son, Chang Hsüeh-liang, was then only twenty-seven and was known mainly for his addiction to

of General Yang Hu-ch'eng, who was to support him in the campaign against the Maoists, but no one was keen to fight because the
anti-Communist action ordered by Chiang Kai-shek was so poorly
ed.

The "young Marshal's" anti-Japanese sentiments even induced
him to give asylum at Sian to all those who were persecuted by
Chiang Kai-shek for having appealed for a national union and
demanded an end to the civil war. This paradox reached the point
where certain Communist leaders being hunted by the Nanking
government lived, in complete safety, in the private apartments of
the man who was leading "the campaign for the extermination of
the Red bandits."[61]

Alarmed by this news, Chiang Kai-shek decided to go personally
to Sian to put things in order. But, suspicious by nature, he did not
trust generals who commanded an army of 150,000 men. Although he was their guest, he indicated to them that he would
make his own security arrangements; he infiltrated Sian with commandos of his secret police and had all the villages in the neighborhood of Lintung, which he had chosen as his headquarters
during his stay in the Northwest, evacuated. No one in living
memory had ever seen such extraordinary precautions taken.
And such ineffective precautions," commented the Lintung station
commander with satisfaction.

Chiang Kai-shek arrived in Sian on December 9, 1936, the very
day on which an anti-Japanese demonstration took place. Deeply
angered, the Generalissimo retired to Lintung and ordered the
young Marshal" to put an immediate end to these "disorders."
Then he summoned all the senior officers of the Tung Pei army
and demanded their absolute obedience. This attempt to supplant
him did not at all discomfit the "young Marshal," who was sure of
his men's loyalty and knew in addition that they detested the whole
traitor" government of Nanking.

---

opium. Despite this habit, he proved that he possessed unsuspected talents:
allying to the Nanking government, he crushed the Japanese faction in
Manchuria. In 1930 he helped Chiang Kai-shek in his campaign against the
Christian General," Feng Yü-hsiang. Despite this, the Nanking government
did not come to his aid when the Japanese invaded Manchuria a year later.
Chang Hsüeh-liang therefore agreed to withdraw his army from the Northeast and left for Europe; there he was cured of addiction and, as a result of
his anti-Japanese sentiments, came into touch with antifascist circles. On
his return to Sian he made many contacts, often friendly, with the Communists.

[61] See Snow, Edgar, *Red Star Over China;* also Smedley, Agnes, *Battle
Hymn of China* (New York, Knopf, 1943), pp. 131–151.

Three days later the "young Marshal" encountered a large mob that was getting ready to march on Lintung. He talked — "very movingly," according to my guides — to a young student who was flourishing an anti-Japanese placard.

"My father was killed by the Japanese and they sacked my house. I have as many reasons as you to want to seek revenge and free our Northeast. I give you my word of honor that your patriotic wishes will be granted. But put your confidence in me and go back to your homes."

As in a tale of the Tang era, the crowd discreetly dispersed. The "young Marshal," no less discreetly, kept his promise. The same night Tung Pei troops occupied Sian with such cunning that the Generalissimo's police commandos found themselves in jail before they knew what had happened. At Lintung, however, Chiang Kai-shek's bodyguard resisted, and the battle raged for several hours. Chiang Kai-shek, far from putting himself at the head of his faithful troops, escaped through a window in bare feet and nightshirt, and in his panic even forgot his dentures. He hid in a fox's hole on Li-san Mountain, where the following day he was found by a young Tung Pei captain. December is very cold in the Northwest; Chiang Kai-shek was half-frozen and had to be carried down the mountainside.

At my guides' request I carefully examined bullet marks and a broken window in the room in which Chiang Kai-shek had slept. Then we climbed up a little footpath to the famous fox's hole. It is difficult to judge from these faint traces, now thirty years old, whether the battle was severe, but one glance at the fox's den confirms that the Generalissimo must have passed an uncomfortable night.

No publicity was given at this time to the less than noble behavior of the Nationalist Commander in Chief; the conspirators had no wish to destroy him either physically or morally. They wanted simply to convince him of the necessity of fighting the Japanese and of forming a common front with the Communists. Chou En-lai came down specially from Pao-an, the Reds' mountain capital, to discuss this with the prisoner of Sian. One can imagine the emotions Chiang Kai-shek must have experienced on seeing his former colleague at the Whampoa Military Academy. In 1926, during the famous "March coup," he had arrested Chou (who escaped at the time of the massacre of April, 1927, in Shanghai) and had never ceased fighting him since. Chiang Kai shek had put a price on Chou En-lai's head and might well have thought that Chou had now come to collect his.[62]

All ended, however, without any bloodshed and even with a general reconciliation. Chiang Kai-shek agreed to take over the leadership of an anti-Japanese coalition and to put an end to the civil war. His about-face was announced to the country in a discreet way so that no one would suspect that the leader's new policy had been forced on him and was not really in accord with his personal convictions. The "young Marshal" Chang Hsüeh-liang even sacrificed his liberty to this salutary unity: he followed Chiang Kai-shek to Nanking, where he was tried for lack of discipline by a military tribunal, and he still remains his prisoner today in Formosa.

The Japanese did not remain inactive in the face of these developments. On the principle that attack is always the best defense they attacked the Chinese garrison at Lukouchiao (Marco Polo Bridge) in the southern suburbs of Peking on July 7, 1937, thus unleashing a war that did not come to an end until V-J Day, in August, 1945.

The Kuomintang and the CP did not try to form a common bloc as in 1924. On September 22, 1937, they both launched an appeal to the nation; but they launched it separately, as two distinct and independent forces which were agreed on "five proposals and four guarantees" essential to the anti-Japanese struggle. The proposals related to the means of mobilizing the nation; the guarantees ensured that officials of both parties could move about in each other's territory without the risk of being arrested and executed.

The Communists renamed their Soviet Republic of China the "Border Region of Shensi-Kansu-Ningsia" (abbreviated as Shen-kan-ning) and put at the disposal of the national army 45,000 soldiers who remained under their command and formed what was now known as the 8th Route Army (and no longer the Red Army). In return they obtained the right to exist if not legally at least freely in Nationalist areas, and were even allowed to open

---

[62] Agnes Smedley, who was in Sian at the time, relates in her *Battle Hymn of China* that the young officers of Tung Pei wanted to cut off their prisoner's head and were indignant at the intervention of Chou En-lai, who saved Chiang Kai-shek's life. As the Soviet press had published attacks against the Sian rebellion, some of them concluded that Chou En-lai had acted on the Comintern's orders. This assumption was not based on any hard fact and credited the Comintern with more perspicacity than they seem to have had.

recruiting offices for their army in certain towns like Chungking and Sian.

I visited the "liaison office of the 8th Route Army" at Sian, and there I learned a lot about the nature of the collaboration between the two partners of the anti-Japanese war. The office was set up in August, 1937, in a little, poorly sheltered suburban house which no conspirator would have chosen as a hideout. But this was still a euphoric period, almost a honeymoon between the CP and the Kuomintang, and people looked forward to the outcome of the war with an optimism that was rapidly curbed by the news from the front. True, the Japanese suffered some reverses in the initial phases of the war, but they were so much more powerful, so much better equipped, that the Chinese army could not hold them. One by one the large coastal cities and the main railroad lines fell into their hands. After the fall of Wuhan in 1938 Chiang Kai-shek was forced to fall back on Chungking, in Szechwan, magnificently situated in the Yangtze gorges, but with practically no road or rail outlets.

Surprised and shaken by the Chinese fighting spirit, the Japanese resorted to unbridled brutality and cruelty. They wanted to punish and destroy rather than conquer. Masses of refugees fled before them toward the most sheltered provinces, spreading the news of the nation's plight. Fourteen million men were torn from their homes by conscription, by bombing, by calamities of every kind, each more murderous than the other.

The traditional army was shown to be incapable of defending China. Only a revolutionary army, harassing the enemy in the rear and mobilizing the whole population against him, could save the country. Mao Tse-tung already had the embryo of such an army and for a long time he had not only thought about the possibilities of this kind of war but had even had some experience with it. Chiang Kai-shek knew this and dreaded the implications, for he had neither the desire nor the opportunity to compete with the Communists on this ground. He was a regular officer, a "man of order"; he had climbed the ladder of power by promising his allies and supporters to protect them from the armed mob raised by the anti-imperialist wave of the 1920's. Could he himself now take the risk, in the name of the anti-Japanese crusade, of unleashing that force again?

Knowing that he could not use revolutionary methods, Chiang Kai-shek was determined to isolate those who employed them and who were gradually winning the confidence of all the youth. Chungking attracted only a few profiteers, faithful to their cynical slogan: "Become civil servants and become rich." In contrast, all those, rich and poor, who believed in China, in its future, in a vision, trekked toward Yenan, the Red capital.

So the Red republic was surrounded by crack Nationalist troops, withdrawn from the front, and put under the command of the most reactionary general of the Kuomintang, Hu Tsung-nan. The liaison office of the 8th Route Army was virtually besieged by the "blue shirts," the secret police who were directly controlled by Chiang Kai-shek.[63] I was shown a model of the district surrounding the office. When a button was pressed, lights went on in the houses occupied by the police — practically every one. They laugh about it today, but it must have taken courage to go to Yenan in those days.

Yet neither intimidation nor the many obstacles put in their way slowed down the activities of the Communist "recruiting officers" of Sian.[64] They adapted themselves quickly to the conditions which were forced on them and equipped their office accordingly. No item of clandestine equipment was lacking, from printing press to radio transmitter. Party leaders like Tung Pi-wu (present Vice-Chairman of the Republic) and Lin Po-ch'ü, chairman of the Shen-kan-ning Border Region, directed it personally. Their ingenuity was certainly remarkable but would not have been enough to break the Nationalist blockade of the Yenan republic. If the blockade was ineffectual, it was because the relationship of the political forces had changed since the beginning of the anti-Japanese war. The real leaders of the national resistance could only be those who relied upon the masses, who were compelled to resist and determined to do so. The Chinese Communists were not wrong in

---

[63] The "blue shirts" were organized like a real secret society: all members had to take a personal oath of allegiance to Chiang Kai-shek. See Carlson, Evans F., *The Chinese Army*, p. 16.

[64] Relations between the Kuomintang and the CP became particularly strained after the "New 4th Army incident" in January, 1941. The Communist New 4th Army, commanded by Yeh T'ing, was operating in Anhwei province and was preparing to move northward when Chiang Kai-shek's troops launched a surprise attack on it. The New 4th Army suffered heavy losses, and Yeh T'ing was taken prisoner. Despite very strong Communist protests, Yeh T'ing was not released until March, 1946. A month later, on April 12, 1946, he died in a plane accident on the way back to Yenan. For the "New 4th Army incident," or "Anhwei incident," see *Mao Tse-tung*, "Order and Statement on the Southern Anhwei Incident," in *Selected Works*, Vol. 3 (London, Lawrence & Wishart, 1954–1956), pp. 225–232.

believing that the Sian incident was a decisive turning point in their history.

THE VETERANS OF YENAN

To the Chinese the "veterans of Yenan" are war heroes and trade union pioneers combined. The Party membership rose from 40,000 in 1937 to 1,200,000 by 1945, and it is reasonable to assume that almost all the new members passed through the Red capital's political school before going to fight at the front in the anti-Japanese war. The veterans, "the old guard," were just numerous enough to instruct them, in theory and by example, and to protect their orthodoxy with periodic campaigns of "correction." Most of the Communist cadres which govern China today are drawn from these "Yenan graduates," with their deeply rooted memories of the heroic days.

These men were of widely differing social backgrounds. Among them were the most enlightened peasants from the liberated areas, young students, and, lastly, a minority of workers who provided the skeleton of the "Sinified" and "Maoized" Party in the distant Northwest. Their common experience in the war years is today the main factor in their political solidarity and their unity. If a mayor, a civil servant, or a factory manager tells you, "I was at Yenan," he is giving you the key to his career and to his political attitudes. I met these men all over China; by listening to them recalling their memories one quickly learns the extraordinary importance of Yenan, this holy city of Chinese Communism.

I knew when, at Sian, I boarded the little unscheduled plane that takes one to Yenan that I would not be landing at any metropolis, but it is such a legendary city that one cannot help feeling a mild sense of disappointment on arrival. So it was here that all those famous heroes lived for such a long time? The landscape is beautiful: hills of loess, faintly yellow, cloven by little valleys with their yellowish rivers. It is harsh, too — vegetation is still scarce in spite of the recent reafforestation campaigns, and the absence of greenery gives a hostile air to the mountains for all their easy accessibility. And the city? Where is the city?

Yenan is 3,000 years old. Originally it was a fortified advance post which protected China from the nomads of the North, one of those advance posts ringed with enormous ramparts, massively thick and celebrated walls, lauded a thousand times for their beauty. Standing on a hill overlooking the city, Yenan's pagoda is one of the oldest in China. It makes an ideal lookout, for it dominates the surrounding mountains. At the foot of the hill runs a stream which protects the city. But all these defenses, natural and artificial, have not been enough: Yenan was sacked in the last century during the bloody Moslem revolt. Then in 1937, following the arrival of the Communists, it was flattened by Japanese bombing. The old pagoda, up there on its hill, is the last remaining vestige of Yenan's ancient glory.

Its new Communist masters were not discouraged by all this. They adopted a defensive tactic practiced in that region for centuries and established themselves in caves which they dug in all the neighboring hills and cliffs. But room was limited, and some of the cliffs are more riddled from foot to summit with caves and galleries than an ant hill, forming strange skyscrapers — partly natural — with terraces, alleys, and picturesque gangways for stairs. As these cliff-skyscrapers were often quite isolated from each other, the troglodyte city was very widely dispersed, but by the same token invulnerable to Japanese air raids. Indeed, the Reds, perfectly protected, wanted to be bombed: with the remnants of the bombs, they made mines and grenades that were much more effective.

It is said that the Yenan caves are warm in winter and cool in summer, which makes them very comfortable in this continental climate and is, no doubt, the reason why the bulk of the population still lives in them today. The city itself is no more than an overgrown market town: two or three streets lined with little wooden houses, a few shops, a hotel, and a stone staircase which leads to a theater that regularly shows films of the intensively active life that was led in Yenan in the days of Mao Tse-tung.

Not all the caves of Yenan have been abandoned to the inhabitants. Those that have some historic interest because a Party leader lived there have been carefully restored and are open to visitors. This restoration has not yet been completed, for there is still a lot to be done — when the Kuomintang troops occupied the city in 1947 they made a point of destroying the places their Communist enemies held most dear. That is why the cave that was used by the editorial staff of *Liberation* and by the Hsinhua news agency will not be opened until the end of 1966.

Today the tour of these historic places is done in three stages: visits to the villages of Yan Tia-lin, Tsou Yan, and Wan Tia-pin.

In the first, which is the farthest from the center of the city, there are only two caves, carved out of the rock and linked by a rather shaky footbridge to a wooden building in which the seventh congress of the Chinese CP was held in 1945. Mao Tse-tung lived here from November, 1938, until November, 1940, as well as during the congress. His cave consists of two rooms: in the first, a large bed with a mosquito net and some very simple toilet articles; in the second, the "work room," a rustic table, a candlestick, and some chairs. No bookshelves and absolutely bare walls. The guide explained to us: "In Yenan we had a generating unit to run our radio station and our press agency. The comrades wanted Chairman Mao to install himself near the unit so that he could have electric lights, but he always refused any privileges. Also, at the art school we had the finest painters in the country; they wanted to decorate the Chairman's living quarters, but he told them they should put their talents at the service of the people and not at his." Our guide wore patched trousers and sandals, which helped to re-create the austere atmosphere of the Yenan epic. The cave next door is fitted out like Mao's; first Chou En-lai and later Liu Shao-ch'i (who, however, came before him in the Party hierarchy) lived there. Why this preferential treatment for Chou En-lai? Because he was Mao's inseparable companion during the Long March and because at that time Liu Shao-ch'i controlled all the underground activity in the Kuomintang zone. Later, when Chou went to represent the CP at Chungking, he handed over the cave to Liu Shao-ch'i, who in 1942 wrote his essay "How to Be a Good Communist" there — an essay that is still constantly quoted today.

Yan Tia-lin is so small that it hardly merits the name of village, but it lies in a lovely setting. In front of Mao's cave stand several trees, including an apple tree under which, said my guide, the Chairman used to read and take his ease. And from the top of the rock from which the caves are cut one can see a small green plain where Mao cultivated a vegetable patch with his own hands after launching a campaign, in 1940, to grow enough locally to sustain the area without importing food. Ever since, the regional secretaries of the Party have had to tend the Chairman's former plot of land solicitously. Foreign correspondents have known the Chairman's vegetable patch well for a long time. Harrison Forman, who visited Yenan in 1944, described it in detail.[65] He reported that

[65] See Forman, Harrison, *Report from China* (New York, Book Find Club, 1945).

Mao grew very good American onions and that the gardener next door, Chu Teh, specialized in cabbages and salad greens. It seems likely that Chu Teh's old patch is tended today by some ordinary mortal, for my guide had no idea who he was.

The second village, Tsou Yan, is a much livelier place. Here there was a whole series of caves which were allotted to members of the Party secretariat. There Mao Tse-tung's neighbor was Jen Pi-shih, Secretary-General of the Party. After the Tsunyi conference at which Mao was elected Chairman, it was he and not the Secretary-General,[66] as in the other Communist parties, who exercised supreme authority and enjoyed the greatest prestige in the Chinese Communist Party.

The accounts of this historical conference do not even mention who was appointed Secretary-General. This position, from which the whole Party apparatus is controlled, is no less important for being less prestigious and could only be entrusted to someone who had the Chairman's confidence. It went to Jen Pi-shih. From the same province as Mao, he first met Mao at Peking University. In 1921 he founded the Union of Young Communists and became its Secretary-General. He played an important role in the Juichin republic and took part in the Long March as political commissar of the Ho Lung army, which reached the Northwest a year after Mao's main column. It would seem that he was Mao's protégé, which explains both the position he held in Yenan (which was confirmed by the seventh congress) and the privileged situation of his cave in the secretariat's village.[67]

One of the surprises at Tsou Yan is the cave that belonged to the present chairman of the Japanese Communist Party, Nosaka — the only foreigner who lived among the top Chinese leaders. But while Mao, like all his fellow-countrymen, had only two rooms at his disposal, Nosaka had three. The third is a bathroom, more than sketchily equipped with a large zinc basin and various toilet

[66] When Snow visited the Red republic in 1936, Lo Fu was still the Secretary-General of the CP. Jen Pi-shih probably succeeded him sometime later, but no one in Yenan was able to pinpoint the exact date.

[67] After Jen Pi-shih's death in 1950, it was another Hunanese, Teng Hsiao-p'ing, who succeeded him. In 1956 the eighth congress re-elected him Secretary-General of the Party. Officially he is number seven in the Communist hierarchy, if one takes as a criterion the order of precedence given to portraits. Teng is preceded by Mao, Liu Shao-ch'i, Chou En-lai, Chu Teh, Ch'en Yün, and Lin Piao. But his activities during the last few years seem to prove that his influence and powers are very great, particularly in relations with foreign Communist parties.

utensils. My guide was unable to tell me whether this "luxury" was a sign of traditional Chinese hospitality or of the Japanese mania for baths.

The village's distinguished residents received their visitors in a little wooden building which stands apart on a flat stretch of ground. Here many notable encounters between Mao and the intellectuals took place during the "rectification campaign" of 1942. The Chairman's talks, which still provide guidance for Chinese intellectuals, were delivered in this room, furnished, like a café, with little tables for four; but every Saturday evening the room was cleared for a dance. According to Anna Louise Strong,[68] all the leaders allowed themselves this distraction once a week. Chou En-lai was a remarkable waltzer, while Chu Teh and Liu Shao-ch'i shone at the slower dances. The American newspaperwoman does not reveal whether Mao also went dancing.

After this almost frivolous locale the third village, Wan Tia-pin, presents the martial face of Maoism. The staff of the 8th Route Army and the war college of the anti-Japanese campaign were stationed there. Mao Tse-tung also had a cave there in which he regularly conducted political courses for the Red cadets. His neighbor was Chu Teh, Commander in Chief and principal strategist. In the big room where the general staff used to meet, my guide talked briefly of Chairman Mao's bravery and insight during the Nationalist offensive in the spring of 1947. Here Mao called together the army's highest-ranking staff officers, demonstrated the necessity of drawing the enemy into the mountain wilderness of Shensi, and ended his lecture with these words: "Yenan will be like a heavy stone which crashes on the enemy's feet." He left the village for the last time on March 18, 1947, a few hours before the Nationalists arrived. My guide concluded: "The Chairman's forecast came true. Twenty-five Kuomintang brigades were destroyed in Shensi province; and one year, one month, and three days after its capture, Yenan was liberated." It seems that Mao never came back again: the decisive battle was then being waged in distant Manchuria.

In Yenan, where Mao spent ten years, one is still shown other relics of his stay — like the notice above the entrance to the Party cadres' school which Mao painted with his own hand and which reads: "Long live revolutionary romanticism and anti-Japanese realism." And they tell you that it was in the mock Gothic cathedral of a nearby village, built by the Portuguese, which then housed the Lu Hsün Academy of Fine Arts, that Mao uttered his celebrated dictum, aimed at intellectuals softened by city comfort: "Digging caves is the first step to the conquest of the Marxist heights."

At that time, indeed, every enthusiastic young revolutionary who arrived in Yenan had to begin by helping to dig a cave. Afterwards they were given stools, with which they attended one of the open-air universities — there were at least six in Yenan — where political science, military science, medicine, and the fine arts were taught. In June, 1939, the military academy had no fewer than 15,000 students. It is hard to believe this when one looks at the yellow Yenan landscape. Where did they live? How did they live? I put the question to Mr. Kao Fan-sian, Vice-Governor of Shensi province, who is, if one dare say it, the super-veteran of Yenan: even before Mao led his Long March troops there Mr. Kao Fan-sian had taken part in the organization of the Red base in the city.

"The Shen-kan-ning Border Region numbered twenty-six districts, covering 50,000 square miles. At the beginning there were only 1,200,000 inhabitants, but about 1946 there were many more than one and a half million. Most of the men stayed here only for their training period and then left, either for our liberated bases in the Japanese-occupied areas, or for the 8th Army, or even for the recently formed New 4th Army in the South. Communication with all the liberated zones was ensured by radio and messenger. Before the Sian incident, in the north of the province controlled by our supporters, a quite radical land reform was decreed, and they began to put it into effect; but after the agreement with the Kuomintang the redistribution of land was stopped. We helped to create peasant mutual-aid brigades everywhere, in the interests of social justice and also to increase production. For at all cost we had to be self-sufficient. The soldiers were particularly prominent in improving virgin land. They managed to produce considerable surpluses, while the cadres, especially those who had just arrived from the city, were able to produce only 60 per cent of their own food.

"At the beginning there was no rationing and practically no money. Each new arrival was assigned to an establishment which took charge of him. According to our calculations we spent ten yuan per month on each [about $4.00]. Gradually we began to put our own currency into circulation, but only in very small notes. Later, when transfers from one establishment to another became frequent, we issued ration cards. No one went hungry, but life was hard. The worst years were 1940 and 1941, for we hadn't had time to organize production. But in 1942, and above all in 1943, the standard of living rose to such a level that we could even sell our farm surplus to the zone controlled by the Kuomintang.

"We introduced rice farming, hitherto unknown in this region, and developed cotton growing considerably. We organized light industry: we manufactured arms — especially grenades and mines — and also medicines, soap, and china, and we prepared leather and furs. All the women were engaged in spinning; at their university, three hours a day were set aside for textile production. We also reopened oil wells that had been abandoned a long time ago by the capitalists, and these kept us supplied with kerosene and other products. All the enterprises were run as co-operatives.

"There were very few foreigners in Yenan. At the medical school, which bore the name of Dr. Norman Bethune, the Canadian Communist who died for our cause, we had two non-Chinese doctors — a Russian, Orloff, who has since left, and an American, Ma Hai-teh, who still lives in Peking. In 1943 or 1944 we welcomed a party of six journalists, mostly Americans, who toured the region on horse- and donkey-back for a few weeks.

"We had a special school for the Japanese prisoners, directed by the present chairman of the Japanese Communist Party, Nosaka. With the help of his pupils we published tracts, and even journals, in Japanese. All the students at this school were volunteers and lived freely in the same conditions as we did. The 8th Army had instructions to suggest to all Japanese prisoners that they should go to Yenan, and if they refused, to set them free. [It must be said, however, that the Japanese were extremely severe with their soldiers who allowed themselves to be captured.] We had no prisoner-of-war camps in our territories, and from 1943, when the Japanese troops' morale collapsed, many deserters tried to reach Yenan.

"All the intellectual elite of the country was to be found at the Lu Hsün Academy of Fine Arts. At first these artists and writers had some difficulty adjusting to the rustic life of Yenan. But Chairman Mao's talks enabled them to get to know and understand the local people and the situation. They wrote and presented plays and organized entertainments of all kinds, as well as exhibitions. Touring shows went to the front to entertain the troops. Believe me, no one was bored in the evening in Yenan. We worked very hard, but we relaxed too.

"We had our radio station (which is now in the Museum of the Revolution in Peking), and the only generating unit in Yenan was allocated to it. The lack of paper was a serious problem; but we succeeded in making paper from grass, and we published a daily newspaper, *Liberation,* and political and cultural magazines. But we were very short of books, and occasionally our troops made very risky sorties into enemy territory solely to commandeer libraries."

In the evening Mr. Kao Fan-sian showed us two documentary films made during the Yenan period, the first about daily life and the second about the village of Nanniwan, which was built entirely by the 8th Army. These old films shot by amateurs had the rhythm and dimension of the classic cinema; they were the best films I saw in China.

They are not devoted to any particular event, although they illustrate in passing several historic moments in the Yenan epoch, such as the seventh congress of the Chinese CP. Watching them, I noticed one small discrepancy: in the congress hall, which I had visited that same morning, the huge red flag is decorated with Mao's profile alone. In the documentary there are two profiles on the same flag — Mao's and Chu Teh's. Mao himself appears for a moment several times. He is seen reading Stalin's works in front of his cave or chatting with a group of peasants, one of them a deaf man who gives the sequence something of a Chaplinesque flavor. He is also seen again briefly giving a lecture to students from the military academy, all seated on the ground.

Yenan is presented as a dedicated community — enthusiastic, impassioned, brave, and resourceful. Everything is shot from life. It is a kind of *cinéma-vérité* which has no room for the stereotyped images of propaganda.

A MISSIONARY'S TESTIMONY

Yenan was not, however, a community whose members organized themselves and helped one another simply to survive. It was above all the center which trained and molded cadres and the brains of a social revolution which was taking place throughout a vast area occupied by the Japanese. It was Yenan which sent regular soldiers to the front, but above all it was Yenan which provided the underground organizers for the liberated bases at the enemy's rear. Thanks to them, in 1945 the Communist Party controlled an area with a population of nearly 100 million.

Madame Fan Chin, deputy mayor of Peking and director of the daily paper *Peking Jih Pao,* was one of these militants who operated in Japanese-occupied territory. Here is her testimony:

"My father, a professor of chemistry at Peking University, later became a high official in the Kuomintang. Throughout my youth I saw that this party was incapable of keeping its promises or carrying out the smallest reform. The insecurity, the unemployment, the oppression of women, the corruption — these were the daily reality, and they never changed in spite of the grand lectures on the rebirth of the nation. Then came the Japanese occupation. I was still in high school, but we were very politically minded; and in my class there were even young Communists who gave me their Marxist books to read. Thanks to them I was able to leave for Yenan in 1937 (I was eighteen at the time).

"I did well at school, especially in literature. That's why I took courses in journalism at the Women's University at Yenan. But I didn't stay there long. After receiving my basic training I was sent to Hopeh province, to the north of Tientsin, where we had a vast liberated base. The towns were occupied by the Japanese, and it wasn't an easy job to organize the press in the countryside. We had no printing press, and the local daily paper which we produced for the peasants had to be written out by hand. It was not until 1943 that we got our first press. We circulated our newspapers right in the towns, and the Japanese tried everything to find out where they came from."

"Who provided you with the news service? Who gave you political directives?"

"The Japanese at first. It was from their radio that we learned the events of the day, which we then interpreted in our own light. Later on we received periodical bulletins from the Hsinhua agency and the Yenan press. We were rarely able to pick up Yenan radio, and of course Moscow radio was even more difficult to get. The Party had experienced men in the region who could advise us, but for us our own way of life was the best school of ideology."

"Were you alone in charge of press problems?"

"We all did everything. As a woman, I had to organize the women's committees of the Resistance. That was even more difficult than producing newspapers by hand. For we women of middle-class background and from the big cities had very different ways from those of the peasant women. No theoretical knowledge will enable you to understand the class-consciousness of a poor peasant; only practical experience does. However, we gradually succeeded in making friends with these women and in getting to know them. In the country the Chinese woman was doubly oppressed — by poverty and by the feudal custom which subordinated her completely to the man. The job of the Women's Federations of the Resistance amounted to explaining to these semislaves that they could be emancipated and to enrolling them in the struggle. First of all we taught them to write; we gave them confidence so that they would tell us in detail about their life, and we told them how to deal with certain injustices that could easily be avoided. Afterwards we organized them in self-defense groups and mutual-aid groups so that they could stand up to the men. The wives of very poor peasants often found their desire to defy feudal custom thwarted by the duties and difficulties of their daily lives. If they devoted too much time to lessons or to social activities, they were unable to do their housework, and their husbands shouted at them and beat them."

"Since you wielded effective power, why didn't you intervene to protect them?"

"The Party exercised no dictatorship in the liberated bases. We intervened as little as possible in the life of local organizations. The women's federations were run by the women of the village themselves. We were only advisers who gave the movement impetus. It is true that certain laws were passed, such as that which forbade the sale of child-brides. But there also we confined ourselves to publishing the laws and made no attempt to supervise every home. We relied above all on education, starting from the principle that destroying one single feudal prejudice is enough to set off a chain reaction, which inevitably leads to the collapse of other prejudices. Daily experience confirmed the value of this method. We often saw women, passive and resigned at first, who a few months later joined the people's militia to take part in the armed struggle. We could see an improvement in the women's cultural lives every day. I can tell you, by way of example, that the present manager of number 5 chemical factory in Peking was one of the poor peasant women in my area and one of those most enslaved by the old customs."

"How were you able to administer this veritable state under the noses of the Japanese?"

"The Japanese occupied mainly the towns. At the beginning they didn't bother about our being firmly entrenched in the countryside. They began to get worried when it became impossible for them to collect taxes, and their soldiers fell into our ambushes. But by then it was too late. We had all the information about their dispositions, and they had none about ours. So they could only carry out big punitive expeditions, which were absolutely ineffective — we knew about them in advance. We knew how to build virtual villages underground, and the Japanese raids were mere blows in the empty air. Certainly they did a lot of damage, with unmentionable brutality: they pillaged, burned, and stole all they could lay their hands on. But they also suffered heavy losses. Our army was there, and even the peasants, whom they regarded as inoffensive, had been well provided with arms and ammunition by us. Toward the end of the war it was we who made raids on the cities, while they no longer dared to come out of their barracks. Later, after they had surrendered, the Kuomintang occupied the towns, and their troops were surrounded in the same way the Japanese had been. If the Kuomintang troops wished to pass through the countryside in order to get supplies it cost them dearly."

"Did you yourselves not have difficulty in getting supplies, particularly industrial products?"

"From the beginning we adopted the principle that we must 'stand on our own two feet.' That is to say, we made everything we could with the means at our disposal, and what we couldn't we took from the enemy."

Madame Fan Chin carries her forty-five years well, and seeing her now in her comfortable office in Peking city hall, it is hard to believe that she could so closely identify herself with the poverty-stricken peasants of Hopeh province. Her intellectual face, very well cared for, bears few traces of the several years of hazardous and trying experiences. Yet she asserts that she has never enjoyed a single privilege and that at a meeting of the Women's Federation of the Resistance I would not have been able to tell her from any peasant woman.

What is more, her revolutionary activities have not prevented her from having a personal life. Her husband is also an intellectual of middle-class origin who studied at a Yenan political institute. They have five children, three of whom, born at the base, were entrusted to the care of peasants. Their parents were too busy with their work or too much on the move to be able to look after them. One of Madame Fan Chin's sons had a miraculous escape from death. He was living in a village which was attacked in a punitive raid by the Japanese, who burned everything and even used gas on the underground hideouts. On the eve of the raid the family to whom this son had been entrusted took him away into the neighboring mountains. Today he is a student. At the time I met his mother he was doing a term of manual work in a people's commune. And Madame Fan Chin told me that she herself spent one month every year working in the fields in the Hopeh area.

THE PIEDMONTESE OF CHINA

When they launched total war against China, the Japanese did not envisage the complete occupation of this country of continental vastness — they did not consider it necessary. The traditional lack of unity of their opponents and the supposed absence of any sense of national solidarity led them to believe that after the inevitable defeat of Chiang Kai-shek's army, China would allow herself to be governed by puppets they had already set up, such as Wang Ching-wei and his like. And, indeed, the Kuomintang government, which had taken refuge in Chungking, did feel itself powerless, militarily and politically, to contest the Japanese presence. Chiang Kai-shek, admittedly, maintained a very important army which received material and technical aid from the United States. But he was building it up for *after* the war, and not for use against the common enemy. Convinced that the Americans would inevitably win in the Pacific, he prudently adopted the old Anglo-Saxon watchword, "wait and see." This immobility frequently provoked his American advisers into outbursts of anger, and their chief, General Stilwell, sent back reports criticizing Chiang Kai-shek. But without result: the Nationalist army never undertook any offensive action against the Japanese.[69] Worse still, when toward the end of the

[69] See Stilwell, General J. W., *The Chinese Adventure* (The Stilwell Papers, White, T. H., ed. — New York, Sloane, 1948).

war the Japanese (although much weakened) decided to take several more provinces in order to improve their communications with Indochina and Burma, Chiang Kai-shek's divisions put up only token resistance.

We have already said that the Chungking government was also completely passive politically. The Kuomintang was never firmly entrenched in northern and northwestern China, which suffered particularly under the Japanese occupation. But even in the districts where the Kuomintang had lately been able to count on many militants and sympathizers, they never showed the slightest intention of changing the social *status quo* in the name of resistance. If the Japanese had been faced by Chiang Kai-shek alone, their original assessment of the situation would have proved right. But the Maoist phenomenon completely escaped them. And that is why they paid such a heavy price, and not merely on the military front. Like sorcerers' apprentices, they rendered easier the very development they had always feared most — the unification of China under Communist leadership.

In 1932 an English socialist, R. H. Tawney, paid a long visit to China to study social and economic problems. He was amazed to find that the state hardly existed, that it was completely unable to defend the country and equally incapable of making any progress whatsoever. The reunification of China under a central authority was, in his opinion, the *sine qua non* of its survival. He wrote: "It is a problem to be attacked piecemeal. China is too vast, too diverse in conditions, and, in the absence of adequate communications, too amorphous and unmanageable, for it to be possible for all parts of the country to advance together. The process of unifying her must be carried out gradually and step by step. There must be provinces which lead and provinces which follow. Some region must play the part of Prussia and Piedmont in the Europe of the nineteenth century, serve as a basis where reform can mobilize its forces, and spread new standards of public spirit, efficiency and good government by the influence of its example . . . Not only governments, but the very idea of government, is unpopular in China. It has every reason to be; it has meant little during the last decade but taxation and war. A state cannot exist without citizens; and, if a Chinese state is to be a reality, it must win the confidence of common men. To win their confidence, it must offer practical advantages, which are clear and unmistakable. It must show results which touch directly the lives of the mass of the population.

It should be least difficult to show them, where government is not a remote abstraction, but stands close to the people. The right policy is to lay a patch of concrete where it can most easily be laid. It is to assemble in the home provinces the material and moral resources which make a modern state, and, strengthened by the prestige which only a visible example of good government can give, to advance step by step towards enlarging the area to which the same methods can be applied."[70]

Professor Tawney understood, therefore, the two essential conditions for the creation of a Chinese state: first, carry out a practical experiment in one area to prove to the demoralized population that this time there would be action instead of empty promises; then rally the whole nation around this model state. "In the China of the past," he wrote, "it was not unknown for communities harassed by tyranny or disorder to request a prince of better repute to accept them as his subjects. If modern Chinese governments relied more on the prestige which public opinion — in China an immense force — accords to positive achievements, and to them alone, they would need fewer bayonets to maintain their power."[71]

After examining the resources of the different regions of China, Professor Tawney concluded that a modern prince would have the best chance of making a success of the experiment in the Yangtze valley. The wretched Northwest, which had just experienced a long famine, did not seem to him to have the potential to be a Chinese Piedmont. At this time Mao Tse-tung and his supporters were far from Yenan and had still not decided to establish their base there. But later, after the Long March, they were not discouraged by the meagerness of material resources in their "new republic."

Their conception of "attractive practical accomplishments" was not the same as Professor Tawney's. In his view, only methodical industrialization would improve the condition of the people, and the valley of the Yangtze, with its natural riches and great communication possibilities, was the site of his choice; if a real bourgeois republic was ever to be created in China, it was there.

Mao Tse-tung was obviously not free to choose the best site for his proletarian experiment. The anti-Japanese war forced him to establish himself in the Northwest, which he was able to defend because of its inaccessibility. One day in Yenan, when Anna

[70] Tawney, R. H., *Land and Labour in China* (London, Allen & Unwin, 1932), pp. 169, 172–173.
[71] Tawney, R. H., *Land and Labour in China*, p. 172.

Louise Strong was praising the capital's climate in front of Mao, he commented simply, "We didn't pick it."[72]

In this semidesert country the Red republic could not hope to command plenty and prosperity. Economically the Northwest was many years behind the rest of China, and no government, even the most efficient, could have caught up — especially in time of war. Therefore Mao could not hope to accomplish big things in the industrial field which would attract the other provinces. Paradoxically it was the handicap of their first base's poverty which provided the Maoists with their psychological-political trump card. Installed in a particularly poor region, everyone from Mao to the humblest Party member was forced to lead the same life as the poorest local peasant: in the Northwest egalitarianism was a necessity, the first condition of survival. There the intellectuals from Shanghai or militants from Wuhan learned by experience, whether they liked it or not, what life was like for the wretched peasants who still remembered the famine of the 1930's and had resigned themselves to facing another.

The idea of "going to the people" has often occurred to intellectuals wishing to rouse the amorphous and resigned peasant masses of underdeveloped countries. In the Russia of the czars, toward the end of the last century, the "Narodnikis" tried to put this idea into practice. They dressed like poor peasants and sometimes even grew patriarchal beards, but they received a limited reception from the muzhiks. These missionaries excited more mistrust than enthusiasm. The simple fact was that despite their disguise, they did not belong to the medieval world of rural Russia.

The Maoists did not make a short-term experiment in northwestern China. They were not idealists who had temporarily given up their comfortable jobs to recruit supporters among the backward population. Mao had told them that the war against the Japanese would last a long time.[73] They therefore prepared themselves to live for years in the same conditions as those whom they wished to convert and mobilize. They asked them to fight against the common enemy, the Japanese, but also to help one another to improve their daily lot. They became part of this peasant world, and at the same time, they transformed it by their presence.

In the Yenan melting pot the traditional divisions between the

[72] Strong, Anna Louise, *Tomorrow's China,* p. 18.
[73] See Mao Tse-tung, *On the Protracted War,* Vol. 2 of his *Selected Works.*

different social classes quickly disappeared. In China, even more than in any other Asian country, the differences between intellectual workers and manual workers were enormous. So were the differences between the regions: the southern Chinese considered the northerners lazy and useless, while the northerners, in turn, regarded the southerners as vainglorious and corrupt. In Yenan no one could hang on to his private attitudes, nor could he expect to enjoy any privileges. Social and regional origins no longer counted in this "model state." True, it was built by a leveling-down: instead of raising the peasant masses to the level of the modern bourgeois republic, the Maoists had to "descend" to the level of the poorest. But it was this experiment which they had experienced that inspired their practical steps, adapted to the war situation and the backward rural economy.

"There are districts," wrote Professor Tawney, "in which the position of the rural population is that of a man standing permanently up to the neck in water, so that even a ripple is sufficient to drown him . . . The individual cannot be rescued by his neighbors, since whole districts together are in the same position. The district cannot be rescued by the nation, because means of communication do not permit of food being moved in sufficient quantities."[74]

The Communists understood that this peasant, in constant danger of drowning, would agree to fight his country's enemies and to act like a citizen only when he was convinced that his leaders would and could lower the level of the water in which he was immersed. Everything was tried, therefore, to convince the peasants and to awaken their political consciousness. For the first time in the history of China the peasants encountered administrators who were not acting for personal gain but as disinterested servants of a collective movement whose fate they shared. These latter by their example gave a new significance to the word "citizen" and made it almost a synonym for "revolutionary." Thus Mao succeeded, in the middle of war, in gathering around his party nearly 100 million Chinese.

The prowess of the Chinese guerillas during the anti-Japanese campaign has been praised even by Western military authorities, and the writings of Mao Tse-tung are closely studied by all specialists in "nonconventional" wars. Anti-Communist American writers have said of Chu Teh that he was "one of the most remarkable

[74] See Tawney, R. H., *Land and Labour in China*, p. 77.

military leaders in all history."[75] It is commonly admitted that it was the fighting spirit of the 8th Route Army and the Red partisans that assured the victory of the Chinese Communists.

There can be no question of minimizing the Maoists' feats of arms during World War II — there is no lack of evidence to attest to their importance. Nevertheless, it seems obvious that the Maoists' main battle was on the political front and that it was their victory in this field which led to their purely military successes. The Maoist army's power was not derived simply from its exemplary conduct toward the ordinary people[76] (something particularly appreciated in a country which had long suffered from military despotism), but also from its ability to help the people materially, politically, and morally.

The methods employed by European Communists in elections and their concept of democratic life make us skeptical about the ability (or the will) of Communists on other continents to do better in these spheres. We are therefore inclined to be doubtful when the Chinese talk of the elections they held in their liberated zones — and in time of war. Can one believe that the CP, usually so quick to monopolize power, agreed to share it with non-Communists and even with their "enemy-allies" of the Kuomintang? Can one believe that in the areas controlled by the Red Army the CP was content with a third of the seats in village and district councils?

We can neither accept the official assertions nor reject them out of hand on the basis that in Europe the Communists have always acted differently. Personally, I am inclined to believe that in this rural corner of China, which had never known democracy, the Maoists learned how to conduct public life in a way that gave these new citizens they were molding a feeling of taking part in regional affairs and even in national affairs connected with the war against the Japanese. And it was this as much as, if not more than, their military successes that gave prestige and power to the Communists, who after the war against the Japanese, seemed in Chinese

---

[75] See Isaacs, Harold, *The Tragedy of the Chinese Revolution,* p. 337.

[76] See Carlson, *The Chinese Army,* p. 37. These are the eight rules of conduct for soldiers of the Red Army: "1) Ask permission before entering a house. Before leaving, thank the occupants for their courtesy and ask them if they are satisfied with the condition of the house. 2) Keep the house clean. 3) Speak kindly to the people. 4) Pay for everything that you use, at the market price. 5) Return all borrowed articles. 6) Pay for all articles which the army has broken or destroyed. 7) Do not commit a nuisance (dig latrines). 8) Do not kill or rob the captives."

eyes to be like the "Piedmontese" — capable of reunifying their country.

THE SUPPLY SECTION OF THE LIBERATION ARMY

When Japan capitulated in August, 1945, Chiang Kai-shek could afford to feel satisfied with the results of his "wait and see" policy. His army was intact and numbered nearly four million men, including thirty-nine crack divisions entirely trained and equipped by the Americans. They also had the biggest air force that any Asian country had ever possessed. During the war the Western powers had renounced all their possessions in China and acknowledged the sovereignty of the Nationalist government over all Chinese territory, including Formosa and all the islands which had been occupied by the Japanese in the last century. Moreover, Chiang Kai-shek was invited to join the United Nations in the privileged position of one of the five founding members of the Security Council. And he was bound by pacts of friendship with the United States and the U.S.S.R. Most of the war lords had been rendered powerless, and the non-Communist opposition had become negligible. On the day of his triumphant entry into his capital, Nanking, Western experts thought Chiang Kai-shek to be "the most powerful ruler in the last two centuries of Chinese history."[77]

In this euphoric atmosphere the Generalissimo was obviously in no mood to accept the proposal of the seventh congress of the Chinese CP that there should be a coalition government. Admittedly he earnestly pressed Mao Tse-tung to come to Chungking for negotiations, but this was simply in the hope of getting at the conference table what he was certain of getting at any rate, even if it meant armed conflict. According to him, the Communists had only 600,000 soldiers and 400,000 militiamen, and the figures which they had published[78] were "exaggerated for propaganda reasons." Confronted with his army, the Communists did not carry enough weight; and Chiang Kai-shek's doctrine was, more than ever, "one party, one principle, one leader."

---

[77] See Belden, Jack, *China Shakes the World* (New York, Harper, 1949), p. 1.

[78] According to Hsinhua, the Chinese news agency, the total strength of the armies controlled by the CP in 1945 consisted of 915,538 regular soldiers and 2,200,000 militiamen.

The reasons for the outbreak of the civil war therefore appear simple and obvious: Mao was ready to make certain concessions consistent with his political power in the country, but he had not the slightest intention of disbanding the Communist armies as Chiang Kai-shek demanded. The Communists had learned the lessons of 1927 too well to place any faith in the promises or guarantees of the Kuomintang. They preferred to be accused of setting themselves up as war lords rather than find themselves disarmed and faced by the Kuomintang's "forces of order." Confronted by the Communists' obstinacy, Chiang Kai-shek decided to wipe them out by military means.

The Chinese historians of today reject this interpretation. According to them, it was the United States which pushed the Nanking government into a trial of strength because they wanted to secure military bases in China, with a view to a future attack on the Soviet Union. Chiang Kai-shek was no more than a tool in their hands. This is why, moreover, the Party decided in June, 1946, to call the Red Army the "Army of National Liberation" (the name it still bears) and to proclaim that its objective was to drive the imperialist Americans out of China.

"Nevertheless," I objected during a visit to the military museum in Peking, "the Americans made attempts to mediate in order to prevent civil war in China."

"What kind of mediator is he who signs military and economic pacts with one of the parties, whose troops he transports in his own planes and warships?" replied my guide. According to him, the United States spent six billion dollars trying to breathe a little life into the moribund Kuomintang regime.

Despite his army's numerical superiority, Chiang Kai-shek represented nothing in the country. His party had virtually ceased to exist, for the corruption of its leaders had disillusioned even its keenest supporters. His inability to govern had alienated even the conservative bourgeoisie, who feared galloping inflation. In the countryside the news that the Communists had been redistributing land to the peasants since May 4, 1946, in the zones they controlled poured out like a powder train and made the work of the Nationalist administrators impossible. "If they hadn't had the Americans," said my guide, "it wouldn't have taken us three years to drive out Chiang Kai-shek and his bunch — a few months would have been enough."

The day after this visit, I had to leave for a two weeks' trip to the Northwest, and my guide strongly advised me to refer to this campaign as the "Third Revolutionary Civil War" — the name given here to the final showdown between the Maoists and the Kuomintang. "Chiang Kai-shek was convinced that we depended as much on the Russians as he did on the Americans, and also he wanted at all costs to take the Northeast in order to cut us off from our allies. And that's where he lost his first big battle."

The Northeast, formerly Manchuria, still bears some signs of the Russian participation in the anti-Japanese campaign. Faithful to the Yalta pact, signed by Roosevelt, Churchill, and Stalin in February, 1944, the U.S.S.R. declared war on Japan three months to the day after the capitulation of Nazi Germany.

On August 8, 1945, Marshal Malinovsky's troops crossed the Amur River and attacked the Japanese "Kwantung Army." Two days before, however, the first atomic bomb had been dropped on Hiroshima, and on August 14 Japan surrendered.

However, the war in Manchuria was no simple walkover for the Soviets. The monuments they have put up pay homage to their soldiers who fell on the battlefields of northwestern China. The inscriptions in Russian are almost always the same: "Eternal glory to the heroes who died for the honor and victory of the Soviet Union." On none of these memorials (I saw five) is Russo-Chinese solidarity mentioned.

The deputy mayor of Shenyang, Mr. Sung Kuang, listened good humoredly when I pointed this out to him. Since 1943 this activist, an intellectual by background and a veteran of Yenan, has worked in Manchuria, which is not his native region. He witnessed the arrival of the Russians and described it to me in detail. But I was more surprised by his biting tone than by what he said.

He has no affection for Russia, particularly since 1960, the date of the hasty withdrawal of Russian specialists, which hit his town hard. It is the Northeast, in fact, which has suffered most severely as a result of Moscow's decision, and it is in the Northeast that attacks against Khrushchev's "modern revisionism" are most violent. However, Mr. Sung Kuang began his talk with a very official eulogy of Communist Russia:

"No one would know how to describe the extent of the moral support the Soviets gave us during our war against the Japanese. Their Stalingrad was our triumph too. The Japanese, who were not, however, at war with the U.S.S.R., interpreted this victory of the Red Army the way we did. They were left demoralized by it, and Stalingrad marked a turning point. Their occupation troops could still hold the big cities, but they already knew they had lost the war and we knew that we had won it. The name of Stalin terrorized them more than that of Roosevelt or Churchill. To us, on the other hand, Stalin was the symbol of our victory. We shall never forget him."

After this preamble, which I had already heard from the mouths of mayors of other towns, Mr. Sung Kuang took a long drink of tea and broke into a broad smile which announced that he had reached the unofficial part of his lecture.

"The Red Army," he said, "undoubtedly cut short the occupation of our region because the Japanese Kwantung Army was a self-contained force, very well equipped and capable of holding out even after Japan's official capitulation. We were very well established among the people, but we were not strong enough to drive the enemy out of their fortified positions. So the Russians helped us to free ourselves. I am no lawyer, and I cannot tell you by virtue of which treaty or which law the Russians considered Manchurian industry to be the spoils of war, transferable to the U.S.S.R. under the heading of reparations. We had had no administrative experience, and at that time the Red Army acted on its own. I'm not saying that its action was illegal; but since the Russians talked a lot later on about all the help they had given us (and which we have completely repaid), it is perhaps not without point to recall how many trains loaded with Manchurian equipment calmly headed for Russia. The Soviets even went to the length of dismantling the tracks of the Shenyang-Tantung line and taking them home. But all these are mere trifles — on the whole they rendered us a considerable service."

At this point Mr. Sung Kuang took another big swallow of tea before recalling a second historic operation on the part of the Russians:

"The Soviets stayed in Shenyang until March, 1946; they were waiting for the Kuomintang's representatives, who were not to be found in this area, to hand over to them the keys of the city. It was all perfectly legal. This manner of handing over power was, in fact, laid down in treaties we did not question. But, of course, the Kuomintang governor did not arrive alone. He was at the head of a crack army, crawling with generals and officers, each more elegant than the other and all accustomed to looting. But the city was empty. The Russians had already carried everything off. You can't imagine the disappointment of these fine gentlemen. Not only did they themselves have a hearty appetite, but they had promised their troops the earth. In their eyes we, who had fought the Japanese for fourteen years, were collaborators with the enemy; while they, who had never fired a shot at the Japanese, were heroic warriors. Here official looting was to have been a punitive measure against the populace. But, as I have told you, there was nothing left to loot. Of course one could always rob the poor, and the Kuomintang troops did so, shamelessly; but it was not enough to get rich. Moreover there was little food and to get any they had to go into the villages and countryside, which were well guarded by our militiamen, who were amply equipped with light arms. Let us admit it in the interests of historical truth, the Russians did not leave us too badly off. All attempts to get out of the city of Shenyang cost them dearly."

Mr. Sung Kuang's face was all smiles, as if the war had left him only happy memories:

"You know, my town was formerly called Mukden, which in the Manchu language means "new prosperity." It was from here that the Manchus set out for the conquest of China, and even when they had established themselves in Peking, all the emperors came back here twice a year to pay homage at the tombs of their ancestors. At that time to travel on horseback from the Great Wall to our town was a matter of weeks. By the time the Nationalist armies were installed here transport was much easier. In theory it is twelve hours by train from Peking to Mukden; yet their supply convoys took as long as, if not longer than, the emperors' horses to get to Shenyang. We controlled almost all of northern China. Even the Japanese traveled by armored train, with constant air-borne escort, to get from one strong point to another. Chiang Kai-shek's troops arrived without any precautions, as if they did not know that to cross Hopeh province from Tientsin to Shenyang they needed Red Army authorization.

"And then it gets very cold here. The Japanese had had time to get used to it, but Chiang Kai-shek's soldiers were mostly people from the South; and moreover they had been trained by the Americans in Burma. When winter arrived, they were as capable of fighting as a fish is of running. But we weren't in a hurry to take Shenyang — the Nationalist soldiers, poorly billeted and badly fed, had gradually begun to leave the town to join us with their arms and kit. We treated them well; we explained to them why we were fighting. Some enlisted in our army. Others we let go free, and they returned to Shenyang; but very often they came back to us within a few weeks. I knew several who shuttled back and forth five or six times, bringing us American weapons of the latest type. It was we who were the first to dub Chiang Kai-shek 'Chief of the Supply Section of the Liberation Army.' "[79]

"However," I said, "there had been some large-scale battles in Manchuria."

"Why yes. During the first year we were ordered to stay on the defensive to build up our forces, and we attacked only railroads to harass the Nationalist transports. Sometimes these delaying actions became pitched battles. Nanking, Chiang Kai-shek's capital, hailed victory after any convoy got through, but our losses were very light in these skirmishes. Later, in 1948, we passed to the offensive and completely cut the Nationalist army off from its rear areas. There some of them resisted, and at Anshan, for example, there was a large-scale battle in which they lost 40,000 men. But that was an exception. At Changchun the Nationalist garrison, led by its Commander in Chief, laid down its arms. They had tried to leave Shenyang to avoid being encircled; but when they realized this undertaking was as desperate as that of the Germans at Stalingrad, they surrendered without any nonsense. They had 90,000 men here, including generals and officers. In all, if my memory serves me right, Chiang Kai-shek lost 500,000 of his best soldiers in the Northeast. When Shenyang was finally liberated on November 2, 1948, our army was already bigger and better equipped than the Kuomintang's."

The Nanking government doubtless drew the same conclusion from its defeat as Mr. Sung Kuang, because two months later, on January 1, 1949, Chiang Kai-shek proposed peace to the Communists in his New Year message. Mao Tse-tung replied to him two weeks later, laying down eight preliminary conditions. The first was the punishment of war criminals, under which heading the Generalissimo himself and members of three families with which he was associated figured — twenty-five persons in all. Very evidently the Communists were no longer at all ready to accept a compromise.

It is true that four days earlier, in central China, the battle of Hwai-Hai had ended with the future Marshal Liu Po-ch'eng, the "one-eyed dragon," and the future Marshal Chen Yi cutting Chiang Kai-shek's crack army of 600,000 men to pieces and taking its Commander in Chief, Tu Yü-ming, prisoner. On the same day

---

[79] Mr. Sung Kuang was boasting a little; in fact, it was Chiang Kai-shek himself who originated the "title."

that Mao Tse-tung laid down his terms, his armies broke Tientsin's resistance and encircled Peking, which surrendered without a shot on January 31.

The negotiations took place all the same, for Chiang Kai-shek had agreed in principle to retire from the scene, but they could not change the situation much. The Communists, who had won the war, claimed the power. The Nationalists could pretend that they still controlled vast areas to the west of the Yangtze, but they knew that these territories were also undermined by the Reds and that a river, however wide, could not protect them. In any case, on April 20, the Liberation Army received the order to cross the Yangtze, and three days later it occupied Nanking, which Chiang Kai-shek had made his capital after the events of 1927. All over China huge photographs are displayed of peasant soldiers, shod in cloth, scaling the walls of the Kuomintang central government headquarters.

A SENTRY IN SHANGHAI

Every epic victory finds its bard, and that of the Chinese Communists is no exception to the rule. Books, plays, and films dedicated to the victory of 1949 are still today the most successful in China. One of these films, *The Sentry Under the Neon Lights,* struck me particularly, not for its artistic value but because it evoked, with a realism mixed with frankness, the atmosphere of Shanghai when the Red troops marched in, in May, 1949.

The main avenue of the wealthy quarter, the Nanking Lu, in the heart of the former international concessions, is still ablaze with neon signs in the American manner. It is lined with luxury shops and night clubs, and it crawls with rich conspirators who whisper to each other: "The Reds are arriving in Shanghai, but they will soon become black here." Such, it appears, is their faith in the power of corruption, which in the past has taken care of more than one conqueror. Then the unit which has been given the job of keeping order on the Nanking Lu, the 8th Prize Company of the Liberation Army, is entirely composed of peasants who have never seen an avenue like this before, probably not even a city. A crowd of admirers, sincere or pretending to be, mob them on their arrival, asking for their autographs and congratulating them. Beautiful students, elegant and perfumed, invite them to dances or to night clubs. Conspirators lie in wait everywhere. Like devils, they watch for the slightest personal weaknesses in order to trap lost souls. A young section commander allows his head to be turned by a counter-revolutionary girl student who wants to use him in a bomb attempt during a New Year's entertainment. Of course Chen Hsi falls for this temptress, played by an actress who invests the part with such obvious treacherousness and wickedness that a child of four would have been suspicious. He is even so bewitched that he forgets the revolutionary merits of his wife (we see her in her village in a series of flashbacks), whom he treats very badly when she spends a few days with him in Shanghai. She seems very coun-trified now, and he thinks only of meeting again the girl who has corrupted him.

Fortunately, Hsu Lin-keh, political commissar of the 8th Prize Company, is on the alert; Mao Tse-tung has personally warned him of the risks facing Chen Hsi and his fellows. Indeed, in March, 1949, the Chairman of the CP had declared in a talk to the Central Committee: "Our victory will soon be complete, but it runs the risk of giving rise to certain dangerous tendencies in our ranks. People of weak character will give in to arrogance, adopt abusive attitudes, and, yielding to the appeal of the easy life, reject austerity. The enemy, who has failed to beat us on the battlefield, will try to win over these weak comrades by flattery. Many of our comrades stood up bravely to steel bullets and deserve the title of hero, but the 'sugar bullets' could be fatal. Let us not forget that the enemy, even disarmed, will continue to fight desperately — let us be ready to fight this new class war."

Struck by these warnings, Commissar Hsu Lin-keh passes them on to his soldiers in innumerable and interminable sermons which completely spoil the film. By these means he succeeds in turning Chen Hsi away from the road to ruin. So all ends well: the Reds stay pure, the Blacks go to jail, and Chen Hsi is reconciled with his wife before he leaves, as a volunteer, for the Korean front.

As I have reservations about the rather too edifying naïveté of the scenario, my guides assert that it was directly inspired by an actual incident. Good. Although that may be so, this film is a document in that it reveals the weakness of the Communists in the big urban centers even at the moment of their victory. Shanghai, the greatest working-class city in China, was the cradle of the CP. On its Nanking Lu during the 1920's countless workers' demon-strations took place, the most famous of them on May 30, 1925. One asks oneself, therefore, why the policing of the Nanking Lu was entrusted to young peasant soldiers completely dazzled by the big city, and not to the workers' militia, recruited in the Chapei district and noted for their revolutionary spirit. It is as if, after the victory of a new Paris commune, the Champs Elysées were guarded by peasants from the heart of France, and not by the workers of the city's Red belt.[80]

But the imagery of this film and the questions which it raises hardly bother the Chinese. Quite the reverse. They find in them the proof of Mao Tse-tung's clear-sightedness and of the accuracy of his conception of the proletarian struggle. "Think a little about the German CP, so powerful during the 1930's and practically reduced to nothing by the Hitlerian terror," said a European Communist who has lived a long time in China, discussing this point with me. "And yet it had only the middle classes against it in the country. Here, in the port cities the repression of the workers was inspired and directed by a coalition of all the imperialist powers and an unbelievably savage upper class. Chiang Kai-shek and his henchmen did not even resort to such means of intimidation as the concentration camp — they executed every suspect. No one knows the exact number of the white terror's victims, but there were tens of thousands each year.[81] This blind repression, actively supported by foreign weapons and money, could have put an end to a bigger, more experienced party than the Chinese CP was in 1927. As in Nazi Germany, it could have demoralized the working class, all the more so because the Chinese workers were living in a colonized country. Nothing like this happened, however, because Mao Tse-tung knew how to choose the field of battle most favorable to the Communists. Not only was the Party not annihilated

[80] Robert Guillain of *Le Monde* watched the Communist troops enter Shanghai and recently described the event in his preface to Roger Pelissier's book: "On the spot it was a remarkable event. Shanghai, citadel of capitalism and of the West in Asia, fell into the hands of her conquerors. And who were these latter? Peasants, peasant-soldiers from the river, poor, badly armed, wearing grass-colored sackcloth. Their army did not fire a shot, and one did not even hear the tramp of their marching feet — they wore slippers. These rustics had undoubtedly never seen a city; they craned their necks to gawk at the unbelievable skyscrapers. They neither stole nor raped; and if occasionally they made a purchase, they paid in cash. This had never been seen before in China." See Pelissier, Roger, *La Chine entre en scène* (Paris, Julliard, 1963).

[81] According to Isaacs, between April and December, 1927, 37,985 Communists were condemned to death and 32,316 to long prison sentences. Between January and August, 1928, 27,699 people were officially executed, but the number killed without trial is unknown. See Isaacs, Harold, *The Tragedy of the Chinese Revolution*, p. 296.

but it again showed itself able to free towns terrorized by the class enemy."

This workers' party had spent more than twenty years in exile in rural China. Did this long transplantation modify it in any way? Did it keep its original character and ideology, which in theory are determined by the special historical condition of the urban proletariat? Foreign students of Maoism often ask themselves this question. According to the Chinese, this is a fictitious problem. The Party, they say, did not need to elaborate its doctrine in the countryside. It had adopted Marxist Leninism from its birth, and this guided it whatever the conditions. Marxist ideology, it is true, finds more favorable soil among the urban workers, but that does not prove that it is inaccessible to exploited peasants or intellectuals. The Chinese revolution was a workers' revolution because it was inspired and directed by Marxist doctrine and cadres. The fact that the majority of those who took part in the revolution were recruited in the rural areas does not, therefore, change its basic character. If the Chen Hsi of the Nanking Lu seems to you to be pure peasant it is because you have not properly understood the situation: his manners were no doubt countrified, but his thinking was absolutely like that of the Chapei workers. Besides, that is why he found himself one day in the heart of Shanghai again — a purely peasant army would never have been able to win the civil war. . . .

These explanations are obviously based on a convention peculiar to the Chinese CP that the ideology has a quasi-autonomous role — a role which the founder of Marxism hardly recognized. But like all *a posteriori* justifications, they contribute less to the debate when their authors have not always corrected doctrinal distortions arising from their experiences. The Maoists succeeded in their revolution with the only weapons at their disposal, and for them the result counts for much more than the vicissitudes of their struggle.

Besides, on their arrival in the big cities they immediately set about organizing the trade unions and other workers' bodies. And Mao Tse-tung assigned to the urban proletariat the task of leading the rural areas, thus admitting by implication that the earlier situation had not been completely normal.[82] It seems, nevertheless, that Mao's tactical principle, "surround the towns by way of the countryside, then take the towns," deeply influenced the thinking of the Chinese Communists, who today intend to apply it on

[82] See Mao Tse-tung, *Selected Works,* Vol. 4, p. 379 (Peking ed.).

world-wide scale. The Western countries, industrialized but firmly
held by the capitalists, are the "towns." The underdeveloped countries, as "explosive" as rural China before the revolution and as
opposed to the bourgeois ideology, are the "countryside." It is in
these countries, therefore, that the anti-imperialist liberation
movement will start, one day to hoist the flag of world revolution
in every capital, as the Chinese Marxist peasant soldiers did in
Shanghai in 1949.

THE NATIONAL FLAG AND THE NANKING
MAUSOLEUM

The Chinese anti-imperialist movement seems to have looped the
loop and returned to its point of departure, that is, to the alliance
of all patriots Dr. Sun Yat-sen had urged as far back as 1924. In
his policy draft on "the democratic dictatorship of the people,"[83]
published three months before the proclamation of the People's
Republic, Mao Tse-tung explains, indeed, that his regime will be
founded on the alliance of the four classes: the working class, the
peasantry, the lower middle class, and the middle class — the very
same classes, one remembers, that Dr. Sun Yat-sen wanted to
unite twenty-five years earlier in the reorganized Kuomintang in
Canton. For its emblem the Maoist republic chose a red flag
adorned with five stars — a large one symbolizing the Communist
Party and, grouped around it, four smaller stars representing the
four classes.

But Mao Tse-tung did not proclaim himself heir or successor to
Sun Yat-sen. He paid homage to him for his forty years of
patriotic struggle, but he also drew up a very critical balance sheet
of his defeats. This was not to demolish him, but simply to demonstrate once more that the national concept so dear to Sun Yat-sen
made no sense in China unless it was embodied in a Maoist-type
socialist revolution, which the Communists were the only ones to
promote.

"We did not adopt Sun Yat-sen's Nationalist flag because he led
to no victory. In its stead we have devised a banner of the revolution because it at last is giving a unified and modern state to the
Chinese." Such was Mao's message to the four anti-imperialist
classes.

[83] See Mao Tse-tung, Vol. 4.

Sixteen years had passed, and I noted that several of my Chinese guides no longer knew the exact significance of the stars on their national emblem. The Maoist regime has undoubtedly been less brutal with the middle classes than were the Bolsheviks after the October Revolution, and it has applied its more cautious, more liberal policy of socialization gradually. However, it is hardly likely that this policy had been approved by Sun Yat-sen or that it corresponded in the slightest to his idea of the alliance between the patriotic classes. True, the great man's widow, Madame Soong Ch'ing-ling,[84] is Vice-Chairman of the People's Republic, and she asserts that her husband would have supported the Maoist regime as fervently as she herself does; but the Communists do not seem to want to link the Kuomintang founder's name too closely with the CP.

Indeed, for them the main point lies elsewhere. The unified modern state that Sun Yat-sen wished for exists today. By paying homage to the patriotism of the Nationalist leader, the Communists extol their own. That is why, on our arrival in Nanking, Chiang Kai-shek's old capital, we were taken on a visit to the mausoleum of Sun Yat-sen, built by the former dictator during the years of the worst anti-Communist repression (1927–1929). It stands a little outside the town, in a park laid out on the slope of one of the numerous hills that ring Nanking.

To reach it one walks along a wide drive lined with trees and climbs a marble staircase. Then one stops in a first pavilion, where it is announced that the Nationalist leader lies higher up; to get to the mausoleum proper one has to climb some 400 steps. Engraved on the granite walls of the mausoleum are quotations from Sun Yat-sen's speeches and from his will, in which he urged his supporters to continue his fight for China's independence. The great man's tomb lies in a little room perfumed with incense, under a beautiful dome in which blue, the color of the Kuomintang, dominates. Sun Yat-sen was not embalmed; his body is buried here under a stone.

From the heights of the mausoleum there is a wonderful view of

[84] Madame Sun Yat-sen, a Christian and educated in the U.S., is the sister of Madame Chiang Kai-shek, of T. V. Soong (one of the chief leaders of the Kuomintang), and of Madame Kung, the most fabulously wealthy representative of the old regime. After the events of 1927, Madame Sun Yat-sen strongly opposed Chiang Kai-shek and broke with her family. However, she was allowed to live in Shanghai and then in Chungking, from which she frequently denounced the Kuomintang. On this subject, see particularly Snow, Edgar, *Journey to the Beginning*.

Nanking and of the Purple Mountain. We lingered there for a long time with our escorts (a guide-interpreter and a historian) and began to talk about Sun Yat-sen.

With assumed innocence I asked if no one had thought of replacing the engraved quotations on the walls, which had been chosen by Chiang Kai-shek, with other, more progressive quotations of Sun Yat-sen's. This suggestion did not shock my guides — they found it pointless: "Sun Yat-sen was not a Marxist. Therefore he could not provide the practical solutions to enable feudal and colonized China to get out of the deadlock. But nevertheless his writings gave people sound aspirations, and there is not a line in them that could embarrass us. Chiang Kai-shek ought to have blushed for shame when he read on the walls of this monument the three 'principles of the people' formulated by Sun Yat-sen: national independence, complete democracy in the interests of the people, and the well-being of the nation. In fact he carried out none of these. For us Communists the national concept has never been inconsistent with our revolutionary and internationalist convictions. Many among us became Marxist Leninists because we gradually learned that it was the only doctrine that could guide us in the fight for a united China. It is probable that Dr. Sun Yat-sen, too, would have understood this if only he had lived a few years longer."

Having uttered this bold hypothesis, my guides prudently added that, even without becoming a Marxist Leninist, one could be a good patriot and help to build the People's China, as the example of many of Sun Yat-sen's disciples proved. "The revolutionary Kuomintang still exists and prospers in China. It has seventy-five deputies in the People's Congress and three Ministers in the government (Postmaster General, Forestry, and Textiles). These men, coming from nonproletarian classes, do not wish to and cannot become Communists, but they are happy to see their country liberated from the foreign yoke and want to contribute to its prosperity and strength. On proclaiming the People's Republic, Chairman Mao promised that the Chinese nation would never again be humiliated, and by keeping his word he has realized the dearest wish of Dr. Sun Yat-sen and his supporters."

Going down the steps of the blue mausoleum, we passed a group of Chinese "not like the others," who seemed to appear providentially to confirm the words of our guides. They wore Western-style ties, suits, and dresses. Without any doubt they had come to Nanking from one of the great Asian cities which have huge — and often prosperous — Chinese communities. In Peking, Shanghai, and other cities special hotels have been built for them — the "hotels for overseas Chinese" — and they are offered every facility to come and visit their reborn motherland. These pilgrimages are expensive, and to judge from their clothes these Chinese from abroad were no Singapore coolies. However, all wore red badges in their buttonholes. From this one could perhaps draw the conclusion that after a century of foreign occupation, ended at last, most Chinese (even those who do not live in China) identify national aspirations with revolutionary aspirations.

It would be taking a rather idyllic view, however, to think that harmony reigns and perfect unity has been achieved between the "Sunyatsenists" and the Maoists. And, indeed, my guides frequently insisted that the class struggle continues in China. How can it have a place under the "democratic dictatorship of the people" proclaimed by Mao Tse-tung? And will it lead to the same excesses which the class war once produced in Stalin's Russia? To put it more bluntly, does a third category exist alongside the Chinese Marxists and those Chinese who are simply patriotic — that of the Chinese who have been consigned to concentration camps?

On this point I put the following question to Prime Minister Chou En-lai: "You often speak of the continuance of, and occasionally of the intensification of, the class war in China. Didn't Stalin say the same thing about Russia not so long ago to justify widespread repression?"

"Stalin's descriptions of the internal situation in Russia often varied," replied Chou En-lai to show that he did not like the comparison and that one can forget Stalin. Then he continued:

"The Chinese revolution did not make the social classes which existed in our country disappear with a wave of a magic wand. They still exist, and if there are classes, the class war will continue. Having passed the stage of the democratic revolution, we created the socialist revolution: we took the means of exploitation away from the exploiters of property, but we neither liquidated nor deported them. The former landlords and the rich peasants, who represent about 7 per cent of the population, still live in their villages, work like the others, and thus are re-educating themselves. Today, after fifteen years, some of them have changed and become good workers. But there are many who still cling to their old ideas and are hostile to the revolution.

"It is different with the middle class, which numbers about a million people. Discontented with Chiang Kai-shek, the middle class either took part in the democratic revolution or sympathized with it or simply did not oppose it. After the liberation, elements of the middle class continued to enjoy all their civic rights. When we came to the phase of the socialist revolution, our policy with regard to the middle class was to buy up their factories, awarding them an annual interest of 5 per cent for ten years.[85]

"It is a fact that former landowners and middle-class elements exist in China. Moreover, the effects of the habits of the former society are still quite considerable. Even among those who have been brought up in the new society there are some who tend to follow the old ways and who even occasionally go in for illegal activities like speculation. It is these people who bring new bourgeois elements into being. Marxists must not ignore these facts or deny them if they do not want such people to corrupt others and commit sabotage.

"There are also external enemies who seek to create trouble. The American imperialists and their lackey Chiang Kai-shek are always sending us a lot of their agents. For all these reasons we constantly remember that the classes exist and that the class war continues. The people must maintain their revolutionary vigilance.

"Previously, whenever they chose, exploiters didn't hesitate to use any means, even the most extreme, against us in order to protect their privileges. Now that we have the power in our hands we rely above all on persuasion. We tell these people that they can be re-educated if they want to serve their country. This is how we do it: in the case of sabotage we imprison as few as possible and execute even fewer. Repressive measures are only used in the case of grave breaches of the law and when the lives of others are involved.

"In Europe you have a long tradition of regicide. Here the last emperor was pardoned. And not only was he not executed, he still sits in the Chinese People's Consultative Conference and he was allowed to publish his memoirs. I could also cite you the case of one of the most important generals of the Kuomintang, Tu Yü-ming, who fought against us for years. During the Hwai-Hai campaign he led an army of 600,000 men, but he ended up by being

---

[85] It was on February 24, 1956, that the Central Committee of the Communist Party of China decided on the "transformation of capitalist industry and commerce in China."

captured.[86] Now he also is a member of the Consultative Conference. All these men — and I could cite you many more — are not and will never become Communists. We do not ask that much of them. All that we demand of them is that they work loyally for their country."

Thus reduced to the re-education of recalcitrants, the political struggle in postrevolutionary China was less than spectacular and the Chinese museums accorded it no place. We knew that the great shift in recent Maoist policy (the "Great Leap Forward," the "hundred flowers" policy, the regime of the people's communes, and the break with the Soviet "modern revisionists") had given rise to bitter debates at the highest levels of the Party, and had perhaps even divided it. In official publications the Chinese themselves described the Central Committee discussions in 1959 and 1961, which ended with the expulsion of the "rightists." We were also told that the "leftists" were called to order at the same time and that thus only the Chinese CP was able on every occasion to adopt a correct line. But at no time did the Chinese explain exactly what the right- and left-wing deviations consisted of and who their protagonists were.

This discretion is hardly surprising. All the Communist parties jealously guard the secrets of their top-level discussions, and dislike making their basic reasons public. The events in China in the summer of 1966 introduced certain innovations which contrasted with the former scheme of things, in that, for the first time, the rank and file were called upon to take action. The Communist countries do not customarily give birth to this kind of mass action. The appearance of the Red Guards is an event without precedent.

It is certain that this innovation was not approved by all the Chinese CP leaders. The Maoist leadership was split by this operation, which led to a reconstruction of the governmental hierarchy and the partial eclipse of the men who controlled the Party apparatus, like Liu Shao-ch'i and Teng Hsiao-p'ing. We do not know the details of this last trial of strength, which ended with the promotion of several of Mao Tse-tung's companions, such as T'ao Chu and Ch'en Po-ta, who until then had not held front-rank posts in the secretariat. We can attempt an explanation: in order to purge the apparatus, it was necessary to appeal to men who did not identify themselves too closely with it, and to the Red Guards, who were not an integral part of any existing body. These young zealots

[86] The battle of Hwai-Hai (November 7, 1948, to January 12, 1949) is considered one of the most important of the civil war.

were able to take their line from the debate which had taken place at the summit, without knowing much about its details. There can be no doubt that this affair will one day occupy an important place in the textbooks and history museums of China.

THE PRECAUTIONS

Jean-Paul Sartre has written: "If an opposition achieves its final triumph, it becomes the measure of history and, while building the future, it decides the meaning of the past."[87a] Every society, even the most democratic, therefore manufactures its own version of history. Chu Teh was not wrong when he replied one day to Agnes Smedley — who was questioning him about Chinese who had betrayed their country — that in America also, during the War of Independence, many Americans had fought on the British side; but "one doesn't learn that at school in the United States."[87b] Nor do the young French find in their textbooks any reference to Pétain's triumphal visit to German-occupied Paris a few months before the Liberation. And no matter what the country, one could find parallel examples.

The Maoist revolution therefore throws its own light on China's recent history. Its interpretation, from all evidence, has been conceived for the education of the masses, who are credited, rightly or wrongly, with a rather elementary level of culture and consciousness. It is reduced, therefore, to basic outlines which, starting from some basic knowledge of the past, enable the intervening changes to be explained — all with the aim of producing action. No one in China hides the fact that this teaching of history is intended to be utilitarian and to produce immediate, concrete results. By studying the rise of their country and their CP, the Chinese are obliged to understand the effectiveness of a certain way of life and system of values which have ensured the victory of Maoism. History is regarded as a means of inculcating in each citizen this "correct political thought" which is — as we shall see later — the key to the whole of the present system.

This educative version of history often appears naïve and even occasionally offensive to us when certain gaps in it are too obvious. It also promotes the cult of personality in a way that

[87a] In his preface to the book by Louis Dalmas, *Le Communisme yougoslave* (Paris, Ed. Terre des Hommes, 1950), p. 9.
[87b] Smedley, Agnes, *The Great Road*.

shocks even those foreigners who sincerely admire Mao Tse-tung's achievements. But to judge this objectively we must put ourselves in the place of the "consumer" it is aimed at. Illiterate until yesterday, he finds in history presented this way the only comprehensible explanation of his life today and of his past misery; it also provides him with the justification for the sacrifices he consents to today and the new direction of his life.

That said, the Communists attach too much importance to history for them to be able to reduce it indefinitely to a mere instrument of primary education. No other society has ever claimed to be the result of objective social laws — which the proletariat, under the Party's leadership, interprets and applies to attain the revolution. To the Communists history is only the analysis of this process, and they cannot tinker with it without running the risk that they might come to repudiate the reasons for the revolution's existence, for enduring it — for its very necessity. As a result, it is more disturbed than any other society when it discovers that its official history has been distorted and falsified. One saw this in the U.S.S.R., where de-Stalinization gave rise to a profound and painful skepticism.

In fact, the Stalinist version of history was not only a simplification but very often a deliberate falsification, intended to justify the struggle within the Party, the vilification and the repression. It was after he had eliminated the Bolshevik old guard that Stalin monopolized all the channels of public information and instruction: he thought himself free to spread his personal version of history and of his clashes with other leaders. The ordinary people had no means of checking his statements or of comparing them with the accounts of others. This was the spirit in which the *Concise History of the CP* (b) [88] was conceived. This publication was more than a history textbook: it also claimed to summarize the doctrine. In the Soviet universities in which I studied we learned "Marxist Leninism" through this basic work. For each chapter we were provided with the texts of Marxist classics intended to justify theoretically the practical steps taken by Stalin, to whose glory all Marxism thus contributed.

This system was perfectly coherent: past, present, and future combined to inspire an admiring confidence in the wisdom of the Party leaders. The system had to be believed in its entirety and with it all the interpretations of history it provided, from the first

[88] *Kratkii Kurs V.K.P. (b).*

congress of the Russian socialists at Minsk at the end of the last century up to the Five-Year Plans, and including the October Revolution, the civil war, the NEP (New Economic Policy), and collectivization: the whole was so tightly knit that the slightest questioning of even a part of it was to risk bringing the entire system down.

After Stalin's death, his successors therefore found themselves deadlocked. None of them could arrogate to himself either the doctrinal infallibility or dictatorial powers of the dead leader without endangering the physical existence of the others. The functioning of the controlling machinery had therefore to be modified and certain repressive methods abandoned. Stalin's heirs were inevitably driven to denounce publicly his methods of government, the product of the inadmissible "personality cult," in order to prove that the new line re-established Leninist norms. This was done in 1956, during the twentieth congress of the Soviet CP.

But Khrushchev, author of the famous "secret report," proposed the revision of only two chapters of the Stalinist history. He believed that the others, which concerned events before 1937, could not be rethought without affecting the coherence of the whole. This was obviously an illusion. The revelations about the concentration camps and other abuses of power, as might have been foreseen, provoked a crisis of conscience and forced the Communists to reflect on the causes of this deviation from the whole system (too often, unfortunately, without their saying anything about it). The madness of one man alone could not explain it, and the inadequacy of the official explanations further undermined the Russians' confidence in their Party. To replace the Stalinist orthodoxy with a credible system it would have been necessary to begin the whole history of the workers' movement again and to throw light on a mass of facts and to "resuscitate" a host of people Stalin believed he had erased from history forever by not mentioning them in his textbooks.

The Soviet leaders neither knew how, nor dared, to go so far. As Stalin's pupils, they applied his own measures to him: on every possible occasion they deleted his name from history. This glaring new falsification merely exacerbated the moral crisis which today still racks a whole generation of Communists both inside the U.S.S.R. and outside it.

Thus the Stalinist conception of history, which for a time was undeniably effective, today has become a brake on both the internal and international activities of the Soviet CP. After such an experience one can no longer judge the Maoist version of history only by its immediate effectiveness and leave it at that; one must examine the repercussions which could bring about its revision in the more or less near future. Perhaps I was the victim of my propensity for always comparing the Chinese Communist experience with that of the Russians, but whenever I noted an omission or an untruth in my guides' recitals I thought of the consequences which the correction of these inaccuracies would have one day on the "political and moral health" of the Chinese. After all, Mao Tse-tung is no longer young, and he even said he is "preparing himself to meet God Almighty" in a recent interview he gave to Edgar Snow.[89] Will the de-Maoization which could shortly appear be comparable to de-Stalinization? Very probably it will not, but the two operations will have at least something in common. Indeed, it hits one between the eyes that the great weakness of the Chinese system of history lies in its attachment to falsifications of the history of the workers' movement imposed by Stalin. During the Soviet dictator's seventieth-birthday celebrations in 1949, his Chinese apologists went to the length of demonstrating his political genius by quoting extracts from his speeches, which proved, on the contrary, his lack of discernment in the matter of the Chinese revolution. If it is true that he said in 1927, "In China the armed revolution is fighting the armed counter-revolution," it is no less true that for him the "revolution" was that of Chiang Kai-shek and his troops, who turned against the workers a few months later. Today quotations of this kind have disappeared from Chinese textbooks and museums, and Stalin is no longer referred to as the gifted analyst of the revolution in China, but neither is he criticized. In 1956, when Mao Tse-tung published two critical essays on the "Historical Experience of the Dictatorship of the Proletariat," one could believe for a moment that the Chinese CP would be the first to open the dossier on relations between Stalin and the foreign parties. But nothing came of it. The Chinese considered it expedient to oppose Khrushchev by defending Stalin, but not by going to the length of carrying out a thorough examination of the latter's actions and theories.

This attitude led, as we have seen, to a complete silence on the Comintern's role in the first revolutionary bid between 1925 and 1927, which is no slight omission. It also leads the Chinese to use a denunciatory jargon stuffed with stereotyped images when they

[89] See his interview with Edgar Snow in *Candide* (February, 1965).

talk of Stalin's enemies, like Trotsky and other opponents from the Bolshevik old guard. But after Chiang Kai-shek's coup in March, 1926, it was the anti-Stalinists in Moscow who advocated the break with the Kuomintang (and the Chinese say today that Mao and his friends wanted the same thing). Similarly, it was Trotsky who was the first to speak in the Comintern of the need to create the "peasant soviets" dear to Mao. Certainly Mao was never a Trotskyite, and the fact that on certain points he had the same ideas as the anti-Stalin opposition in Moscow did does not prove that he sympathized with them. But one can see from this that the loyalty of the Chinese to the Stalinist version of the struggle within the International prevents them from telling all about this debate which was decisive for the future of the workers' movement and, more particularly, for their own revolution.

If one day, therefore, the Chinese study their real history, they will be forced to modify several important points in the version they disseminate today. Similarly, in the jealously guarded dossiers on the Maoist administration, they will find the answer to mystifying questions. At the time of the "Great Leap Forward" the Maoists made dazzling promises they were unable to keep. "Certain errors" have been officially admitted, but in such cryptic and vague terms that a more advanced and more aware population would not have stood for them. Serious research into these matters would doubtless reveal anomalies in the working of the Chinese Party and in its relations with the masses.

There is no doubt that the Chinese of future generations are due for some shocks that will lead to a crisis of conscience when they are able to draw up an accurate account of their elders' activities before the revolution and during the early days of the new China. However, there is no doubt either, in my opinion, that these discoveries will be less painful than those made by the Russians after the twentieth congress. For Maoist history is not haunted by the ghosts of prominent Communist leaders executed in a bloody struggle for power. In contrast to Stalin, Mao neither liquidated his predecessors nor terrorized his comrades in arms with purges: the Chinese revolution did not devour its young. And one is even surprised occasionally by the stability of the team which has governed China for nearly eighteen years. Moreover if one recalls with what calm assurance Chou En-lai declares that there are no concentration camps in China, one is convinced that the revelations that could be made after Mao's death or later will have less serious consequences than those made at the Russian CP's twentieth congress.

The comparison between the Maoist and Stalinist experiences could even be of very great advantage to Mao. Stalin's defenders, in fact, explain that his repressive methods were "forced" on him by the economic and political underdevelopment of Russia, which he wanted to modernize and industrialize in the shortest possible time. But in 1949 China was hardly more developed than Russia in 1917, and Mao's ambitions were no less than Stalin's; yet this does not seem to have "forced" him to resort continually to violence. The basis of his system is an intensive indoctrination, but the ideological coercion one sees being exercised in moments of sharp political conflict never develops into bloody persecution.

It is within this framework that one must also place the Red Guards movement, which in a sense is more shocking for the novelty it represents among Communist regimes than for its "excesses." The recourse to action by the masses to speed up a social process may disturb because of its brutal simplifications, but it can in no way be compared with bureaucratic and police repression. A movement such as that of the Red Guards, which gains considerable liberty of action, represents a very big calculated risk for the leadership. Mao must really believe in the completely positive role of egalitarian pressure from the rank and file to undertake such an enterprise. And if the Red Guards have revealed social conflicts and do not behave like characters in a well-directed ballet, it is because the germ of those conflicts existed in the society, and the Party, which helped to lance the abscess, has agreed to pay the price of the operation by sacrificing some of its own cadres. Mao's prestige in the eyes of the people has undoubtedly risen, for he has demonstrated once again that he is the champion of a cause and not the head of a new governing group.

Certainly Mao's position in his party has never been that of Stalin's in his party. Mao did not have to push himself forward and boost his merits above those of more distinguished comrades better placed than himself in order to lay claim to power after the victory of the revolution. No Trotsky faced him. It was neither Ch'en Tu-hsiu, nor Li Li-san, nor Wang Ming, nor Chang Kuo-t'ao, nor any other leader of the CP who assured victory: the triumph of Communism in China was due to Mao Tse-tung and his strategy, and no one contests this. Neither did Mao have a venerated predecessor like Lenin with whom he might be constantly compared — he was spared Stalin's role of spiritual son, scrupulous executor, and sole faithful successor. He is his own Lenin, and that, by all accounts, has very much simplified his relations with his comrades-in-arms.

Neither was Mao guided by a theory firmly established by the circumstances of the Chinese revolution. In an interview he gave to Anna Louise Strong in 1946, Liu Shao-ch'i — present Chairman of the Republic — remarked that Marx and Engels developed their theory on the basis of conditions in European countries, and that they rarely spoke of Asia.[90] Their general principles concerning the class war and historical development were certainly universally valid, but a Marxist theory of revolution in Asia had still to be worked out: Mao was therefore compelled to make his own decisions, to make a class analysis of Chinese society and to work out a revolutionary strategy rather vaguely derived from Marxist principles. He made the peasantry the driving force of his revolution, for example, and to ensure the cohesion of his army he established a purely moral "code of conduct" — one may ask if these solutions conformed to the Marxist doctrine. To him the goal was certainly the establishment of a socialist society, but he alone chose the means of attaining it. And that has been the case not only during the civil war, but since he came to power.

Some may therefore ask if this "Asian Marxism" of Mao's would have been acknowledged by Karl Marx as a contribution to his system. But this problem will not be felt in its full intensity until China becomes an industrialized society with sufficient productive forces at her disposal to envisage the practical realization of the Marxist utopia. Only then will it be possible to learn if the Maoist innovations help to bring about an egalitarian and free society conducive to the complete development of man, as Marx envisaged it. For the time being, the aim of Mao's theoretical generalizations has simply been to ensure the cohesion and development of an essentially peasant country which until yesterday was still steeped in highly antisocial Confucian values. The Maoist ethic ought, in principle, to inspire in the Chinese the pattern of behavior they must observe in order to create this future society and make it work. It is too soon to decide whether this ethic is imposing a discipline based on obedience rather than on reflection, and whether it does not risk producing sterilizing effects.

[90] Marx spoke of the "Asian method of production," however, and this concept led to many controversies among Marxists up until the 1930's and again during the course of the last few years. But the Chinese, like Stalin in the past, prefer to ignore this problem and to stick to the European historical period.

But Mao's companions are no younger than he and while one may admire the stability of the leadership group, it must also be noted that little fresh blood has been introduced into it. During the next few years younger men will necessarily take over and it is legitimate to ask if they will have the same breadth of mind as those who "made the revolution." In the United States people predict that there will unquestionably be a struggle for power and that the revolutionary ardor of Mao's successors will probably be less fiery.

It would appear that the Americans are mistaking their wishes for reality and that their predictions are inspired by fallacious comparisons between Russia after Stalin and the China of today. The systems of these two countries are radically different. There is no evidence to support the assertion that Mao's death will lead to the situation that followed Stalin's death; nothing indicates that those who relieve the "old guard" will be less Messianic, that they will be less ardently dedicated to the cause of "Asian Communism." Rather is it to be feared that they may be less flexible than their predecessors.

Finally, we gained the impression, admittedly from rather slender clues, that the present leaders are deeply anxious to ensure a harmonious succession to the great man. This anxiety has, for example, prompted the Chinese Communists "not to publish an official history of the CP of China, but only a chronology of events and a collection of documents permitting the separate study of the various problems."[91]

This decision, taken two years after Stalin's death, when rumors about the great revision were coming from Moscow, seems to show that the Maoists are aware of the provisional character of the history they teach today. Perhaps they envisage modifying it soon to meet the demands of a more educated and more curious generation whom the simplifications, the naïvetés, and the omissions of the present textbooks will not satisfy. If the Maoists succeeded in bringing about such a revision without provoking too many shocks and crises, they would be demonstrating that de-Maoization could be an enrichment and not a denial of the writings of the man who was together the promoter, the theoretician, and the historian of the Chinese revolution. And thus it would be proved once more that the Russian experience is a much richer source of education for the Chinese than they care to admit.

[91] See Pischel, Enrica Collotti, *Le origini ideologiche della rivoluzione cinese*, p. 284. Note also that the committee of state in charge of the publication of documents is presided over by Chou En-lai.

CHAPTER TWO:

Ideology in the Countryside

THE PEASANT ENCIRCLEMENT

No recent statistic gives the exact total of the Chinese population. Some official speakers talk of "750 million Chinese," others of 600 million or 650 million. Their uncertainty is understandable: there are no precise facts about the growth of the population.[1] But whatever the total, it is certain that the peasantry represents 80 to 85 per cent of the population. That is, 120 million Chinese families, each comprising about five persons, live in the country. In China the countryside is not a hinterland cut off from the urban centers. Here the towns are "encircled by the countryside," islands constantly washed by the immense sea of peasants. Even in the urban islands, the peasants are firmly established. Certain people's communes are, in fact, included within the boundaries of the towns which they supply; and when it is said, for example, that Kunming, the capital of Yunnan, numbers 1,200,000 inhabitants, it should be understood that this means about 800,000 are townspeople and 400,000 live on the land. I do not know if these 400,000 "urbanized" peasants are counted in the 120 million rural families, but even if they are not, the fact remains that the real China is always peasant China.

This China is not easy to penetrate — first of all because of the lack of transportation. Except in the Northeast (formerly Manchuria) and in the neighborhood of the very big cities, China has neither a railroad nor a highway system that meets its needs. Professor Tawney calculated in 1932[2] that even if 10,000 miles of railroad were built every year it would take 180 years for the Chinese to have a rail network as comprehensive as that of Britain. Since 1949 many main lines have been built in China, and the

[1] In the interview he gave to Edgar Snow (*Candide,* February, 1965), Mao Tse-tung admitted: "Some say that China has 680 million to 690 million inhabitants, but I don't believe it." He remarked that peasants were responsible for a certain confusion in the statistics. They do not always immediately register a death, in order to use the dead person's ration card for a few more months.

[2] See Tawney, R. H., *Land and Labour in China.*

most important towns are now linked up. However, the building of lines to distant rural regions has not yet been considered.[3]

China is a country of great rivers and great lakes. Water transport, therefore, makes up a little for this lack of road and rail. One Yangtze is worth many highways, particularly where freight is concerned. And almost everywhere people work en masse to build roads by the most rudimentary methods. Near Nanning I saw soldiers, students, and workers, working with pick and shovel and carrying the earth in straw baskets, add a few hundred yards of road to the national network within a few hours. It is true that this was in the outskirts of a provincial capital, and I doubt if an effort of this kind (although both spectacular and moving) would be enough to cover the whole region with real traffic-bearing roads. In any case, it is practically impossible at present for a foreign visitor to reach a people's commune that is very far from an urban center.

I cannot accuse our guides of wanting to prevent us from seeing these far-off communes. True, they indicated the difficulties of such and such a trip and the price (to hire a car is ruinous). But when we insisted on visiting one of these communes in Yunnan, in the far southwestern part of the country, and studying the problem of national minorities on the spot — there are several in this province — they allowed us to do so. Our Polish car, a Warszawa, which seems to be as tough as a jeep, could not make it all the way to the commune; we had to abandon it on an impassable path and cover the last few miles on foot behind a guide who came to meet us.

In the village the whole populace awaited us. Half of them Chinese, the other half Sanyis (representatives of the national minority), and they seemed to be in a state of indescribable excitement and curiosity; apparently no one here had ever seen a white man in the flesh before. We were installed in a large hall which served as a school, and the chairman had two or three pounds of sunflower seed, the main product of the village, roasted in our honor. Every ten minutes the village boys, having escaped the vigilance of their teacher (who tried to keep them in the central square) crowded into the hall to examine at close range our astounding long noses. None of our hosts had ever traveled by train, and most had never seen an electric light. The Kunming newspaper, which arrives twice a week, is read collectively; thus

[3] The Chinese railroad network has been practically doubled since 1949 and now extends to 25,000 miles. In comparison, France, eighteen times smaller in area, has more than 30,000 miles of railroad.

these peasants, who know practically nothing of the technical developments of the age, are perfectly aware of the war in Vietnam and take an interest in world politics. The chairman of the commune wears a likeness of Ho Chi Minh in his buttonhole. Painted on the school walls, alongside portraits of Marx, Engels, Lenin, and Mao, are political slogans.

This contrast between technical backwardness and the most advanced political awareness is to be seen everywhere. In the Northwest, in the very places in which Mao and his general staff lived for years, we saw peasants tilling the soil with wooden ploughs; at night the "celebrated caves" are not lit up — there is electricity in the area, but it is used mainly for the irrigation system and seldom for domestic lighting. Nor is any railroad planned, at least in the immediate future.

Obviously I did not expect to find American-style model farms in China. While still incomplete, the statistics on agricultural mechanization and rural electrification are eloquent enough. Besides, I never dreamed, however, to what extent all China is marked and formed — one could almost say imprisoned by — the poverty of the countryside.

"Whoever wins the peasants will win China. Whoever solves the land question will win the peasants." The basic premise of this thirty-year-old formula of Mao's was proved true during the civil war. By promising them land, Mao Tse-tung channeled peasant unrest and used it to defeat the old regime. But after the victory the promise to solve the land problem had to be kept. But his opponents claimed that this problem was absolutely insoluble in China and the U.S. State Department did not hesitate to assert this categorically in its famous White Paper presented and compiled under the direction of Dean Acheson.[4]

Traveling today through rural China, one realizes that the U.S. leaders were not making this assertion out of sheer bad temper, in the way that one might curse someone. They had made apparently legitimate deductions from precise figures. How do they manage to get enough to eat and provide a surplus for the state?

In this country, which is not much bigger than the U.S. but three and a half times more densely populated, only 10 per cent of the land can be farmed. An area of 296 million acres must feed 120

[4] *United States Relations with China* (U.S. State Department, Washington, 1949).

million peasant families, without counting the urban population. In the Yunnan commune there are 720 acres of mediocre land, practically no agricultural machinery or artificial fertilizer, and 359 families to feed. One tells oneself that even if this land were distributed in the most equitable way, it would not be enough: how can China escape periodic famines?

And yet, despite the hardship of the years from 1959 to 1961, which was due to particularly severe natural disasters, there has not been even a hint of famine in China. Must one therefore believe that the Maoists have so effectively "solved" the land problem that farm production will be sufficient from now on to feed the country and provide the surplus necessary for its industrialization?

Wu Chen, Vice-Minister of Agriculture, provided me with economic facts at the end of our tour of the rural areas. But the real answer, which we got from him as well as from all the other Chinese we questioned, is a political answer. "We freed the peasants from exploitation. They found the means of organizing themselves into mutual-aid groups, then into co-operatives of an advanced type, and then into communes. This new organization increased the productivity of the land and ensured that there was food for all. Nothing is beyond man: what you call the 'miracle' is only the result of the setting up of the communes, and we foresaw it a long time ago."

A Western mind, instilled with respect for technology, finds it hard to be content with this explanation. This stubborn defiance would not have been enough to solve the problem. Yet everywhere we went food supplies were secure. In fact the replies of the Chinese we met indicated the keystone of their system: intensive politicizing, which enables resources to be utilized to the maximum, guaranteeing subsistence for all and allowing social growth. This constant political preoccupation becomes at the same time a value — the first in the Chinese ethical scale — and an undeniably effective means of social organization.

In no other country in the world are the peasants as constantly and as systematically educated and indoctrinated. In the most backward villages, where the inhabitants have only antiquated equipment, we found Marx's portrait and anti-imperialist posters. But political education cannot be dispensed to millions of peasants like a vaccine. Teachers depend on their pupils and have to learn from them in order to understand them. In a country as dependent on the peasantry as China, Communist propaganda would become a brake on the energy of the producers and paralyze production if it appeared to be simple coercion. Because they lived for a long time among the peasantry and because more than 60 per cent of Party members are drawn from it, the Maoists know it better than the Communists of other countries and they have understood how to create real bonds between it and their Party. Further, the experience of Yenan not only enabled the Party to gain a better knowledge of the countryside, it erased differences between urban and peasant political elites. The Party wants to preserve this unity at all costs: it is the political and moral foundation of the new society which is pursuing a great egalitarian course. This leveling, which has eliminated the dreadful inequalities of the old China and foreshadows the realization of a Communist society in which the differences between town and country would be abolished, has not taken place, as my Chinese contacts say, without errors and some fumbling. At the beginning the Maoists had hoped to unify society by "depeasantizing" the countryside through industrialization. They relied on the members of the peasant communes rapidly becoming part factory worker and expected that, at one blow, the speedy industrialization of the country would be accompanied by a general "proletarianization." This was the result they expected from the 1958 experiment. But technology has its own demands and its own logic, which cannot be twisted or juggled with. Industrial operations can only be carried out in relatively concentrated areas endowed with sufficient infrastructure and not in villages that have hardly any communications and are deprived of adequate equipment. The "back-yard blast furnaces" of the "rural steelworks" did not take long to go out. And while the people's communes survived this blow, they are almost exclusively agricultural today.

The Chinese do not like talking about this episode. They admit rather reluctantly that they had hoped in 1958 for a rapid growth of production which was held back by a run of bad luck. But whatever the reasons for their setback may be, it is possible that the Chinese were trying to solve, or at least they have a very strong awareness of, a social contradiction which exists, unobserved or tolerated, in the other socialist countries. In fact, the rural cooperative organization — as, for example, the Soviet kolkhoz — always uses family forms of production and consumption, and by this fact retains a backward social character. A kolkhoz represents a simple grouping of a number of peasant families, who live separately and exploit the communal land with the sole aim of achieving higher individual incomes. The socialist transformation of the rural areas will sooner or later call for a modification of present production methods and social relationships between the peasant producers. It was this that the Chinese in 1958 believed they were already able to do.

Their attempt failed, but they do not admit defeat (perhaps they are waiting until their economic development is more advanced in order to try again): although molded by primitive farming methods, the peasant mentality must be changed, and if the fusion of town and country cannot be achieved in the sphere of production, it must be achieved in matters of opinion, culture, and the system of values. A didactic and egalitarian society cannot have two systems of education or two moral codes, one for the towns, the other for the countryside. The unity of China manifests itself in everyone's personal experience, through the compulsory periods spent in the communes, through the manual work imposed on the cadres: if the differences within the society cannot be abolished at one swoop, then everyone must experience them personally so that he will not forget, whatever his role in society, the painful essence of the alienation of manual labor and of underdevelopment.

That is why the peasantry is still present throughout China. As the utopia of the communes could not be realized and the peasant is not yet able to become an industrial worker, all the others must draw nearer to him, "the most advanced helping the backward." A political order of the day can only be effective, according to the Maoists, if it can be followed in both towns and communes at the same time. The attitude toward work, toward country, and toward other people, the concepts of marriage and divorce — in short, the ways of life and of thinking — must be, if not identical, at least extremely close, if one wants to overcome the inevitable "contradictions among the people" and avoid all divisions between the different social layers. It is self-evident that such a concept does not favor urban elites. It is also in this sense that it is true that in China today the towns are still "encircled by the countryside."

I was often told in Peking, "To understand Chinese Communism you must understand the peasant problem and study the people's communes." The first of the three "Red banners" of the Party line proclaims, "Long live the communes!" The government declares that "agriculture is the basic element of the Chinese economy." And many of the doctrinal conceptions of what Liu Shao-ch'i calls "Asian Marxism" are dictated by the fact that in China the real country is the peasantry.

In the future, perhaps in twenty years, the Chinese edifice will be profoundly modified by industrialization. Work and moral values will not be the same, and China will think differently. But today one must still begin with the land if one wishes to understand Chinese socialism.

A SHORT CUT TO COMMUNISM

In April, 1958, in a district of Honan province, a few hundred miles from Peking, 43,000 peasants belonging to twenty-seven farm co-operatives decided to amalgamate, not simply to work the land more efficiently but also to set up local industries, dig irrigation canals, build roads, build schools — in short, to speed progress in every aspect of their economic and cultural life. A little later, the peasants of Liaoning province in the Northeast did the same, and they in their turn were imitated by the co-operatives of the South and Southwest. If one is to believe what is said today, the Chinese peasants spontaneously felt the urge to set up a new social organization to meet their material and spiritual needs.

The pioneers of Honan, who created the first people's commune in China, named it "Sputnik" to show the world that their experiment would have as much impact as the launching of the first satellite. On August 7, 1958, they published their statutory articles, which were to serve as a model and which can be regarded as a declaration of political and economic intentions. Everyone sixteen years of age and older who enjoyed civil rights and lived on commune land could become a member of the commune and be paid for his work.[5] While maintaining the principle of collective ownership of land, "Sputnik" decided to pay wages monthly as in industry. It was also anticipated that members would, like factory employees, work fixed hours, with two days off per month for men and three for women. They would eat in canteens and leave their children in nurseries, as city workers do. The commune would build new dwellings for peasant-workers and deduct the rent from their salaries. It would also be responsible for education and pro-

[5] The others, that is to say, the former landlords, could work in the commune but did not have the right to vote and could not be elected to positions of authority.

tection. To begin with, it would provide primary education; then later, secondary; and still later, higher education for all its members, whom it would also organize in people's militias.

Mao Tse-tung and other Party leaders visited the area to study the project and supervise the first stages of development. Then the Central Committee met in the resort of Peitaiho, where on August 29, 1958, it adopted its "historic resolution" saluting the birth of the people's communes and recording its wish to see them multiply. By the end of the autumn that year 740,000 farm co-operatives disappeared to make way for 26,000 communes, all organized on the "Sputnik" model.

The speed of this reorganization was due, according to the Chinese, to a tremendous, spontaneous push by the rank and file; to some foreign observers, however, it proves that the operation was very carefully prepared a long time ahead. Be that as it may, the fact remains that in a few weeks 500 million Chinese peasants radically changed their way of life; a revolutionary transformation of such magnitude and carried out at this pace has no precedent in history.

From the day they took power the Chinese Communists showed themselves to be extremely cautious in everything that concerned the rural areas. Without ever openly criticizing Russian methods of collectivization, they constantly repeated that they envisaged different solutions which would take into account China's special characteristics. And it is a fact that the first co-operatives (organized very rudimentarily at the beginning, then shortly after on the pattern of the kolkhozes) were set up without violence. The brutal methods used to enforce the creation of the communes contrasted with the former "kid-gloves" approach. This time the Maoists seemed to be in a hurry, as if they were racing against time. Yet in the U.S.S.R., despite Stalin's extremely violent methods, it took nearly three years (1929–1932) to organize kolkhozes and sovkhozes. Why at this point did Mao speed things up, and how was he able to establish the commune system widely at such a pace?

To begin with, to set up the communes it was not necessary to group individual farms (as had to be done in Russia for the creation of the kolkhozes): the Chinese peasants, who had already lived for five years in co-operatives of different kinds and were therefore used to collective life, were not called upon suddenly to give up their personal effects, nor did they have the feeling that a tough and painful change was being forced on them. In addition, in the CP there were eight and a half million peasants, perfectly integrated into their environment and capable of "winning over" their fellows, while in the U.S.S.R. it was the urban militants (like Davidov, hero of Sholokhov's *Seeds of Tomorrow*) who were responsible for this task. Finally, in the U.S.S.R., collectivization began at a time when very poor food deliveries to the towns were dangerously slowing down the whole of the economy and the implementation of the Five-Year Plan. In China, on the contrary, the 1958 harvest was little short of miraculous,[6] which is why Mao chose this moment to launch his new agricultural policy.

All this doubtless explains why China's communes were born relatively painlessly, whereas the Russian kolkhozes were created at the cost of merciless terror. This success reinforced the Maoist conviction, already firmly rooted, that "production relationships" must be given priority over "productive means." From 1955 on, Mao had criticized those who thought it essential to have tractors and other modern machinery to run the farm co-operatives.[7] According to him, the new relationships established among agricultural producers were enough to offset the lack of machinery and increase the countryside's output. After the launching of the communes, which for him represented another stage in the uninterrupted progress of the revolution, he seemed to decide that thanks to these improved relationships China would be able to overcome its economic backwardness very quickly and put an end to its underdevelopment. The new organization of the rural areas not only had to produce the "socialist capital growth" needed to finance the industrialization plan — as previously in the U.S.S.R. — but also had to change the nature and capacity of rural production. This conviction that the age of plenty was about to arrive very soon showed clearly in the final phases of the Peitaiho resolution: "It seems that the realization of communism in China is no longer a distant prospect. We are going to avail ourselves of the people's communes in an active effort to open new roads leading to the communist society."

Encouraged by this optimistic prophecy from the top, the Com-

[6] The harvest of 1958 was estimated at the time to total 375 million metric tons. The following year it was, in fact, estimated to be only 250 million tons, but even this figure is a record which has not been equaled since. The 1962 harvest, which was excellent, totalled 210 million tons. (Unpublished figures supplied privately to journalists, including Edgar Snow.)

[7] Mao Tse-tung, *The Question of Agricultural Co-operation* (Peking, Foreign Languages Press, 1956).

munist theoreticians began to work out the time it would take to achieve the ideal society. "Even recently peasants in their fifties feared they would not live long enough to see communism put into effect. Today even the octogenarians firmly believe that they will have the good fortune to live under communism," said *Jenmin Jih Pao*. Ch'en Po-ta, close collaborator of Mao Tse-tung, explained that thanks to the communes the productive forces of Chinese society were going to develop at a speed unparalleled in history, and they would eliminate distinctions between industry and agriculture and between manual and intellectual work, thus making possible a harmonious transition from socialism to communism. The Marxist classics were invoked and long extracts from Engels were quoted to support these statements. It appears that some leaders — their names are not known — expressed doubts about the possibility of carrying out such an ambitious program so quickly. They were called right-wingers, and Marx's celebrated epigram that humanity poses itself only problems that it can solve was recalled for their benefit.

Needless to say, local leaders, encouraged by all these theoretical explanations, stepped up their efforts. In some communes they even dreamed of rapidly reaching virtual economic autarchy, of doing away with money, and of distributing food, clothes, and all necessities free. The Party cadres formed in Yenan recalled that during the great days money had practically disappeared and that after the Liberation the CP leaders for a long time received almost no salary. According to them, salaries had to be quickly eliminated, and the free distribution of goods had to be introduced. Mao Tse-tung himself, visiting a commune in Anhwei province at which free rice was being distributed, said: "Since one commune can put into practice the principle of rice without pay, others can do the same. Since rice can be eaten without pay, clothing can also be had without pay in future."[8]

And so the Chinese Communists thought they had found a miraculous recipe which was going to enable their country, in conformity with Karl Marx's prophecy, to "leap twenty years in a day." The Chinese peasantry suddenly seemed possessed of unlimited energy, capable of such productivity that the most optimistic forecasts were surpassed. The reports which arrived in

[8] Bowie, Robert R., and Fairbank, John K., eds., *Communist China 1955–1959, Policy Documents with Analysis* (Cambridge, Harvard University Press, 1962), p. 28.

Peking from every corner of the country described the establishment of little local steelworks, paperworks using craft methods, and even factories making ball bearings. Everywhere new farming techniques produced undreamed-of results, to the point where, in a country traditionally overpopulated, a reduction of the acreage under cultivation was now envisaged.

The enthusiasm was such that in November, 1958, the official Party journal had to issue a clarification explaining that China had not yet reached the stage of communism.[9] The top leaders traveled about the provinces nonstop, and in December, 1958, they met at Wuhan to draw up a balance sheet of the commune experiment. Their new resolution began with a phrase such as one rarely finds in political documents: "A new social organization, fresh as the morning sun, has appeared over the vast horizons of eastern Asia."

After this poetic introduction, the Central Committee drew up a catalogue of what must be done and what must not be done. Thus it was decided that the system of monthly salaries, established in terms of output, should be applied universally in conformity with the socialist principle of "each according to his labor." The eight-hour working day, plus two hours for study, would be maintained, and workers would always have at least eight hours' sleep and four hours for meals. There was no question of shortening the working day, even in districts where manpower was plentiful, nor of extending it where labor was short. In short, it was premature to dream of applying the principle of "from each according to his ability, to each according to his needs"; for "every Marxist ought to understand that the transition to communism is a long and complicated process."

The communes were then called upon to allow their members to own their own homes, their personal work tools, their domestic animals, and even to make bank deposits. Further, commune members were authorized to have second jobs in addition to their collective work and to do what they liked with gift parcels from relatives living in Chinese or foreign cities. Complete egalitarianism, therefore, was not at all the rule and would not really be so for a long time to come.

Having laid down that the organization of the rural areas would remain socialist, the Central Committee urged the communes to industrialize themselves "on a grand scale": "The development of industry in the people's communes will not only contribute to the industrialization of the whole country but also lead to the reduc-

[9] Hsü Li-ch'ün, in *Red Flag* (November 16, 1958).

Mao Tse-tung proposing a toast to the wife of the Polish Prime Minister, 1957.

Mao during the Long March. Photograph by R. Bury from a picture in a museum.

House in Shao-shan, Hunan, in which Mao was born. It is open to the public.

Room in which Mao was born. Pictures on the wall are of his parents.

Mao's cave (the one with the door open) in Yenan. In the cave on the left lived Chou En-lai, and later Liu Shao-ch'i.

Mao's bedroom inside the cave.

Peasant working in rice paddies near Kweilin, Kwangsi province.

Rice paddies, near Kweilin.

Chinese-made tractor in Yunnan province, south of Kunming.

Yenan: a family having their lunch.

Author arriving at a people's commune eighty miles from Kunming.

Yenan: planting time.

Author talking with leaders at the people's commune near Kunming.

People's commune in central China, Honan.

Inside a peasant's house in northern China.

"October" commune near Nanking.

"October" commune.

Meeting of poor peasants in the same commune.

Street in Canton.

Two students and the British lion in front of the city hall of the International Concession in Shanghai.

The Bund, or waterfront, in Shanghai at 6 P.M.

New bridge at Wuhan, the only rail and road bridge over the Yangtze Kiang.

Children in Kweilin carrying the hats they will wear their whole life.

Peking: streets and a market with Peking-style ducks.

Electrification of a commune near Nanning, Kwangsi province.

Evening class in reading and writing.

"Spring Festival": the Chinese New Year celebration in Canton.

tion of differences between town and country. . . . Each commune ought, according to its ability and in line with the general plan, to develop its production of chemical fertilizers, insecticides, tools, building materials, and machinery. . . . The industrial production of the communes ought to be strictly linked to agriculture, but it ought equally to aim at satisfying the rural population's needs in textiles and other consumer goods."

More and more farm workers were therefore to be moved to the industrial sector of the communes, in which the Chinese peasants were going to prove that it was possible to unite the traditional and craft methods of the countryside with the modern techniques of urban industry. But all this had to be planned on a national scale, "for all China is a single chess board" and no local "boss" can aspire to autarchy. On the contrary, co-operation between communes was to be rapidly expanded.

Last but not least, "manpower and the communes' material and financial resources must be used rationally, cost prices must be reduced, and waste combated."

These specific directives, spelled out in great detail by the national and local Party press and based on the communes' many months of experience, indicate better than anything else what the Maoist hopes for the transformation of rural China were. These hopes were based on the astonishing belief that it was possible to urbanize the rural way of life and production speedily. And that it was going to be done entirely through the peasants' own efforts, without any major help from urban industry. As is known, these hopes, expressed seven years before my arrival in China, were dashed. But I specifically wanted to find out why the commune system had changed and what had become of it. It must be said here that I had no difficulty in documenting 1958, the year of "the enthusiastic launching of the communes." Most Party resolutions and handbooks published at this time are still on sale in Peking. For, paradoxically, and despite evidence which can't be ignored, the Chinese leaders assert that their ideas on agricultural policy have not changed.

THE COMMUNES TODAY

A people's commune today is a state in miniature. It has its "central government," which supervises the whole enterprise, manages its finances, decides its investments, controls its relations with the outside world, and administers the "nationalized sector" — farm machinery centers, repair shops, minor ancillary industries, etc. But the "central government" does not dominate the productive activities of the lower levels or look after payment. For this it delegates part of its powers to subdivisions, or brigades, which form a kind of "county" that in turn supervises the "municipalities" which are the basic units, or teams.

These teams generally have about one hundred members, who live in the same village. In a very big village there can be two teams, but this is rare, villages containing on the average from fifty to sixty households. Each team sends its delegate to the commune's general assembly, a sort of "parliament" which meets at least twice a year to discuss the production plan and the "investment policy." The plan is submitted by the district delegates, who draw it up on the basis of the results achieved by all the communes of the region; but each commune has the right to suggest modifications before it is adopted. Next, the work tasks are allocated to the teams, which are free to organize themselves as they wish. If a team produces more than its allocation, it receives a bonus. If it produces less, it can be penalized, except when natural disasters have been the cause. The team gets a lump sum which it divides among its members according to their individual contributions, which are calculated in "work points." In a commune the incomes of different teams are not, therefore, the same, nor are those of individual workers within a team. The variations can be quite big. A brigade is usually made up of a dozen teams, and it undertakes all kinds of work: irrigation, electrification, processing of farm products. It is responsible for large-scale animal husbandry and can "board out" pigs or water buffaloes with team members, who get "work points" for looking after the animals. It is the brigade which co-ordinates all major tasks and ensures that the most advanced teams help the backward ones.

The "central government" of the commune draws some of its resources from minor industries (brickworks, cementworks, etc.) and meets its budget with the profits from its brigades and teams. It is the "central government" which builds schools, hospitals, and meeting halls, and which invests for the common good. It also has a special fund to help large families and to prevent too great a disparity between incomes. The permanent staff of this central administration is not very big, and during the busiest farming seasons the staff works in the fields like everyone else; but the rest of the time it is paid monthly.

This brief outline shows that the structure of the Chinese rural economy is a complex one, and it illustrates how extremely difficult it is to judge a commune's situation after having seen only the headquarters or a single team. Conditions, as we have seen, could be very different in other brigades, or even from one team to another. As a result, what we observed here and there in different communes and the figures we collected are not enough in themselves to enable me to describe the material state of the communes with any accuracy. I shall simply try, therefore, to say what they represent ideologically and politically.

A few days after my arrival in Peking I drove for one and a half hours under a gray February sky to my first people's commune, which bore the name Chi Tsi Tchien, or "Green All Year." Established in 1958, Chi Tsi Tchien comprises 8,100 families or 36,000 persons, who, divided into twelve brigades and 125 teams, farm 6,570 acres. The director, Mr. Kao Hsiao-cha, greets us at the entrance to the commune headquarters and leads us to a little room where many other foreign visitors are already admiring examples of exceptionally fine vegetables which "Green All Year" proudly produces. Modestly, Mr. Kao Hsiao-cha denies that his commune is a model one. He is thirty-eight years old and is of peasant origin. He has met many journalists, knows what interests them, and talks with great facility, quoting figures and the like without notes, whereas some factory managers have to read their set pieces. Mr. Kao is a "very urbanized peasant."

"Before the commune was formed," he says, "there were eleven farm co-operatives on this land. Despite their efforts and intentions, the members of these organizations were in no position to undertake the large-scale operations needed to increase the yield. This district suffers regularly from bad droughts, and even during the 'good years' the scarcity of water doesn't allow us to cultivate huge areas. Since setting ourselves up as a people's commune we have begun work on irrigation. We have dug a six-mile canal which irrigates 1,300 acres, and forty-one electrified wells which enable us to water 95 per cent of the commune's land!

"Fortunately, all that was carried out in record time, for in 1959, and for the next three years, we experienced the worst drought we've had since the beginning of the century. Previously a less severe drought would have been enough to drive the population away. This time no one suffered, and even better, our commune's income, which was eight million yuan in 1958, rose to more than thirteen million by the end of the three years.

"How was this possible?" continues Mr. Kao. "First of all, thanks to planning, we chose the crops that were most resistant to drought. We reduced the acreage allotted to cereals in order to grow more vegetables, and we achieved remarkable results. We continued the irrigation and reafforestation operations. At the moment we have 498 electric sprinklers and thousands of fruit trees. Our fruit production is sixty-five times what it was when the commune was founded. We have been able to scrape up enough to build hothouses and buy tractors and other agricultural machinery. In 1964 we sold 115,000 metric tons of vegetables to the government board which handles wholesale goods.

"Now do you want to know how the commune members live?" Mr. Kao goes on. "In 1964 each worker earned on the average 600 yuan, while other benefits totaled from six to eight yuan a month. Seventy per cent of them have bicycles and 60 per cent have radios; and if I can't tell you exactly how many watches they have bought, I can tell you they have bought plenty. On top of that, all the children go to school, and practically every adult has learned to read and write. We have, in fact, seventeen primary schools for 6,500 pupils and three secondary schools for 2,650 pupils. Evening classes for adults are held three times a week. Finally, we have a hospital and eleven clinics which give free medical care and employ thirty-two doctors. For entertainment there is a mobile movie theater and our own radio station, for our commune has a transmitter."[10a]

Having ended his talk with several phrases of thanks to Mao Tse-tung, Mr. Kao invites me to visit the hothouses, which are run directly by the commune administration and bring it considerable profit. They are heated by coal and produce two crops of vegetables each winter, one at the end of January and the other at the start of the spring.

To be truthful, the commune's general appearance does not reflect the prosperity with which Mr. Kao is so pleased. On our way to the hothouses we meet many very poorly dressed peasants, and the children appear to be infinitely less well cared for than in Peking. Nor do the two old peasants who greet us at the entrance to the hothouses have the look of people who own watches and

[10a] René Dumont had visited the same commune a year before me and collected much more detailed information, which did not always tally with that given to me by Mr. Kao (particularly in the matter of incomes). See Dumont, René, *La Chine surpeuplée* (Paris, Editions du Seuil, 1965).

bicycles, but they are extremely proud of their setup and of their produce. They kindly offer me a cucumber, which I eat to please them — and also because I am very fond of cucumbers — and they promise to send me vegetables at the Hsin Chiao Hotel in Peking.

Encouraged by the general friendliness, I feel I shall be able to ask them a few questions about their past experiences and talk to them, for instance, about hopes that have not materialized, so that I can better understand the evolution of the commune system. So I ask if the commune has built the canteens which, it appears, were to be a stimulus to collective life. The two old peasants continue to smile amiably, but they leave the job of answering to Mr. Kao: "During the busy seasons we organize meals in the fields, but generally people prefer to eat at home. During the winter the kitchen stove heats the house, and that's much better than a canteen." Seeing that I will not get a straight reply by this subterfuge, I tackle the subject head on: "But in 1958 canteens, communal dwellings, and other communal facilities were foreseen. An industrialization drive was also planned. How did this go here?"

Consternation. The two old men concentrate on their cucumbers and discreetly disappear. Mr. Kao retains a half smile and his *sang-froid* and, as if he has not heard a word, suggests going to look at the tractors and the repair shops. The spell is obviously broken. I shall not receive my vegetables from the "Green All Year" commune.

About ten days later I find myself near Nanking in an even more hospitable commune, where I am asked to lunch. What is called "lunch" in a Soviet kolkhoze or in a Chinese commune is a banquet copiously laced with vodka or local wines. I remember in particular a meal of this kind in 1959 in a Moscow suburb which completely knocked out the members of a British Labor Party delegation, with the sole exception of Aneurin Bevan, who didn't turn a hair. I am therefore a little uneasy, but on the other hand alcohol loosens tongues and leads to confidences. My host, Li Tsun Win, director of the "October" commune, appears to be particularly frank, and even before seating us at the table, he has established a kind of old-soldiers' bond with us. Mr. Li arrived in this commune after his demobilization; he fought for years in the Liberation Army, and he is very agreeably impressed when I reveal my military past in the U.S.S.R. This time, therefore, I feel certain that I shall get some information about life in the communes during the "Great Leap Forward."

Oddly enough, "October," which is only about a third of the size of "Green All Year," seems to me to be more prosperous, although its income is lower — 220 yuan a year per worker. But perhaps I get this impression because the weather is especially fine and because Mr. Li Tsun Win is evidently delighted to entertain foreigners and does not subject us to a recitation learned by heart.

We drink a slightly warmed *vin rosé* in a toast to friendship among the peoples of the world in general and between ourselves in particular. Each toast is followed by a *kan-pei,* which means "dry bottom." We even drink a *kan-pei* to the Albanian people, who supply turnip seeds to Mr. Li's commune. It goes without saying that the French are *kan-pei-ed* after each course and sometimes even during a course. Thus we quickly arrive at the point where my host and his deputy, Mr. Lin Ma Yen, announce that they are ready to tell and show me all I wish. I repeat my delicate question about the past.

The director is not too worried. He takes off his cap as if this ought to help him think, then launches into a speech of several minutes which our interpreter carefully notes down before translating it at one go: "It is not accurate to say that our attempt at industrialization wasn't successful. It would be more correct to say that we carried out certain projects and not others. For instance, we built a small cementworks and a glassworks which still function and bring us appreciable benefits. We also make certain farm tools and have a repair shop for our eight tractors. But it is also true that we abandoned some undertakings we had already started. There was a simple reason for this: natural disasters hit the country and our region in particular. We were therefore forced to restrict ourselves to the construction of reservoirs and above all to efforts to produce a good harvest. Today 50 per cent of our land could be considered proof against possible disasters, but there is still a lot to be done. Our farm production (5,250 kilograms of cereals per hectare[10b] on the average) could be increased considerably. So we give it priority. Perhaps there was a little waste during the initial period, when we tried to do too many things at the same time, and there is still some. The little ventures we set up are still running. During this period we developed the education sector

[10b] 11,555 pounds per hectare, one hectare equaling 2.47 acres.

considerably and improved the living conditions of commune members. Above all we found we could manufacture things the peasants of old China would never have believed they could produce themselves."

I asked if the "urbanization of the countryside" did not mean the construction of canteens, the introduction of fixed hours — in short, the same conditions that applied in the towns? Had they not run into some opposition? Had they not failed? "I personally prefer the country," replied Mr. Li without hesitation. Then, with his natural good humor, he launched into his military reminiscences, explaining that he had always preferred to fight and live in the country: "What advantages do the towns enjoy? Electricity? We have that here today. The cinema? There is one in the village that is open even in the afternoon. We can go there now if you like." But instead we moved from one point to another (despite the vigilance of our interpreter, rather a pedant, whom I suspect of "sweetening" his translations). If Mr. Li did not sit in judgment, he at least vented quite severe criticisms of some of the ventures during the great wave of "communal" enthusiasm.

He was not director of the "October" commune at that time. It was part of a very much bigger grouping — too big — that in 1960 was divided in four.[11] Then "certain well-intentioned but overzealous comrades imagined that large-scale operations could be carried on throughout the year — they wanted to go too fast. But in the country one must make haste slowly. Finally, the ground had not been sufficiently prepared, and some peasants from a comfortable background or, let us say, less poor, did not see clearly the goals we wished to reach. At present we are taking our time. Each new major scheme or commune reorganization is discussed with all the members, brigade by brigade, team by team, and sometimes I even go from door to door to persuade a few stubborn types who mistrust all innovations on principle."

The subject is exhausted. Mr. Li puts his cap on again, lifts his glass for a last toast, and proposes, if we like old things, to show us something "the likes of which you have never seen before." It turns out to be a monastery which is indeed one of the most beautiful we have visited in China. It is called Chi Chsa and dates

---

[11] There are at present 74,000 communes instead of the 26,000 initially established, but the subdivision has not been automatic. Among those I visited, two ("Green All Year" and Huang Tu, near Shanghai) have retained their 1958 area.

from the sixth century, from the Sui dynasty.[12] It contains one of the most important collections of ancient books, and in its courtyard magnificent Buddhist sculptures are set into the rock. Mr. Li does not have the keys to this marvelous place, which still belongs to the Buddhist community, but he is received with honor. This is because the commune has given large sums toward the restoration and upkeep of the monastery. "Religious superstition must be combated, but this is a cultural monument," explains Mr. Li.

We are not the only visitors. Young peasants stroll in the park. Have they come to pray? Mr. Li assures me that they have not; he knows them, and they are definitely not religious. They are walking about simply because they find the place pleasant.

The village does not seem to be humming with activity, and leaving the monastery, we go to take a look at the movie theater. In the middle of the afternoon it is crowded with an audience watching a report on the recent session of the People's Congress in Peking, as spellbound as if they were watching a detective film. Mao Tse-tung gets a very big hand.

After the movie theater comes the glassworks, small but full of activity. Then the primary and secondary schools, and finally, in the annex of the latter, in a large conference room, we come upon a full meeting of the "poor peasants of the commune." There are 300 of them, perhaps more, men and women, sitting on stools or on the floor, listening to the brigade leader talk about spring sowing plans. Today they are no poorer than the other members of the commune; but they were particularly poor under the old regime, which is why they are considered "the backbone of the present collective." They have priority in the discussion of every project; but once it has been adopted, they are also "the first to be mobilized for its implementation."

The last to learn about these communal plans is always the ex-landlord, who works and is paid like the others, but who does not enjoy the same rights. I went to see this former village magnate. He is a very old man who lives with his children and grandchildren — fourteen people in all — in a little three-room house, and he was not expecting visitors. The whole family, therefore, set about tidying up and busying themselves to make us comfortable. It cannot be said that the landlord's clothes are patched — they are made up of bits and pieces of different materials and colors. The

[12] The Sui dynasty reigned from 581 to 618 A.D.

room we are in is dark, and its grayish walls are bare of all ornament — not even a portrait of Mao Tse-tung.

"Tell them how much you have earned this year, you and your family," says Mr. Li before I can ask a question. The old man reflects, calculates, then argues with Mr. Li about the figure to give. The difficulty arises — if I understand it correctly — from the fact that Mr. Li wants the ex-landlord to include the income from his little personal plot of ground, while the other wants to count only the sum he has received from the commune. They end up by compromising and announce that the figure was 1,000 yuan, but without giving details of how this sum has been reached. Mr. Li is delighted, and after having extracted a declaration from the old man that he is satisfied with his standard of living, he gives me the floor. I must admit that I am rather chilled by this episode, and, further, I get the impression that the ex-land-lord looks on me with hostility. To speed things up and cut the visit short, I ask him if he lived in this house "before" and how much land he used to have.

"I have always lived here," replies the old man. And he casts a glance around him — at the dirty walls, at his daughter, at the young children hanging about the kitchen entrance — as if he wishes to let it be known that it wasn't the same then or to indicate politely that my question is stupid. "Do you believe that a landlord with self-respect would have lived in such a modest house?" suggests the look on his shriveled face. Then, after a moment of silence, he adds: "I had eighty *mou* of land."

Eighty *mou*, hardly twelve acres. Is it possible that someone who owned so little could be regarded as a landlord? I check the figure with the interpreter, for experience has taught me that figures are often distorted in translation; but the old man insists that he possessed a good eighty *mou*. Embarrassed and not knowing what other questions to ask, I end the interview.

Once outside and walking across the fields on our way to see the work teams, I ask Mr. Li how much his family owned before the revolution. "They owned nothing. We were tenant farmers, and we worked for the wealthy, people like the man you just saw." "So there were a lot of landlords in your part of the country?" Mr. Li is walking in front of me along a narrow footpath between two fields, and I cannot see his round face, on which one can some-times read his reply without waiting for the interpreter (who, it may be said in passing, does not stop taking notes, even while walking, which slows down the conversation). Mr. Li takes a moment to reply.

"Five or six had lots of land and exploited us, but the others escaped at the time of the Liberation or were tried for their crimes against the people. I can't give you the exact details — I was in the army at the time. On my return I found only the one you have just seen, who was the least bad." I explain that I am not unaware of the misdeeds of the old regime, but I go on to ask if after so many years these distinctions still make sense, and if a family ought to pay for generations for the sins of its fathers. Despite my careful phrasing, the question makes him indignant. After swearing that the landlord's children go to school and even to the university, like all other young Chinese, and that the old lack for nothing if they work, Mr. Li raises his voice: "No, you don't know anything about the old China! If you really knew, you would be rather surprised at our leniency with these people! In their day they didn't hesitate to crush those who were poorer than themselves, to exploit their misery, to trample underfoot the weak, who died from hunger. Today they pose as victims because they are obliged to work in order to live, like the rest of us. But they didn't allow the others to live at all. They don't like to talk about the past. But we do! We're not ashamed to have been poor, to have been forced to do goodness-knows-what to survive. In their world there was neither mercy nor law nor justice. We can talk about the past because we did not trample on those who dropped from exhaustion and hunger. We were the real victims — they have never really suffered. That is why they can never understand what it is we desire and what we are doing."

Our conversation was interrupted by the songs of a group of young peasant girls who were working in a field and seemed to be enjoying themselves. I do not know if this good humor was explained by the fact that the work was coming to an end or if Mr. Li had previously warned them of our arrival and suggested that we be greeted with music.

We left late, after having visited the agricultural research station and strolled in the fields with some optimistic young agricultural scientists. "In a few years, by using more fertilizers, by bettering our seed selection, and by mastering nature even more, we shall be able to double or triple our production," they concluded as they invited us to come and see them again. Mr. Li, the perfect host, escorted us to the boundary of the commune.

THE RECITALS OF BITTERNESS

He is called Shu Chi-chen. He is sixty-seven and has a sharp, birdlike face. Mr. Kao of the "Green All Year" commune, having assured me that I can talk to any peasant I like, has led me to his house with a firm hand. Old Shu waits at his door and invites me in with a gesture; it seems that he has something to tell me. I perch on a stool against a wall covered with pictures of Mao and patriotic posters. The room, very clean and very narrow, is sparsely furnished: a little table, a chest of drawers, and some stools — all new. A young woman with a long black pigtail, whose clothes are worn but freshly ironed, brings us tea. Mr. Kao, his party, and Marc Riboud leave for livelier and more photogenic locales, leaving me alone with my interpreter and the old man.

Mr. Shu Chi-chen wants to tell me about his good fortune — it is the first time in his life that he has lived in his own house. He never owned any land; he never owned anything. He had always worked for others and lived in atrocious accommodations provided by his employers-exploiters. The crowning calamity: his wife, now dead, presented him only with daughters. The one serving tea is the youngest, but there were five others, three of whom died in infancy. He worked like a slave to feed his family, knowing only too well that he would be forced eventually to beg until he died of hunger once he was no longer strong enough for heavy work. Who would support him, who would care for him in his old age? A daughter in the old China became at best her husband's slave. She was never able to support her father. Nor could Shu rely on his employer's charity: landlords had never known this word. Even in his wildest dreams Shu had never imagined that he might spend his old age with his family in his own house and with enough to eat. It was this he wanted to tell me about, so that I might understand that he owes everything to Chairman Mao and that he loves him as if Mao were his father.

No, he no longer works; or rather he helps his two sons-in-law, who live with him, to cultivate their individual plots (one *mou* of land), and he looks after their pig. He has no grandchildren, but he still has hopes; his surviving daughters are still young, and they have survived because they had the good luck to grow up after the Liberation. The youngest is not married yet. At present five members of the family work "for the commune" and earn enough to have built this house with their savings. Until then they had lived in commune accommodations; it wasn't bad, but it wasn't as good as this brand-new, comfortable house, complete with electricity.

"Ask me questions about the past," says Mr. Shu Chi-chen and immediately provides me with one: "Ask me why I didn't drown my daughters, as others often did at that time." It was because he had a presentiment that things would change, that this wretchedness and injustice could not last forever. Of course, he wasn't a Communist at that time, and he was unaware of the existence of Chairman Mao; but he knew that he wasn't the only one to hate oppression and that the people were going to wake up and drive out the bandits who were sucking their blood. After the Liberation he learned to read and write — only a little, admittedly, because it's difficult — and now he understands the past and the present better. He would like me to explain in my country that if "the imperialists and their feudal lackeys try to return to China," he, his family, and the whole nation will crush them like snakes.

We left off there, but one cannot get rid of the ghosts of old China in a single conversation. Several other witnesses in communes and factories conjured them up for me. Throughout my stay I came across — be it by chance or by the ingenuity of my guides — men and women who insisted on telling me about their former lives and sufferings. The story of Madame Chang Chiu-hsiang, formerly an illiterate peasant, today a deputy of the People's Congress and a member of the Academy of Sciences, deserves a place of honor in this category.

I met Madame Chang Chiu-hsiang rather by mistake. Before going to Sian, I had asked an Italian colleague, Gino Nebiolo of the *Gazetta del Popolo,* for the name of people I could interview in this town, from which he had just returned. In the list he gave me, Madame Chang's name appeared, followed by this note: "Very well informed on the changes in the rural areas." That was all — neither her titles nor her age were mentioned. In Sian my guides welcomed my request for a meeting with her, but they did not speak of Madame Chang with the tone of voice and respectful phraseology usually reserved for important political personalities. Their reaction seemed to me to be of the same kind that greeted my request to see a basketball match rather than the opera — part surprise, part satisfaction. (They too were basketball fans.)

This sharpened still further my curiosity about this woman who was "very well informed on the changes in the rural areas," and I declared my readiness to go to Pa Li-tien, her village, thirty-odd miles from Sian. The road to Pa Li-tien is hardly passable, but by chance Madame Chang had to spend an evening in Sian after giving a series of lectures at the Institute of Agronomy.

So we met one evening in the lounge of the People's Hotel. My first reaction was one of amazement: the very well-informed deputy is an old, worn-out peasant woman with a kind of kerchief tied around her white hair, and she talks in a very low, almost inaudible voice. My interpreter, Mr. Wang, who is assistant professor of French in the School of Foreign Languages, is almost forced to put his ear to Madame Deputy's mouth, and even so he seems not to understand everything or not to understand her dialect. Puzzled, I am not too sure how to broach the question of the "changes in the rural areas." But Madame Chang, despite her shy and reserved manner, is perfectly at ease, and without waiting for my questions begins to tell the story of her life.

"I was born in 1910 in Shantung province, but at the age of eight I came to the Northwest. Floods destroyed my native village, and my parents, completely ruined, left to seek their fortune in Shensi. But famine raged everywhere, and my father could not get enough to feed us. So one day he sold me for thirty-three pounds of grain to a peasant who was a little less poor than he was. My new father was kind to me, but his wife did not like me. She beat me, made me work very hard, and forbade me to go to see my real father and my family. My new family wasn't exactly rich, and what wealth it possessed continually declined because the head of the family smoked opium and his business suffered as a result. We had little to eat, and there was more water than rice in my bowl. Soon we didn't have even this bare minimum, and my adoptive father was forced to sell me as a bride to an officer. Having done so, he took pity on me. I was thirteen; I was too immature to consummate the marriage, and my adoptive father helped me to escape before the wedding night. So I took to the roads of Shensi as a beggar. Those were famine years. Many other waifs like me tried to throw themselves on people's pity, but no wanted anything to do with us. There was no question of getting oneself adopted or even of obtaining some kind of permanent shelter with the peas-

ants, who were also starving. One day in a half-deserted village I
ran into my adoptive father and his family, who were begging like
me: the famine had driven them from their home. We were thrown
together again.

"Passing through the village known today as Pa Li-tien, my
adoptive father got to know a tenant farmer to whom he sold me
as a wife. My husband was a very good cotton planter, but he had
no land of his own and he was very poor. Moreover, his two
brothers were hiding at his house to escape conscription and didn't
earn their living. Fortunately the rich peasant he worked for
agreed that I should help at the farm, without pay, of course, but
for a little food. Eventually our position improved because the
harvests were good for several years in succession, and my husband was able to save enough to open a mobile cigarette stand. It
wasn't a real business; he sold only a few cigarettes retail, but for
us it was a period of relative affluence all the same.

"In 1935 I had my first child, a daughter, and five years later I
had a boy. We had only one bed on the floor, as you must have
seen yourself in peasant houses, and our clothes were always in
rags. In winter we shivered because we had only a single blanket
so patched and worn it hardly gave any warmth. But the worst
was to come in 1943. One evening Kuomintang soldiers arrested
my husband because he had insulted their officer, who had stolen
cigarettes from him. My husband explained that it wasn't he but a
customer who had complained when he saw the officer taking
cigarettes without paying, but his protests were of no avail and he
was put in prison. I did everything I could, and I even sold our
stand to be able to bribe them with jars of wine; but I only partly
succeeded. My husband was freed for forty-eight hours on condition that he himself find the guilty man. The same evening we
escaped to the hills. It was mid-winter and there was snow everywhere. We took shelter in ruined temples and begged in the villages. A dog had bitten one of my children, and we were not
merely hungry and cold but afraid of everyone.

"Eventually we learned that the Kuomintang soldiers had left
our village, and we returned there; but we had nothing there but
debts. I was therefore forced to sell my eight-year-old daughter to
a rich peasant for fifty yuan and a bale of cotton. It was a fresh
start for us; we began to make cotton slippers, and that kept us
alive. But my daughter was too unhappy in the family which had
bought her. She came to me sometimes to tell me how she was

being mistreated, but there was nothing I could do to help her. One day she even tried to hang herself, and neighbors saved her at the very last moment."

Madame Chang bursts into sobs. Very moved, I murmur some words of sympathy and advise her to stop reviving old memories. But instead of translating this, my interpreter motions to me to be patient, that our narrator will calm down on her own. As for the local political official taking part in the session, he has from the start been deep in a dreamy contemplation not far removed from sleep, and the scene evokes no word of comment from him. Is this Chinese discretion, or do both of them already know this tale? I have a strange feeling. I have every reason to believe that Madame Chang is telling me a true story (I have heard others of the same kind elsewhere), but at the same time it seems to me as if I am taking part in a well-organized entertainment in which the actor's part and that of the public are preordained and codified. The tearful outburst is no doubt spontaneous, but at the same time it serves as an intermission, perfectly justified by the length of the recital. I haven't the heart to face Act Two, and with all possible circumspection I request that we move on immediately to the present day.

So Madame Chang enumerates her present possessions: "Seven of us live in a four-room house and we have seven blankets. I have a pair of quilted trousers for winter and another lighter pair for summer. My husband is the commune constable and my son is an electrician. My daughter-in-law works in the same team as myself, and we get on very well together. My three grandchildren go to school or are looked after in a nursery. They always have clean clothes and don't know what it is to go hungry. Our village, which once was poor, has become a prosperous and happy place thanks to Chairman Mao."

Madame Chang rattles off, in addition, the menu of her daily meals and of holiday meals. Her face has become as happy as it was tragic a minute before; but her voice remains as low and weak, and her vocabulary is extremely simple — almost poor. How and why did this woman come to be elected to the Academy of Sciences and the People's Congress, foremost centers of Chinese culture and politics?

"We have achieved very good results in cotton growing and we have succeeded, by our own methods, in developing giant plants, while before the Liberation only 'dwarf cotton' was known in our province," Madame Chang explains. Then follow statistics illustrating production increases, and at that point I think I understand that this shy woman is a great innovator in the field of agriculture.

"So," I say, "you have discovered a new way of growing cotton, and you are now teaching this in science institutes such as those at which you have been lecturing this week?"

"Other communes have achieved results as good as ours," Madame Chang replies modestly. "There's not very much to be learned from me. At the Institute of Agronomy I simply told the story of my life so that the young people of today will know what China was like before the Liberation and how much we suffered then."

I give up trying to understand the deep reasons behind Madame Chang's career, but before leaving her I ask what has become of the daughter she sold. Another surprise: this daughter lives with the son of the man who had formerly bought her, and she is perfectly happy with him. They have five children and all belong to the prosperous commune of Pa Li-tien.

During the war against the Japanese, and later during the civil war, the Communists used a simple and effective technique to awaken the peasants' political consciousness: they gathered the villagers together and invited the poorest of them to tell their life stories. These "Speak Bitterness Meetings" illustrated social injustices in striking fashion, and the listeners learned that they themselves ran the risk of becoming the victims one day unless they grouped together to defend themselves, as they were advised to do by the CP. By listening to the misfortunes of others, the peasants understood better what caused their own, which they often hid out of shame and which they tended to attribute to a specific piece of bad luck. Thus these sessions of "collective analysis" took the peasants out of their closed family world and brought them closer to their neighbors, and even to the inhabitants of other villages and other provinces who came to talk to them.

It was the results produced by the recitals of bitterness which enabled the Communists to set up women's associations, to build up their army's morale, and to undermine the morale of the Kuomintang soldiers. The women, who had never had the opportunity to complain to anyone, could at last vent their grievances publicly; they came out of the meetings inspired. Kuomintang prisoners, who were not treated as enemies, were also invited to recount their misfortunes to the Red soldiers.[13] A life story became a simple but powerful political argument, capable of destroying old habits and of shaking out of their apathy people who would have rejected doctrinal lectures.

This technique has proved so effective that the Communists continue to use it to combat what still remains of the old regime. Madame Chang is not the only one to narrate her misfortunes to the young people. Hundreds if not thousands of others do the same on radio, on television, in the factories, or in the principal schools. In all the communes I visited I listened to recitals about merciless landlords, exploited peasants, and children drowned, sold, or dying of cold and hunger. And everywhere displays of photographs of the atrocities of the old regime are used to illustrate these stories. They have gone further — a few relics of the old days have been preserved: thus, practically in the center of Shanghai one can visit one of the most miserable shanty towns in the world, which is still preserved as a "museum" today.

It is probable that for one generation of Chinese these denunciations of the past still have educational value. They guard against any relaxation of discipline that would risk facilitating a return to the hell that was, and they encourage a greater appreciation of the achievements of the regime which has given a minimum of well-being and considerable security to these people who not so long ago lived in atrocious misery and in dread of the morrow. And last but not least, these recitals recall that the worst of the present difficulties are nothing compared with the hardships of former days.

Before I went to China I was personally convinced that the old regime was morally and politically indefensible. But it was an abstract conviction. I admit that I never really saw the horrors of Madame Chang's world. And even after having heard about them I found it hard to imagine the hell that once had been the daily life of the Chinese peasant — in the same way that someone who has never known what it was to be in a concentration camp can never fully comprehend the sufferings of the inmates; it is virtually impossible to "feel" a way of life so radically removed from one's own.

[13] Jack Belden, in *China Shakes the World,* has stressed the part played by the "Speak Bitterness Meetings" during the civil war, which he covered from the Red Army side.

At the same time these testimonies cannot be treated as simple "historical curiosities." It is often said that the Maoists are more the continuers of certain Chinese traditions than they are disciples of Marx. And, indeed, it would be absurd to deny that a traditionalist element informs their methods. But what other country in the world has known such a radical break with the past? The Russian rural areas were profoundly changed by the October Revolution, then by collectivization. But in the time of the czars the peasants did not sell their children or their wives and did not live in a permanent state of near-famine. And never in the twentieth century did a system so openly based on the oppression of the "poorest" by the "not so poor" obtain in rural Russia. In the U.S.S.R. and the European people's democracies I have met people who had known misery but never anyone with such a dreadful history as Madame Chang.

The Chinese revolution has advanced the peasantry — that means the vast majority of the population — more than "twenty years in a day." At one swoop it abolished hateful centuries-old customs. It has made an unprecedented break with the past, and to the new generation of Chinese that past will be (it already is) as incomprehensible as it is to us. I even ask myself if, for example, the young people who have grown up since the revolution fully understand why Article 3 of the 1950 marriage law states that the sale of children is rigorously forbidden in China.

LOVE AND POLITICS

The youth club in the Ma Tchi-tse commune, near Sian, is a vast wooden barracks outside the village, almost in the open fields, and this afternoon the spring wind was buffeting it unmercifully. The club was deserted. The commune manager had warned me that the young people came there only in the evening "to sing revolutionary songs and to have discussions among themselves." But I asked if I could visit it all the same.

Neatly laid out wooden benches seemed to prove that in fact there was more discussion than dancing here. The walls were covered with notices in hand-lettered black characters on red paper and a wall newspaper written in the same manner. "Let us develop scientific education to combat superstition," proclaimed one notice. Another advised, "Let us lead a hard-working life even during the spring festival." I noticed that a manuscript article in the newspaper was illustrated with several drawings of a couple holding hands. In this country of strict morals such illustrations invite a closer study of the text. Here is the translation:

"In the province of Heilungkiang in the extreme northeast of China there was a young woman, Hu Shu-tsin, who after living in a big city and finishing her secondary schooling, went to work in a people's commune. At the beginning she found the work very hard, but she was brave, determined, and politically educated. She clenched her teeth: 'I have hands like the others,' she said, 'therefore I ought to be capable of service like them. Practice makes us tough just as school educates us.' Not only did she not dodge work, but she sought the hardest tasks.

"Impressed, the commune members took a liking to her and discussed her case among themselves. Some of them asserted, 'She is too pretty and talented to marry a peasant.' However, Hu Shu-tsin fell in love with a young farm worker, Chao Tsia-min.

"Chao Tsia-min was from a very poor family, and all his childhood he had lived alone with his mother in wretched poverty. There was no question of his going to school. Only after the Liberation did he learn to read and write. Then he became interested in agricultural techniques, but what he preferred above all was to work in the fields. He excelled at this. A member of the Communist Youth and a dedicated worker, he became head of one of the commune's brigades.

"Hu Shu-tsin quickly noticed the young brigadier's qualities — his honesty, his initiative, his capacity as a worker. Often she said to herself, 'I am better educated than he is, but I don't have his good points. We could complement each other and so become revolutionary peasants of a new type.' Moreover, she fell in love with him. Chao Tsia-min loved her also, but he was convinced that a girl like Hu Shu-tsin would never want to marry him. So they worked together side by side and often went for walks without ever daring to reveal their feelings. One day Hu asked Chao, 'What kind of woman would you like to marry?' 'I'm a peasant; I would like to marry a girl who loves working in the fields.' 'Do you know anyone who would suit you?' Chao thought, 'Yes, you,' but didn't dare tell her and simply replied, 'I think so.'

"A little later, during another stroll, Chao in his turn asked Hu if she had a boyfriend and if she was expecting to get married. Hu replied, 'I intend to spend all my life in the country, and I would like a young peasant who loves his work.' This time they understood each other and decided to marry.

"It must be added that since Hu Shu-tsin's arrival in the commune several 'cadres' from the city had made advances to her, but she had always repulsed them. When she was asked why she didn't want to marry someone from the city, she explained, 'These men didn't displease me, but I didn't know them well enough. I knew Chao Tsia-min very well, and I was sure that I would be happy with him.' "

Who, then, is the author of this surprising love story? My interpreter, Mr. Wang, knows everything: "It's taken from the well-known handbook, *Love, Marriage, and the Family,* published on the fifteenth anniversary of the revolution, which all young people study today in order to understand better their rights and their duties in this sphere." He added that the point was that this was "not a story, but an extremely significant real-life episode, which is soon going to be filmed." The director himself, although no longer young, knows the handbook well. Unfortunately no copy exists in the club, and I will have to look for one in Peking or Sian.[14]

I cannot leave such a piquant situation in mid-air until I get a copy, so I ask my escort to explain to me the importance of the text which merited a position on the wall newspaper and even illustration by the local artist. The commune director opens fire:

"For centuries," he says, as if addressing a meeting of peasants, "marriage in China was the business of parents. Myself, I was married without ever knowing my fiancée, and indeed although I came from a rather advanced background, I think my parents bought her for me. It is only since the Liberation that young people have had the right to marry whom they please. I am not saying that there aren't still arranged marriages in the old style. Unfortunately there are, and that's why young people must get to know their rights and refuse to accept the decisions of patriarchal families."

The last phrase was pronounced in a tone of exhortation that almost called for applause.

"Very well," I say, "but how is the story of Hu Shu-tsin and Chao Tsia-min so instructive in this respect?"

It is my interpreter, a young teacher, who takes on the job of answering this time, basing his reply, by his own admission, on the

[14] This handbook, by Mr. Tsan-tsin, has not been translated into any foreign language.

handbook, which he has studied deeply (he is a bachelor and therefore very interested in the question of marriage):

1) The object of love is marriage. But one must not marry lightly. A young Chinese ought not either to accept the choice of his parents or to marry someone, no matter how right she might be, whom he does not know well enough. In some villages the elders take a dim view of girls and boys working and going out together, and even say unkind things about them. The young ought not to pay any attention to these prejudices, which are survivals of the old regime; but before making a lifetime commitment they must get to know each other well, like Hu Shu-tsin and Chao Tsia-min.

2) Some young peasant girls want at all costs to marry the sons of workers or cadre members because they think that life in the towns is much easier. There are also young girls who before giving their consent demand gifts — sometimes even expensive gifts, like watches and bicycles. The point here is again that these are bourgeois habits, based on selfishness and on greed for money, which must be actively combated. It is the husband that a young Chinese wife must love, not money. She must neither be calculating nor hope for material advantages — it is unworthy of a free person whose work renders her independent. It is true that workers and cadre members are the most ideologically advanced elements, but young peasants like Chao Tsia-min contribute as much to the building of socialism and are equally worthy of being loved. By her conduct Hu Shu-tsin proved that she had broken free from all petty bourgeois prejudice and calculation.

3) The best bond between a couple is the interest they have in the common task and their full agreement on political matters. Chao Tsia-min would not have loved Hu Shu-tsin if this educated girl had despised manual labor. And on her part, Hu Shu-tsin would not have loved Chao Tsia-min if he had been a bad worker without initiative. Both shared the same outlook and knew that the advent of communism was the best guarantee of their happiness. And they had the assurance that their love would help them to become revolutionary peasants of a new type, who would contribute to the building of socialism.

"Don't you think, by any chance, that Hu Shu-tsin's beauty also played a part in this business?"

Everyone began to laugh. We were installed in the club and apparently no one was in a hurry to resume the tour of the commune. Love remains interesting even when it has political over-tones. Nevertheless the director quickly recovered himself, stopped laughing, even seemed slightly embarrassed at having given way to laughter, and began to talk very seriously about feminine beauty. "One cannot be insensible to it," he conceded, "but too much importance mustn't be attached to it, for it is ephemeral and the prettiest women aren't always the best." Wang the interpreter, who is a bachelor and therefore must have had some views on the subject, carefully kept quiet. I asked more "daring" questions, wrapping them up as much as possible to avoid offending the company. In order to find out if young peasants have sexual relations before marriage, I expressed anxiety about the fate of girl-mothers. But the director apparently did not know the meaning of the term. I therefore asked him if there were children whose paternity was not recognized. He answered with a lengthy discourse on the privileged position of children. So I raised the question of abortion, as birth control is not a forbidden topic. The manager replied that in fact abortions are authorized, but bad for the health. "Here we prefer sterilization, but again it is difficult to explain to people." We are far away from love and we shall not get any nearer to it before touring the commune.

This was not the only time that I was able to discuss the amatory side of life in China. At the Hai Ye ("Sea Swallow") studios in Shanghai I was shown a film which treats the subject with a certain humor. It was the story of Li Hsung-hsung, a beauti-ful young peasant woman of Honan province. Li Hsung-hsung has only one child. She works with her husband in a prosperous com-mune and enjoys a rather high standard of living. Her house is roomy and clean and her child as pretty as it is well cared for. But all is not going as well for other members of the commune, some of whom want to retain the old customs. Li Hsung-hsung, who holds no official position and whom we do not even know to belong to the Communist youth organization, clashes with these backward elements and helps to free the young people from the family yoke. Her husband, much more timorous, would rather live in peace with his neighbors and doesn't approve of his wife's militancy; this leads to scenes, a short provisional separation, and various repercussions. Finally the husband gives in, and the cou-ple, reunited in perfect understanding, resume the common strug-gle for the common good.

Onto this central anecdote are grafted episodes which provide

Li Hsung-hsung with the opportunity of helping young people. Some of the young people, in fact, are ready to let their parents arrange their marriages — these are the ones who fear they are incapable of choosing the right companion. Li Hsung-hsung tries to dissipate these absurd fears and advises them to start going more often to the youth club or to other groups organized by the commune. The more one takes part in youth movements, the more one becomes active in politics, and the more one has a chance of finding a life partner in the proper manner; such is Li Hsung-hsung's first lesson.

Li Hsung-hsung's next concern is with young people who are a little more aware. These know perfectly well that they have the right to marry whom they please, but they want to avoid quarrels with their parents and they say, "If they choose badly, we shall get divorced later." My interpreter explained later that if the young people took up "this absolutely incorrect position" (which Li Hsung-hsung easily persuades them to abandon) it was because they interpreted incorrectly the policy followed earlier by the Party in particular historic circumstances; at the time of the Liberation, indeed, the Party encouraged women who had earlier been married against their will and had had an unhappy domestic life to obtain divorces. This in no way means that the Party had ever intended to devalue marriage and extol divorce.

Finally Li Hsung-hsung comes to the case of Ho Mei-fei, a charming young girl who is very worried. Her parents have decided to marry her to a truck driver who brings chemical fertilizers to the commune once a week. Without consulting their daughter, who is secretly in love with a young peasant, they open negotiations with the truck driver. It should be explained here that the parents, who are from a rather comfortable background, are arranging this marriage in the hope that later they will be able to use the driver and his truck for illegal speculative deals.

Ho Mei-fei, in terror of her parents and weeping bitter tears, is about to submit to their wishes. But Li Hsung-hsung has still one card to play — to appeal to the truck driver's conscience. So she goes to wait for him on the road some distance from the village to talk to him on his own. The driver arrives, in Sunday best and loaded with presents: he has come for the betrothal. "What!" says Li Hsung-hsung to him. "You, the workers, who ought to set an example in political consciousness, now accept feudal morality and arranged marriages? Don't you know the old proverb, 'Fruit taken by force has a bitter taste?' How can you hope to have a socialist partnership with Ho Mei-fei when you hardly know her?" Convinced, the truck driver turns back and the stubborn Ho Mei-fei's family, which has gathered for the betrothal feast, waits in vain for her fiancé. Li Hsung-hsung has won. Ho Mei-fei, emboldened by this last-minute rescue, at last dares to marry the man she loves, and the film ends with a shot of the young couple working spiritedly as they sing a song composed by the commune manager in Li Hsung-hsung's honor.

After the showing one had to comment on the film. This time we were not in a lonely club in the heart of the countryside but surrounded by intellectuals in one of the biggest studios in China. The director started off by explaining that the scenario was inspired by a true story. I cautiously expressed some reservations about the detail: "Is kissing on the screen forbidden in China to the point that Li Hsung-hsung isn't even allowed to embrace her husband when she sees him again after a separation of several weeks? Isn't this puritanism in contradiction to what you call the lived experience?"

"This is not puritanism," replied the director. "It is a kind of discretion we have always observed in our country. Basically the film is not at all puritanical. It urges the young to emerge from the narrow family circle, to become independent and choose their own marriage partners. Do you think it is necessary to show how people kiss to put this across?"

The conversation rapidly took a polemical turn. Ever since we first met, the Chinese film-makers and I had disagreed on practically everything. The question of puritanism could only divide us more. In their view present-day China is, on the contrary, antipuritanical because it wants to break with the superpuritanical Confucian morality which prevailed throughout the countryside. Furthermore, the emancipation of women helps to combat puritanism. Today everyone, man or woman, is free to marry or divorce as he or she wishes.

But to us the word "puritanism" does not mean the same thing. I am not talking of the right to marry but of sexual freedom, which does not exist in China because the problem of relations between men and women — with all their psychological implications — is either dealt with in a misleading way or its existence is denied. As in Stalinist Russia, personal questions (including sexual questions) seem to belong to the accursed realm of bourgeois thought. May

the members of a socialist society therefore be miraculously protected from complexes and neuroses? May they never have to
resolve personal moral problems?

It is true that in the sphere of private life the Chinese do not
seem to pose the same questions we do in the West — at least if
we can judge from their literature. Certain Chinese literary classics
are very erotic, but those in which the sentiments of love are
analyzed are unknown. Mao himself said to Edgar Snow, "I just
don't know what your romantic novels are about." Is this lack of
understanding real? One may doubt it: Mao has in fact been married four times. In his last divorce he broke with the woman who
had accompanied him on the Long March in order to marry an
actress from Shanghai (herself a Communist and "Yenanist"). Can
this be explained simply by "family functionalism" and politics?

This desire for simplification, born of a belief in a mythical
"moral and psychological simplicity of the poor," is useful today to
a regime which wants to guide the young toward a "family functionalism" that corresponds with the immediate interests of society. The individual is therefore freed from the yoke of the patriarchal family but at the same time must submit to the demands of
collectivism. It is undoubtedly an advance, but it results from the
evolution of the social role of the family, and not from a freer
concept of sexual relationships.

In the old China the family was really the "social cell" and the
unit of production. The Confucian rules established the relationships between father and son, between the elder and younger
brothers, and laid down in detail the duties of each member of the
family. The stability of society was guaranteed by the strict observance of these rules. Paraphrasing the former president of General Motors, one might have been able to say then: "What is good
for the family is good for China."

This rigid family structure, already seriously shaken by the civil
struggles of recent decades, no longer corresponds today to any
economic or social reality. There is no longer anything to justify its
existence. The family is no longer a unit of production; it no longer
feeds its members alone. Today the ancestral temples serve only as
commune meeting halls, and peasant life is no longer based on
family ties.

Chinese dramatists often find surprising ways of saying this. In a
provincial theater I saw a one-act opera entirely dedicated to a
discussion between a husband and wife about how to use the

animal manure that they had saved up. The wife, more conservative, at first wants to fertilize their personal field. The husband replies that their land is already fertile enough and that they must give this manure to the commune, in whose prosperity everyone shares. The mother-in-law intervenes and recalls with her recital of bitterness that selfishness risks bringing back the old chaos, thus tipping the balance in favor of the husband. This opera would hardly appear breath-taking to a Western audience, but nonetheless it expresses a fundamental truth: that today life, the future, and the security of every peasant depends on the commune and no longer on his family's productivity.

What is more, everyone has now become independent within the collective whole, and society is no longer divided into clans, faithful to their own ancestors. The division today is horizontal; men and women group themselves in terms of age or professional interests, much as they do in the West. The Maoist advice to young Chinese — "Be independent, choose your own marriage partners" — is not basically very different from that which has been given for a long time to young Europeans. The experience of people like Hu Shu-tsin or Li Hsung-hsung can certainly give us a better insight than that of Madame Chang or one of those women with bound feet whom one still meets so often in China.[15] One can even say that the politico-love stories quoted as examples to the young Chinese are not unlike some stories in our romance magazines; whereas the accounts of pre-Liberation life take us back to a medieval world.[16]

What strikes one about these "model" stories is the fundamental role played by the women, who dominate the game and impose their will. Even in the commune of Hu and Chao, where the conflict is least acute, it is the woman who takes the initiative. As for Li Hsung-hsung, she has the role almost of a good fairy. It is certainly not just by chance that the women are given such prominence. Their emancipation is symbolic of the liquidation of old prejudices, for woman was the principal victim of the Confucian code, which did not accord her any rights at all. It is possible,

[15] The custom of binding the feet was widespread in China about the fourteenth century and was intended in particular to confine the woman to her home. The Communist government has obviously banned it. For the best interpretation of the origins of this practice, see Etiemble, *Connaissons-nous la Chine* (Paris, Gallimard, 1964).

[16] See the extraordinary account by Gold Flower in Belden, Jack, *China Shakes the World*, pp. 275–307.

therefore, that among the new generation the women are, in fact, the most enthusiastic supporters of the reformed family system.

Our film-makers' arguments in favor of the Maoist moral code would therefore be difficult to refute if the choice in this sphere was only between this and the previous code. But the neo-puritan side of Maoism is self-evident and offends so much more because it is taught not only in the countryside but also in the towns, where the traditions to be countered are not at all the same. Since before the war, millions of urban Chinese have broken with the patriarchal family concept. Thanks to the growth of secondary and higher education they number tens of millions today, and one wonders what value there can be for them in Li Hsung-hsung's advice on the best way to find a fiancé.

Admittedly, we don't know how the regime's moralistic regulations are applied in Shanghai, where I saw courting couples strolling on the Bund, or in Peking, where young people do not seem to spend all their time discussing productivity. Behind the rigid façade of official puritanism there exists, perhaps, a certain semi-clandestine freedom of morals comparable to that which I knew in Stalin's Russia. This idea often struck me because the Maoist family directives are very much like those the Soviet regime lavished on us and which we applied, it must be admitted, with a minimum of discipline. But China is no doubt better organized and even more rigid than the U.S.S.R. was. "Dissolute morals" are condemned here without appeal, and adultery is punished by law, which was never the case in Russia.

But then it seems obvious that the Chinese leaders are preoccupied with population growth (the Russians did not face this problem), and their concept of the family reflects this. For example, when they advise young people to marry late (thirty years old for the man and twenty-five for the woman), it is not only because "one must be ripe for marriage and one must know oneself well" but above all because it is a means of limiting the number of births.

Let me add, finally, that before leaving China I was able to acquire a copy of the famous handbook *Love, Marriage, and the Family,* and among other warnings in it against "dissolute morals" I found this one: "One must not court and promise marriage to several people at the same time. A young man who does this does not make progress in his studies, works badly, does not take a big enough part in the collective life. He even risks falling into traps

set by the enemy in this epoch of the class war in which we live."
Loose morals, therefore, are not denounced in the name of religious or lay morality but only because they could threaten the
balance of society. Sins in China do not lead to hell, but they make
easier the task of a political demon — "the bourgeois and feudal"
ideology which permanently menaces collectivity and which everyone must guard against.

THE DEMONS

No one in China intrigued me so much as Miss Kao Mei-tsun, a
student at the Petroleum Institute of Peking. Originally from Shantung province, she was six years old at the time of the Liberation.
Her parents were poor peasants, and it was thanks to the new
regime that she was able to become a student. She is an excellent
student, but that doesn't prevent her from taking a very lively
interest in politics and especially in the problems of "modern revisionism."

It was "revisionism" which provided us with the pretext for a
long discussion at the student center. In the room which Miss Kao
Mei-tsun shares with six other young women I noticed that a portrait of Stalin hung above the worktable in the very place reserved
everywhere else for Mao Tse-tung's picture. Why? Miss Kao Mei-
tsun blazed: "I hope that you don't believe the calumnies which
modern revisionists have spread about this great Marxist Leninist?"

In this country where everyone is extremely polite it is very rare
to be attacked in this way at the first question, and my very
intelligent interpreter, In Sun-lin, could not hide his surprise. The
others present — the director of the Institute and Kao's room-
mates — settled down on stools and wooden beds (the only furni-
ture in the room) as if for an entertainment. Then they waited in
silence, looking very expectant.

Kao isn't what one would call a beauty, but her round face is
very expressive, and in the heat of discussion she begins to look
more and more like Li Hsung-hsung, the heroine of the film I
mentioned earlier. She expresses herself with complete assurance,
basing her views, it is true, on official texts which she knows
virtually by heart. However, she could not have known either that
we were going to visit the student center or that I would be particularly interested in Stalin's portrait. No. But to judge from the

extent of her knowledge, it was clear that she was following the great debate between her country and the U.S.S.R. with passionate interest.

I did not succeed in the slightest in shaking her convictions, first of all because they were solid enough to be proof against persuasion and secondly because Kao refused to pay any attention to my arguments if they were not supported by the facts as they are presented in Chinese publications; in other words, she refused to believe practically everything that I could say about Stalin. The audience, which grew every minute (it overflowed into the corridor), approved this method of discussion and encouraged Kao by looks and smiles. The director himself nodded his head as a sign of approval. Stalin was so firmly defended by these young Chinese partisans that I decided to leave him in peace. At the end of the session I asked Kao if she held any position in the Institute's Komsomol.

Instantly she lost all her verve, all her spirit and aggressiveness. Sadly and without daring to look me in the face, she confessed: "I am not yet worthy of membership in the Young Communists' League. I have not yet succeeded in throwing off feudal and bourgeois ideological influences." Suddenly I became indiscreet. How was it at all possible that a model student, of peasant origin and educated by the new regime, could succumb to these evil influences, and how did they manifest themselves? Had this young admirer of Stalin had a war lord or a landlord in her family background? Could she perhaps have fallen in love with a capitalist or, worse still, a foreign visitor?

Nothing like that. Kao Mei-tsun assured me of the purity of her proletarian origins and swore that she had never known a war lord, a landlord, or a capitalist. I believed her, but that merely heightened the mystery. Had she read the wrong things? No, she read only scientific books and Party documents. After various guesses I ended by asking Kao outright what in the devil's name she could be considered guilty of.

"Nothing in particular, I assure you," she replied in the most natural way. "But we are living in a period of acute class war, and the feudal and bourgeois ideology of the old society is still very much alive. I fight it strongly, but I am not sufficiently liberated to be worthy of becoming a member of the Komsomol." I was compelled, therefore, to accept the idea that every Chinese, young or old, carries within himself the dangerous germ of bourgeois ideology and that even if he strives to eradicate it for the preservation of his moral and political health, this is extremely difficult for him and does not depend solely on his will. In China one does not choose one's own ideology; rather ideologies take possession of souls. The good ideology, the proletarian, has taken hold of the great majority, but the bad one, the feudal-bourgeois, still possesses a considerable number. This poses grave problems not only for individuals like the student Kao Mei-tsun but for the whole society, whose future depends on the success of the good ideology and the defeat of the bad.

I do not base this conclusion on an isolated case, intriguing though it may be. When one talks with the Chinese about this class struggle, which has a high priority in their program, one comes up against explanations which defy our concept of social conflicts. Not all the former property owners are considered as enemies to be defeated. There is no order which specifies that former wealthy peasants must be physically destroyed, as when Stalin liquidated the kulaks in Russia. Today's class struggle is therefore not a simple extension of yesterday's; it does not represent the liberated peasants' desire for revenge on their one-time exploiters. Such a concept would be debatable for Marxists, who define classes in relation to their actual part in production, and not according to their past activities. But for the Chinese this is not the point.

For them it is mentality which determines membership in this or that social class. A formerly rich man converted to Marxism becomes an irreproachable proletarian; conversely, a worker or poor peasant who clings to old customs falls into the bourgeois or feudal category. Admittedly, the former property owners are more likely to have bad ideas in their heads and to be cool toward the new society than its proletarian beneficiaries. But there are plenty of exceptions to this rule, so much so that I sometimes asked myself if the "bad class" is not mainly composed of workers who fail to absorb the collectivist principles.

These explanations amaze us and sometimes offend us. Yet the problem of the growth of social groups or elements in a society such as China's is a very real problem. True, there are no "classes" in China in the Marxist sense of the term, but there are certainly different social positions and functions, which by their very nature give rise to different outlooks and can promote aspirations to new privileges. It is not by chance that Mao Tse-tung has always been more preoccupied with this problem than the other Communist leaders in power. China approached socialism from a much lower standard of living than the countries of Eastern Europe. In China the social hierarchy was more complex and less dependent on the economic situation than elsewhere. The mandarins, who had almost unlimited powers, were not always wealthy proprietors. And even the powers of village landlords were often determined more by their social position than by the amount of land they owned. In entrusting administrative functions to the beneficiaries of the revolution, Mao was aware of the danger of arousing "contradictions among the people," and the booklet which he published on this subject at the time of de-Stalinization represents the first original examination of the problem since Trotsky.

Mao explained that the revolution did not abolish social conflicts and that these are even the driving forces of progress during the whole period of transition to communism. His theory was very much more complex and subtly shaded than Stalin's former theory about the aggravation of the class struggle during the building of socialism, and it did not have as its aim the justification of abuses committed by the Party apparatus. Mao's aim was diametrically different.

According to Mao, the revolutionary drive inevitably encounters the resistance of "demons": there are first of all the old demons, such as arrogance, selfishness, the lack of courage on the part of subordinates, and conformism or submissiveness; then there are new demons, such as the temptation of privilege, which manifests itself among those who hold positions above the rank and file, the taste for an easier life, and finally the appearance of more fastidious consumer appetites. China must therefore combat all these demons; and this vast fermentation working from the bottom to the top is called the "class struggle."

To illustrate this strange situation more explicitly I have combined in one narrative several accounts of the class war in the rural areas. I was given these accounts not only in the communes but sometimes at universities.

In China at the time of the Liberation the population consisted of roughly 73 per cent poor peasants, 20 per cent moderately well-to-do peasants, and 7 per cent landlords and kulaks. These inequalities were ended by land reform and collectivization, and the communes offered every peasant a chance of a better life. Although this policy is in the interests of the great majority, and the majority exercises political power, the mental attitudes inherited from the old regime did not disappear overnight.

Then, again, the commune system is not as rigid as some foreigners think. It is molded each day by the commune members, who enjoy considerable freedom of action. The peasants, for instance, own their own animals, their own tools, their own individual plots of land (very much smaller, it is true, than those of the members of Soviet kolkhozes). They are free to sell their products in the market and to buy industrial products like chemical fertilizers.

Moreover, in a commune the wage structure is a complex affair which depends a great deal on the co-operation and honesty of every member. It is impossible to fix productivity norms on a national scale, since agricultural production is strictly conditioned by the quality of the soil, the quality of the equipment, and climatic conditions. It is equally impossible to fix the peasants' incomes in terms of hours worked, since farm tasks vary considerably. The communes therefore have to employ a mixed system — some work being paid by the job and some by the hour — and allow the teams a great measure of autonomy.

Thus the "misled" peasants have a chance not only to give priority to the tasks they do for themselves and to devote themselves to commercial activities which border on the illegal but to cheat the commune or misappropriate part of the collective production. Experience has shown that collective ownership is not enough to prevent variations in income, the formation of groups of *nouveaux riches,* and the exploitation of honest peasants by these latter-day profiteers. In the communes where this happens, the rural "magnates" of yesterday regain their influence and can even indoctrinate the young people by dazzling them with promises of the "easy life." According to my guides, although there are no private farms, one can talk in some cases of a virtual restoration of capitalism in the sense that it is capitalist practices that govern the relations between peasants, and that collective ownership serves to make a minority rich.

If, on the other hand, the rank and file is imbued with the collectivist spirit (as is usually the case), the social relationships become more and more communistic. So in the villages where everyone really puts the collective good first, it is possible to abolish the whole business of internal accountancy by letting each member of the team determine the value of his own work. This is what is done, for example, in the Tachei brigade in the Northwest, which, while achieving remarkable results in the improvement of virgin land, has succeeded in raising the living standards of its members very considerably. When this stage is reached, the individual plot of land loses its importance for the peasants, the spirit of mutual help develops and eliminates all differences, the young concentrate mainly on acquiring new know-how which will enable them to serve the collective whole better, and the commune can invest greater and greater amounts in the collective equipment and in the development of its cultural division.

Thus the communes, starting with the same internal structure, can develop in very different directions, according to the ideological leanings of their members. A whole literature and art are dedicated to showing the consequences of the good or bad behavior of commune members.[17] In certain cases, when things really get too bad, the Party is forced to intervene by mobilizing the poor peasants; but its ability to control "from the top" is rather limited. "It is impossible to inculcate correct political thought by decree or to force the peasants by means of administrative measures to live and work by standards they have not yet fully assimilated," a very high personage in the regime told me frankly. "Education is therefore the only useful and effective weapon."

But in the countryside the Communists represent only a little over 1 per cent of the population. They are not priests charged with the preaching of the gospel to the peasants. They would be sermonizing to no effect if the masses did not feel the need to find new solutions to their problems.

In the matter of political education, therefore, the Chinese

---

[17] I saw several operas and a number of films dealing with this subject. One of the most typical, *The Village of Fan Choun Lin,* told how a demobilized soldier, Li Yung-hu, found after three years' absence that his village was completely dominated by a former kulak, Yen Wan-chen. The poor peasants were impotent against him because he had succeeded in dividing them and corrupting several, including the brigade leader, who was Li Yung-hu's brother. The kulak's clique stole the chemical fertilizer intended for the brigade in order to sell it on the black market and, with diabolical cunning, accused the honest peasants who tried to resist them of committing the crime. The latter were therefore at the mercy of the *nouveaux riches* of the village, who were not content to live the high life (wine and meat at every meal) but went to the length of organizing evening debauches for the young (card games in particular) and making them read harmful books. The young soldier, Li Yung-hu, was compelled to organize secret meetings to wrest power from these "village capitalists," but, naturally, he triumphed in the end.

peasants are first and foremost self-taught. Those among them who are already Communists help them a little, but it is by their daily experiences, by the constant battle with the backward or those beyond redemption, by the search for solutions to practical problems that the political consciousness of the workers in the people's communes is molded. They are the only and the best judges of what they ought to do.

Why does this peasant self-education yield such good results in some communes and negative or even disastrous results in others? Because the old morality and customs are difficult to eradicate. Then, if vigilance toward foreign ideologies is relaxed, be it only for a moment, and if one abandons for a second one's demands on oneself, the enemy will seize the opportunity to reinject his poisons in the hope of setting back the entire venture.

This "enemy" is not always a secret figure who must be unmasked. Sometimes he is to be found in the minds of well-intentioned militants who want a breathing space or want to avoid a clash. For the old Chinese proverb rightly says: "To learn is to row against the stream; when one stops, one drifts back." That said, excessive zeal is also a mistake: "A good Communist ought to march at the head of the masses, but without ever detaching himself from them and without trying to hurry them too much on the road they are still not very familiar with."

Specific examples were always cited in support of these propositions, which were often put to me. Dozens of times the names of communes, brigades, and villages were hurled at me to dispel doubts I had and to prove that the class war in China is neither an attitude of mind nor a bogey but a daily experience lived by millions of Chinese peasants. It is on its outcome that the success or failure of the commune system depends.

What can one say in reply? This way of looking at things and of tackling problems is obviously preferable to Stalin's, for it does not involve the physical destruction of "socially guilty elements." But it would be naïve not to see, despite assurances about the autonomy of the collectivized peasants, that this Chinese struggle between the new mentality proclaimed by the Communists and that of the previous epoch is accompanied by society's constant pressure on the individual. The class war is not a bloody one in China, as Chou En-lai proudly stressed to me, but neither has it been reduced to an ideological discussion on the merits of the proletarian ethic. Rather it is a kind of rigorous and massive education which affects every citizen, even the best. The present faith of the Chinese in the almost unlimited potentiality of education is based, according to some experts, on an ancient Chinese idea: "Man is born good, but he can lose this quality if he is badly educated." Conversely, therefore, a good education can make him perfect. Mao Tse-tung has inherited this traditional outlook, and his famous saying "China is a blank page on which everything can be written" is the old maxim brought up to date.

THOUGHT AND THE HARVEST

I had an appointment with Mr. Wu Chen, Vice-Minister of Agriculture, at the International Club in Peking a few days before I left China. I had asked him if we could simply talk without my submitting a questionnaire, and he had agreed. Our meeting was therefore devoid of all ceremony. No one on the Chinese side took any notes. Mr. Wu Chen had no files on hand and only quoted a few figures from memory to give me an idea of the present over-all state of Chinese agriculture and its potential. He started off by asking me for my impressions of the rural areas and the communes I had seen during my stay.

I did my best to extol the beauty of the landscape, that of the South in particular, which is among the most beautiful in the world. After which I added frankly that the living standards of the Chinese peasants seemed to me to be very low and that their equipment and methods were extremely old-fashioned. I did not stress the mediocrity and scarcity of the overcrowded living accommodations or the modesty of the communal buildings. I talked mainly about the work, almost always done by hand or with tools so worn and so out of date they would not be out of place in a museum. Certainly I had been told and had seen for myself that everywhere today the Chinese peasant eats his fill, which for him is the victory of victories. But one cannot always be harking back to the past, and men's bellies cannot be filled by memories of old wrongs. Yet given the Chinese population, their growing needs, and the extremely low level from which they started, I do not see how they will be able to overcome their crippling heritage of underdevelopment without more modern equipment and agricultural techniques.

Mr. Wu Chen listened to me patiently and without any trace of surprise: "In comparison with other countries, indeed," he said, "our agriculture is still only slightly mechanized. However, in comparison with other more modern countries, our agricultural production isn't too bad. Not so long ago all the work was done by hand. Today we have about 120,000 tractors, and we use about seven million [metric] tons of chemical fertilizers. It should be kept in mind, too, that some crops, such as rice, do not need heavy agricultural machinery. In the rice paddies we need only simple machines which are not at all 'spectacular.' However, it is true that we lack even this equipment. The biggest effort up to now has been put into irrigation: the building of canals and reservoirs, and the installation everywhere of electric pumps and diesel engines. The result — today we no longer fear drought, or at least we fear it much less than other natural disasters."

"If your agriculture is already achieving satisfactory results, is the main objective of the mechanization of the rural areas to liberate manpower for industry and to reduce rural overpopulation?"

"The potential of our communes is immense, and without having done a complete check, we already know that the modernization of agriculture can double present production. In the experimental farms and research stations certain communes get up to nine [metric] tons of rice per two and a half acres, and this occurs even in regions known previously for their mediocre yield. Further, we envisage the improvement of immense tracts of land still lying fallow. At present in China 296 million acres are under cultivation, but work done by our agricultural scientists indicates that we could till twice as much. We are not very actively engaged on this problem — that will be dealt with later. Today we are concentrating principally on stepping up the production of land already under cultivation, and we have every reason to be optimistic. Let us not forget that science often progresses more quickly than one expects; and before we have carried out our present plans, we shall certainly have discovered new ways of mastering nature."

Mr. Wu Chen is, as can be seen, in complete disagreement with the Western experts who estimate that even if Chinese harvests are considerably increased, they will not be enough to feed the population should it continue to grow at the present rate. Mr. Wu Chen did not even wish to bring up the problem of birth control and overpopulation; he left that to a specialist I was due to meet later. He confined himself to stressing China's enormous and still unexploited agricultural resources. According to him, modernization is only beginning; and great though the present efforts are, it will take at least twenty years to solve the four basic problems (mechanization, electrification, manufacture of chemical fertilizers, and irrigation) and four other hardly less serious problems (improvement of seed selection, widespread use of insecticides, more effective protection of the harvest, and development of methods of making the land arable).

With great authority, the Vice-Minister assured me that even taking periodical natural disasters into account, Chinese agriculture could increase its production by 6 per cent a year for many years, during which the use of still more sophisticated techniques will undoubtedly step up this percentage. But having supported his claims by citing the example of Japanese agriculture and others, Mr. Wu Chen suddenly declared that the real problem lay elsewhere.

"Our optimism," he told me, "is not based solely on the use of better techniques. For us the state of man's morale counts as much if not more than methods, no matter how perfected these may become. After all, it is the man who applies these methods; it is he who uses the techniques; it is he who decides the pace of work. If his decisions are right, if they are dictated by solicitude for the collective good, everything progresses: production, society, and the individual. We believe, therefore, that moral strength increases physical strength and that in fact Marxist Leninism is the best recipe for obtaining good harvests. That is the central principle of Chairman Mao's teaching, and where his ideas are correctly applied the harvests improve noticeably."

I could not hold back a smile, which I hid by burying my face in my notebook. However, nothing in this declaration on "the productive effectiveness of Marxism" ought to have astonished me. I had already heard it more than once, but nonetheless these assertions about the direct relationship between Marx, Mao, and the harvest always induced a strange ticklish feeling inside me. Fortunately Mr. Wu Chen interpreted my silence as a sign of my deep interest, and he continued.

He explained to me that the commune system is founded on the three-cornered relationship between the individual, the collectivity, and the state, which are interdependent. The rank and file enjoy the democratic rights and liberties of organizing their own work, deciding certain investments, and distributing money among the general fund, the social fund, and the wage fund. But they cannot solve these problems in a satisfactory way unless they are conscious of the role of the state, which represents society, and of that of the communal collectivity, which guarantees the security of everyone. All signs of selfishness, lust for gain, sectarianism, or narrow-mindedness are obviously prejudicial to collective society and, in the long run, to the individual. "Thus," Mr. Wu Chen said to me, "you have surely noticed that the communes do not all achieve the same results, and that within the same commune the teams can have very unequal productivity and therefore very unequal pay. That is inevitable, since we apply the principle 'to each according to his labor,' but we are working on this. How can such differences be avoided? Ought the state to give the same pay to those who are less successful — and often less successful because they don't have a correct attitude toward work? That would be absurd. It is the commune members themselves who ought to ensure that inequalities do not get worse, by transferring very good workers to the most inefficient teams and by helping those who are handicapped by illness or by a large family. This demands sacrifices of shock workers and of the collective; but our men have a strong political consciousness, so they do these things readily. And help from comrades is always more effective than financial aid."

"Nonetheless," I said, "from what little I have been able to see, the differences among communes are always very great. I saw a commune in Yunnan province where they earned an average of fifty yuan a year, and another near Peking where they earned 600."

The figure of fifty yuan surprised Mr. Wu Chen, who told me that very probably in this Yunnan commune they pay some of the "work points" in kind. He admitted, however, that the differences remain considerable, particularly between the communes in fertile provinces and those in provinces where the soil is poor. But he added that mutual aid among the rank and file and the intervention of the state (which reduces the taxes of the weaker communes and sends them experienced cadres) allow them to narrow the gap. "It is by reinforcing their political leadership that we best help the communes in difficulty," he concluded, reaffirming the priority of ideology over technique.

I do not question what Mr. Wu Chen told me about the internal democracy of the communes: a lot of incontestable evidence confirms that the rank and file in the communes is very often consulted.[18] But it remains to be seen whether this "democratization" is related to the fact that the peasants have a highly developed political consciousness or if it is only made possible by the rather primitive conditions in which the rural population lives. The two explanations are not mutually exclusive. A primitive collectivism can be a step toward a more complex form of peasant collective democracy. A certain experience of communal life can, if it is rounded off with a real political education, inculcate in those who are living it those habits of active participation in social life thanks to which it will be possible for them to arrive at the "higher collectivism" of tomorrow.

But what is less understood about the Chinese system, I noticed, is the part played by the little personal plots of land allocated to everyone. It is said that in order to cultivate them the peasants neglect a little the work they owe to the commune; and the plots make possible this "free market" which itself leads to the speculations denounced daily in the name of the revolution. Is it true that the peasants tend their own plots more carefully than those of the collective?

"Here, in contrast to what happens in the U.S.S.R.," replied Mr. Wu Chen, "the size of the private plots is strictly limited. They are never bigger than half a *mou* [about 380 square yards]. In fact, they are only kitchen gardens of a few score square yards. Our statistics don't take into account their production, which is really negligible. But these kitchen gardens improve the food supply of the family, allowing it to live a little better. Nowhere does their existence create a problem because no one dreams, as you would say, of 'living off his own land.'[19] This land is distributed as a sort of bonus. And in this way people can use their spare time productively. It is a secondary problem. The existence of these plots has some immediate economic effect but no real influence on the political life of the village. The class war does not weigh those who work more on their own land than on the collective land against those who do the reverse. It weighs those who love the people's communes (and who are in the great majority) against those who do not like them because they are still bound to the anticollectivist

[18] Jan Mydral's *Report from a Chinese Village* (New York, Pantheon, 1965) provides important evidence on this point. The author lived for two months in a village in Shensi province and collected the stories of all its inhabitants.

[19] However, the Western experts estimate that the private plots provide 5 to 7 per cent of the food consumed by the peasantry.

ideology. As for the free market, it also plays a positive role by making peripheral barter easier and by slightly influencing the prices of seasonal or marginal products — the prices of necessities being, as you know, fixed and guaranteed by the state."

There is, therefore, no internal contradiction in the commune system, which, according to Mr. Wu Chen, as early as 1958 was conceived in the form it has now reached. This last assertion seemed a little rash, and I recalled for Mr. Wu Chen the resolutions of Peitaiho and Wuhan on the industrialization of the countryside "on a grand scale." He admitted that some mistakes had been made and that natural disasters had killed certain hopes, but according to him, the basic principles concerning collective ownership of the land and proportional pay for labor are the same as in 1958. Our disagreement became more serious when I remarked that the Soviet kolkhozes were based on the same principles.

This comparison deeply offended Mr. Wu Chen. According to him, the Soviet system is based solely on the use of fallacious material incentives and does not allow the kolkhozes any political, administrative, or educative tasks. On the contrary the people's communes play multiple roles and are the authentic nucleus of collective life. "The Russians' agricultural difficulties prove clearly that it is useless to rely on material incentives to transform rural production and obtain good harvests. Their system is in full recession; it is economically ineffective and is no longer a means of attaining the communist society." With an amused satisfaction which he scarcely tried to disguise, Mr. Wu Chen added that China already exports considerable amounts of meat to the U.S.S.R. and that she has even suggested sending agricultural advisers "to help the Soviet comrades to overcome the deadlock."

Afterwards we touched on less burning topics, such as, for example, the production of the meat which China exports, although its cattle breeding had not seemed to me to be in a flourishing state. Mr. Wu Chen admitted that meat consumption in China is still very low: thirty-three to forty-four pounds a year per person. But even in this sphere considerable progress has already been achieved. Before the Liberation the Chinese peasants were convinced of the truth of the old proverb, "Vegetables and soya ought to be enough to keep one alive." Today meat is no longer rationed, for production is enough to satisfy the domestic demand and even to export some. "It follows," continued Mr. Wu Chen, "that the cattle-raising potential is far from exhausted, and in this field, too, we are only at the beginning."

The question of rationing and the importing of cereals was also rapidly dealt with. For a long time to come there will be ration cards in the towns to control consumption. But the rations have already been so increased (between forty-four and fifty-five pounds a month for workers, thirty-nine pounds for students, and thirty-five pounds for cadres) that most workers do not take advantage of their entire ration. As for imports, they are accounted for by logistical considerations (they facilitate the supplying of food to the big port cities like Shanghai and Tientsin) and not at all by the inadequacy of production, which this year topped 210 million metric tons.[20]

But Mr. Wu Chen was in a hurry to reply to the criticisms of Chinese agriculture made the previous year by "the revisionist Suslov." He dared, indeed, "to reproach us for paying too much attention to agriculture. He no doubt believes that God the Father will send us bread and raw materials for our industry." Point by point, eloquently and ironically, Mr. Wu Chen demolished the Soviet conceptions of the priority given to heavy industry at the peasantry's expense. He declared them "anti-Marxist, unrealistic, and characteristic of the ideological confusion of the modern revisionists."

I interrupted: "Weren't you yourselves influenced by these concepts before your quarrel with the Soviets?" Mr. Wu Chen reflected for a good minute: "We had some Soviet advisers who pushed us along this road, and perhaps their influence caused us to make some mistakes. But as early as 1957 Chairman Mao clearly explained to us that we ought to consider agriculture as the basic element of our economy. You will find, therefore, the complete reply to your question in his celebrated talk 'On the Correct Handling of Contradictions Among the People.'" Before parting I promised to reread this text.[21]

20 For several years China has not published any agricultural production figures, but it seems that their 1963 harvest was 180 million metric tons, that of 1964 more than 200 million. As for the continual importation of cereals from Australia and Canada, the "logistical" explanation does not appear to take account of the fact that China certainly needs foreign currency to buy industrial equipment, which is more difficult to produce at home than wheat. But cereal imports represent nearly 30 per cent of China's total imports, and it is difficult to believe that China would spend such huge sums, except in the case of overriding necessity.

21 Here is the extract to which Mr. Wu Chen referred: "As China is a great agricultural country, with over eighty per cent of its population in the villages, its industry and agriculture must be developed simultaneously. Only then will industry have raw materials and a market, only so will it be

It was late when I left Mr. Wu Chen, but I went for a long walk in the deserted streets of Peking. I tried to reconcile Mr. Wu Chen's optimistic statements with what I had seen in the communes. No person, no speeches, no reasoning could wipe out the signs of poverty that I had seen everywhere in the Chinese countryside. These rural areas had seemed to me more primitive and poorer than the areas in Russia where I had helped with the harvest during the war. The Chinese villages make one think of the forgotten world of the submerged tenth, but there is one outstanding difference — one never sees children with rickets, people dying of hunger, or beggars. The schools, the nurseries, the dispensaries, the research stations are all still on a modest scale, but they testify to the progress made and above all to the will to escape the curse that is underdevelopment. But what a long road remains to be traveled before this country attains the era of prosperity!

And since for the Chinese the solution of the agricultural problem depends above all on the acceptance of socialist ideas by the peasantry, these ideas must be adjusted to the level of the latter, which obviously is still extremely low. Certain European economists believe that the present effectiveness of the communes is due to the system of subdivision employed: the team, which is the basic unit, is responsible for a few dozen acres and its members can identify themselves with, understand, and discuss the practical problems of the organization of work in an area of this restricted size. This view, which is probably an accurate one, tends to support the theories that an elementary democracy exists within the communes and, on the other hand, that the intellectual backwardness of the peasantry imposes a burden on the whole country.

---

possible to accumulate fairly large funds for the building up of a powerful heavy industry. Everyone knows that light industry is closely related to agriculture. Without agriculture there can be no light industry. But it is not so clearly understood that agriculture provides heavy industry with an important market. This fact, however, will be more readily appreciated as the gradual progress of technological improvement and modernization of agriculture calls for more and more machinery, fertilizers, water conservancy and electric power projects and transport facilities for the farms, as well as fuel and building materials for the rural consumers. The entire national economy will benefit if we can achieve an even greater growth in our agriculture and thus induce a correspondingly greater development of light industry during the period of the Second and Third Five-Year Plans. With the development of agriculture and light industry, heavy industry will be assured of its markets and funds, and thus grow faster." Mao Tse-tung, "On the Correct Handling of Contradictions Among the People," in Bowie, R. R., and Fairbank, J. K., eds., *Communist China 1955–1959,* p. 294.

For paradoxically the pressure from the rank and file — let us not doubt that it exists — does not at present make either a much greater democratization or the raising of cultural standards in China any easier. To advance his peasant revolution, Mao is forced to adjust the other sectors of life to the level of those who still represent the vast majority of the population and who form the essential element in his economy. But, as we shall see, this policy of adjusting national development to the needs of the countryside gives a very special flavor to the Maoist ideology and is carried out at the expense of the intellectual and technical elites who, it is said, "do not have the right to separate themselves from the masses."

CHAPTER THREE

The "Correct Political Thought" for Towns

"The sun rises in the east of China four hours earlier than in the west. When the Ussuri, in the extreme eastern part of the country, is bathed in the golden rays of the morning sun, it is still night in Tien Shan and in the Pamirs, in the far West," the official Chinese textbook on geography tells us poetically.[1] But all watches in China are on Peking time. So great is the government's anxiety to ensure the unity of the country, it does not even heed the sun's course. Everything, absolutely everything, must help to obliterate the old divisions and fragmentation. Mao wants China to be a single entity for all her citizens and wants them all to live at the same tempo and under the same conditions.

The least significant news released in Peking is immediately disseminated throughout the whole country with remarkable speed. In the capital in March, 1965, we saw the first illustrated posters denouncing the suppression of anti-American demonstrations by Asian students in Moscow and the expulsion from the U.S.S.R. of Chinese nationals wounded by Soviet militiamen. The next day we were in Shanghai — the same posters were already in place. Ten days later we came across them in Kunming, in the far Southwest; they were already yellowed by the weather and quite plainly had been posted here, as on every wall in China, on the very same day as those in Peking.

"We are 650 million and we are united as a single man," the orators proclaim before huge crowds summoned periodically to protest "against the imperialists' deeds in the Congo or Vietnam or Santo Domingo." A political demonstration in China is not at all the same thing as in Europe or America. It lasts for several days and sweeps like a tidal wave across the country. Eighteen or twenty million people take part in turn in these marches of unity and indignation. They are not always the same people, for a considerable number of workers must always stay at the factory or the university; but a party representing the employees is delegated, and

[1] See Jen Yu-ti, *Geography of China* (Peking, Ed. Langues Etrangères, 1965).

Chinese students consider it an honor to be chosen for these groups.

We saw a demonstration of this kind at the beginning of February, just after the first American air raid on North Vietnam. It was fascinating. In Tien An Men Square, on improvised stages, the actors from the Peking Opera mimed scenes depicting American villainy. At every street corner amateur troupes did the same, while to the delight of the children military bands played marches at full blast. An endless stream of demonstrators flowed along the city's main avenue, as wide as the Champs Elysées but much longer. On the second day these processions and incredible displays had become so familiar to us that we hardly batted an eye. If, on the third day of the demonstration, there had not been a huge meeting in which Mao Tse-tung took part, we should have stayed in our hotel. So it is hardly surprising that foreign journalists who live permanently in Peking rarely bother to attend these demonstrations and devote no more than a few lines to them in their dispatches. The result is, however, that people abroad have only the vaguest idea about these great frenzied gatherings of the Chinese.

But is the object of these demonstrations to impress foreign countries? In my opinion, no. It seems to me that the Chinese need to keep repeating to themselves, in order to convince themselves, that they are "united as a single man," so close and painful is their memory of recent dissension. Foreign intellectuals who have made China their new motherland all told me repeatedly that with our European minds we could not grasp this permanent and extraordinary preoccupation of the Chinese with unity. We live in a world where, for a very long time, the ideas of national unity and of the centralized state have been taken for granted. In Europe we are preoccupied with the diversification of society. To call for the unification of the nation makes no sense, and when such appeals for national solidarity are made, they inevitably come from the conservative right, making a hollow and suspect sound.

In China the concept of national unity within the framework of a centralized state is new, or rather it is being revived after centuries of a pseudo-union based on the values of peasant civilization and which, in fact, sanctioned the fragmentation of the country. Every great mandarin was his own government, and on the pretext that he represented the emperor, he demanded loyalty to his own person.[2] Under Chiang Kai-shek's republic even this tenuous unifying factor had disappeared, and millions of peasants in the outlying regions had never heard of Chiang Kai-shek or the Nanking government. An old peasant in the Sian region explained to me that neither Chiang Kai-shek nor the Shensi war lord had ever really existed for him, and that in his eyes supreme power was embodied in a great landlord nicknamed "Number One Devil" and in his sons, Devils Number Two, Three, Four, etc., according to their age. Only these "Devils" succeeded in making him afraid and therefore in collecting taxes from him. Before 1949 Madame Chang Chiu-hsiang had never heard of the governments of Nanking or Yenan. To her the name of the Kuomintang did not connote a regime or a political party but the soldiers who, passing through her village, had arrested her husband. In short, before the Communists came to power, the Chinese population had only the very vaguest notion of the state.

Today the Chinese are no longer isolated, closed off in their villages or in their provinces. The differences of dialect should not be a barrier for long to a vast intermixing of the population; for in every school the children are taught the same dialect, *pai-hua,* the spoken language of Peking.

Talking with students, one finds out that they come from every part of the country. At the Steel Institute in Peking we met some youths who came from Wuhan, a city which in fact has its own Steel Institute. In Sian we met students who came from Shanghai, which with Peking is the biggest university city in the country. The same applies to industrial cadres: the director of the heavy machine tool factory in Kunming is a northerner from Shenyang, and the assistant director of the metallurgical combine at Anshan is, on the other hand, a Shanghai man. Among the skilled workers at Wuhan there are quite a few Manchus who are teaching machine operation to young peasants who have often come from distant villages.

[2] In his *Une Barbare en Asie* (Paris, Gallimard, 1945), pp. 178*ff*, Henri Michaux tells this story which illustrates the relations between citizens and government in the old China: "Confucius and his disciples one day met a good woman. They learned that her father had been carried away by floods, her husband killed by a tiger, her brother stung by a snake, and one of her sons taken in a similar misadventure. Confucius, disconcerted, asked: 'And you remain in such a country?' It was a small state within China which one could easily leave for another. The good woman then gave this delightful Chinese reply: 'The government isn't too bad!' Which is to say that business was good and taxes moderate."

Economic necessity justifies the movement of skilled manpower. In the old China, industry was almost exclusively concentrated in the coastal zone (Shanghai, Canton, Tientsin) and in the Northeast. Now the government intends to industrialize every province, and it has set up factories in Mongolia, as well as in Szechwan, Shansi, Yunnan, and other provinces. It was normal and necessary that the inhabitants of regions which had been industrialized for a long time should help in the starting up of new factories and in the training of peasants turned workers. Nevertheless, it seems that the transfer of workers from one region to another might be taking place on a greater scale than is absolutely necessary. Undoubtedly one can see in this great intermixing of the population an indication of the government's intention to wipe out, at all cost, the invisible boundaries which until recently separated the Chinese.

Apparently people move about quite freely in China. In the stations, in the trains, in the airports, I never saw travelers' papers being checked. I was assured that students and technicians could choose to work anywhere. But the Party and the government often appeal to their "devotion to the well-being of the country" to induce them to accept a place of employment or study other than that of their choice. However, ration cards for certain necessities are honored only in the town in which they have been issued, and this limits one's chances of moving elsewhere. Nevertheless, none of the "transplanted" workers we questioned ever expressed any homesickness, and they even declared they were delighted at their good fortune; although this rosy outlook most often seemed to be manufactured on order.

In addition to this horizontal mixing of the population, there is what one might call a vertical mixing, the most visible sign of which is the rule that students, intellectuals, and the cadres must do a spell of manual work during the year. In the spring particularly one sees whole columns of townspeople, carrying rucksacks, taking the road to the country to work in the fields. In some areas at harvest time three quarters of the inhabitants pour out of the towns to help the peasants. Here again practical necessity is not the only explanation of the CP's desire to ensure that everyone does his share of manual work; there are also ideological reasons, the most obvious of which is the elimination of other invisible boundaries — those which separate different social classes — and all this with the aim of strengthening the unity of the country.

No matter what is said, I do not believe that this stint on the farm is spontaneous and that intellectuals and cadre members are really enthusiastic about spending several months a year in a commune to be reinvigorated among the people.

No one in China denies that living conditions in the country are much tougher than in the towns. While Hu Shu-tsin, the young student who went to live in the country and married a peasant, is cited as an example, usually it is the country people who want to move to the town. In 1958, when industrialization was in full swing, there was a huge movement of peasants into the towns. Two years later, after the "Great Leap Forward," the pace slowed down, and a considerable number had to be sent back to their villages; they were not too pleased about it.

In fact, town-dwellers are under pressure to spend some time in the country, while only a small proportion of the peasants get a chance to go to work in the new factories or to study at a university. The attraction of the town for them is still growing, and if one day the government allows a really spontaneous population movement, it will certainly be the reverse of the kind they are at present encouraging: the peasants will flood into the towns.

There is no hope of closing the gap between urban and rural standards of living for a long time to come. Party theoreticians are perforce resigned to this, but they are doing everything in their power to lessen the effects and to even them out.

It follows that large-scale migrations, sometimes encouraged, sometimes held back, are only possible because of the existence of a powerful administrative machine which decides, anticipates, and supervises the execution of its directives. The Chinese freely admit it and they even declare themselves proud to have been able in such a short time to build a great centralized state such as their country has never known before in its history. They do not give us figures for the number of cadres employed by this state organization which governs 650 million people. But even without having obtained such details we can assert that a state of this kind carries within it the germ of bureaucratization. The Chinese we talked to denied this and explained that civil servants live as modestly as the workers and are obliged to do some kind of manual work so that they remain close to them.

The Red Guards' rage, however, is directed against the people in the Party apparatus, and now at last official publications reveal the existence of cadres who abused their power, who made mistakes, and who cut themselves off from the masses. No doubt young zealots are not the best judges of the behavior of men who sometimes can boast a proud history of militancy. But the fact that Mao considered it necessary to purge the Chinese state machine with the help of the Red Guards proves that conflict between the new bureaucracy and the masses existed and was in danger of getting worse as time went on.

THE STREET

There are in China, which is essentially a rural country, ten cities of more than one million inhabitants. Two of these, Shanghai with ten million inhabitants and Peking with seven million,[3] are two of the greatest cities in the world. Urban China on its own comprises an enormous, complex, and varied country. But all big cities in every country of the world possess a common character, and a European feels less out of his element in the big Chinese centers than in the countryside.

In the morning, watching the Chinese workers set out for work on bicycles or public transportation (very often carrying their lunches), one recaptures a little of the atmosphere of any other metropolis. Some cities still bear traces of the century they were "open to foreigners." In Shanghai in particular one sometimes gets the impression of being in a little corner of Europe or America that has been transplanted bizarrely to the Far East. From the period of friendly collaboration between China and the Soviet Union remains the legacy of a few huge buildings in a non-Chinese style that is associated with a certain Russian cultural epoch.

As these elements of the city seem so familiar, one often tends to assume that what happens here is equally similar — a profound mistake. Chinese society functions totally differently from Western societies and from the communist societies we know; it operates according to principles which have practically never been applied elsewhere. This is perhaps even more obvious in the towns than in the countryside.

To begin with, Chinese towns bear the stamp of the country's economic backwardness. Our guides make no attempt to hide this from us; and when we are out walking, they make no detours to avoid the poor quarters. There are few cars in the streets; and when you arrive at night in a big Chinese city, the silence and darkness are almost as profound as in the heart of the countryside.

[3] This figure, as I have already explained, includes a certain number of suburban communes.

Apparently everyone goes to bed at sunset here. Hardly a lighted window is to be seen, and the wide avenues, often lined with several rows of trees, are deserted. Arriving at a hotel in the evening, you do not really see it until the following morning, for both its façade and the street are plunged in darkness. Even the hotel's interior, lit only by the dimmest of bulbs, is a shadowy world.

Early in the morning you are awakened by a concert of automobile horns so thunderous that you have the feeling some catastrophe has brought fleets of ambulances into the street. But no; these are simply buses and a few taxis plowing their way through the crowds of cyclists and pedestrians on their way to work. The use of car horns is not only authorized but obligatory, and the drivers observe the regulation with enthusiasm.

Among the crowds whole brigades of road-sweepers, brooms in hand, tidy both main and back streets throughout the day with as much solicitude as if they were cleaning the corridors of a palace. Often children, also armed with brooms, take part proudly in this meticulous street-cleaning on their way to school.

At exactly ten o'clock a new din accompanies another national exercise: at every street corner loudspeakers broadcast rhythmic music and commands urging the population to practice mass gymnastics. The buses keep moving, however, and some pedestrians continue on their way as if nothing was happening; but many others stop and start hopping, shadow-boxing, and doing other exercises in the middle of the street.

In the schools, offices, ministries, and factories there is a quarter of an hour's break; everybody goes down to the courtyard or the street or out on the terrace where instructors lead the mass physical culture class to the shrilling of whistles. It is exactly at ten o'clock, too, that the big state department stores open their doors. In the provinces it sometimes happens that customers are already waiting at the doors — the only queues that we saw in China. However there is no lack of shops, and every town has its shopping streets, lined with stores of all kinds with attractive window displays and clerks as helpful as in any private enterprise business. These shops are most often co-operatives and occasionally joint "private-state" enterprises, the owner having sought government participation in his concern and being, in effect, more manager than co-proprietor.

One also sees open-air and covered markets, all overflowing with vegetables and remarkable for their cleanliness. Most restaurants are not visible from the street but are usually tucked away in courtyards and contain several small rooms where families or parties of friends can eat privately. The more modest ones are directly on the street and have only public rooms.

Places of entertainment are open from midday. In Shanghai a crowd of fans line up outside the "Great World." This place, which in the days of foreign control was the biggest night club–gambling house–brothel in the Far East and even in the world, is a huge many-storied building with terraces and gardens. Today it houses eleven movie houses, as well as theaters, music halls, and operas.[4] For fifty fen (twenty cents) one can stay from midday until ten o'clock at night, moving from one hall to another, chatting with friends if the shows are not to one's taste.

In Peking the equivalent of the "Great World" is situated near the famous Temple of Heaven, in a very populous quarter. While in Shanghai to go to the "Great World" is practically obligatory, nothing is done here to attract the foreign visitor. It was almost by luck that we discovered it. Spread over several bustling alleyways, this immense amusement center is made up of numbers of small booths which seem to be temporarily installed, like stands at a fairground. Here one must pay admission at each one, but it is very cheap. There are magicians and acrobats, who seem to draw the biggest crowds, but the "revolutionary operas" are also popular.

Marc Riboud and I went without an interpreter from booth to booth, then ended up in a little, very cheap Mongol restaurant. The waiter put in front of us some lamb cut into very thin slices and raw vegetables; then he placed in the middle of the table a kind of circular and horizontal samovar. In the center was a charcoal-heated chafing dish around which were compartments full of boiling water (various sauces are served separately) — and we had to manage on our own. It was delightful and Marc Riboud assured me that in no other country in Asia, which he knows well, would he have dared to touch the food in a similar place.

Twice, and at some length, we strolled through this district where thousands of people of all ages come to enjoy themselves, to eat, and to drink. Not once did we see any sign of the police or even a single militiaman. This well-behaved crowd is as dense every day because factories close for the weekly rest day in rotation. Only schools and public departments are closed on the tra-

---

[4] The biggest drama and opera companies have other theaters where it is often very difficult to get a seat.

ditional Sunday. In the street it is very difficult for a foreigner to place a Chinese "socially" by his clothes, but aside from that, the uniformity of the Chinese crowd ("the blue ants") has been very much exaggerated by Western journalists — there is a great variety of colors and styles in people's clothes. By dint of mixing with this not-very-well-off throng one can eventually spot the poorest (who are never ragged or lice-infested), but in effect there is no way of telling at first sight a factory manager from his workers or a young university professor from his students. Nowhere else have I seen this sartorial egalitarianism. Neither have I witnessed anywhere else such enormous curiosity. The Chinese seem to be born gapers. All that one of them has to do is look up at the sky, and a dozen others will stop and do the same. A European with his astonishingly long nose, can sometimes walk about without attracting attention, but it only needs a few children to follow him to get a closer look at his extraordinary proboscis for a curious crowd to gather. All this is not perhaps particularly Chinese, but nonetheless the Chinese man-in-the-street seems to have a marked herd instinct. For example, in Wuhan I was on my own at the edge of an old district of rather tumble-down little shacks, Marc Riboud having gone off with our interpreter in search of a spot from which he could photograph the famous Yangtze Bridge. To begin with, only a few urchins took an interest in me. I said "good morning" to them — one of the thirty Chinese words I know — then one of them passed on the word that a foreigner who could say *Ni hao*[5] was among them, and in a few seconds an unbelievable number of people came out of their houses and gathered around me. All wanted to shake my hand and hear me say *Wo bu hui suo chung kuo hua.*[6] All appeared very amiable, and I felt I was surrounded by friends, but so many of them that it was becoming rather disturbing. Our interpreter at last turned up to rescue me, but he was reluctant to answer when I asked him how so many people could live in such tiny dwellings.

THE SPOTLESS ANTHILL

In every town we were shown modern apartment buildings for the workers built near new factories, generally some distance from the center. Shanghai is ringed by a virtual belt of satellite housing

[5] "Good day." Literally, "Thou well."
[6] "I do not speak Chinese."

projects comprising European-style houses, three or four stories high, with gardens, parks, and recreation areas. At Kunming, around its principal precision machine tool factory, which is still expanding, a huge new district has shot up. One could give many more examples. The people who live in these new apartments seem to have a more comfortable life and more living space than those in the older districts, which are admittedly more picturesque but obviously overcrowded. The building of homes for workers in a still-growing industry is carried out according to rational and precise plans. But in order not to show too much favoritism toward those benefiting from industrialization (and also in order to rehouse the greatest possible number of slum-dwellers) the living space allocated to each family is very limited even in the new buildings. One sees six or even eight people living in two rooms of very modest size.

In Peking we had a long interview with Mr. Chu Yung-yan, Deputy Director of the Office of Urbanization, who knew by heart the number of new buses put on the roads, the exact measurements of Tien An Men Square, and many other statistics, but who, unfortunately, did not know the ratio of inhabitants to living space in his own city. We were luckier in the provinces.

In every town I visited I asked to meet the mayor, and generally this was very easily arranged. If the mayor was not available, one of his deputies welcomed me and often talked with me at length. Only in Nanning, capital of the Kwangsi-Chuang region, bordering on North Vietnam, did my hosts ask me to submit written questions. Caught unawares and anxious to avoid matters of general policy, I confined myself to vague questions such as, "What is your town's economic situation?" Two days later the mayor, Mr. Yuan Hun-tzan, solemnly read me a long report on the situation similar to that which the chairman of a big corporation periodically presents to his shareholders. To begin with, he painted a picture of the lamentable state of the town under the old regime, harshly blaming the Nationalist militarists and principally Li Tsung-jen,[7] the most powerful and redoubtable man in the region. Then he spelled out the progress achieved and ended by describing at length

[7] After an exile of fifteen years in the United States, General Li Tsung-jen returned to Peking in 1965 and was very well received. Originally from Kwangsi province, Li Tsung-yen always retained a strong position, even after going over to the Kuomintang in 1927. Under the Nationalist regime he played a major role and was even President of the Republic in 1949.

the shortages and difficulties still to be overcome. He particularly stressed the poor accommodations: "We have at present twenty-six and three-fourths square feet per person; we must increase this to at least thirty-two square feet.

Twenty-six square feet per person! Even in the most over-crowded Soviet towns the estimated living space is seventy-four square feet per person, and everyone there complains, not unreasonably, of the housing crisis inherited from Stalin's day. In China it is just incomprehensible how people are able to conduct family life in such conditions. Yet Nanning does not appear to be more overcrowded than other towns. It is rather in the central regions, in Changsha and in Wuhan, that one gets the feeling of being in a human anthill. This critical lack of living accommodations goes a long way toward explaining the modest living standards of the Chinese and certain aspects of their way of life; for example, they are forced to go to bed early in winter, and in summer, on the contrary, to stay up as late as possible to make the most of daylight and fresh air.

It only remains to answer the question which constantly comes to mind in China: how has the regime succeeded in disciplining people who suffer great privation and live in conditions which in all countries and at all periods of history have led to squalor and encouraged crime?

For it is a fact — China is clean. There have been innumerable jokes about the extermination of flies (and rats, bugs, and other parasites that went with the filth of former days) but no one denies any longer that China has become clean. In this country where before 1949 there were no sanitary facilities to speak of and where everything was "doubtful," one can today drink tap water in any hotel.[8] No longer are there the epidemics which periodically ravage underdeveloped countries. No other country on the Asian mainland has yet achieved comparable results; and the person most impressed by the Chinese success in this field during my visit was an English journalist permanently based in India.

Further, China has become honest. It is no longer necessary to keep an eye on one's pocket either in the "Great World" or in any of the other crowded public places usually frequented by pickpockets. One can leave luggage and packages in an open car in the street without any risk of their disappearing. A taxi driver whom

[8] Even in Peking and Shanghai there was neither drainage nor running water outside the European quarters, and the streets, which rarely had an asphalt or concrete surface, were never cleaned.

an Italian journalist, Gino Nebiolo, had by mistake given 20 fen (eight cents) too much looked for him all evening to give the money back. Nebiolo was not even aware of his mistake, and no third party had witnessed it.

It has reached the point where it is even difficult to throw away or "forget" intentionally something one wants to get rid of. For instance, during a stroll in Yenan one day I bought a packet of roasted sunflower seeds. By the time I had eaten half of them, I had had enough. At first I tried to give the bag to some children playing in the street, but they refused them. So I left them on a rock, convinced that the children would take them when I had disappeared. About 300 yards farther on a girl of fifteen caught up with me, the bag of seeds in her hand, her face flushed with running and anger, and gave me a sharp lecture. From her gestures if not her words (I was without an interpreter), I gathered that one must not dirty the streets by throwing things away, nor should one tempt children by leaving near them something nice which does not belong to them. I carried my bag of seeds back to the hotel, and the following day when I moved on I left them on my table. The next day, as I was boarding the plane, a waiter from the hotel overtook me at the boarding ramp; out of breath, he handed me the half-full bag of sunflower seeds.

In a foreign country, particularly if one cannot do without an interpreter, as is the case in China, it is extremely difficult to form any idea of the extent of crime and prostitution. Some skeptics among the Peking diplomatic colony warned me against premature enthusiasm and showed me a Shanghai newspaper in which it was reported that a factory making anti-theft locks for bicycles had surpassed its production target by 20 per cent. "If there weren't any thieves in China, why would they manufacture anti-theft locks?" they said, not without apparent reason.[9]

Other skeptics of the same breed told me that a knowing sailor from Hong Kong or Singapore always has a few good addresses where he can find a temporary soul-mate.

---

[9] In Peking I was told the story of a diplomat who had decided to put Chinese honesty to the test. A few yards from the hotel he "lost" his wallet, in which he had left only his visiting card and twenty yuan. Twice his wallet was brought back to him the same evening. The third time, to his great surprise, it contained fifty yuan when it was returned to him. When he inquired about this, the Chinese authorities admitted to him that only his card had been found in the wallet and that on an off-chance they had put fifty yuan into it so that he would not be left without any money.

One could reply that the bicycle locks are perhaps intended for export, and when it comes to girlfriends the boasting of sailors the world over is proverbial. But one might as well admit what the skeptics say — and admit it without any embarrassment. It would be miraculous indeed if in fifteen years a country as densely populated as China had radically wiped out all crime and prostitution, and it would be surprising if they were to succeed in doing so in the near future. Suffice it to say that today one has to search to find thieves and prostitutes and that anyone who knows what Shanghai was like, for example, in 1949 would have to be blinded by prejudice to deny that amazing results have been obtained.

In any case, even the strongest opponents of the Communist regime admit this, although they attribute these results to Mao's repressive policy and to the system of spying and informing on one's neighbors which he has imposed on the population. They assert that the Communists have deported hundreds of thousands of "contaminated suspects" from Shanghai and other cities and that they have established a whole network of district committees, street committees, and even block committees which strictly control everyone's conduct. Only by suppressing all individual liberty, they say, could Mao have achieved such results.

It is indeed more than likely that there has been repression; and when the Communists boast of having "re-educated" a record number of delinquents at record speed, they are obviously speaking euphemistically. But in no part of the world has repression alone put an end to crime or prostitution. And it must be said right away that not many countries as economically retarded as China can afford the luxury of a British-style parliament and the strict observance of the rights of man. Most backward countries are under more or less tough dictatorships, and everywhere the "strong men" in power have tried to stamp out crime and prostitution without success.

Even in China itself, before the war Chiang Kai-shek decided on a great anti-vice campaign and in February, 1934, personally launched the "New Life" movement, urging the Chinese to restore the four traditional virtues of their civilization, represented by the four characters: *Li* (politeness), *I* (mutual aid), *Lien* (honesty and respect for the rights of others), and *Chih* (loyalty and honor). "If these virtues are observed," declared Chiang Kai-shek in a manifesto to the nation, "begging and stealing will be eradicated. Civil servants will be honest and patriotic, corruption will end, and people will work more and harder. If these virtues are observed, social and administrative disorder will cease and the people will acquire a more military spirit. To begin with, we must learn habits of order, propriety, simplicity, frugality, and punctuality."[10]

The Generalissimo pointed out further that the virtues extolled by the "New Life" were inherent in the Chinese character and that they had been at the root of the success of the two ancient and celebrated kingdoms, Chi and Chu. But Chiang did not rely on these virtues flourishing suddenly and spontaneously in the hearts of his compatriots. He carried out a series of Draconian measures, going to the point of forbidding young Cantonese men and women to stroll together in the streets or to eat together at the same table in restaurants. In some provinces the police had to daub paint on the arms and legs of women who wore sleeves or skirts too short. Among other measures (in Shantung, for example) was the shaving of women's heads if they wore their hair short or waved. In Nanking civil servants were forbidden to frequent "houses of pleasure" under pain of instant dismissal. National cleanliness weeks were organized during which it was forbidden to smoke in the streets and other public places.[11]

Thirteen hundred local associations created throughout China taught the ninety-six principles of the "New Life" and supervised their application. War against rats and flies was included in the program. Foreign observers reported innumerable comic incidents that resulted from this policy, but the coercion with which it was applied also gave rise to some sinister episodes. According to the noted American liberal historian John King Fairbank, Chiang Kai-shek attacked the problem of the social regeneration of China "with the methods of a commander in chief of the Military Academy."[12] Even supporters of the Nationalist dictator deplored "his intention to refashion China with sword and ax."

But the Kuomintang's "morality" drive was doomed to failure.

[10] See Lachin, Maurice, *La Chine capitaliste* (Paris, Gallimard, 1938), p. 178.

[11] Roger Pelissier, *La Chine entre en scène,* p. 267, quotes the evidence of a French journalist: "The New Life movement is spreading throughout the country. . . . From the moment he arrives at the mouth of the river on which Shanghai is built, the traveler is assailed by slogans exhorting him to be clean, dignified, simple, and honest. If he goes as far as Nanking, he finds these slogans stuck on the telegraph poles, in the boats, buses, and other public vehicles. . . . In the overcrowded areas a sanitary inspector visits each house once a week and sticks up a poster saying 'clean,' 'nearly clean,' or 'dirty,' whichever is the case."

[12] Fairbank, J. K., *The United States and China,* p. 191.

The deterioration in standards of behavior was the result of the deterioration of economic and social relationships; neither preaching nor repression could remedy the decline.

If the Communists have succeeded where their predecessors failed, it is because the total reform of society they have effected undoubtedly favors the flourishing of the virtues advocated by the "New Life" campaign. One is tempted to conclude that the application of Marxist-Leninist principles has been much more effective than the evocation of the principles of the Chi and Chu dynasties; but the matter must clearly be more complicated than that, for in the sphere of "virtue" the other Communist countries have not always scored such successes. Stalin even gave incontestable proof that appeals to Marxist Leninism alone are not enough to persuade people to lead an exemplary life. Despite sermons, threats, and violence, he was indeed powerless to check crime and kill the antisocial spirit in Russia, particularly during the years of World War II. It is true that the U.S.S.R. experienced frightful difficulties and that its economic infrastructure was completely disorganized at times. Draconian laws against speculation and common-law offenses were not enough, under such conditions, to prevent people from violating "socialist morality." They were practically compelled to resort to any means to combat poverty; had they observed legality they would not have survived. Young Soviet citizens brought up in the relative prosperity and the more balanced society of the post-Stalin period cannot imagine that their elders were constantly forced to risk breaking the law, written or moral. Having talked with them, I can testify that (although the U.S.S.R. is still by no means a model country where hygiene and honesty are concerned) the raising of living standards has had very marked "cleansing" effects.

The history of both China and other countries yields ample proof that repression and the preaching of noble moral principles cannot induce people to forget the necessities of daily life, and that these are what determine people's behavior. Economic progress in itself is certainly not enough to improve moral standards, as is abundantly proved by the growth of crime in some highly developed countries. It does, however, create necessary conditions for the effective assimilation of social education.

In Maoist China this education has borne fruit. One is bound to state that despite its visible poverty, this country has been able to solve a number of basic economic problems and to achieve an economic balance which enables its citizens to respect the social rules. This raises the question: how and on what basis was it possible to establish this balance in a society where, according to our estimates (approximate but erring on the side of optimism), annual income per head is still only $120?

It would be risky in answering this question to depend only on official publications. But if one does not find *the* answer in these, there are at least partial answers to be discovered by studying three aspects of Chinese political and economic life: first of all, *planning*, at the same time very centralized and very flexible, which has solved some marketing and food-supply problems; next, the constant attention the Chinese pay to the *improvement of the quality* of what they produce in order to be able to export, which undeniably raises the living standards of the masses; finally, something absolutely basic for the Chinese — the elimination of material incentives and the *raising of the level of political consciousness* of the workers.

What I saw and the conversations I had did not completely enlighten me, and I find certain aspects of China's economic life are still an enigma. The fact is, however, that not only does it "work" but, while the explanations are not always satisfactory, the results obtained are impressive.

FLEXIBLE PLANNING

During recent years few travelers have been authorized to visit the southwestern provinces, and the general assumption has been, therefore, that to the west of the Yangtze China was less "presentable" than the rest of the country.

As a result, having secured permission to enter this region, and in particular Yunnan province, we arrived there especially "vigilant," on the alert for any sign of poverty or wretchedness and eager to compare Kunming (the biggest city in the Southwest) with the "show cities" like Peking and Shanghai.

In fact, Kunming stands up well to the comparison. To begin with, it is favored by nature: situated almost in the tropical zone but at an altitude of 6,500 feet, Kunming enjoys a springlike temperature almost all year round. Everywhere there are trees and gardens. The city is literally festooned with flowers, and its beauty is rounded off by a great lake of an astonishing green. It was not by chance that the French colonials chose this place as an inland resort and linked it to Indochina by railroad at the turn of the century.

Since then — and particularly since 1949 — Kunming has changed a lot. The old city, formerly ringed by a famous wall, today represents only a third of the whole.[13] Everywhere broad tree-lined avenues have been laid out; modern houses and a large theater have been built. Among the showplaces are "parks of culture," a zoo, and a permanent exhibition which records the industrial and agricultural progress of the province. Its many shops are well stocked, and its inhabitants are rather better dressed than the other Chinese. In short, the city is not at all the wretched place we had expected.

Kunming numbers more than a million inhabitants; it is the capital of a province with a population of more than 20 million and is as big as Poland, yet no railroad connects it with the rest of the country. Its only rail link is the line to Hanoi built by the French, which passes through 200 tunnels and whose route is described in old guidebooks as one of the most picturesque in the world.

Of course Kunming is not completely cut off from the rest of China. The famous Burma road by which the Americans supplied Chiang Kai-shek at the end of World War II passes through Yunnan. Nevertheless, given the low level of motorized transpor-

[13] "The main port of entry for all Americans into China [during the war] was Kunming, capital of Yunnan. . . . Its streets, its alleyways were filthy; it was one of the national strongholds of the opium merchants. Almost up to the outbreak of war its prostitutes were penned in a street chained off at both ends; rich families bought girl slaves to serve in the household. The province was ruled by a curious character named Lung Yun, one of the most devious and shaky supports of the national government. . . . Of the 70,000 Americans in China probably half were stationed for a longer or shorter period in the Kunming hostels. . . . Six to eight men, crammed into one room, slept on double-tiered bunks; helmets, gas masks, foot lockers, barracks bags, tumbled about in the dust and confusion of the little cubicles. The Americans were nauseated by the filth, grease, and general putrefaction of the messes, which, however, were cleaner than anything the Chinese army had for itself; almost every American who ate at them came down with some variety of dysentery or diarrhea during his stay in China. . . . The American soldiers worked during daylight hours and saw the city usually after dark. Once or twice a week, or as often as they could get a pass, enlisted men would pour into town in search of wine, women, and entertainment, and Chinese touts and racketeers would pluck them clean. . . . Venereal disease rates soared." White, Theodore H., and Jacoby, Annalee, *Thunder out of China* (New York, Sloane, 1946), pp. 160ff.

In *Journey to the Beginning*, Edgar Snow also describes the unhealthy conditions and bandit morality which ravaged Kunming when he passed through it before the war. He writes particularly of children working in the tin mines and of the banditry which made it practically impossible for anyone to venture outside the city.

tation, one could expect that supplies to this city whose population has quadrupled since 1949 might be erratic. They are nothing of the kind; Kunming's prosperity is one of the most striking illustrations of the gigantic efforts China has made to narrow — and even abolish — the tremendous inequalities which still existed among different provinces only fifteen years ago. According to Mr. Li Wei, deputy mayor of Kunming, Mao's government has done everything "to enable the outlying provinces to walk on two legs — one provided for them by the central government, the other made by themselves."

The "government's leg" is obviously heavy industry. Before the war Kunming had some embryonic industry. The region's copper and tin mines (the latter produce two thirds of China's exports of this metal) had long been worked. Today deposits of iron and coal have been discovered in the province, and a large steelworks has been built. And a factory (owned by a capitalistic bureaucrat) had been processing imported raw materials since 1938. After 1949 this was converted for the manufacture of mining equipment. It now makes heavy machine tools — in 1958 it was the first factory in China to produce these, and it made the four 5- to 9-ton models sent to the Chinese exhibition in Paris.[14]

This key factory (it even publishes its own newspaper) obviously depends on the Ministry of Heavy Industry, but its development has stimulated that of the whole industrial sector of Kunming and Yunnan province: ancillary enterprises have been set up; new factories have been equipped with its machinery; roads, technical schools, and new housing have been built.

Up to this point Kunming's history conforms to the classical pattern of industrialization carried out by the center around a number of regional pilot plants. But the example of Kunming be-

---

[14] The factory manager Fan Tzi-tan, a former metallurgical worker from Shenyang, talked to us at length about the visit of Soviet experts who in 1957 had been called in to give their advice on the possibility of producing precision machines of this type. The Russians offered negative advice: "With the equipment at your disposal and given the slight technical training of your workers, you cannot manufacture precision machinery." They particularly stressed the absence of workshops with a constant temperature, necessary for this kind of manufacture. But according to Mr. Fan Tzi-tan, the Russians underestimated the ingenuity and capacity for innovation of the Chinese. "We have a constant temperature almost all year round in our city," he said. "That was already a start." If he is to be believed, the factory produced its first precision machine barely a few months after the pessimistic Soviet experts' visit. Since then it has obviously perfected its equipment and it is continuing to expand.

comes particularly significant when one notes that this rapid industrial growth has not caused any of the imbalances which accompany a massive influx of manpower (remember that the city's population increased four-fold in fifteen years). It was mainly about this phenomenon that I questioned Mr. Li Wei.

"Responsibility," he explained, "is shared by the central government and the municipality. In Peking, for example, they decide to increase the production of machine tools or to set up new factories in Kunming, but it is we who are responsible for the well-being of our population. As a result we have our say on the sites of factories — they mustn't be built on cultivated land, or be too far from the commercial center, or inconvenience the local people in any way. It is we who hire the new workers; we have to provide their accommodations, transportation, medical care, and, of course, food supplies (the latter by assessing the potential of the people's communes in the suburbs). All this is expensive. So that we can cope with this expenditure the government allows us to deduct part of the allocation provided for by the development of factories. We are therefore the people most interested in the success of the government plan — if the production of the central industry goes up by a foot, the living standards in our town are raised by an inch.

"Besides the government plan there is a plan at the provincial level in which we take part under the same conditions, and we ourselves work out our own plan. We carry this out with what we have 'earned' by our participation in the other two plans and which enables us not only to meet social expenses but also to establish factories which are directly under us. Certain industries (processing agricultural products, textiles, clothing) need only relatively light investments which, moreover, are quickly amortized. In order to make these light industries profitable it is enough to use the raw materials rationally and adapt them as much as possible to the needs of consumers. Besides, we get help and advice at the start from provinces already specializing in whatever it is we are undertaking."

Mr. Li Wei is originally from Shanghai. In 1937 he went to Yenan. Although since the start of his revolutionary career he has done at least two days' manual work each week without fail, he has the air of a 100-per-cent intellectual. He has a very systematic manner but never gives the impression that he is reciting a catechism. He acknowledged that the present Chinese economic system is very complex and that it has been formed in stages, not without serious mistakes having been made. By his own admission, Kunming is still a long way from being perfectly satisfactory, for certain municipal industries have not yet attained the standards of quality specified by the national plan. It seemed to me that if the government imposed certain requirements, the municipality did not enjoy as much autonomy as Mr. Li Wei claimed.

"No," he replied. "The prices of goods are fixed on a national level in terms of their quality. For instance, cotton goods must possess certain characteristics before the distribution people will buy from us to sell at the fixed price. They can reject our product. Our municipal enterprises are only profitable if the quality of production satisfies government standards, which are those of the consumers." What is true for industry is equally applicable to agriculture. Kunming is supplied with fruit and vegetables entirely by the suburban people's communes with a minimum of middlemen and transportation costs, which places them at a lower rate than the average national rate. A third of the meat and cereals consumed are also provided by the communes, and Mr. Li Wei intends to reduce "imports from other provinces" still further in the future.

Escorting me back to my hotel, Mr. Li Wei complained about the inability of foreigners to understand the Chinese system. A French journalist to whom he had revealed his preoccupations and expressed the desire that his province might become self-sufficient lectured him on this obnoxious policy of "relying on his own resources." According to this journalist, China was a very backward country because she fell back on herself, with no desire to learn from abroad. Mr. Li Wei found this way of looking at things absurd and false.

"If," he said, "we can produce here the kind of goods the old war lords of Yunnan never dreamed existed, it is thanks to the national plan and the state's help. It is the state which has enabled us to exploit our own resources and to develop ourselves. Even when we come to satisfy all our own needs, we shall not be doing so as regionalists. We shall be contributing to the economic life of the country. In the same way China can only contribute to the economic life of the world if she is first of all able to develop her productive capacity."

For the last six years China has not published any more economic statistics. It is very difficult to estimate what her total production might be and even more difficult to estimate her production in specific sectors. The Soviet experts who worked in

China until 1960 took a dim view of the enormous waste resulting from a multiplicity of abortive experiments and trials.[15] But it would be euphemistic to say that their evidence is not always impartial.

In a country as big as China and which has an extremely limited transportation system, it is probable that in fact only the production of consumer goods in the different provinces could prevent too great an inequality in the living standards of their respective populations.

We have no means of judging the efficiency and profitability of a system which, while aiming at and achieving great centralization, at the same time encourages local enterprise. But we can state that the quantity and quality of goods available in all the towns we visited satisfy the demand and even seem to exceed it.

At the Kunming industrial fair we saw radios, bicycles, ready-made clothing, textiles of all kinds, and a mass of metallurgical products — all made in Yunnan, although fifteen years ago none of these were manufactured in the province. The retail price of these goods is high, particularly if compared with that of agricultural products.[16]

[15] One imagines, in fact, that at the time that each people's commune had to "industrialize" itself by its own efforts, the municipalities, large or small, had to undertake minor projects which went against "industrial logic." In the towns, however, they would have had to distinguish very quickly between viable and nonviable enterprises.

[16] Here, by way of example, are some prices displayed in state shops. The yuan is worth about forty cents (or three shillings or two French francs). It is divided into ten mao and one hundred fen. The note of highest value in circulation is worth five yuan (two dollars, fifteen shillings, ten francs), and the smallest coin is one fen. These indications are necessary, but the Chinese consumer and pay systems are so different from ours that any comparisons made on the basis of figures alone would not be valid.

Agricultural Products

Rice: 1 kg—20 fen (rationed)
Potatoes: 1 kg—5 fen
Cabbage: 1 kg—10 fen
Tomatoes: 1 kg—2 fen
Eggs: 10—45 fen
Spinach: 1 kg—5 fen
Butter: 1 kg—8 yuan 40 fen
Szechwan salami: 1 kg—4 yuan
Milk: 1 liter—20 fen (for children)
Wine: 1 liter—1.5 to 3.2 yuan

Manufactured Products

Trousers (linen): 9.12 yuan
Trousers (gabardine): 36.50 yuan
Shirt (man's): 6 to 8.70 yuan
Shoes (canvas, man's): 4.45 yuan
Shoes (leather): from 15 to 36.80 yuan
Fancy jacket (woman's): from 31 to 37 yuan
Printed cotton (woman's): 3.20 yuan
Heeled shoes (chic): 16.30 yuan
Radio (4 valves): 60 yuan
Bicycle: from 166 to 190 yuan

But nowhere did we see any signs of scarcity, such as the lines outside shops one still sees in socialist countries much richer than China. Foreign diplomats in Peking who know the countries of eastern Europe admit that the centralized machinery in China operates much more flexibly.

This success and what one might call not abundance but the steady satisfaction of vital needs obviously act as an incentive to the population and cement national unity. A young Chinese person of today knows he will never again be cooped up in his village, or even in his province, and he knows that his work contributes to the raising of everyone's living standards — and therefore to his own.

This last phrase runs the risk of sounding like a propaganda slogan. Perhaps, and so much the worse. Any traveler could write it after having spent some time in China, on the condition, of course, that he was sincere, that he had a vague idea of what China was like only fifteen years ago, and that — it is not much to ask — he had intelligence enough not to hark back constantly to the superabundance of the well-fed countries of Europe and America.

THE THICKNESS OF A SLICE OF MUTTON

The best place for Mongol cooking in Peking is an old restaurant in the heart of the city; it is in the covered market of Tung-An, always swarming with customers who forage among the widely varied stands which include stalls selling foreign-language books. The restaurant in question is relatively small and its "productive capacity" is limited by the fact that it offers its patrons not just one private room for a party but often two. In the first room you eat the dishes that have to be boiled (you do this yourself on the self-service principle); in the second there are miniature charcoal stoves on which you grill mutton that has already been cut and prepared for you. By European standards the succulent meals served here are not very expensive (five yuan per person at the most), but for the Chinese they are obviously a luxury.

Madame Hélène Marchisio has compiled a list of comparative prices in several towns (mainly concerning food products) which is more comprehensive than the above table. It shows that differences are slight from one province to another. See Bettelheim, Charles, Charrier, Jacques, and Marchisio, Hélène, *La Construction du socialisme en Chine* (Paris, Masero, 1965), pp. 122–124.

But a few years after the Liberation (I was not given the exact date), at the time of the socializing offensive, the authorities suddenly become worried about the "select" character of this restaurant and decree that it must be opened to a wider cross section of the people. There is one way to do it — serve many more meals and thus bring down the prices. The old chef, who has always cut up the meat himself and, when necessary, helped out the less dexterous customers, flatly declares that he cannot accept the new working conditions. He is a man of principle, remarkably uncompromising, and no one is able to change his mind. So he is replaced by younger, more dynamic cooks who agree to the lowering of prices, which they think will be offset by a big increase in the number of customers. At the start there are, indeed, crowds of new customers, then fewer, and finally practically none at all; even the regulars no longer come. No one can understand why; indeed, the Mongol restaurant serves only raw ingredients which are still supplied by the same wholesaler and are therefore of exactly the same quality. So an investigation is carried out, and eventually the reason for the customers' dissatisfaction is revealed — the new cooks do not possess the right touch with a kitchen knife and fail to cut the mutton into thin enough slices, which are absolutely essential for good Mongol cooking.

It turns out that one of the disappointed regular customers is a friend of Chairman Mao and that he has told him about the whole affair. Mao gives his view: "The old cook must be reinstated and allowed to do things his own way. It's much better to progress slowly than to sacrifice quality. As for the young cooks, they shouldn't be dismissed but should learn from the old chef how to slice mutton properly; and when they have mastered the art, it will be possible to open the restaurant to a wider clientele."

This Solomon-like judgment of Mao's was known not only in Nan Hai (the park next to the old imperial city where the country's top leaders live). It was also familiar to all the cadres, who applied its moral in their own particular spheres — so one is told and no doubt it is true, for according to the Chinese (and for the Chinese), basic lessons can be taught by simple examples. Thus (according to the Chinese friend who told me this story and guaranteed its authenticity) Mao, by his judgment in the case of the Mongol restaurant, had recalled an idea that he had propagated during the heroic Yenan days: "All that the old China could do the new China will do — and better." Was this resolution forgotten in the excitement of preparing and implementing the "Great Leap Forward" of 1958 to 1960? The reply one gets from the Chinese, despite their capacity for self-criticism, is never categoric. It is either "Yes, errors were committed" or "Yes, we lacked experience." The important point, they say, is that most errors were corrected during the period of readjustment (which came to an end in 1964) and that the promise made by Mao in Yenan has been kept. After which they tell you that in all branches of industry the quality of Chinese products is improving as quickly as their quantity is increasing, and they assure you, although offering neither figures nor statistics, that this is saying quite a bit.

How can one check up? If a comparison with the past is made, one must admit without hesitation that the Chinese are right. Their country today produces more varied goods, heavy industrial equipment, and even atomic bombs — something beyond the old China's dreams. But whether the quality of Chinese production (particularly in the sphere of heavy industry) is up to the standard of other countries and is advancing by leaps and bounds is a question even a technician would find it difficult to answer.

We visited various factories, particularly those manufacturing chemical products, which were completely equipped with machines made in China. We saw that most of the equipment in factories as complex as one in Shanghai that makes optical goods was also made in China. At Wuhan and at Shenyang we were taken around giant factories which manufacture heavy machinery for the new steelworks. Finally, at Ming Hang, a Shanghai satellite town, we were invited to admire the 12,000-metric-ton hydraulic press, one of the most difficult pieces of machinery to install correctly (there are only nine in the whole world), which the Chinese built "by relying on our own strength." And the assembly lines of trucks at Changchun and tractors at Loyang (legacy of Russia's pre-1960 aid) include Chinese machinery and parts. In 1949, at the end of the civil war, China produced only 158,000 (metric) tons of steel a year. Today, according to conservative estimates, she produces more than 15 million tons and can build on her own each year new steelworks producing a million and a half tons. This puts China among the great industrial powers; the fact that she now imports very little quality steel proves that the range of her own steel production has been greatly increased.

Paradoxically, during the first nine years of the regime, while the CP followed a "moderate" economic policy, no one denied that the Chinese were making tremendous progress. The results they achieved during the period of economic reconstruction (1949–1952) and during the first Five-Year Plan (1953–1957) impressed even the most anti-Maoist of experts. After sifting Peking's official statistics, the American economist William H. Hollister concluded that the Five-Year Plan had raised the gross national product of China by 11 per cent a year, while during the same period India's rose by only 4 per cent.[17]

Other critical U.S. observers, like A. Doak Barnett, admitted that "Communist China . . . may be able, within a relatively short time, to build a heavy industry base stronger than that of Japan, which today is the only industrialized state in Asia."[18]

But when, in February, 1958, the People's Congress in Peking approved the new Five-Year Plan which proposed to put the "Great Leap Forward" into effect and to advance at a pace never before attained, in defiance of all the classic economic laws, practically the whole world expressed skepticism, which was soon justified by the facts. We have already seen that the bid to industrialize the people's communes had to be dropped. Many other projects also had to be abandoned: too much ambition, too much zeal led to waste and brought only disillusionment.

After drawing up the balance sheet of its achievements in 1959, on the occasion of its tenth anniversary, the Chinese government decided not to publish any more statistics.[19] Since then it has been

[17] Hollister, William W., *China's Gross National Product and Social Accounts, 1950–1957* (Glencoe, The Free Press, 1958).

[18] Barnett, A. Doak, *Communist China and Asia* (New York, Harper, 1960), p. 38.

[19] Here are some extracts from the speech Chou En-lai made at the time: "According to the adjusted planned figures for 1959 (it can now already be foreseen that most of planned targets will be fulfilled), the total output value of industry and agriculture will be 5.3 times that of 1949; of this total the value of industrial production will be 11.7 times larger. Steel output will reach 12 million tons, 76 times the 1949 figure of 158,000 tons; coal, 335 million tons, more than 10 times the 1949 figure of 32,430,000 tons; electric power, 39,000 million kilowatt-hours, more than 9 times the 1949 figure of 4,310 million kilowatt-hours; and cotton yarn, 8.2 million bales, 4.5 times the 1949 figure of 1.8 million bales. In 1958, China jumped to seventh place in the world in steel, third place in coal, eleventh place in electric power and second place in cotton yarn production. Even though modern industry had been introduced for nearly a century, fixed industrial assets totalled less than 13,000 million yuan by 1949 in old China; in the ten years of New China the value of newly added fixed industrial assets

possible to speak of the failure of the "Great Leap Forward" and question the reality of progress in China. Further, as the Chinese were forced to cancel certain big projects already under way, following the departure of the Soviet technicians in 1960, one can logically assume that there really is a "Chinese crisis."

We were struck by one fact, however — more than half the heavy factories we visited had been built (and many others noticeably enlarged) during the time of the "Great Leap." It seems, therefore, that China made considerable progress during those ill-fated years which, as is known, were further overshadowed by a series of natural disasters.[20]

The Russians even take the view that there has been overproduction in China's heavy industry. According to them the bottleneck occurred during the "Great Leap" because China could neither utilize nor export the heavy machinery she blindly manufactured with the sole aim of producing as much as possible. To me the Soviet arguments do not appear convincing, all the less so because they tend to justify the Russians' hasty withdrawal by explaining that their counsel of moderation fell on deaf Chinese ears. However, a number of detailed examples were cited for us which show that in the Northeast, for example, industry encountered the same kind of trouble as the Mongol restaurant: the enormous increase in output was neither matched by a comparable improvement in quality nor related to demand.

This impression seems to be borne out by some Chinese explanations. "We thought that eight to ten million tons of good-quality steel of adequate type was more essential than eighteen million tons of mediocre steel," said Po I-po, a vice-chairman of the government and chairman of the State Economic Commission, justifying the industrial "readjustment" policy.[21]

---

amounts to around 45,000 million yuan. . . . Now we have ourselves begun to produce about 500 types of steel and 6,000 types of rolled steel . . ." Chou En-lai, *A Great Decade* (Peking, Foreign Languages Press, 1959), pp. 3, 5.

[20] "It hits one between the eyes that the famous 'Leap Forward' in 1958, even if it finished badly, was not the complete failure it is sometimes said abroad to have been. It has at least left behind a considerable number of buildings, establishments, and constructions of all kinds — factories, to begin with, and an incredible number of housing projects that were begun at the same time. On top of that, there is a huge number of public buildings and heavy construction projects." Guillain, Robert, *Dans Trente Ans la Chine* (Paris, Seuil, 1965), p. 24.

[21] Strong, Anna Louise, *The Rise of the Chinese People's Communes* (Peking, New World Press, 1964).

And in his report to the People's Congress of 1964, Chou En-lai declared that this policy had been "carried out for basic reasons" and that the range of Chinese production "had been expanded over these last four years to about 24,000 new varieties, that is to say, three times more than during the great expansion of 1958 to 1960." According to Chou, quality was very much improved and "in the case of certain products we have attained, or almost, the level of the world's best."[22] In the same report the Chinese Premier spoke also of the increase in total production, which in 1964 was 15 per cent higher than that of the previous year.

Obviously Chou En-lai's claims have not been enough to dispel the doubts of foreign observers, who are still awaiting the publication of the precise figures on the third Chinese Five-Year Plan (1966–1970), which is already — in theory — under way, and the "discretion" of Chinese officials on this subject is the constant theme of conversations in Peking's diplomatic community. This significant silence confirms all assumptions. "Perhaps this plan doesn't even exist," say some. "Without the help of Soviet economists the Chinese weren't capable of carrying it out and they don't dare admit it." According to others, the Chinese are keeping mum to hide their colossal military expenditure from the world. Still others allege that if the Chinese gave the exact figures on their economic potential, they would risk revealing the strength (or the weakness) of their atomic arsenal. Yet another group — the most cautious — confines itself to the suspicion that the Chinese have not yet solved their overproduction crisis and have failed to use to the fullest extent their existing heavy industry.

The Chinese government itself is plainly responsible for this climate of skepticism, for it does not even attempt to offer a plausible explanation of its silence. "Our statistics are solely for internal use," say the Chinese leaders, assuming that this reply closes the matter. It is not for us to explain (and still less for us to justify) this attitude, but it is certain that it induces a certain malaise. While visiting factories, even the best, we were on our guard and tempered our enthusiasm. At each workshop "closed for repairs," each machine "temporarily out of order" we became more suspicious. For instance, when we visited the metallurgical combine at Anshan, obviously no "Potemkin village," its great rail factory was "refitting" for several hours. Perhaps this was perfectly normal, but in view of the doubts that nagged us, this stoppage intrigued us, shall we say.

22 *Pékin Information,* No. 1 (January, 1965).

That aside, we never had the impression, despite our professional "distrust," that the Chinese factories were operating at low pressure and failing to exploit their full potential. Without accepting official declarations on the expansion and continuing development of industry, we can say that everything we saw convinced us that the biting skepticism of the Peking diplomatic colony was unjustified. There is no doubt that Chinese heavy industry is no longer developing as fast as at the start of the "Great Leap" — at that time it had absolute priority — and not even at the end of the third Five-Year Plan will China's total production overtake Great Britain's. However, she is advancing quickly all the same; one need only see the enormous quantities of heavy machinery destined to equip China herself which leave the factories of Shenyang, Wuhan, Anshan, and Kunming — not to mention the factories of Shanghai, which remains China's first industrial city. It is astounding to see how a country able to produce such equipment has "got off the ground," taken such a decisive step along the road to industrialization, even if in certain circumstances the pace of its development can slow down. Thus it seems today that if China is producing less it is because she is giving priority to quality — which suggests a new leap forward in the near future.

During our "inspections" of Chinese factories our guides always insisted that we examine the plates on the machinery indicating the place of manufacture. Most often they wanted us to verify that they were of Chinese make. But on other occasions they also wanted us to see that they were of Russian origin so that they could "deny the lying assertion of Suslov, who in his report of February, 1964, declared that the Chinese were trying to wipe out the traces of Soviet aid." And it is a fact that all the machinery of Soviet origin still carries inscriptions in Russian.[23]

In verifying these "identity plates" on machines we had a few surprises. In Changchun we visited the big "Liberation" factory, which makes four-ton trucks and which was entirely equipped by the Russians during the first Chinese Five-Year Plan (1953–1957). In the engine workshop four new machines bore the legend "Made in U.S.A."[24] "Yes," explained our guide calmly, "we

---

[23] Our guides did not fail to make plain that "what Suslov calls Soviet aid the Chinese paid a stiff price for." No doubt, but it is certain the Russian equipment considerably facilitated the start.

[24] On one of these machines there were even the words "Property of the U.S. Government."

bought them because this workshop has been very much enlarged; we manufacture many more engines than trucks. The surplus is used for irrigation pumps in the people's communes." "But what about the American embargo?" The guide smiled: "That's their affair, not ours."

One also sees machines that have come from Europe and Japan. Always without the slightest embarrassment the guides explain: "We always rely above all on our own productive capacity, but when it is necessary we buy abroad." Quite often foreign technicians come to install and start running the machinery supplied by their country. Even in our hotel in distant Harbin there was a Swiss engineer who was "accompanying" his machinery. And in Peking there are many more foreign technicians than foreign journalists or foreign guests.

The Chinese still avoid relying on one supplier and spread their foreign orders around. This allows them to encourage competition among Western firms and protects them from the whims and political changes of foreign governments. No European country is the "most favored" in China, and the *rapprochement* with France has provided no special conditions for French businessmen and industrialists. "Business is business": despite its hostility to the Wilson government, China gives large orders to Britain (notably in the chemical industry field).[25] And Japanese, Italians, and West Germans, no matter how pro-American they might be, are all trying to secure a foothold in the Chinese market,[26] on the one hand because the market offers very profitable outlets for certain industries facing difficulties[27] and on the other because the Chinese, while they are exacting customers, already have a reputation for being particularly "correct."

Observing this expansion of foreign imports, which today total

[25] According to the London *Sunday Times* of October 17, 1965, of fifteen complete factories ordered from Western countries by China, four were being supplied by Britain. The first (a chemical fertilizer plant by Humphreys and Glasgow) is already under construction in Szechwan province. All are of an average value of three million to four million pounds (about eight to eleven million dollars).

[26] During the winter of 1965 the West Germans contracted (despite U.S. opposition) to build a new steelworks in China with a capacity of 4.5 million tons. As for the Italians, they have secured an order for an oil refinery, and they are already supplying chemical fertilizers.

[27] This seems to be true in the case of the French firm Berliet, which sold six million dollars' worth of trucks to the Chinese (and ought to sell still more) at a time when it envisaged a serious reduction in the working week.

about $1,700,000,000 a year, one comes naturally to ask the question: Where does China find the tremendous sums of foreign currency to meet these bills?

Some accuse the Chinese of being "fed" by their rich compatriots in Southeast Asia and of benefiting from "very capitalistic" commercial deals in Hong Kong. The British also supply them with a certain amount of currency to ensure the supply of provisions to their colonial enclave in China (they even buy drinking water from Canton). These explanations would have been sufficient when China hardly traded with the capitalist world: this was still the case from 1953 until 1957. In effect, trade with the U.S.S.R. then represented 56.39 per cent and trade with the people's democracies 19.1 per cent of China's total foreign trade.

But the volume of trade with the U.S.S.R. has continued to decline since 1958, as has trade with the people's democracies more recently. Today the greatest part of Chinese foreign trade is with non-Communist countries; and if one is aware of the aspirations of Japanese[28] and European businessmen, it is possible to foresee that in the not-too-distant future Chinese imports will represent almost three billion dollars annually. It is obvious that such a sum cannot be provided each year by a few rich foreign Chinese or by a few secret deals.

No. If the Chinese can import more and more it is because they export more and more. Not only, as in former days, raw materials, precious metals, and agricultural products such as soya and tea, but also textiles of all kinds, craft products, and manufactured goods.

In May, 1965, an English colleague who had come back from the Canton biennial fair assured me that foreign buyers had bought up 700 million dollars' worth of Chinese goods. As the fair lasts only a few days, one could suspect the Englishman of exaggerating a little. However, it is a fact that in all the textile factories we visited the packaging departments were filled with goods marked "Made in China" and therefore obviously not intended for the domestic market. It is also a small but telling point that in the center of Hong Kong there is a three-story Peking government

---

[28] The Japanese Foreign Minister, Mr. Etsusaburo Shiina, declared at the beginning of 1965 that he hoped Chinese-Japanese trade would reach one billion dollars before 1970. Some time later, when the Sato government refused to give the Chinese credit to buy ships, the order for the latter went to the French, who, ready to grant facilities for payment, were surprised to find the Chinese paying in cash.

enterprise permanently as crowded with shoppers as a Western department store on Christmas Eve, in which one can literally find any article and at quite low prices. But Hong Kong is without doubt the world's best shopping center for imported consumer goods; it is not the place to try to sell poor-quality goods, even at cut-rate prices.

Which brings us back to our sheep, or rather to "the thickness of the slice of mutton" in the Mongol restaurant in Peking whose story reveals the Chinese concern with quality.

Light industry, say the Chinese economists, acts as a link between agricultural production and heavy industry. One can also say that it is their light industry which is enabling the Chinese to take their place in world trade.

If light industry isn't the dynamo of Chinese progress, it provides the current which drives it. Having acquired most of their experience in the past in light industry, the Chinese are putting this to good use. Hearing them talk of "the need to provide the people with adequate supplies of goods" or saying that "there is no point in increasing their wages if at the same time we do not make available the commodities they need," certain analogies come to mind. Following the civil war in 1921, Lenin and his group used very similar language. Their country was put to a terrible test: for several years they had lived under "war communism" conditions, which were marked by the total mobilization of resources and population. There had to be a respite, and the Bolsheviks organized one. This was the NEP (New Economic Policy), under which consumer goods reappeared for a time. Long after it had been abandoned in 1927 a whole clandestine folklore recalled the NEP period as the good old days. True or false, it was still being whispered about in 1939 when I arrived in the U.S.S.R.

After the effort of the "Great Leap" would the Chinese have concluded, like Lenin forty years earlier: ". . . we had advanced too far . . . we had not secured a sufficient base . . . the masses had sensed what we ourselves could not as yet consciously formulate . . . namely, that the direct transition to purely Socialist forms, to purely Socialist distribution, was beyond our strength, and that, unless we proved able to retreat and to confine ourselves to easier tasks, we would be threatened with disaster."[29] And

[29] See Deutscher, Isaac, *Stalin* (New York, Oxford University Press, 1949), p. 221.

doesn't the Chinese period of "consolidation and readjustment" of the economy correspond to that of the Soviet NEP?

Perhaps. But in the U.S.S.R. in 1921 the economy was still not entirely a socialist one, and it was enough to abandon the "war communism" restrictions for private enterprise to take over production and distribution of consumer goods. The Russian rural areas had still not been collectivized, and the ending of compulsory requisitioning allowed a return to the traditional market economy. Certainly heavy industry, banks, and the transportation system remained in the hands of the state, which did not lack the means of controlling the other sectors, but basically the NEP sanctioned the creation of a mixed economy.

In 1960 nothing like this was possible in China.[30] The government and the CP had no one to whom they could delegate powers to "restore" the consumer goods industry and domestic commerce. They were compelled to do it themselves within the existing socialist framework, which they had no intention of modifying. The task was not easy. For confirmation one need only recall the disappointments experienced by other socialist countries confronted by the same problem. It appears that China's leaders have found solutions which permitted the "purely socialist" production and distribution of goods capable of competing on a worldwide scale.

The importance of this success should not be exaggerated. Indeed, it is known how many doubts there have been for some years about the possibility of producing a diversified range of consumer goods and of distributing them effectively without having to resort to private enterprise and without bribing the workers with material incentives.

Many Westerners in favor of the nationalization of all the means of production have come to the conclusion that light industry and

---

[30] It is only fair to underline the fact that China began to apply her policy of "readjustment" under conditions incomparably better than those prevailing in the Soviet Union. In 1921 Russia had been ravaged by seven years of war, national and civil. The working class was decimated, the peasantry ruined, and the bourgeoisie either in exile or in prison. They were the worst conditions in which to carry out a policy of rapid socialization. China herself encountered difficulties more than ten years after the new regime had taken over, following a period of growth that was too "spontaneous" and too costly, but which in no way impoverished the country. It sufficed occasionally to slow down the rhythm of the "Great Leap" for economic tension to be reduced. And, in any case, the means of "consolidation and readjustment" existed.

commerce ought to be left to the capitalists, the only people able to make them work. Even in the U.S.S.R., where such a return to the past is impossible, economists are trying to bring the mechanism of competition and market forces into play to "revitalize" these sectors.

China is perhaps the exception which proves the rule, but her consumer goods industries and services function well without recourse to material incentives. Certainly, enterprises are authorized to conclude bilateral contracts between themselves, and wholesale trade is controlled by very flexible regulations; but it does not appear that producers share profits or that the staff receives any commission on sales. It is a small point, possibly, but no one in China ever accepts a tip. Another point is that hotels for foreigners are more than merely adequate, which is more than one can often say about hotels in other socialist countries. But (and it is no longer a question of small points) it seems to me rather unlikely that in provincial towns, for example, Nanning or Kweilin (which see six foreigners a year at the most), they might have stocked the shops simply to impress us. At Nanning we went into a popular restaurant where the staff was holding a political meeting, and out of pure curiosity we took a look at the menu; sixteen different fish dishes appeared on it, none costing more than fifty fen (twenty cents).

Of course, there is a dark side to this picture. Very often in shops there are more salespeople than necessary. In an antique shop in Changsha which did not seem to do a lot of business (three times we went there, and three times we were the only customers) there were six assistants, each more attentive than the last. In provincial hotels, built when there were plenty of Soviet technicians around but deserted today, it looks as if they have kept on practically all the staff. In the big department stores there is an incredible number of salespeople — most of them apprentices, explain the Chinese when one expresses surprise; they could also add that all this tends to prove that they do not worry too much about service costs, and in the short run the consumers can only gain from this state of affairs.

Foreigners often explain the efficient functioning of light industry and distribution in China by the country's old commercial tradition and also by the attention which the new regime pays to efficient cadres, even when they are former owners. In fact, the Communists have been extremely indulgent toward those who have rallied to their side, and as we have already seen, the "national bourgeoisie" is represented by a star on the Red flag. The old capitalists — there are 90,000 in Shanghai alone — still work, and I interviewed one of them — in Shanghai, of course.[31] Mr. Liu Lei-i receives 5 per cent annual interest on the value of his enterprises (nationalized in 1953) but in money which cannot be converted or invested. Which means, in effect, that he deposits practically all of this money in the national bank, and the government allows him only to satisfy his individual needs as a consumer. This does not cost the country very much compared to the great experience and technical know-how Mr. Liu Lei-i puts at its disposal.

Yet another explanation of China's success in the field of light industry seems to be that she was driven by sheer necessity. "Our country suffered various disasters," I was told by Mr. Yuang Lung-kwei, one of China's greatest economists. "The disaster of our mistakes, the natural disasters of the years 1959 and 1960, and

[31] Son of one of the biggest capitalists in Shanghai, Liu Lei-i studied at Cambridge. He sympathized (discreetly) with the Communists before their victory because, he said, "At any rate, things cannot go any worse than they did in the Kuomintang's last days." He is at present vice-president of the Chamber of Commerce, manager of a factory, and a deputy of the People's Congress.

The policy of tolerance toward big capitalists certainly helped in the reconstruction of the economy when the new regime was being created. It is probable that Mao Tse-tung envisaged the continuation of this policy over a long period, as he had announced in his essay on the new democracy. But for several years circumstances have forced him to put the emphasis on egalitarianism and political incentives, now considered the main driving force of development. Within the social framework which has evolved there is no longer any place for the capitalists, and their presence now strikes a jarring note.

I admit that this contradiction in Maoist policy was crystal clear: on the one hand they preached an almost evangelical egalitarianism, and on the other they preserved the privileges of several thousand Chinese who were entitled to a very much higher standard of living simply because they were already wealthy before the revolution. This contradiction could obviously be resolved in a manner less violent than that employed by the Red Guards. From the end of August, 1966, they besieged the homes of big capitalists, demanding that they hand over all valuable possessions to the state and begin to lead a really proletarian life. Even Dr. Sun Yat-sen's widow, although no capitalist, and despite the fact that she is still Vice-Chairman of the Republic, was taken to task by the young egalitarians because her house in Shanghai appeared to them to be too bourgeois. Chou En-lai had to defend her during a rally in Peking. Madame Sun Yat-sen will no doubt be able to continue living as before, but it is more than likely that capitalists like Mr. Liu Lei-i will no longer be paid their annual 5 per cent interest.

finally the Russian disaster." And he added that China owed a
great debt of gratitude to Khrushchev. "We know he wanted to
destroy us by recalling his technicians and canceling all the contracts between us. But in doing so he merely compelled us to rely
on our own strength and to find original solutions." There is certainly some truth in this caustic explanation, but it must also be
added that since 1960 China has been forced to increase imports
from the non-Communist world in order to avoid collapse and that
she can only pay for them with the products of her agriculture and
light industry. Agriculture is therefore considered today to be the
"basic sector," but gradually consumer goods are moving to the top
of the list of Chinese exports. This absolute necessity for China to
concentrate her efforts on a sector generally neglected by other
socialist countries (at least in the first stage of their development)
has been to the Chinese consumer's advantage. For China to be
competitive in the markets of Southeast Asia she has had to
improve the quality of the goods she exports, and at the same time
she has also had to improve those intended for the home market.
All the Chinese I talked with refused to admit any of these explanations of their success; they will not concede that what happens
inside China might depend, however little, on either international
trade or the technical legacy from the old regime.

According to them, their economic success in all fields is entirely due to a strict adherence to the wishes of the masses. They
talk at length of the opportunities that consumers have to express
their preferences before the final version of the article is put on
sale, of the control exercised by the distributive organizations over
producers, and of the law which punishes those who supply goods
that do not conform to the written contract. In short, they wish to
prove that the economy functions according to a democratic
mechanism.

They do not always succeed in convincing you because a great
number of comparable measures have been taken in other spheres
without producing very striking results and because all socialist
countries always boast that their economy is a democratic one.
Besides, how did it happen that the "democratic mechanism" was
unable to avoid the "calamity of errors" at the time of the "Great
Leap Forward"? The Chinese do not allow themselves to be
bothered by this kind of question. "None of our concepts has
changed since 1958, and the 'Great Leap' continues. It is always
featured among the three red banners of the Party." How, then, is

one to understand the policy of readjustment and the successes it has achieved?

"One thing certainly helped you when you were in trouble: you are the heirs of an ancient civilization rich in experience and capable of adapting itself," I say to the man who told me the story of the Mongol restaurant, partly to provoke him. "Wasn't it the old chef who saved the restaurant because he had always known how to cut the mutton in thin enough slices?"

"Not at all. In this matter it is the Party which played the decisive role because it was very close to the masses and knew how to satisfy their demands. It was the Party which enabled the old chef to put his talents at the people's service, and it was not to make money that he took up his job again."

Whomever one talks with in China, one always ends up listening to the same assertion: "So that the socialist economy may work, every citizen must be animated by the socialist spirit. All must be *Red* and *expert*. And in the battle for quality of production the 'political consciousness' factor plays an even more important part than it does anywhere else." And this is saying a lot when one knows what role it already plays "elsewhere."

THE "FIVE HAOS"[32] OF THE CHINESE WORKER

They all look alike, these socialist factories, whether they are Russian or Chinese, Czech or Polish. They were built "at top speed," and the builders had no time to give them a fancy finish. It's not that they are ramshackle. No, everything runs well, and often excellent products are manufactured before our eyes, but one always wonders by what kind of miracle. Even quite new factories age quickly and show premature signs of wear and tear. This is because no one ever dreams of fixing them up. The machinery is carefully maintained, but no one worries if the rest of the factory cracks, grows dirty, or otherwise deteriorates.

In China, as if to compensate for the aesthetic deficiencies, Red slogans are posted everywhere. And when I say everywhere I mean everywhere. They cover the inside and outside walls of workshops, canteens, and administrative offices. As they are written in Chinese, they have something of the quality of abstract paintings.

[32] *Hao:* the concept of "good" is represented in Chinese by the following characters — woman + child = "good."

Amateur artists also illustrate the billboard spaces with their drawings. They are inspired by political events: scenes from the war in
Vietnam; cartoons against the U.N., that spider which attracts victims into its web, where the Americans wait to devour them; U.S.
planes falling in flames (there is no shortage of red chalk in
China). Alongside these vengeful drawings are more peaceful
illustrations. The production race (the inevitable "socialist emula-
tion") is symbolized here by races among airplanes (or occasionally horses) identified by the colors of workshops or teams —
the same colors as those little flags found in the factory, fixed to
the machinery. Even in the busiest workshops there is always a
quiet corner where the workers can retire during breaks; here there
are handbooks decorated with Mao's portrait and which contain
excerpts from his works — and judging by their dog-eared appearance these handbooks are very much read.

Another feature of the socialist factory is the roll of honor, the
size and position of which vary according to the enterprise, but
which in China is always red with gold lettering. It displays the
portraits of meritorious workers, gilded and often garlanded with
flowers. Visitors are welcomed in specially laid-out rooms in which
samples of the factory's products are displayed and progress
graphs often hang. A host — but more often a hostess — offers
visitors tea and cigarettes. It is quite common for the manager or
one of his deputies to come and talk about the factory, but they
never invite you into their offices. Once, however, we did get into a
managerial office, Marc Riboud having insisted on photographing
the manager at his desk. It was a Shanghai factory which makes
three-wheeled delivery trucks. The office was furnished with a very
simple wooden desk, chairs, and a few leather armchairs which
obviously dated from the old regime. On the table were a single
telephone and a few pencils and ballpoint pens. On the walls,
which could have done with a touch of paint, were posted slogans
that had come half unstuck. The stove was lit, a luxury in Shanghai, where even schools are not heated because it is claimed that
the climate is too mild to warrant the waste of fuel.[33] Nothing in

[33] This factory, the "Shanghai Automobile Manufactory Works," is situated in the An Tin industrial district, nearly twenty miles from the center
of the city. It makes three-wheeled vehicles (fifteen a day) based on a popular Japanese model but "adapted to Chinese conditions." The factory was
built from a big repair workshop that had belonged to a "bureaucratic
capitalist." It is having to expand rapidly, and several workshops were already under construction when we visited it.

the furnishings gives one a clue to the importance of the office's occupant. It is exactly the opposite of what happens in the U.S.S.R., where everything is done to accord status to the man in charge and to differentiate him from others according to the principle of *Edinonatchalstvo* (power embodied in one man). The Soviet boss is installed in a luxurious office and is distinguished from his inferiors by his demeanor and his style of dress.

In a Chinese factory one is always in danger of taking the manager for a laborer and vice versa. It sometimes seemed to us that the workers, who do not know the managers personally, also make the same mistake and in any case are not required to show any sign of respect — nor do they.

One other thing surprised us during our visits to factories: our host never seemed to be in a hurry. This was understandable when the host who greeted us was the public relations man of the enterprise (or at least the person who carried out this function, for the job as such does not exist); but it was less so when the director himself took charge of us, which happened frequently. He would guide us through the workshops, canteens, workers' apartment buildings, and practically through the nursery. This would take him a good half day, and no one would come to call him away during the tour. Further, when this key figure recalled proudly that in conformity with Party rules he worked two or three mornings a week as a simple worker in order not to cut himself off from the masses, one began to wonder when he found time to run the factory. Occasionally, our confidence encouraged by the friendliness of these bosses who put themselves out for us, we risked asking them a silly question: What does a factory manager's job consist of? They replied without taking offense and even without any sign of surprise.

A manager's role is limited by the fact of his subordination to the Party committee, which forms in each undertaking the "decision-making nucleus," as they term it. This committee numbers up to fifteen members, elected for a period of a year by the Communists working in the enterprise, and they can be subsequently re-elected. It is these men who exercise the leadership in all aspects of the factory's life and settle all the important problems, from the production plan to the organization of leisure. The manager is then responsible for carrying out these decisions. He is also responsible for maintaining contact between the enterprise and the higher central authorities who are his immediate superiors.

But in a large enterprise unforeseen problems which urgently need to be solved must often crop up. Do the fifteen people, who work in different workshops and not necessarily on the same shift, have to meet to deal with these problems? Or are they handled by the secretary of the committee — its only permanent member? If so, must he be considered the real manager of the factory, the manager in name being no more than the head of the technical section? It is not that simple, the Chinese reply. For a start, the manager is usually a member of the committee. Then the workers also have their committee, which is elected by a two-level ballot[34] and must be consulted about every new decision. Finally, I was told, "Authoritarianism is severely frowned on in China and no one has the right to give orders based on his personal solutions. To find the correct solutions it is better to discuss the problem with several people and at length rather than to act quickly and in a rash manner." I was in a bad mood and I said rather foolishly, "I hope this principle doesn't apply to the fire brigade." My informant did not flinch, "Yes. It *also* applies to the fire brigade."

Management, therefore, is the corporate responsibility of the administration, the Party committee, and the workers' committee. But who referees the disputes which can break out among these three branches? "There are no disputes," they tell you, "for everybody works toward the same goal." I insist: "But the workers' committee has the right to oppose decisions of the Party committee if it makes a decision which upsets the workers?" Reply: "The Party committee never makes decisions which upset the workers." I try again to argue the point, but my informants refuse to abandon one iota of their case that the committees are perfectly representative and that perfect harmony reigns among them.

However, not everything goes before them for discussion. In China a factory is never an autonomous unit, and there is no question of its managing itself completely independently for the workers' benefit. It operates within the framework of the central plan (or within that of the local plan, which comes to the same thing, as this is integrated into the central plan), and it must accept the norms and regulations fixed for all industry. If these are not adhered to, sanctions follow, and these are almost always individual. An entire committee cannot be fallible, but "a manager

[34] Plenary meetings of workers are rare in the big enterprises. But the workers are divided into teams, and the elected chief of each team takes part in the election of the workers' committee.

is and must undertake his responsibilities." This phrase was the only one in which my informants connected the words "manager" and "responsibility," making it plain to me that the manager plays an important role all the same: he is the one who must see that the norms and regulations are complied with.

But what does a manager do when he realizes that the factory's equipment is too worn or inadequate to carry out the plan for which he is responsible? He calls a meeting of the Party committee, which investigates the factory's budget to determine whether it is large enough to buy new or more advanced machinery, assuming that the machinery is available. This is not always the case, and such simple solutions are not always applicable. The Party committee then decides to solve the problem "by our own resources" and consults the workers' committee. This always ends up with an appeal to the "veteran workers," very real people who have become a legend. I was told in Shanghai that they have "pianists' fingers," and despite my technical ignorance I can testify to their astonishing dexterity and to their ingenuity. One or more of these "veteran workers" come to take a look at the faulty machinery. If they are not too familiar with it they operate the machinery for a few days. Then they begin to tinker with it, and their pianists' fingers, it appears, work miracles. If the machinery is really beyond repair, however, an appeal is made to the center.

The following incident illustrates the skill and ingenuity of these veteran workers (and of Chinese workers generally). In the old quarter of Shanghai, which has been partly rebuilt but still bears the marks of its shanty-town history, in a narrow lane of beaten earth stands a huge hangar-like building, partly roofed and with the tumble-down air of anything but a factory. To enter it one goes through an unlit wooden lean-to, finally emerging in the main building; there, in an incredible clutter of junk, several hundred workers are going about their tasks industriously. One says to oneself that in this dump the most they can make is nails. Wrong. They are manufacturing seamless steel tubes of every size and shape — even irregular patterns which involve particularly difficult and delicate precision work. The tools and machinery they use have been so modified for their present function that one could say they virtually invented them. The whole place is a pure masterpiece of improvisation; one says to oneself that it is impossible to do precision work with such old, patched-up machinery, and yet the tubes emerge at a great rate.

Mr. Tsao, manager of the factory,[35] lively and talkative, is thirty-nine but doesn't look it. Son of a farm worker from Shantung province, he enlisted in the 8th Route Army in 1944 and came to Shanghai with it. He has never had any formal education, of either the normal or the technical kind; he "learned everything in the army." But he knows his factory like the back of his hand and can describe in detail every invention of his veteran workers and general handymen. "Some doubted that it would be possible to make these tubes in such a small factory," Mr. Tsao tells me. I don't know if I should be shocked by this skepticism or admit that although they are being made before our very eyes, I still harbor some doubts myself. But I simply ask, "Don't you have any technicians here?" "Yes. Some veteran workers have been promoted to technician, and a few rather gifted young ones are studying at the Institute of Technology while continuing to work in the factory," replies Mr. Tsao, who then goes into the well-known refrain: "Our success is due to the combination of three factors — the leadership of the Party, the workers' initiative, and management's energy." I had not asked for details of the practical operations in the factory. Mr. Tsao showed me a tube of particularly delicate manufacture which the factory had produced after six months of trials.

A few weeks later in the Northeast, at Anshan, visiting another seamless tube factory, where everything was modern, mechanized, and enormous, I thought with vague nostalgia of that Shanghai shed where the workers manufacture the same tubes practically by hand. And each time that I was shown a modern factory after looking around an older semicraft enterprise in another town, I experienced the same feeling. Admittedly the Anshan factory produces much more than Mr. Tsao's hangar. Admittedly the modern truck plant at Changchun[36] produces more than this factory at

[35] The "Yung Chin Seamless Tubes Factory of Shanghai" was built in 1957 from a workshop specializing in the finishing of imported tubes. It now produces 900 different types of regular tubes and 80 types of irregular patterns. There are 340 workers in the factory, 24 of them women. The average pay is 68 yuan. Mr. Tsao, father of five, earns 104 yuan a month. His wife is a textile worker who earns 82.5 yuan. The latter's mother lives with them in an apartment with 430 square feet of living space, in the old part of the city.

[36] "Truck Factory Number 1" in Changchun was built from 1953 to 1956 under the direction of Soviet technicians. It is a smaller version of the Li Khatchov factory in Moscow. Its present production is the subject of discussion, as according to some technicians, it ought to be able to produce more. It seems that between 80 and 100 trucks are produced a day. The section of the factory devoted to the manufacture of light cars was "restocking" during our visit.

Shenyang or that old Liberation Army workshop at Nanking,[37] which "with bits of string" are making very sturdy tractors in the first case and one-and-a-half-ton trucks in the second.[38] But we have seen modern factories in Europe, and it is obviously in these improvised factories where the most striking evidence of the resourcefulness, patience, and incredible dexterity of the Chinese workers is to be found. Hence our liking for them — a "tourist" taste, it must be admitted, and one that the Chinese certainly do not share because these factories are less profitable than the others and are evidence of the backwardness of the country, forced to use its slightest resources to the limit. Nonetheless — and this the Chinese freely admit — they are an excellent school for young workers, who learn not only how to work on an assembly line but also to use their initiative.

In the modern factories it is difficult to see how even the most ingenious of the veteran workers could introduce innovations. It is even more difficult to visualize, in view of their lack of scientific education, how they would man an electronic control panel.[39] Even in such factories, however, our hosts continued to talk of "the initiative of the masses," but nevertheless without citing very convincing examples of its results. At Anshan, unable to claim that a veteran worker had perfected the Martin furnace, they showed us samples of types of steel which China had not produced before. And they continued to tell us that all their successes were due to the alliance of Party, masses, and management.

In fact, in the advanced sector the workers' contribution to progress is their conscientiousness and the effort they make to train themselves; this last point is very important if one thinks of the enormous number of Chinese workers who come straight from

[37] Russian technicians had also asserted that it was impossible to build trucks here.

[38] Among factories of this type the place of honor must go to the Sian agricultural machinery works. Built in 1931, during the heroic days of the Kiangsi republic, it was taken on the Long March to Yenan, where plant equipment seized from the Japanese was added to it. In Yenan it produced mines and grenades. In 1949, 100 workers set it up again in Sian in a former weaving mill, which was so inadequate that they had to work partly in the open air. Today it employs 1,300 workers, 12 of them Yenan veterans. The factory produces twin-share plows and twelve-row seeders.

[39] The manager of the Wou-chin chemical fertilizer factory talked to us about one of his workers, Tsou Tchin-ying. Of peasant background and three-quarters illiterate, Tsou obviously could not read chemical formulas written in Roman characters. By dint of patience he invented his own system for deciphering them. Thus, to him CO became a half zero plus a zero. Thanks to this he became capable of controlling a machine.

the rural areas into the factory and the serious problems this kind of migration creates everywhere. I had the impression, therefore, that in China some kind of internal democracy within enterprises and the constant liaison between management and the rank and file make both the integration of the peasants and the education of the workers easier.

But is the "socialist conscience" alone enough to rouse the people's energies or are other methods being tried? And who are these workers whose names appear on the roll of honor? I ended up by putting this question to Mr. Tsung, who showed us around the number one machine tool factory in Peking, and naturally I phrased it in the following terms: "Who are your Stakhanovites?"

To my complete surprise, Mr. Tsung, fifty years old and a member of the Party since his youth, did not understand my question — he had never heard of Stakhanov.[40] I told him who he was. "Here we have something different," explained Mr. Tsung. "It's not the workers who simply surpass the norms whose names appear on the roll of honor. It is those who best observe the 'Five Haos.' "[41]

Not unhappy to note that while he does not know about Stakhanov, I am equally ignorant of the "Five Haos," Mr. Tsung led me to the roll of honor, on which they are posted. Here they are:

1. Be politically correct in one's thinking.
2. Practice mutual help among one's comrades to reinforce the collective unity.
3. Learn from the most advanced and teach the most backward.
4. Learn how to innovate and economize at work.
5. Fulfill production norms.

"Fine," I say to Mr. Tsung, "but only in the case of the fifth can one tell without any possible error if the rule has been complied with. How can you decide by the other criteria that one worker is more meritorious than another?"

"We decide nothing," replies Mr. Tsung. "It is the workers themselves who decide. Our workers are organized in teams (of

---

[40] Alexis Stakhanov, Russian miner of the Donbas who was cited as an example to all for having dug fourteen times the amount of coal required by the norm.
[41] See note on p. 235.

104 members at the most) who form the basic collectives. Each team elects its chief and allocates the work among its members. The monthly salaries are not all equal: there are eight categories which correspond to the different levels of ability, and it is the workers of a team who decide who moves from one category to another. They also decide, when a team has earned a collective bonus for having surpassed its norm, whether this will be divided among them all or only among the most meritorious. Finally, it is they who recommend to the workers' committee that not merely those who work fastest but also those who best observe the 'Five Haos' should appear on the roll of honor. Then the committee chooses from among the candidates recommended to them by the teams."

This is quite a program, and it prompts some questions: if it is the team which promotes its members from one wage category to another, it must also therefore decide each individual's income. Doesn't this almost automatically risk leading to disputes with the management, which pays the workers? And if — without mentioning bonuses — a team receives a fixed sum each month, doesn't the way in which it is distributed risk fostering differences among its members?

Mr. Tsung listened to me with a smile and a look from behind his glasses that said very clearly I knew nothing about socialist man; then he told me, "Our workers don't work for money but for an ideal. They think first of all of the collective good, of socialism — such mean and selfish quarrels as you describe cannot happen here."

In twenty-five factories I asked the same questions. Twenty-five times they told me the same things with a discreet astonishment that I could for a moment suspect that socialist workers were interested in their pay and could quarrel about it. May I say that the twenty-fifth time I also greeted their replies with discreet astonishment?

For after all, what does a Chinese worker earn? In Peking the average monthly pay is sixty yuan; in Shanghai and in the Northeast, seventy yuan; in Kunming, fifty-two yuan. Minimum pay varies from twenty-eight to thirty-eight yuan. Apprentices get only nineteen yuan to pay canteen and dormitory expenses. Family allowances, which are reduced after the second child as a form of birth control, enable the heads of families to increase their budgets; and if one adds certain other benefits (overalls, which are very cheap, are free for apprentices), one concludes that the lowest-paid workers earn enough to feed and clothe themselves but absolutely nothing more. Unless a couple gets double pay[42] or either of them receives regular bonuses, it is virtually impossible for them to buy a bicycle at 180 yuan — and a bicycle can be considered an item of prime necessity.

I am not quoting statistics to denigrate the Chinese system — the simple fact that every Chinese today has the guarantee that he can and will continue to be able to live on his pay represents considerable progress — but I simply wish to show that the desire to earn a little more money would not necessarily be antisocial. None of the twenty-five factory officials with whom I spoke — many of whom, it should be recalled, were of peasant or proletarian origin — would accept this idea for a second. "Our workers," they said, "know that increased production will bring about a rise in living standards for us all. It is for this that they must help one another, learn from the most advanced and teach the backward."

Is it through class instinct that they know these truths about everyone's part and duties in society?

"Their social origins indeed predispose the workers to good behavior. But in order for them to be able to act conscientiously and consistently for the good of the country and for their own well-being, they must be motivated by 'correct political thought' — which is the fundamental criterion in the factory, as in the rest of one's life."

You may search for all the explanations you wish of the behavior of the Chinese masses; the managers and cadre members will allow you to do so without hostility but with a derisive smile. For them one thing, and one alone, counts — "correct political thought," keystone of the Maoist system.

LEARN FROM LEI FENG

Arriving in Canton we saw enormous portraits of a young soldier posted on every wall. Usually a soldier has a grim air, brandishes a rifle, and cries, "Attack the enemy!" The Canton soldier had some books rather than a gun under his arm; not only was he not shout-

---

[42] In 1958, and up until the "Great Leap," most women worked. When the pace slackened, they were the first to be dismissed. Today only 50 per cent of the women in the cities go out to work.

ing anything, but he wore a benevolent smile. "Who is that?" I asked. "It's Lei Feng, the idol of Chinese youth," the interpreter replied. "Why? What has he done to deserve this honor?" "Nothing very special. He helped the people because his political thought was correct."

I did not press the matter. A week later in Peking we asked some workers what they did with their leisure. Practically all of them had been the previous Sunday "to see the film about Lei Feng," and they had found it remarkable, wonderful, very good. We now looked with even more respect on this soldier, Lei Feng, whose poster appeared on every wall here, too; by all accounts this idol of the young was also a hero to the adults. We already knew what "correct political thought" was, and we asked for an interview with this young soldier who practiced it so well. "He died last year in a car accident," our interpreter told us. "But go to see the film which portrays his life story — it has been taken from a personal diary which Lei Feng kept. You will learn everything about him."

That same evening we went to the movies. In the opening sequence Lei Feng meets a group of Young Pioneers[43] and plays with them until one of the youngsters notices three scars on the soldier's hand. "Which battle were you wounded in?" he asks. A shadow falls across Lei Feng's face. Flash back: a tumble-down cottage in the snow, shaken by the winter wind. It belongs to a family of poor peasants, but only a barefoot child in rags is there. His father, a narrator explains, has been tortured to death by the Japanese; his mother has committed suicide after being raped by Kuomintang drunks; his elder brother has died of tuberculosis contracted by working in a factory from the age of ten. His younger brother has died from malnutrition. At the age of seven Lei Feng is alone in a hostile world — and already the audience is on the edge of its seat.

Little Lei Feng leaves the shack to gather some dead wood. A hideous witch catches him — she is the landlord's wife. She drags the child to the front door of her huge, well-heated house. Her landlord husband comes to meet her: long silk robe, pipe in mouth, and all the wickedness of the old regime written on his face. The hag suggests that they cut off the little thief's hand. Her lord and master agrees. Slash, slash, slash — a billhook falls three

[43] Equivalent to the Boy Scouts.

times on the orphan's hand; dramatic music; the audience trembles in horror.

Back to Lei Feng the adult, surrounded by the Pioneers, who wipe away their tears with their red neckerchiefs. "Each time that I look at my hand," Lei Feng tells them, "the hatred of my class enemies is revived within me." But these enemies are defeated by the People's Army, and Lei Feng is taken in hand by the new regime. He is fed, clothed, nourished, and cared for. "Those were the first decent clothes I ever wore," he will note later in his journal. Then, despite his tender age, he takes part in the fight against the landlord, revealing the wrongs he received from him, and finally helps to share out the landlord's ill-gotten goods when they are distributed to the poor.[44]

Then Lei Feng goes to school, learns the trade of driver-mechanic, and eventually finds himself in the motorized section of the Liberation Army. He writes in his journal: "I have been saved at the cost of the blood and life of my revolutionary elders. The great Communist Party and Chairman Mao saved me! I have decided to dedicate my life to the communist cause." But with the inexperience of youth Lei Feng imagines that to dedicate oneself to a cause is to fight rifle in hand. Learning from the radio one day that a group of Nationalist saboteurs have infiltrated a coastal province, Lei Feng rushes to the political commissar and volunteers to go and fight them. Touching naïveté — to defend herself China does not rely on spontaneous gestures by soldiers; she has enough troops everywhere to wipe out "Chiang Kai-shek's malevolent envoys." With good-humored patience the commissar explains to Lei Feng that times have changed; today the peaceful front of socialist construction is the most important for the Party. Lei Feng leaves with four volumes of Mao's works — a gift from the commissar — and reads and understands them: a soldier must help the people in their work and in their life. In the glorious tradition of "Paluchun," the 8th Route Army, he must live for the community without thinking of his own comforts, his own interests, or his own fame, and he must refuse all reward and even any thanks for the services he renders. "It isn't I who must be thanked," he says, "but our army and the Party which molded and inspired it." In short, he assimilates the "correct political thought."

---

[44] This episode does not appear in the film, but the phrase quoted came from an article by Madame Soong Ch'ing-ling, Vice-Chairman of the Republic (*Peking Review*, May, 1965).

The result is a perfection which enables him to accomplish an interminable list of good deeds: his truck is the best maintained in the army, he drives like a champion, he carries a peasant's child for miles in a heavy downpour, and he cannot go near any work site without rolling up his sleeves and rushing in to help the workers. He has reached such a state of unselfishness that he refuses even to buy himself a lemonade, so that he can send all his wages to flood victims.

While being so virtuous, Lei Feng asserts no superiority over comrades who are less so; he does not even preach to them. He helps the lazy by doing their work while they sleep, which, contrary to what one might believe, does not encourage their laziness. Lei Feng's gesture moves them, awakens their conscience, and does more than long discussions to make them better citizens and more collectivist in outlook. On this point the example of the soldier Wang Da-li is characteristic. Tall, handsome, a keen basketball player, Wang Da-li is a lighthearted figure. He spends all his pay on amusements, never sending anything to his aged mother, to whom he never even writes. If we are not told that he is a lady's man it is because such a thing is unthinkable in the Chinese cinema, the most puritan in the world — but he has the look of one. One episode shows to what extent Wang Da-li's thought is not "correct." Several Sundays running Lei Feng goes to work at a yard, without revealing his name, of course, in case they want to reward him. Determined to find out the name of this admirable volunteer, the yard manager goes through Lei Feng's jacket and finds an envelope addressed to Madame Wang Da-li (you will soon see why); assuming that she is Lei Feng's mother, he writes out a superb testimonial to Wang Da-li and sends it to his regiment. Far from refusing this unearned tribute, Wang Da-li accepts it without batting an eyelid and even glories in it — to the loud hilarity of the audience.

Sequel: his village is flooded, and Wang Da-li is given a long leave to go help his family. Ashamed of himself for not having written or sent a penny, he wonders uneasily how his old mother will greet him. She falls on his neck and thanks him with floods of tears for the letters and money she has received every month — from Lei Feng, as you have guessed. Wang Da-li also guessed it; scales fall from his eyes, inspired by "correct political thought," he carries children, parcels, and old people through the rain and helps the blind to cross the street. So good does he become that when

Lei Feng dies he is deemed worthy to inherit his four volumes of the works of Chairman Mao.

The audience leaves wet-eyed. Gino Nebiolo even told me that in a movie theater in the suburbs of Sian he saw the audience rising in unison at the end of the film and chanting for a full five minutes, "All honor to Lei Feng!"

The next day our guides asked us what we thought of the film and the character of Lei Feng, and subsequently intellectuals and executives frequently put the same question to us — we did not know where to look. According to the circumstances, we took the coward's way out and either muttered quickly, "The best ever," or avoided replying. Several times, when we thought we could do so without offending those who asked, we gave them to understand — in much more moderate terms than I employ here — that the kind of cult dedicated to this communist saint who reeked of virtue seemed rather foolish to us. No one fully understood us. "But," said one, "we haven't invented anything. Lei Feng really existed and everything told about him is true. Besides, there are hundreds of thousands of Lei Fengs in China, and we congratulate ourselves on this; it is only with such men that we can advance toward the collectivist society." So be it. But must the lives of saints be used to dictate to the Chinese people their daily conduct? And must socialist education really consist of preaching happiness by self-renunciation, ascetic altruism, and the boy-scout code? In China it appears to be so, at least for the time being.

The subject of the conversation changed. Our Chinese companions tried to convince us of the superiority of political incentives and of "correct thought" over the material incentives advocated by the revisionists while we questioned ourselves about Lei Feng's qualities. Without doubt the story of the little orphan whom the revolution has given a vast new family is a moving one. Lei Feng's intense love for his fellow men and his desire to merge into the collective whole of the nation are edifying. But of what is he a militant model? When do his "political convictions" manifest themselves, how does he envisage the future? In short, in what respect is he an exemplary Communist?

The Chinese have no difficulty in convincing us that the socialist society functions so much better because it is more capable of gaining the conscientious compliance of every citizen: this is one of the basic ideas of socialism. We also fully appreciate that in China, where the material advantages are very thinly spread, the political consciousness of the workers must play a decisive role. Without it, the complex system of centralized planning (within which, however, vast sectors are left to regional or local initiative, and all decisions are discussed by various committees) would never work: it would be paralyzed by rivalries, with each region, each city, each enterprise trying to secure the maximum for itself without any thought of the others. Workers who are asked to go from one province to another to "help the backward," without receiving any raise in pay, must believe in a collective ideal to accept such sacrifices. The slogan which declares that one must be "Red and expert" therefore seems perfectly adapted to the conditions in which Chinese society is developing.

However, the lesson that can be drawn from the story of Lei Feng is a moral lesson and not a socialist lesson. Lei Feng never discusses politics with his comrades. He converted the frivolous Wang Da-li not by explaining political principles to him or by conjuring up the picture of a better future, but simply by practicing what he preached, altruism. Is socialism in China therefore only virtue?

One must believe so, since Mao Tse-tung in person launched the slogan "Learn from Lei Feng" and since we often heard Chinese who were highly cultivated and anything but naïve talking without the slightest trace of a smile about the outstanding value of this hero, assuring us that Lei Feng could not have become what he was without having assimilated the essence of Mao's political works. *Before* reading Mao he was merely well intentioned; *after* reading him he understood what his duty was and the part he must play in society; and so he became virtuous, therefore Communist.

In his funeral tribute to Bethune, the Canadian doctor who had been a member of the 8th Army, Mao declared: "A man can have greater or lesser abilities. If he is devoid of all selfishness he is already a noble and pure person who has rejected vulgar feelings, a person useful to the people." He added that such a man would never "pick up a light load and leave the heavier ones to others," that he would be keen and warm-hearted with his comrades and with the people. Then he asserted, "Those who are not like this cannot be regarded as Communists or, at all events, as pure Communists."

Lei Feng, the "Five Haos," "correct political thought" — all the usages and customs of present-day China are determined largely by this Maoist definition of the "ideal man" and the "pure Communist." Mao does not ask his compatriots to accomplish great exploits, he simply asks them to be virtuous and "devoted to the people" (for anyone can do good deeds in the Lei Feng manner without either difficulty or genius). And since Yenan he has never ceased to preach this new morality with evangelistic fervor. There is no lack of "heavy loads" in China, and she needs plenty of "saints" to shoulder them voluntarily in the service of the common cause. Perhaps she was able to emerge only by creating this climate of collectivist religiosity by asking everyone to renounce concern for the self. Although she may greatly need technicians and Stakhanovites, China cannot afford the luxury of maintaining a "technico-Stakhanovite" elite; she must therefore appeal to the altruism and disinterestedness of everyone. Contrary to what some Westerners claim, these principles are neither absurd nor in opposition to economic laws; this way of doing things is perfectly adapted to a poor and overpopulated country that is seeking to overcome its underdevelopment.

For all that, the politico-moral education given in China often appeared to us excessively simplistic and sometimes even impoverishing. Even if Mao thinks he can inculcate altruism into 650 million people, would it not have been possible for him at the same time to inculcate into them some other qualities necessary to Communist man, and could he not have chosen a model a little more complex than Lei Feng?

These questions lead us to another basic problem facing China — that of the "great cultural revolution." It was already under way during our stay; in the spring of 1966 it intensified, and today it is still developing. It will not be considered accomplished, we were assured, until all the Chinese have become Lei Fengs[45] — which will not be for a long time.

[45] In 1966 the Chinese press revealed the existence of several other posthumous heroes whose "correct political thinking" was enshrined in their personal diaries. The most important among them is Wang Kie, also a soldier and also killed in an accident.

CHAPTER FOUR:

The Elusive Proletarian Culture

THE "PERMANENT REVOLUTION" IN CULTURE

In August, 1966, the world was astonished to learn that the Red Guards were attacking historic monuments, the poetic names of Peking streets, and precious *objets d'art* of the past. This storm worried even China's friends. Yet since the turn of the century the Chinese intellectual elite has been rebelling against the old civilization and disowning it absolutely. Ch'en Tu-hsiu, a man of great learning, who yielded nothing in intellectual style to the most cultured scholars of the West, already in 1915 urged Chinese youth to destroy the entire traditional culture and considered it expedient to insult Confucius publicly.[1a]

Why does this iconoclastic rage sweep China every so often? Why do the Chinese revolutionaries advocate a complete break with the culture of their country? Why today are the Maoists giving the "cultural revolution" a significance which goes beyond that of culture in the sense in which we understand this word, regarding it as a means of radically changing the people's mores?

Because for centuries culture in China served to preserve the established order, as perhaps in no other part of the world. For more than two millennia the Confucian rules constituted the only real cement binding the Middle Kingdom together, making up for the deficiencies of both religion and state. They were of a kind which smothered all impulse toward progress and provided a sort of invisible structure for this country that is as big as a continent. China was shaken by tremendous social shocks, and peasant revolts periodically heralded the doom of dynasties which "had lost heaven's mandate," but no new concept ever penetrated this closed civilization based on the perpetual inequality of men and the submissiveness of the governed in the presence of the governing elite.

Shut off from the rest of the world and from its own society, this splendid culture became the very image of the immovable China. Revolutionary ferment, instead of rising up from the depths of the tortured country, could only come from outside. It is in this respect that the Chinese revolution already differs from those which have

[1a] See p. 44.

taken place in Europe. When, during the French Revolution, the Jacobins placed the goddess Reason, a magnificent bare-bosomed woman, on the altar of Notre Dame, their destructive attacks against religion were made in the name of a philosophy deeply rooted in the country, one which had long preceded the revolutionary eruption. In Russia, too, the culture of the revolution infiltrated the liberal and then the socialist elements of society and gave birth to ideas which were the real components of Russian culture well before October, 1917. In China there was nothing like this. The Chinese revolutionaries had no cultural heritage to exploit. Neither Dr. Sun Yat-sen nor Mao Tse-tung could draw from it: "China was a blank page."

China's revolutionary culture must therefore be produced in a painful upheaval. And at the same time nothing less is demanded of it than that it should become the new cement to hold society together. It is therefore the concern of the whole country, the alpha and omega of its social progress. For us, used as we are to a consumer civilization which regards culture as one of the products of consumption, and certainly not as the basic product, it is not easy to understand the fierce passion the Chinese display in regard to everything that concerns ideas. We comprehend neither their complete confidence in "good" values nor their complete distrust of ideas they consider "malignant." Our respect for the past and present of culture is colored by a great skepticism as to its real influence on the fundamental mechanics of life. In China, ideas are all; what else besides its faith in the new values can this dispossessed people mobilize in its fight to change its way of life? Throughout the Maoist struggle the word "revolution" and conduct according to the new rules were synonymous.

The Chinese drama does not lie so much in the desire to destroy the old culture as in the difficulty of defining the new culture which must be put in its place. "Destruction is accompanied perfectly naturally by construction," the young Chinese assert proudly, but we did not always get the impression that this was quite true. And when one moves from economic matters to broach cultural problems, discussion with the Chinese becomes difficult. In a factory we could be skeptical or admiring, but we understood the arguments of our guides. It was not at all the same when we visited cultural institutions, and this difficulty was not solely due to our foreign point of view; it has produced strange upheavals within even the Chinese intellectual elite itself.

In fact, the "new proletarian culture" which the Maoists conceived in the great fervor of their revolution seems to be taking shape very slowly, cruelly dashing their perhaps utopian hopes. Sometimes they approach it patiently, sometimes with a surgeon's haste. But, since in neither case are the results either quick or always happy, the intellectuals are blamed.

Men of bourgeois or petty bourgeois origin are of weak character — this is inscribed in all the Chinese textbooks, and a thousand more or less verifiable examples are cited to support this thesis. Then the Chinese we meet give us to understand that the great majority of Chinese intellectuals are still precisely of bourgeois and petty bourgeois origin. One is forced to conclude that the regime cannot rely 100 per cent on the combativity of its intellectuals, who, because of their "blemish," are in danger of revealing their shortcomings in particularly difficult circumstances. Yet China needs intellectuals, who are the "engineers of souls," as Stalin once said — and Mao has taken over this formula. How can such a contradiction be resolved?

The answer is as uncertain as the premises of this dilemma. In principle, the intellectual can temper his soul by contact with the people and, by joining in manual labor, he acquires characteristics which guarantee his future revolutionary stability. He can even become a model Communist, free from all selfishness and vanity. But in practice the purges which hit "weak" intellectuals play havoc in exactly those circles of Communists and artists who over the years have proved their devotion to the cause and their spirit of self-sacrifice. Patently, the explanations we are given are too simplistic.

During our stay in Peking we were received by Kuo Mo-jo, the prestigious president of the Academy of Sciences, celebrated historian and dramatist, who did not join the Party until 1958, but who had fought alongside the Communists for more than a quarter of a century. Our interview with him took place in a room in the great People's Palace, where only personages of the first rank receive visitors. Despite his age (seventy-eight) Kuo Mo-jo was in good form, very sure of himself and in a witty mood. He even regaled us with antirevisionist anecdotes and ceaselessly praised the superiority of the Chinese system. A few months later we were dumbfounded to learn that this same Kuo Mo-jo had declared that all his life's work deserved to be burnt.

Madame Fan Chin, an editor of Peking's two daily newspapers and deputy mayor of the city, was no less expansive when we talked to her at length about her experiences as a militant during the anti-Japanese war (see pages 110–13) and about her present work. She assured us, among other things, that she had never ceased doing her annual stint in the countryside, where she always felt at home among the peasants. Thanks to her, we visited the *Peking Jih Pao* (the Peking morning paper) and the *Peking Wan Pao* (the Peking evening paper), and the editor in chief of these two papers, Mr. Hue Chuan, talked to us for a long time about the Chinese press's fight against revisionism. A few months later, Madame Fan Chin was relieved of her post and the editorial direction of the two newspapers was "reorganized."

Lastly, we visited the universities of Peking and Nanking, where the atmosphere was one of peaceful study, giving no hint of the "wave of anger" soon to be unloosed by the students against their rectors, who were both dismissed as revisionists.

All these measures show that the "great cultural revolution," as defined in the spring of 1966, has had many victims among the people who had appeared to us to be the faithful guardians of Maoist orthodoxy, and who did not seem to have selfish leanings or petty bourgeois weaknesses. However, while I am unable to explain the reasons for these individual misfortunes, I think I can say that we had a vague presentiment of this purge which has been under way since April, 1966. For all the people we interviewed stressed the inadequacies of the cultural front, which was falling behind in the struggle to mold socialist man in China. The official in charge of higher education told us frankly — as you will see later — that the proportion of students of proletarian origin was still not big enough in the universities and that the whole system must be reorganized to reinforce the bonds between manual labor and study. The directors of propaganda and of culture deplored to us the fact that real Communists represented only 20 per cent of all intellectuals and they declared that this number had to be increased through the rigorous ideological struggle. Other statements led us to understand that the majority of intellectuals were not quite up to their task and that the Party was not happy about this state of affairs.

These complaints appeared paradoxical to us, it must be admitted, for we got the impression that on the contrary the cultural life of China was already politicized to the limit, and that the intellectuals there were already mobilized "in the service of the people" to a degree rarely reached in the other Communist countries. We were not shocked by the fact that they are required to join in manual labor in the fields and in the factories, for in view of China's special situation such an obligation to share "the sufferings of the country's underdevelopment" is perhaps morally justified. After all, in a society in which the vast majority of citizens must make the maximum effort for the common good, it is normal that the elite "who work with their brains" should show their fellowship for and understanding of the rank and file. But I find it hard to see how such a system could be enlarged even more or how an intellectual would be able to do his creative work if, instead of doing two months on the land, he had to spend eight months in a people's commune. Similarly, I asked myself how efficient the Chinese education system would be when all the students end up spending twice as much time in the fields as they do in college.

And then, reading the list of accusations in the spring of 1966, one could ask oneself if it was merely a question of this eagerness to keep the intellectuals at the same level as the masses. For we derived the impression that the Chinese creative workers are in process of becoming scapegoats held responsible for all the setbacks which occur in the molding of "these socialist exemplars," who according to the Maoists are indispensable to society.

To the Chinese Communists, the class struggle — as we have seen — consists above all of the confrontation between the men of "correct political thought" and the upholders of the old mentality who repeat superstitions and cling to the values of the old society. According to them, a dispossessed landlord even today can corrupt a whole people's commune by supplying the young people with harmful literature and by encouraging them to gamble and lead an antisocial life.[1b] One scabby sheep is therefore capable in certain circumstances of tainting the whole flock and of causing incalculable damage to the social progress of the country. What is more, this sheep is not necessarily of bourgeois origin and easy to unmask. Very often it is of proletarian origin and contaminates itself involuntarily through failure to understand an opera or a book. One might say that in the Maoist view the masses still resemble a child, which can easily become delinquent if exposed to bad influences, but which, on the contrary, can become very brilliant if given a good education.

No one will spell out such a definition of the masses in China, where the poor are extolled to the skies as having potentially the

[1b] See note on p. 187 on the film *The Village of Fan Choun Lin.*

greater virtue, but reading the doctrinaire Chinese, or talking with them, on the subject of the influence of art and literature on the masses, we got the impression that this is precisely the approach.

The Maoists in fact judge artistic creation by two criteria. First, they want each work to be within reach of the people and to please them. Second, they try to determine the effects of a work as a means of developing good collectivist sentiments among its audience. "Research" has shown, for example, that the traditional operas had a bad effect on the masses by parading emperors, princes, and their concubines before them. Such works reinforced superstition and helped the "class enemy" as a result. The theatrical repertoire was therefore radically revised at the request of avant-garde activists who had drawn attention to this phenomenon.

During this period it was established that even certain modern operas, which at a particular moment in time had played a positive educational role, must be seriously revised if they were to continue to arouse the people's finer feelings. Thus *The White-Haired Girl,* the celebrated opera created in Yenan in 1944, for long the glory of Chinese drama, was considered twenty years later to be clearly inadequate. What in fact is the story of this young peasant girl, the slave of the local petty squire, who was found in a forgotten mountain village by the Liberation Army? This peasant girl's father, as poor as he was illiterate, was tricked by the wily squire into putting his fingerprint to a contract which gave the squire possession of his daughter. The wretched father realized his mistake too late and killed himself through grief. His daughter, reduced to real slavery, could look to no one for help, and that is why her hair was white despite her tender years. The libretto, one observes, merely denounces the cruel manners of the old China.

But today that is not enough. The peasants must not be presented as passive beings, even if that is what they were at a particular period (*The White-Haired Girl* was taken from real life). It was therefore decided that the father would not commit suicide, but would be killed by the squire's henchmen after a desperate and heroic struggle. The village peasants also show their anger at his death, and an entirely new character — he did not exist in the previous version — in the person of a Communist Party agitator comes to rouse them and recruit them into the Red Army. As for the white-haired girl, she is no longer a mere slave, but a sort of prisoner of war who continually demonstrates her hatred for her landlord enemy. She conducts herself with a dignity which impresses the audience with the strength of her class feeling and, in the finale, she herself joins the Red Army and leaves, rifle on shoulder, to fight for the total victory of the revolution. After such a finale, every member of the audience understands perfectly what his duty is and how to follow the heroine's example.

The authors of the previous version of *The White-Haired Girl* have not been accused retrospectively of revisionism for having turned out an opera that was not didactic enough. But this kind of accusation is common enough, particularly since the purge that began in April, 1966. The most glaring case is obviously that of Teng Tao, who until recently occupied key posts in the Chinese press. Director of *Jenmin Jih Pao,* he was in fact the country's number one journalist, and his writings were widely published, even outside his own newspaper. Thus in 1961 Teng Tao published a series of reports in the Peking evening paper (then under the direction of Madame Fan Chin) which he later assembled in an anthology entitled *Evening Observations in Yenchan.* In one of these articles, called "Preoccupying Oneself with Everything," he referred at length to the Tonglin party, which represented the progressive wing of the landed gentry under the Ming dynasty. In another he wrote of "persons of great culture of former days"; and in yet another of the rational use of manpower during the era of the "fighting kingdoms." Obviously all these historical reflections enabled the author to draw a moral for the present, but his conclusions did not attract the attention either of his Party superiors or, for that matter, of the foreign experts who scrupulously study the Chinese press. It was only in 1966, five years later, that the more vigilant critics in Peking discovered that Teng Tao's aims were revisionist, that he had praised the opponents of the Ming dynasty in order to incite the Chinese Communists to form an opposition against Mao, and that he had paid tribute to persons of great culture as an invitation to the intellectuals to rebel against the Party, which he had even accused of misusing manpower in present-day China.[2a]

"We are determined to completely liquidate all the old ideas, all the old culture, all the old manners and habits through which the exploiting classes poisoned the consciousness of the people for thousands of years," Chou En-lai answered in Bucharest, on June

---

[2a] Judging from the extracts which the Chinese press has published, Teng Tao certainly used very subtle methods of expressing his unorthodox views on Party policy through the medium of historical allusion. But I did not read his text in full and I still wonder how even such disguised criticism escaped for so long the keen eyes of Party watchdogs.

18, 1966, when asked what the "cultural revolution" in his country consisted of. This explanation makes one think that the Chinese Communists' present battle is restricted to the cultural modernization which has preoccupied the intellectual elite of the country for years.

But if one looks more closely at the Communist cultural battles of the last quarter-century, one notices that the victims were not the traditionalists, bound by the old morality, but on the contrary the avant-garde intellectuals who were among the first to answer the call of the revolution. This paradoxical fact deserves to be briefly examined in order that we should better understand that the real problem of today's cultural revolution lies in the Maoists' desire for a certain type of intellectual who comes from the people and is capable of helping the Party to mold socialist man as they have imagined him. The "men of great culture" — except scientists, perhaps — seem to be too steeped in "nonproletarian" values to be able to "serve the people," and whatever their desires and efforts (and God knows they do what they can) they fall into disgrace one after another as involuntary carriers of the germ of revisionism.

THE RELUCTANT SONG OF THE MONGOLIAN LARKS

"In those dark days of the repression in 1927 a great number of intellectuals of petty bourgeois background who had joined the Communist Party, but who lacked determination, left the Party," it is claimed in *Stories of the Chinese Red Army,* published in Peking in 1961. It is enough to look at the biographies of the principal Chinese intellectuals, however, to reach the exactly opposite conclusion. With the exception of Hu Shih,[2b] the great liberal philosopher, who, never having been a Communist, could not therefore desert the ranks of the Party, most of the prominent essayists, novelists, and poets drew nearer to the Party after Chiang Kai-shek's savage repression in Shanghai. Kuo Mo-jo, Mao Tun, Yü

[2b] Hu Shih, who was a friend of Ch'en Tu-hsiu and fought like him against traditional culture, never accepted Marxist philosophy and, unlike Ch'en Tu-hsiu, chose the Kuomintang. He was Chiang Kai-shek's ambassador during the war and was President of the Academia Sinica in Formosa until his death in 1962.

Ta-fu, Chou Tso-jen, Pa Chin, Chao Shu-li, Ting Ling, and many others followed the example of Lu Hsün and proclaimed more than ever their determination to engage in politics. Everything drove them into the arms of the Communists, the only consistent opponents of the established order, and whatever their objections to certain of the cultural premises of Marxism they all found themselves in the Shanghai League of Left-Wing Writers, directly inspired by the CP. These people, who were in touch with foreign intellectual circles and were imbued with Western libertarian theories, could not accommodate themselves to a regime of medieval repression which accorded no place to culture, whether traditional or modern. Nowhere else have cultural claims and the revolutionary struggle been so completely and automatically united as in China after Chiang Kai-shek's treason. The celebrated slogan sums up the spirit of the Chinese intellectual elite of this period, "From revolutionary literature to the literature of the revolution."

The petty bourgeois or bourgeois origin of these men did not prevent them from conducting a clandestine struggle in Shanghai first and later moving to the Communists' spartan capital at Yenan. When one today sees Yenan, which has really nothing of an artistic and cultural center, it is hard to believe that the finest Chinese intellectuals lived there for years in conditions more primitive than merely rural, working the land to provide some of their needs. This was nonetheless true, and the case of Ting Ling, the woman writer, not exceptional in itself, is worthy of mention because of the vicissitudes she suffered later.

Originally from a comfortable family in Hunan, Ting Ling was the childhood friend of Mao Tse-tung's first wife, Yang K'ai-hui, and like the latter had studied in college. Then she settled in Shanghai, where her early writing won her great success. She had no regard for Chiang Kai-shek and moved in left-wing circles, although she was not a member of the Party. But her nonconformist ideas were sufficient for the dictator's "blue shirts" to take an interest in her. One day in 1931 she was kidnapped, taken to Nanking, and thrown into jail. It was easy enough to disappear in Shanghai at this time. Ting Ling's husband was among the forty writers of the Left-Wing League who were mysteriously murdered in the street.

But Ting Ling had friends, particularly Agnes Smedley, who, when she found out about her disappearance, launched a great campaign of protest in the United States and elsewhere abroad.

Confronted with the indignation of the intellectual world, Chiang Kai-shek was forced to give in. In 1933 Ting Ling was set free and she returned to Shanghai, this time a convinced Communist.

She was one of the first to join Mao Tse-tung in Yenan. Mao evidently greeted with open arms the most celebrated woman writer in China — as Snow described her at the time — and entrusted to her the editorship of the literary section of the CP's main newspaper, *Liberation*.

Naturally the intellectuals were not the only ones to take the road to Yenan and the influx of activists swelled particularly in the years 1940 and 1941. The Party leaders then decided to speed up the political education of the newcomers. Their writings were almost entirely devoted to the question "How can one become a good Communist?" and they answered it by adopting methods of collective study, criticism and self-criticism, altruism, and work among the masses. In February, 1942, by inaugurating the Party's Central School, Mao laid down the "style of life" which he demanded from everyone, stressing the practical approach and the need to help the people in every sphere.

One month later an eminent intellectual, Wang Shih-wei, published his essay, "The Wild Lily," in which he declared that "even on the sun there are spots" and that only criticism could help to get rid of them. Wang Shih-wei was courageous enough to launch this offensive: he was well-known for his translations of the Marxist classics, but until 1938 he had been very close to the Trotskyites. The Party had pardoned him but it was perfectly capable of reopening his old dossier and declaring that this rebel theory had been influenced by Trotsky's writings.

No one dreamed of addressing any such reproach to Ting Ling, who also hurled herself into battle: on March 8, 1942, she published an essay, "Thoughts on Women's Day," denouncing the glaring contradictions between the Party's statements of principle and its deeds. Three days later the well-known poet, Ai Ch'ing, entered the lists with an article which caused a sensation, "On Knowing and Respecting Writers." In it he explained that the writer is not "a Mongolian lark which never sings anything but praises." Other writers published similar articles.

The information we have on this crisis, which took place at the height of the war and in a region completely isolated from the rest of the world, is necessarily fragmentary. It must be noted nonetheless that the intellectuals' discontent was not provoked by material difficulties, which none of them mentioned, but by the degree of cultural control, which had suddenly assumed proportions they considered unacceptable. And, paradoxically, their claims appeared in the official journals of the Party, which seemed to accept the start of real discussion on the intellectual's role in a society controlled by the CP. It is true that the leaders and the intellectuals lived very much together in the Maoist capital, that they were like one big family. It is said, for example, that Mao Tse-tung often saw Ting Ling, with whom he had always been very friendly.

But this climate of unusual tolerance could not turn the Communist leaders from their goal. They had a very clear conception of what they wanted from the intellectuals and after three months of palaver Mao Tse-tung invited them to a "talk on art and litera-ture" on May 3, 1942. A week later he had a second session with them behind closed doors. Then on May 21 he reached his conclu-sions and put an end to the controversy. The cultural doctrine that he formulated in the course of these talks is more strongly in force today than ever before in China.

Mao condemned every art form that did not have its roots in the people and did not serve their political education. He exhorted the intellectuals to be tough with the enemy but to be "meek as the ox before the child" in their dealings with the people, in accordance with the precept once used by Lu Hsün. According to him, every work of art reflects class feeling. Nonpolitical art never existed and never will exist. The proletariat must have its own revolutionary art, inspired by its profound popular wisdom and helping to fulfil its historic mission. As the Party represents the highest expression of the proletarian will, therefore of proletarian ideology and culture, it is the sole judge of the proletarian character of every work of art, of its usefulness and quality. It has the right and the duty to criticize creative workers, but it is by definition protected from criticism. For to criticize the Party is to criticize the prole-tariat and to offend against the people.

Many experts have thought that they discerned a very special Chinese emphasis in the Yenan talks and they have even maintained that they marked the start of the "Sinification" of the CCP. However, what is particularly striking about this text is Mao's very strict adherence to Soviet cultural orthodoxy, formulated by Stalin after his victory in the U.S.S.R. The concept of a politically determined "utilitarian art" and the condemnation of bourgeois theories of art for art's sake have been taught in all Soviet schools since the 1930's. The right of the Party — that is, of its leaders — to consider itself as the embodiment of the proletariat and the guardian of its spiritual virtues was also proclaimed in the U.S.S.R. long before the Yenan talks.

If there is any originality, therefore, in Mao's text, it lies primarily in his frankness and in his faith in the virtues of persuasion. Mao did not hesitate to assert that the intellectuals' first task was to popularize culture and that the raising of the cultural level could only come afterwards. He also explained that it was always better to "cure ideological illnesses than to kill the sick." It must also be noted that Mao's tone was infinitely more moderate than that of the Soviet doctrinaires, which was furiously abusive. In his Yenan talks, although he indulged in polemics and refuted the intellectuals' criticisms, Mao did not attack any of them by name or resort to threats.

This mild method was undoubtedly effective and although many intellectuals in Yenan probably questioned the possibility of creating an art inspired by folklore, they accepted with enthusiasm the task assigned to them by the leader of the Party. After all, he was asking them to "bring some warmth to those who suffer from cold," and no one in China could be insensible to the problem of bringing culture to the masses. Then again, Mao promised them a kind of spiritual happiness if they learned how to make themselves useful to the people; he even explained to them that through such conduct they could one day become the champions of a modern and higher culture than that which previously existed.

The intellectuals rushed headlong into the sessions of criticism and self-criticism organized as part of the Cheng-feng ("rectification of errors") campaign, hoping that this collective introspection would enable them to reach the same level as that of the people they wished to serve. Only Wang Shih-wei refused to join the movement. Even after the talks in May, 1942, he still wanted to argue his own point of view. He was accused of Trotskyism and the most persuasive pressures were brought to bear on him. On June 2, 1942, he resigned from the Party and from then onwards worked as an ordinary hand in a match factory. He has never made any self-criticism.[3]

Among those who approved of Mao from the bottom of their

[3] See Goldman, Merle, "Writer's Criticism of the Party in 1942," *The China Quarterly*, No. 17.

hearts, one must cite Chou Yang. A writer and literary critic, Chou Yang was born, like Mao and Ting Ling, in Hunan. He had studied in Shanghai and then been active in the League of Left-Wing Writers. Chou Yang has always championed a national culture, realistic and within reach of the people. In Yenan, where he was Director of the Department of Education of the Shensi-Kansu-Ningsia Border Region (in effect Minister of Education), he took part in the struggle against the "modernists" by translating *Relations Between Art and Reality,* by Chernyshevski, a nineteenth-century Russian critic who was an admirer of Fourier and an advocate of "art for the masses." After the Yenan talks, Chou Yang was appointed supernumerary director of the Lu Hsün Academy of Fine Arts (in order to ban abstract painting, which, it seems, was spreading there in an alarming way), and he became — with Ting Ling — co-chairman of the Writers' Association of the Northwestern Republic.

After this spring gale in 1942 all was calm on the cultural front for several years. The war was being fought; the intellectuals dedicated themselves completely to their work as activists and propagandists in close touch with the people — no longer could they have any doubts about serving the cause, which continued to gain ground and win over whole regions, while the People's Army went from victory to victory. Ting Ling, for example, accompanied the Red Army in the North and organized the distribution of land there. She has recounted this experience in her novel, *The Sun Shines on the River Sang-kan,* which won the Stalin Prize in 1952 and was translated into fourteen languages. Mao apparently cited her as an example to the whole literary world.

The Chinese sector of the latter expanded considerably after the proclamation of the People's Republic. The All-China Federation of Literary Art Circles had been founded in Peking on July 10, 1949, with Kuo Mo-jo presiding. The Communists made sure that they held the key posts although they were plainly a minority within the membership. Later it was decided to form an association of writers presided over by Mao Tun, another veteran of the Communist struggle and a former companion of Lu Hsün. Chou Yang was the active vice-president. But, paradoxically, in the arguments which broke out, the Communists were opposed not by the least politically minded intellectuals but above all by Communist writers. As usual the battle was over the role of culture in the new society and the relations between the intellectuals and the Party leaders. These debates were held on various pretexts: once it was a question of the significance of a film, *The Life of Wu Hsun,* another time the attitude to a literary classic, *The Dream of the Red Chamber,* but in fact the leitmotiv was always the same: what degree of autonomy Communist intellectuals can have, and how they can best contribute to the building of socialism. It followed that those who did not share the same concepts as the Communist leaders were denounced as "evil minds."

Ting Ling was one of the latter. A member of the staff of *Wenyi Pao,* the country's main literary journal, she was accused by the ever-vigilant Chou Yang (who had been co-director with her of the Writers' Association of the Northwestern Republic) of having "used the authority invested in her by the Party and the people to form a small clique, with the aim of satisfying her ambition to rule the literary world," and of having, with the connivance of Feng Hsüeh-feng, editor in chief of *Wenyi Pao,*[4] made this journal "their private property" and "reacted angrily to anyone who intervened."

But Ting Ling and Feng Hsüeh-feng were certainly not without friends, and the Party, which had no wish to alienate the intellectuals, did not hurry matters and hesitated a long time before dismissing them from their posts. However, in 1953 Feng laid before the Second Congress of Writers a report in which he criticized, point by point, the government's policy since the Liberation. This time the orthodox decided things had gone too far: the report was thrown out and a new editorial staff was put in charge of *Wenyi Pao.*

Feng and Ting Ling bowed to this judgment, but Chou Yang did not let up on them. "They always considered the reorganization of *Wenyi Pao* as an act of vengeance by the Party directed against their persons," he wrote. "They harbored deep resentment and had only one idea in their heads — to reverse the Party's decision and get their jobs back."

Those not familiar with the Party will find it hard to understand why there is anything shameful about an editor who has been dismissed feeling hurt and wishing to regain his position. In orthodox eyes, however, to have such feelings is to defy the

---

[4] Feng Hsüeh-feng, writer and militant Communist since the 1920's, never went to Yenan; arrested in Shanghai in 1936 by Chiang Kai-shek's "blue shirts," he spent seven years in a Kuomintang concentration camp. During the Shanghai League of Writers period he was known as an opponent of national culture; in his "Essay on Foreign Infiltration" he wrote that "even rape would produce its fruit."

authority of the leaders, the only competent judges of what is good for one and all. It is not enough to accept their decisions — these must be greeted with pleasure and even gratitude, under pain of being accused of disloyalty to Party and people. Indeed Ting Ling and Feng Hsüeh-feng, encouraged by their friends, not only did not say "thank you" but even, it is said, considered starting their own journal. If this in fact was the case, one must conclude either that China at that time was more "liberal" than the other Communist countries or that the two "rebels" were able to rely on solid support from within the Party hierarchy.

This happened in 1953. While in Moscow Stalin's death was bringing about the start of the "thaw," in China the struggle to socialize the economy and root out the old morality grew more bitter month by month. Once more the intellectuals were mobilized and "individualists" subjected to stronger and stronger pressure. The idea of going among the people to help them in their task once again became the order of the day. Ting Ling was not opposed to this program. On the contrary, in an article, "Life and Creation,"[5] she explained that the writer must live among the people he wishes to depict and that he can only translate an experience if it is his own. What she objected to, however, was that the verdict on the resultant work should come from the summit of the cultural hierarchy, which is not always guided by valid criteria.

At the same time another prominent Communist writer, Hu Feng, sent a 300,000-word memorandum to the Central Committee in protest against "the five daggers plunged into the writer's head." The memorandum opposed: (1) the need to adopt a Marxist view of the world, (2) the merging of writers with workers and peasants, (3) the remolding of thought, (4) the employment of a national style in the arts and letters, (5) the use of literature for political ends. It will be seen that Hu Feng went much further than the previous rebels in his claim for the autonomy of the writer and that he even demanded that cultural matters should be taken out of the hands of the state. This did not prevent his memorandum from being published and even being distributed free as a supplement to *Wenyi Pao,* the journal formerly run by Ting Ling.

Then on February 5, 1955, Chou Yang staged a counter-offensive and harshly criticized the memorandum at the Writers' Union congress. Hu Feng agreed to make a self-criticism and the affair appeared to have been disposed of when suddenly the *Jenmin*

[5] *Chinese Literature,* No. 3 (Peking, 1954).

Jih Pao of May 16, 1955, published letters that Hu Feng had sent to several of his friends inciting them to counter-revolutionary action. On May 24, under the heading "Second Series of Facts about the Hu Feng Clique," further letters even more compromising than the first ones appeared.[6] Letters from Hu Feng's wife were also published. This correspondence bristled with serious insults against the Party and even against Mao. The newspaper did not explain how it came by all the letters. As it is highly unlikely that some twenty correspondents of Hu Feng would all, spontaneously and at the same moment, send letters to *Jenmin Jih Pao,* it is obvious that they were obtained by police methods — which were condemned in principle.

For his part, Chou Yang in February, 1956, inferred the general lesson of the incident: those who do not follow the Party line have counter-revolutionary tendencies, and those who have such tendencies sooner or later end up engaging in counter-revolutionary activities. Every writer must understand after such a statement that he risks sliding down the slippery slope of counter-revolutionary activity when he deviates from the official line.

There was therefore plenty of self-criticism in Shanghai and Peking. Ting Ling and Feng Hsüeh-feng added theirs. The past of such militant intellectuals made it impossible to doubt their courage; above all, they were determined to take part in the building of the socialist society. As a result, they submitted once more to discipline and agreed to give up their independence — in the hope, no doubt, that it would be only for a time.

They did not think any the less about it, as one understands by the cry of relief they uttered when, in February, 1957, Mao Tsetung invited them to speak freely.

China had been less shaken than the other Communist countries by the revelations about Stalin at the twentieth congress of the U.S.S.R. Communist Party. Although they had effusively lauded Stalin's merits, the Chinese leaders had not adopted a servile attitude; they always made their own political decisions and consequently never automatically made the same mistakes as the Russian Communists. China did not owe her existence to the U.S.S.R.; for her Stalin's infallibility had never been a dogma, and as a result the revelations did not have such a shattering effect. Nevertheless, at that time she was still a member of the great

---

[6] Simone de Beauvoir in *La Longue Marche* (Paris, Gallimard, 1957), p. 382, gives her opinion that this correspondence was apocryphal.

Communist family and the events in Poland and Hungary (to mention only the countries most affected) forced her leaders to ask certain questions. In every one of the Communist countries it became necessary to revise certain ideas, and the Chinese, like the rest, decided to liberalize their regime. Besides, Mao had foreseen the de-Stalinization storm; even before Khrushchev made his accusations, Mao, in January, 1956, gave a talk (that was not published) in which he evoked for the first time a principle dating from the time of the "warring kingdoms":[7] "Let a hundred flowers bloom, let a hundred schools contend."

But it was not until February 27, 1957, during the eleventh plenary session of the Supreme State Conference, that he explained clearly how this famous historical formula could be applied in the new China. He invited his fellow-citizens to criticize, without fear or restriction, what was not going right in the system in order to bring out new ideas which would "facilitate the socialist transformation." He added: "Marxism is a scientific truth and does not fear criticism. If Marxism feared criticism, if it could be demolished by criticism, it would be good for nothing." Finally, he attacked the "oversimple methods" used to solve problems of a spiritual nature as being "not merely ineffective but even detrimental." The "opposition" triumphed, and a new "campaign of correction" began in which, this time, it was those who had been previously accused who were the prosecutors.

Thus Ting Ling openly attacked her old enemy Chou Yang and demanded that he define what he meant by "loyalty to the Party and the people," which he had so often evoked to ban all criticism and discussion.

Other writers made even more violent attacks, as can be seen from the following extracts from articles published in cultural journals. "In our literature there is not one sincere word, no word that comes from the heart, because in our society creative work is not free. . . ." "A writer who cannot take one step without first looking furtively to the right and the left to make sure that he is not being watched cannot relax enough to write. . . . He can have the most moving or most important idea in his head, but he dare only express it in a dull way for fear that it may offend." "The stronger the organization is, the weaker the individual is. . . ." Socialist realism demands that the writer see reality only through the 'socialist spirit,' which is a subjective and abstract

[7] From 475 to 221 B.C.

concept. If he does so, his work has no literary value and can only serve as a vehicle for certain political ideas. . . ." "The Soviet literature of the last twenty years is at a level very distinctly lower than that of the twenty years before 'socialist realism' was invented." "Literature has become impoverished in the fifteen years following the 'Yenan talks.' "[8]

The intellectuals were not the only ones to utter criticisms. For a few weeks in the spring of 1957 everyone could write to *Jenmin Jih Pao* or the local newspaper to voice his complaints, no matter how bitter they were; and the letters were published without comment. No subject was taboo; the letter-writer could denounce an injustice of which he had been the victim as well as proclaim his opposition on principle to communism. The papers even published caricatures sent to them ridiculing prominent leaders. In one of these the Maoist team is shown grouped on the top floor of a fortified tower which stands on a rock separated from the country by a series of huge moats. The caption reads simply: "Applying the politics of the mass."

Never has the Communist press (or, in a general sense, the political press) opened its columns so tolerantly, and with something approaching humility, to criticisms which, in fact, could relate to anything. But it is precisely this acceptance of all criticisms, published without any differentiation between serious articles and passionate outbursts, which makes one doubt the purity of the intentions of those who launched the "hundred flowers" campaign. Didn't they wish to discredit all the discontented by lumping the serious critics together with the eccentrics, the regular grumblers, and the crackpots? Didn't they wish to prove that all who criticize reject even the idea of socialist construction and advocate a return to the old regime? One can more readily raise these questions in view of the fact that in China the Party apparatus was in control of the situation, and the country was not going through a crisis like those experienced in 1956 by Hungary and Poland, where censorship, even during this fluid period, stifled the more virulent critics.

It was obviously through neither masochism nor compulsion that the Chinese CP's newspapers published openly anti-Com-

[8] I have taken these quotations from Wu Tsu-kuang and Tsing Chao-yang in the indictment of the "right-wingers" issued by Chou Yang, who was restored to power after the abandonment of the "hundred flowers" policy. Chou Yang, *Un Grand Débat sur le front littéraire* (Peking, Ed. Langues Etrangères, 1959).

munist articles, such as one which reminded the Maoists: "China belongs to the 600 million people, including the counter-revolutionaries. It does not belong to the Communist Party alone. . . ."[9] The Maoists certainly had an idea at the back of their minds when they indulged in this astonishing tolerance. What was it?

It is difficult to believe that Mao launched this campaign to trick the discontented into revealing and denouncing themselves. Such a Machiavellian plan could only have germinated in the mind of an arch-policeman, and Mao never has shown any signs of being that. Even admitting that power might have corrupted him and changed him into an unscrupulous dictator, one knows that in a police state such as Stalin's suspects are arrested and their confessions are extorted from them. The heads of police states usually prefer discretion and prevent their being publicly criticized by their future victims.

It must be admitted that we have no satisfactory explanation of the "hundred flowers" affair, for which no parallel is to be found in the other Communist countries. Let us simply state, therefore, that in June, 1957, the era of open criticism was succeeded by one of self-criticism by the former accusers. Here again one could remark the most extraordinary excesses. Even the two leaders of the Democratic League, Dr. Lo Lung-chi and Chang Po-chün, who had never been Communists, nevertheless confessed their great sin: of having made criticisms "detrimental to the great Communist party."

Meetings of the different cultural associations multiplied, and the malcontents were violently denounced as rightists and even as secessionists. According to their orthodox accusers, their actions had not been motivated by a spirit in keeping with the formula "unity-criticism-unity," which allows constructive discussion. Chou Yang even declared to the Association of Chinese Writers that Ting Ling, Feng Hsüeh-feng, "and their clique" had deliberately prepared a secession for the next National Congress of Writers, which was due to be held in October, 1957. As he was once more in a position of strength, Chou did not hesitate to revive some very old stories, going so far as to reproach Ting Ling for the circumstances in which she had left a Kuomintang prison in 1933, insinuating that she had put herself in pawn to the enemy. Then he

[9] See Snow, Edgar, *The Other Side of the River* (London, Gollancz, 1963), p. 395.

examined Ting Ling's complete works, from the novel *Journal of Miss Sophie* (whose heroine is "a nihilist and fervent individualist") to *I Was in Hsia Village* (in which Ting Ling "idealizes a woman used as a prostitute by the Japanese"),[10] touching on the critical works of the Yenan period in passing. Chou Yang concluded: "The fires which the rightists have lit in literary circles have burned more strongly than fifteen years ago in Yenan, but today the forces of the revolution are also very much greater than they were fifteen years ago. The arsonists have burned themselves, and Ting Ling and her like are completely unmasked. . . . The only solution for the rightists is to repent and make a fresh start. The Party and the people are ready to help them to reform."

The road of repentance usually leads to a people's commune where manual labor is compulsory,[11] but it appears that Ting Ling was in Peking for two more years. Her final disgrace dates from 1959, according to unofficial sources, and she was linked with the dismissal of Marshal P'eng Teh-huai, the Defense Minister, who was accused of "rightist tendencies." We do not know all the details of the conflict which ended with the removal of this figure, one of the most prominent of the Maoist old guard. More politician than soldier, P'eng Teh-huai certainly harbored no Napoleonic ambitions, and it is considered that his disagreement with the other leaders had mainly to do with the attitude to be adopted toward the U.S.S.R. and on the question of the modernization of the army. His feats of arms during the civil war are still glorified in museums and textbooks, but in 1966 the Chinese press quite clearly attributed rightist and revisionist tendencies to him.

Agnes Smedley linked P'eng Teh-huai and Ting Ling in a chapter of her *Battle Hymn of China,* the latter having escorted her through the former's army. She presents them both as exceptional personalities, and she sees them as living symbols of the revolution, which united in the same struggle a refined woman intellectual and a general who sprang from the most backward

[10] Ting Ling's prize novel, *The Sun Shines on the River Sang-kan,* was not condemned retrospectively because it had been "written with the help of the Party."

[11] "A Very High Official told me quite flatly that only persons engaged in counterrevolutionary 'acts of violence' were arrested and that no mere dissenter, individualist or critic of party mistakes was punished," writes Edgar Snow in *The Other Side of the River,* p. 403, pointing out that in the Chinese view, public confessions and other humiliations are not considered as punishments.

ranks of the peasantry.[12] It would be unfair to be ironic about this judgment, but on rereading these pages which recapture the atmosphere of the heroic epoch, one is inevitably forced to say that this "marriage" of the intellectual elite and the revolutionary peasantry contained within it the germ of future dissension. The war and the revolution had certainly been a wonderful school for the peasant masses, but not everyone has the talents and high intelligence of a P'eng Teh-huai, and the passage of Mao Tse-tung's "teaching army" did not ultimately cure the awful backwardness. That thousands of intellectuals went to live in these primitive villages was a symbolic gesture and no doubt necessary to overcome the prejudice against "literates," but this in itself was not enough to wipe out illiteracy. It was practically impossible to bridge the gulf which separated the intelligentsia of Shanghai and Peking — polyglot and internationalist, open to all the currents of modern thought — and the mass of poor peasants who formed the Party's troops and the revolution's striking force.

To spread culture among the masses was a much bigger and more difficult problem in China than anywhere else. To teach hundreds of millions to read, write, and count a little is a frightening task and, as we shall see, the Chinese Communists have begun it with a determination which is to their credit. But it will take more than a generation before the general level of culture is raised to the point where the masses have access to real literature and art. At present they respond to works which are so elementary that in our eyes they are hardly worth considering as art or literature. Millions of copies of the journal of the model soldier Lei Feng have been printed, but it has yielded first place in the Chinese bestseller list to *The Journal of Wang Kie,* the model citizen of 1966. Having established that such books "do good," the Chinese leaders demand that intellectuals concentrate on this elementary level within reach of everyone. They even declare that only this literature and art are revolutionary because they inspire the peasants, workers, and soldiers to behave in an altruistic way that benefits the collective whole.

But such a task is beyond the capacity of men molded in another cultural tradition and marked by their own knowledge and

12 During his childhood, P'eng Teh-huai was almost executed by his family, assembled in judgment, because he had offended his grandmother. Miraculously saved by the intervention of one of his uncles, he had a brilliant military career and, according to Agnes Smedley, biographer of Chu Teh, was the real brain of the Red Army.

taste; despite all the stints in the communes, they cannot transform themselves into peasant-writers. Their works are necessarily too complex or "artificial" and they readily fall into the category of "old ideas which demoralize the people."

Simone de Beauvoir, who was in China during the good period of the "hundred flowers," has already remarked that the postulates of the Maoist cultural policy were impracticable. She wrote in her *Long March:*

"The only authentic action open to the intellectual is precisely that of writing: serving a longer probation, sharing the labor of workers and peasants would always be a way of *informing* oneself and not of *living* . . . It is right to think that as long as they confine themselves to 'going among the masses' writers will remain powerless to put them into words; they will have to 'come from the masses.' There are already young authors who come from the lower ranks of society; only, with rare exceptions, they are not really writers; without tradition, without assurance, hardly masters of the language, when faced with the blank paper they suffer from that dizziness which usually attacks uncultivated people: they are the first to yield to conventions and clichés. One notes a divorce between matter and form; the older ones possess the instrument, but have not lived the experience they propose to interpret; the young ones, in whom the movement of history is embodied, lack technique and knowledge. Chinese literature will have its opportunities when a reconciliation is brought about; one day culture will become a familiar thing for the workers and peasants; the language will not intimidate them any longer; then they will be able to talk frankly among themselves. In the meantime, the literature can hardly be more than a preliterature; this was what Mao Tse-tung foresaw when he said in Yenan that culture will be able to raise itself only when it is universally distributed."[13]

But Simone de Beauvoir could not have foreseen that this slow birth of the new culture would be accompanied by a kind of "permanent revolution" which at each stage eliminates some creative workers of the old school — all veterans of the revolution — and that it would produce a veritable storm of self-criticisms and accusations against "nonproletarian" writers. Since 1966 we have

[13] In *Literature and Revolution* (Michigan, Ann Arbor Books, 1960) Trotsky demonstrated the incoherence of the champions of proletarian culture. It was this which made the Chinese, beginning with Mao, attribute to him the theory of "proletarian politics, bourgeois art," which never was his.

been witnessing a strange spectacle which makes plain the Party
leaders' irritation with the intellectuals who know too much and
"set themselves above the people"; it is almost as if the former
meant to push their insistence on egalitarianism to the point of
demanding that all Chinese have the same cultural level.

It is almost symbolic that Kuo Mo-jo's self-criticism followed
shortly after the congress of writers of working-class and peasant
origin during which Chou Yang made the inevitable eulogizing
speech about Lei Feng and Wang Kie. Kuo Mo-jo promised in
vain to go "among the people" to acquire, with all humility, their
profound wisdom; he swore in vain that he was not afraid to dirty
his hands in the mud of the countryside, but he will not write *Lei
Feng's Journal* and he probably knows it. Besides, he is only the
latest in a long list of "veterans" considered useless from now on,
the men who have failed to adjust to the cultural climate of the
proletarian and egalitarian China of today. One year before him,
the great Mao Tun, most famous Chinese Communist writer of the
century (Lu Hsün not having been a member of the Party), was
dismissed from his post as Minister of Culture and fell into
disgrace. Then it was the turn of Yang Hsien-chen, a Communist
philosopher, deputy director of the Party's School of Cadres, who
was publicly accused of being a "conciliator" and supporter of the
theories of Deborine.[14] And these days, in the spring of 1966, the
tone is rising: the victims are both more numerous and more
violently taken to task; they have even been accused of fomenting
a plot against the "security of the state."

The drama of this whole generation of Communist intellectuals
is all the more distressing in that they in no sense refused to play
the part of "Mongolian larks" but desired, for the most part, to
sing the praises of the Party which has transformed China and is
curing her underdevelopment. The simple fact is that the Party
finds that their tune is no longer any use, that it contains too many
complicated notes which baffle the people. It finds reluctance, even
sees revisionism, where it is no more than a question of the
inherent complexity in the writer's profession.

I would have liked to meet some of these "deviationists,"
particularly Ting Ling, whose case is, in my view, the most typical.

---

[14] A. M. Deborine, Menshevik philosopher, joined the Soviet CP in 1928
and directed the review *Under the Banner of Marxism,* but his doctrinal
interpretations angered Stalin. He returned from exile in 1955 and is regarded as a victim of the errors of the period of the "personality cult."

I had drawn up a questionnaire on cultural problems, together with a list of personalities (including Mao Tun) who I thought would be able to answer it. Nothing came of it.

"But our leaders themselves are intellectuals!" exclaimed a high official of the Ministry of Foreign Affairs laughingly after reading my question about the relations between intellectuals and the Party. "Chairman Mao Tse-tung is a historian, poet, and philosopher . . ." he repeated to convince me that my preoccupation with this aspect was pointless. But then he promised to get in touch with cultural officials to find me "valid informants." A few days later he gave me the good news: the director of the Department of Culture and Propaganda of the CP Central Committee was going to answer my questions in person. "What is his name?" I asked. "Chou Yang," the official replied. He added that if I was interested in Chinese culture I must know the name, and in a sense he was right; no one has done more to defend orthodoxy than Ting Ling's former accuser. Even on the bookshelves on every floor of the Hsin Chiao Hotel one found speeches of his to the intellectuals in which he explains "the combat tasks which have to be tackled by workers in philosophy and the social sciences," or again "the path of socialist literature and art in China."

And this orthodox militant's pamphlets were also to be found in the stations, in the airports — everywhere. They were the authorized texts whose function was to enlighten the people as to the regime's aims and principles. My high official was right; no one in China could have been better qualified to instruct me in the official concept of cultural life.

THE "MARXISTS," THE "HEGELIANS,"
AND THE "PATRIOTS"

Reading his speeches, I imagined Chou Yang to be tall, thin, austere, with a wrinkled face and, no doubt, glasses. The man in front of me is stocky, rather broad-shouldered, with a round face and thinning crew-cut hair, and he smiles almost continuously. Very relaxed, he sits next to me as if with the intention of tapping me on the shoulder in a friendly way from time to time in the Slavic manner. There is something Russian in his appearance and manner — to the point where I even think for a moment of talking to him in Russian — but he doesn't understand it. Next to him is a charming interpreter in tight slacks, slimmer and more elegant than those whom we have encountered up to date. Chou Yang announces that the interview will be conducted in French. Seated at a table, two Chinese observers, one of them representing the Foreign Ministry, take notes.

No doubt because he is used to speaking in public, Chou Yang punctuates his phrases with swelling cadences which invite applause. At the end of each sentence he chuckles with satisfaction and turns toward me to see if I am impressed and convinced. In fact, I am completely surprised, for nothing is happening as I had imagined it. I begin by asking a question meant to be tricky and embarrassing: What does Chou Yang think of Soviet cultural interventionism and of the quality of Russian socialist realist art? Far from smelling a rat, Chou Yang welcomes my question with relish, as if it brought him unhoped-for pleasure.

"Certainly Soviet art and literature count for nothing." (A sweeping gesture underlines this assertion.) "They are dull and lifeless, unviewable and unreadable."

I prick up my ears; the previous night I had read an article by Chou Yang in which he bitterly accused Ting Ling (and her clique) of lack of respect for Soviet culture. I do not dare to remind him of this, but nonetheless I ask him to expand a little what he has just said about Russian culture.

"It is very simple. The Soviets opted for an absurd theory. According to them, after the nationalization of the means of production, the class struggle stopped and harmony reigned between what they call the workers, the peasants, and the 'intellectual workers.' The conflicts which, always according to them, no longer exist in life must not be found in either art or literature. That is their vision of 'socialist realism.' Marxist Leninists see things very differently. To begin with, the spirit and ideology of the propertied classes survive a long time after the revolution and cannot be eliminated by decree. The role of the Communist Party is to analyze correctly class relationships in order to disclose the antagonisms which remain. Even the working class has its internal contradictions. The peasantry is even more divided, and as for the intellectuals, they do not even form a class; they are a social stratum divided according to political attitudes. The Soviets were incapable of making this analysis. That is why they were unable to conduct the struggle against the bourgeois ideology or to train a new generation of proletarian creative workers. Their art is neither realistic nor socialistic — it is simply a version of bourgeois art."

This is strong stuff. I then ask how, half a century after the October Revolution, the Russian intellectuals have relapsed into bourgeois attitudes, and what has brought about this reversion.

Chou Yang is not in the slightest embarrassed: "It is very simple. Incapable of directing cultural life, the Soviets first tried to compel writers and artists to work to order, and they took repressive steps against those who rebelled. Chairman Mao has often explained to us that this policy is both unworthy of Marxists and absolutely ineffective. Marxists cannot be produced by force. The only weapons are education and persuasion. In the U.S.S.R., predictably, this bullying has produced no results, and after sterilizing a whole generation of creative artists, the Soviet leaders have resigned themselves to buying works of art which conform to their concept of a harmonious society. Yes, buying — at a price. Do you know how much a Soviet writer is paid?" cries Chou Yang, his face contorted with indignation. "Do you know how much an academician earns? Compare them with the pay of a Russian worker and you will see that the differences are even much greater than they are with you in France."

Chou Yang is in full flight. There is no question of getting a word in.

"In this way they created an intellectual layer completely cut off from the people, ensconced in their *dachas*, thinking only of money and comfort. Is it surprising that in these conditions the most down-at-the-heel bourgeois ideas have been revived? Read what the Russians write. Do you think they discuss the class struggle or colonialist oppression? Not at all. They preach universal reconciliation, a so-called harmony between all men, rich or poor, exploiters or exploited, imperialists or colonized. They call that humanism! And it is — the most bourgeois kind possible, the same kind that Marx and Lenin denounced as the very expression of bourgeois trickery and hypocrisy. They tell us today that there are universal values, independent of social class, that human nature is unchangeable, and that one of its basic traits is an inborn selfishness. Believe me, it was one of their cultural leaders who told me that. What can you expect? They are all conditioned by their life of luxury and their *dachas* and no longer realize that their pseudo-universalism comes straight from Kant, and not from Marx."

Having dealt with the Soviet intelligentsia, Chou Yang reassumes his benevolent smile and asks me if I have followed his argument. I answer with a question: At what point, in his opinion, did this Soviet decadence set in? This time Chou Yang is well aware that I have laid a trap, but he keeps on smiling.

"Are you trying to say that all that is Stalin's fault? That is partly true. We have already said that Stalin committed serious errors and that he often adopted very unpleasant methods. For example, we consider his 1935 constitution indefensible, and it certainly contributed to the degeneration of Soviet cultural concepts. But Stalin was nevertheless a Communist, a revolutionary, and he led the U.S.S.R. under particularly difficult conditions when she was subjected to capitalist encirclement. During this period no one had had any previous experience with building socialism, and such a gigantic undertaking could not go forward without mistakes. But Stalin was unmovable on certain fundamental principles. He was not a capitulationist like Khrushchev, who thought only of reconciliation with the imperialists and under whose leadership the Communist Party of the U.S.S.R. abandoned all revolutionary and Communist aspirations. That is the truth!"

This truth I am aware of — it was thrown at me whenever I mentioned Stalin in China. It is useless to argue. I return to Chinese cultural policy: "Since you condemn interventionism and pass such harsh judgments on Soviet practice, why did you renounce the policy of the 'hundred flowers'?"

"Who told you we have abandoned this policy?" replied Chou Yang, sincerely astonished, and with the spirited approval of the observers. "It is not true. We are still faithful to the principle 'Let a hundred flowers bloom, let a hundred schools contend.' We do not tell our artists how — or what — they must paint or write. All can freely choose their themes and the form of their works. We often publish very controversial books and occasionally even books that are frankly deplorable, like, for example, those by a certain Nikita Khrushchev. Soon we shall also be publishing the writings of Chiang Kai-shek."

Chou Yang's observers enjoy the joke, and the pretty interpreter laughs as she translates it but my laugh is visibly forced. Chou Yang is conscious all the same that he has not really replied and he adds: "Of course we have our own idea of culture, and we don't leave artists and writers to their own devices. In order for them to serve the people as we wish, the political consciousness of creative workers has to be developed. That's the key problem of the cultural policy. If the artist accepts collectivist values, if he assimilates Marxism, his work will necessarily reflect our epoch and will be useful to the people. Thus, instead of telling writers what they must write and painters how they must paint, we give them a political education and make them understand the true facts about our country and the world."

"In other words, you advise intellectuals only in the political sphere?"

Chou Yang looks at me out of the corner of his eye, vaguely uneasy. Perhaps he understands French or senses the irony. He becomes very serious.

"The great majority of our intellectuals, about 90 per cent, favor socialism and want to contribute to its success. They are patriots who know how much our country suffered before the Liberation. But these same intellectuals are mostly of middle-class or lower-middle-class origin and do not have the integrity of the proletarian class. True, they try hard to assimilate Marxist Leninism, but it isn't easy for them. Today a minority among them, 20 per cent at the most, have succeeded in assimilating the dialectical method and know how to use it to analyze and to create. They are true Communists. There are others, about another 20 per cent, who are ideologically very close to us but who are not yet complete Marxists. Their dialectic remains more Hegelian than Marxist. As Chairman Mao said in his 'Yenan talks,' some can hear the message of proletarian ideology all their lives without ever really absorbing it."

Chou Yang, with a grave air, retreats within himself for a moment. What he has just said about the difficulty of getting beyond Hegel perhaps evokes a memory of personal friends who have not surmounted it. . . . On my part, I am calculating: 20 and 20 are 40, and I ask who the other 60 per cent are.

"It is simple," replies Chou Yang. "They are still ideologically uncommitted. As patriots, proud of the achievements of the People's China, they are for us, for socialism. But stamped by the old anticollectivist prejudices, they do not always understand the people and sometimes yield to ideological influences foreign to socialism. Some of them, about 10 per cent, are even systematically hostile to us. That is why, as I have already told you, one cannot consider the intellectuals as a homogeneous class or abandon the struggle to bring as many as possible into our camp."

Without my raising the question, Chou Yang then explains to

me his own personal case. He also is of nonproletarian origin, and he has had a lot of difficulty in becoming a conforming Communist. He was lucky in that the Party helped him in his "first political steps," but he appreciates the difficulties all the same: "We had no preparation to enable us to adapt our consciousness to the new production relationships, to the economic infrastructure of a society such as had never existed before in history."

Paraphrasing Mao, he explains to me that there are things one cannot learn from books and which only practice and life can teach. By this subterfuge he moves on to the basic principle of the Chinese doctrine: the necessity of manual work for the intellectuals and the cadres.

"Do you believe that this so-called 'forced labor' is indispensable to our economy? Quite the reverse. Our economists will even tell you that the opposite is true: the participation of intellectuals in production costs more than it brings in. The intellectuals' productivity in manual jobs is low, but they continue to get their usual pay while in the factory or at the people's communes. No, it is not a question either of exploiting or of harassing them. Our aim is to produce intellectuals who know about life, for society greatly needs such people."

I ask who decides when and where an intellectual must go to do his manual stint. Chou Yang's reply is rather vague; it seems that this varies considerably according to locale and circumstances. But Chou Yang insists on the fact that everything is always arranged in a friendly way and that all problems are ironed out by discussion and persuasion.

"Occasionally we are obliged to convince not the intellectuals but the commune members, who are not keen to accept them. A few days ago I had to deal with the case of a writer. He wanted to prolong his term in the fields, but the commune members felt that they were losing too much time teaching him how to work the land. In some sectors of our society the divisions are still very marked and prejudices die hard. The peasants are still not used to seeing intellectuals working with their hands. In the old China the literati let their fingernails grow long to show that they belonged to a superior class which did not dirty its hands. The people still remember this, and that is another reason why we want the intellectuals to prove that those days are over and that the barriers erected between men must go."

I admit that such spells of manual work may be useful for the social unification of China, but I ask if there is not a risk that they might be detrimental to creative work.

"In our view an intellectual must know his country and his time from the inside in order to understand them and reflect them in his work. Goethe rightly said that the writer develops at the same pace as the world in which he lives. If the world is progressing, the writer flourishes; if the world is regressing, the writer retreats within himself. We are living today in the ascendant period of the socialist era. We are therefore convinced that our intellectuals are in a privileged position and that they will be able to create a proletarian art, which until now has never existed. But to achieve this they must be participants, combatants, and not observers who describe the new social developments from the outside. That is the difference between our concept and that of the Soviets, who suggested to their writers that they go into the kolkhozes and the factories to see peasants and workers at work. The 'observer' of this kind can only produce dull, static works; those who play a full part in their world by doing manual work are, conversely, able to portray it with power and richness."

Frequently recalling the "Yenan talks," Chou Yang lyrically conjures up a picture of the proletarian art to be born from a merging of the intellectuals integrated with the people and the new society which inspires them. When he finishes, I mention the exhibition of contemporary painting I saw in Peking and the academic (I dare not say "Soviet") aspect of the canvasses on display. Then I recall the Gramsci criticism on the "common sense" of the people. I know that the authority of the founder of the Italian CP does not equal Mao's, but I need to lean on some authority, and I even attribute more to Gramsci than he has actually said. In vain; Chou Yang, who has probably never heard of the famous Italian Communist, remains chilly. But his ignorance affords me a slight advantage. Not knowing just who Gramsci is, he does not dare to reject my arguments as "revisionist" or "Hegelian." He tries to circumvent the obstacle and is willing to admit that Chinese painting is terribly academic. But what to us is the inevitable result of the conception of art known as proletarian is to Chou Yang merely the result of errors committed in the application of the present cultural policy.

"At the start," he says, "we did not give enough importance to manual work for intellectuals. That is why some of them didn't know the people very well. As a consequence their works are not always good, and we criticize them, as you have just done with good reason."

"What I criticize are your principles," I say. "I strongly fear that they lead inevitably to formalism." And I add that I think it is dangerous to judge the quality of a work solely on its popularity. Chou Yang leaps.

"But there is no other criterion! An artist cannot work only for his wife and his niece. He must serve the people and accept their judgment. Each class creates its own art and culture. The proletariat, which is in power and in the process of transforming China, has the right to have its own art and culture. And they will be very much better than those of other classes because the proletariat is nobler, more just, and morally more correct than the bourgeoisie and all the other classes who dominated the old society."

Suddenly I feel as if I am at a meeting, and to change the atmosphere I quickly switch the subject. I ask Chou Yang to tell me about certain articles which have recently appeared in China and which, if the translations published in Europe are to be believed, express very harsh judgments on Shakespeare and on European literature and music, both classical and contemporary.

"That's not completely true," replies Chou Yang. "In our theatrical schools Shakespeare and Molière are read and performed, and we in no way denigrate classical culture. The problem for Marxist Leninists is not to accept or to reject the heritage of previous ages. What we want to do is to analyze these works and explain their social and political origin in order to bring them within reach of our people. The classics can be extremely useful if, thanks to them, the people better understand the societies in which they were created. But they can also be damaging if they are published just as they are, without interpretation, for they run the risk of giving readers prejudices which no longer belong to our age. In short, we intend to be the masters and not the slaves of our cultural heritage. We do not believe that there are works which are unassailable, unsurpassable, and above all criticism. In our view there are things which cannot be learned from the classics. Shakespeare was great, but he had not been through the experience of socialism. Our young people need a theater which reflects this experience, for it is theirs."

Then, to contrast this Marxist-Leninist attitude with that of the "revisionists," Chou Yang quotes the case of Lukacs, "this veteran revisionist," who praised the bourgeois literature of the nineteenth century in an extravagant manner and held it to be without equal.

"Why did he commit these errors and why is he so appreciated in Russia?" asks Chou Yang. "Because neither he nor the other revisionists believe in the possibility of socialist art. Their respect for the bourgeoisie even prevents them from imagining that the collectivist society may give birth to an art which is a thousand times superior. Without denying that bourgeois individualistic humanism played a positive role during a certain historic period, we are convinced that proletarian humanism will play a much greater part. Admittedly the bourgeoisie dethroned God in order to put man at the center of the world. That is to their credit. But the man they thus placed on a pedestal is *their* man, a bourgeois egoist steeped in the values of a monetary society. In our opinion this man is neither admirable nor, fortunately, eternal. In our society a different and very much better man is in the process of being formed. Lei Feng was such a man, and there are millions of others like him. Therein lies our hope."

I record this in silence (which is interpreted as approbation) and I take my leave.

The old Russian proverb says: "Happy is the man who believes — his faith keeps him warm." Chou Yang, with his "proletarian culture" of the future, seemed to me to belong to this happy category. No doubts seemed to disturb his sense of certitude and no argument from a "nonbeliever" could shake his clear conscience as a scourger of revisionist or simply nonproletarian heretics. When in the spring of 1966 the Chinese press indicated discreetly that "a high cultural authority" had for a long time protected wrong-thinking intellectuals, I hazarded many guesses at the possible identity of the man in question but the thought never crossed my mind that it might be Chou Yang.

However, a dispatch from Agence France Press on July 1 revealed that, according to the monthly review *Red Flag*, "Chou Yang opposes the literary and artistic line laid down by Mao Tse-tung. He protects the anti-Party clique which favors capitalist and feudal literature and art." And this was only the beginning. As the "great cultural revolution" progressed, the attacks on Chou Yang increased. No one was more violently taken to task. During August, 1966, the Central Committee's propaganda department even launched a pathetic appeal: "Let us hold high the great Red banner of Mao Tse-tung's thought and vigorously denounce Chou

Yang, grand master of the black gang in literary and artistic circles." And here is how the Chinese press has since described the fallen leader: "Representative of the bourgeoisie, insinuated into the ranks of the Party"; "representative of the landed proprietors and degenerate elements"; "hundred-per-cent counter-revolutionary revisionist"; "recruiter of deserters and renegades"; "criminal"; "admirer of Khrushchev"; "old fox"; "fierce wolf"; "a viper of good appearance"; "the bourgeoisie's god of justice"; "Lucifer."

What strikes one about this list of charges is that both the tone and the vocabulary contrast with the moderate accents which characterized Mao Tse-tung's "Yenan talks." In those days Mao Tse-tung employed a modern and international idiom and was sparing with Chinese references. Today's documents are as violent as they are systematic and draw on images that seem to come directly from the "superstitious past," as, for example, "In the spring of 1957 monsters and demons of every kind appeared one after the other." Although they swear fidelity to the thought of Mao, Chou Yang's accusers appear to have a naïve and simplistic concept of culture and of the intellectual's role, a concept that can hardly be found in the writings of Mao himself.

But why did this proletarian left — for this is how the accusers describe themselves — choose Chou Yang as the principal target of its fury? In the articles about him one first of all notices a certain number of puzzling polemical falsifications. Imputed to the miserable Chou Yang are ideas he sharply attacked during my interview with him. He is accused, for example, of having considered the "bourgeois realism of the nineteenth century" as the summit of the arts, while in fact he told me exactly the opposite. It is claimed that he was in agreement with Ting Ling during the Yenan controversies of 1942 and that he was her protector during the "hundred flowers" crisis in 1957, although in fact he was her main opponent. He is presented to the world as an admirer of Khrushchev, although in fact he talked to me about the former Soviet premier with complete contempt.

It is probable, however, that Chou Yang committed crimes which are much more real in the eyes of the Red Guards: while he was a supporter of art in the service of the people, he seems to have claimed a certain autonomy for the cultural sector, an "indirect co-ordination," and a more cautious indoctrination. He may, as they allege, have declared, in defending books which were not strictly political, that "it is not by talking all the time about Chairman Mao that one best applies Mao's thought," and that the artist must be free to choose the subject of his work. And he may also have maintained that the quality of a work of art does not depend on its content alone and acknowledged the importance of artists, of great intellectual personalities and of specialists.

These attitudes in no way contradict his main theory on the utilitarian character of culture. In a free discussion Chou Yang would probably have been able to demonstrate that his way of treating the intellectuals would have been more effective than that used by the Red Guards. But the proletarian left does not share his anxiety to win the intellectuals, precisely because it no longer accords to men of culture a special role which objectively differentiates them from others. Rightly or wrongly, Chou Yang considered that intellectuals form a social stratum. The proletarian left holds that what separates them from the rest of the people results from the heritage of the previous epoch and must be abolished and not sanctioned under any other system.

It is this, in my view, which would explain the Red Guards' fury against Chou Yang, supporter of different methods and a different way of handling intellectuals rather than advocate of an anti-Maoist theory of art and literature. And if so many long articles are written against him, it is because the question of the intellectuals in particular enrages the Red Guards. They have also attacked other privileged groups, the remaining capitalists and the bureaucrats, but as the influence of these on people's minds is nil, their neutralization is a simple affair. The intellectuals, on the contrary, possess the means of persuasion, know how to bewitch minds, and remain, whatever one may do about it, a social stratum. Chou Yang already wanted every peasant and worker to become a writer and thus beget the proletarian culture. The proletarian left goes further: while waiting for the whole nation to become intellectuals, it refuses the right of existence to an elite, even one that springs from the people.

"We don't want any specialists," cry certain young Chinese workers, while the students demand that the period of study should be reduced. It would be wrong to see in these manifestations only a contempt for culture. The same antispecialist workers throw themselves into higher mathematics in order to manufacture, for instance, steel oxygen bottles, which China was forced to import at exorbitant prices and which Chinese specialists thought impossible to make in China.[15]

The students know that a long period of study at higher educa-

15 *Peking Review*, No. 30 (July 25, 1966).

tion levels means a strict selection system that favors the most gifted and creates a lifelong differentiation. But culture remains an aristocratic fact which ensures privileges for those who know, and therefore can; who question themselves, and therefore doubt. But culture remains the great goal of the new man, and a society in mid-development cannot base itself on the principle "Culture for all or for no one." We are witnessing, therefore, a convulsion which runs the risk of doing considerable damage and which is the product of a singular haste to do away with human inequality. China has suffered so much from privilege that she seems to prefer to impoverish herself — momentarily, one hopes — in an all-out and utopian bid for equality rather than allow social differences to be re-created within her society.

A HUNDRED FLOWERS OF THE SAME KIND

Never in any theater in China, either in Peking or in the provinces, did I see an empty seat. Everywhere the auditorium was packed and everywhere my neighbors were workers straight from the factory or peasants who had come in from suburban communes. In short, China's efforts — according to the hallowed formula — to bring culture to the people are an undeniable success. I ought to have been less surprised than most at seeing the working classes in the theater in a Communist country. During my "Soviet period" I witnessed the tremendous efforts made by the Russian regime to enable all sectors of the population to attend the most varied forms of entertainment.

At the height of the war the Russians continued to go to the theater and crowd into the movie houses; when a town was liberated, the places of entertainment were always among the first buildings to be rebuilt.

Although I had lived through this experience, I was often struck in Chinese theaters by the truly proletarian character of the audiences. The nature of the entertainment and the surroundings accentuate their popular character. The halls, particularly in the provinces, are often extremely modest affairs, built with the sole purpose of accommodating the largest possible number of spectators. No foyer, no bars. During the intermission most of the audience usually stay in their seats. Another odd feature: to help the audience to understand it, the libretto of an opera is projected onto screens on both sides of the stage.

But if the "normal" show in China is stripped of all the usual Western trimmings, it is a vastly different matter at gala performances in the concert hall of the People's Palace in Peking. Our visit coincided with the change in the theater's repertoire, which in keeping with the authorities' decision must henceforth reflect the day-to-day preoccupations of the Chinese. Diplomats and journalists were therefore invited to attend the premières of a ballet whose story was drawn from contemporary themes and of some new operas in which the action takes place abroad, in the Congo or Vietnam. These festivities always attract an elegant audience and are conducted according to the international rite, with long discussions in beautifully decorated salons and buffets. For foreigners they provide a rare opportunity to meet Chinese officials privately and to chat about things sometimes very far removed from the theater.

Our hosts' curiosity about these ballets and new operas was as great as ours. Everyone claimed to be very pleased at the modernization of the repertoire and explained that Chinese audiences were bored with the old shows peopled with princes, emperors, and their concubines. The contemporary operas which we attended were of two types: one was inspired by revolutionary literature and recalls the days of resistance to the Kuomintang and to the Japanese. The others were directly inspired by present-day Chinese or world events. The number of different shows staged in a few months gives a lofty impression of the fertility of Chinese dramatists, but to see them is to realize that they are often merely variations on the same theme.

Thus *The Red Rock* and *The Red Lantern,* two operas taken from recent history, contain several scenes which are virtually the same. In one it is the Kuomintang police who interrogate the Communist prisoners, in the other it is the Japanese; but their methods (at first, attempts to corrupt, then torture) and what they say to their victims seem identical. We came across the same scenes in an opera of the second type in which it is the Americans and the South Vietnamese in their pay who apply these methods to their N.L.F. prisoners.

Another similarity is that occasionally the hero has been captured through the treachery of a "weak" comrade, who (by chance, no doubt) is always an intellectual. Despite their stereotyped form, the war operas are full of very lively action and are never boring. The audience is always completely absorbed. In Sian, where we saw *The Red Rock,* our neighbors sobbed when Sister Chiang, a Communist militant, was first tortured in the headquarters of the "Sino-American Co-operation Organization" and then shot by the Nationalists on the Red Rock. However, these fervent theatergoers do not react like those of the Middle Ages who, after seeing a passion play, would try to stone the actor who played the part of Judas. In Shanghai the role of the Japanese colonel in *The Red Lantern,* a negative and odious character, was played by Yuan Chi-kai, who is an extraordinary actor. Fascinated, the audience applauded each of his tirades (which is rare in China), irrespective of their content. It was quite surprising, but it was an indication of their taste for good theater.

However, the masterpiece of art dedicated to recent history is *The East Is Red,* a super song-and-dance production which in four hours retraces the entire Maoist epic. Tremendous resources were made available for this outstanding spectacle, which was put on for the fifteenth anniversary of the People's Republic, with a cast of 3,000 actors. We saw just extracts from this work, which is staged in its entirety only on important occasions.

Another contemporary ballet, *The Red Detachment of Women,* tells the story of a peasant girl from the island of Hainan. Oppressed by her landlord, beaten by his henchmen, abandoned half-dead in a forest, the heroine is saved by a detachment of partisans composed mainly of women. Her first experience as a soldier is rather unhappy: unable to understand guerilla tactics, the good peasant girl fires on the enemy at the wrong time, ruining the plan to wipe out the landlord and subjecting her detachment to unnecessary losses. The political commissar forgives the new recruit, who in time becomes an exemplary soldier and even succeeds him when he is killed in action. The theme of this ballet slightly resembles that of *Die Massnahme* (*The Measures Taken*) by Bertolt Brecht, in which a young soldier, keen but raw, shows himself unable to respect the rules of the collective struggle, misfires, and seriously endangers the safety of his comrades-in-arms. But while Brecht makes a tragedy of his hero's inability to fit into the group, which ends up by killing him with his own consent, the Chinese ballet has a happy ending and tends to demonstrate that with a little patience and a lot of persuasion those combatants the least amenable to discipline can be reclaimed. This "eulogy of persuasion" has served as a theme for several other Chinese productions.

The Red Detachment of Women would be as successful in Europe as the production recently presented there by the Peking Opera. The décor and costumes are beautiful, the pace very quick, and the "battles" danced by ballerina-acrobats in uniform are astonishing. The quality of this ballet seemed to me to be superior in every way to that of most of the shows based on contemporary events.

In Yenan during the war Chinese artists were already staging didactic and propagandist drama. They continue today; the villains are obviously the Americans. During demonstrations in Peking we saw an impromptu performance in the central square which featured Lyndon Johnson, his ambassador to Saigon, Maxwell Taylor, corrupt South Vietnamese politicians, and American airmen who were prisoners of the Vietnam partisans. We also saw whole operas about the events in Vietnam (*Letters from the South* and *Fires of Wrath Under the Coconut Trees*) and about the Lumumba struggle in the Congo (*War Drums Below the Equator*).

Some European modernists for a long time championed the impromptu play on political themes, and Brecht, for instance, considered that only this kind of theater had a future. But this type of theater, if it is to have the value which Brecht wanted to confer on it, calls for constant innovation, while in China plays contain little of this quality and thus one gets the impression of hardening arteries. When you have once seen Johnson shouting abuse at Taylor, who then shouts abuse at the American Commander in Chief (always slightly drunk), who in turn shouts abuse at the trembling South Vietnamese puppets, you have seen it all.

By chance I accompanied the British Labor Party delegation to Moscow in 1959. It was invited to the première of a Soviet ballet on a contemporary theme, *The Paths of Thunder,* which takes place in Africa. The British politicians were very upset to see their compatriots (or characters who strongly resembled British military types) portrayed on the stage as always fortified by whisky and radiating stupidity. Between acts they allowed themselves to express some reservations about this aspect of the ballet without thinking that this would raise doubts in the minds of their Russian hosts about their anticolonialist and antiracist feelings. The incident even threatened to reach serious proportions when the Labor leaders refused to listen to their hosts' anticolonialist lectures. Benefiting from this experience, I preferred not to tell my Chinese escorts that their stage imperialists staggered a little too much and that their talk was rather too stereotyped.

The operas and plays which deal with Chinese domestic problems are sometimes didactic to the point of audacity. How can one fail to salute the courage of a dramatist who is given the task of explaining to the peasants that they must not keep the manure for their gardens but must give it to the commune, and who actually succeeds in creating a play on this subject. A whole repertoire deals with the most down-to-earth problems in an artless way that Soviet Russia never in my experience dared to employ. In Kunming, capital of a province in which there are important national minorities, we saw an opera denouncing the superstitions of the Yis; in Sian we saw one about the way shepherds must protect their sheep during storms; in Wuhan, another one about the training of women aviators; and so on. In all these works there are always several unpleasant characters (generally of bourgeois origin) who enable the playwrights to create suspense and to explain even better at the end why the good guys were victorious.

What is painful in these operas are the moments devoted to the Mao cult. The heroes meditate in front of his portrait so that no one is left unaware that it is he who inspires them to their good deeds. In the opera about the women aviators, after a training accident, the political commissar decrees: "All flights are stopped for five days and everybody must immediately get down to the study of Chairman Mao's works." Next the trainee pilots are seen deep in Mao's books — after which there are no more accidents. A hundred similar examples could be cited, and in view of the prevailing climate in China there is nothing really astonishing in this. Yet when presented on the stage, this intense Mao cult offends much more than it does in everyday life.

The graphic arts more than the others serve to feed the cult. In the place of honor in official buildings and in every working-class or peasant home a portrait of Mao is displayed, whether a giant photograph or a normal-size likeness. The ones most often seen show Mao in a peasant house, talking to the people, with his host smoking a pipe and the children crowding at the door while everybody looks at him eagerly, except the cat which, being a mere animal, turns its back; or Mao inaugurating the People's Palace in Peking, surrounded by representatives of all nationalities; or Mao walking at the head of the Red Army column which ended the Long March so victoriously; or Mao alone, in a short white shirt, with a straw hat in his hand and a smile on his lips.

Contrary to what one might expect, these pictures are not ugly (except for the second one, which is frankly hideous); and while they may be "socialistically realist," one detects the influence of the old Chinese pictorial tradition and a certain touch; they have a minor charm which Russian paintings in the Guerassimov manner never have.

With the dramatists, film producers, and all the other artists we met we tried to avoid "doctrinal" discussions like the one I had with Chou Yang and to find out about the living and working conditions of the intellectuals.

But proletarian art, "a thousand times superior to all others," never failed to come up for discussion, as well as the decadence of Soviet art, not to mention Western bourgeois art. Listening to these speeches, we suddenly felt the strength of the isolationist tendencies which daily become more marked in China. Everything that comes from the U.S.S.R. and the Communist bloc (excluding North Korea and Vietnam) is revisionist and corrupt. Everything that comes from the West is at best bourgeois, at worst, imperialist, and must therefore be considered suspect, if not actively combated. There only remains Chinese proletarian art.

We met several rather elderly people who were familiar with foreign literature and who could talk about Brecht, Sartre, Ibsen, or Shaw; but the young people did not even know their names. While Mr. Chao-sin, Communist secretary of the Theatrical Association of China, could explain to us, for example, to what extent Brecht was influenced by the Chinese theater, a young Shanghai producer did not even know Brecht's name. And while the artistic director of the Hai Ye studio, Mr. Li Tse-wu, thought that there was good and bad in Sartre's work, a young scenarist had never heard of him.

But "the old ones who know" defend the same theories as the "young isolationists," and sometimes with even more fervor. Practically all of them are of bourgeois origin, and they do not fail to indicate it by the tone of their avowal.

"Did you like *The Red Rock?* What can you expect? It was a worker who wrote it and it is still our best book," a writer of the "old epoch" said to me very sincerely.

From others, too, came the same line about the proletarians

who know more about life, are "politically better," and consequently superior in all spheres. One day I tried to console some of
them on this point by recalling that Marx was of bourgeois origin
and yet knew a lot more about many things than many workers,
but my words fell on deaf ears. Besides, Chairman Mao has
already explained in his "Yenan talks" why Marx was able to
become Marx even though he was bourgeois.

The intellectuals' only hope of erasing the stain of bourgeois
origin is manual labor, which brings them into contact with the
masses. So they tell you about it and show you the immediate
results. "Here are the paintings I did before and here are the ones I
did afterward," said a painter. They were landscapes which did not
look very different to my eyes, but I didn't dare to make any
comment.

A well-known actor at the Peking Opera, Li Hu-tsan, who is
himself of very humble origin, has nevertheless benefited considerably from his stint in a factory: "I am forty-three and I have
worked at the opera since I was nine. Four months ago I was
playing the role of a provincial governor when suddenly I was
entrusted with the principal role in a modern opera, *We Must Not
Forget!* I know very well that people want to see this kind of
opera, but I was scared — I didn't know if I was capable of por-
traying a worker. The Party advised me to go to a factory, and for
six weeks I worked as an ordinary unskilled laborer. Then during
rehearsals I invited my factory comrades along and asked for their
opinions. They laughed at me: a worker would never talk like that;
why do you make gestures like this? etc. Then they showed me
what I had to do to play the role authentically, and, thanks to them,
I was a great success, as was the opera."

Criticism from the rank and file, self-criticism, work in contact
with the people — there is no lack of new customs and rituals in
the Chinese cultural world, which is separated more and more
every day from foreign cultural influences by a widening gulf.
Paradoxically, even the members of remote communes asked us
about ourselves and the country we came from while intellectuals
never treated us to the basic courtesy of answering our questions
with their own. Dramatists never inquired about the plays being
staged in our country, nor film-makers about our films, nor writers
about our literary tastes. I got the impression that they did not
want to know and, above all, that in their eyes people who do not
practice either criticism or self-criticism and who do not engage in

manual labor cannot have any taste or even, to tell the truth, a real existence.

"We more easily find a common language with Africans or Asians than we do with Europeans," I was told by a young Shanghai intellectual who, it turned out, had never been out of China and doubtless had met only a few delegates in transit. But (as was the case in the U.S.S.R.) it is precisely these young products of isolationism who always adopt the most peremptory tone in discussions and proclaim their country's cultural superiority with the greatest assurance. When they get into a muddle while quoting Marxist classics, their elders fly to their aid and take up their arguments on proletarian culture (sometimes carrying things to the point of absurdity), so much so that I often wondered if they were trying to imply that all this must not be taken too seriously. For is it possible that a man in the theater who has lived for a long time in Europe and in the United States can assert without irony that the best film he has ever seen is *Lei Feng* and that his dearest ambition is to be able to adapt it for the stage?

One must believe so. What is certain in any event is that no artist or intellectual ever made the slightest criticism of the present regime in my hearing.

Another factor is that political enthusiasm here is ten times greater than it ever was in Stalin's Russia, and intellectuals accept infinitely greater material sacrifices. Coercion alone cannot explain the frenetic activity of the men who are building China's "proletarian culture." These men have not been heaped with honors as were the bards of Stalinism. They do not have private cars, or luxury apartments, or *dachas,* or shops better stocked than the others reserved for them; and they actually go out to work on the land, and afterward they beat their breasts in self-reproach because they are not proletarian enough. They must therefore believe that their efforts will bear fine fruit. Are we perhaps too blasé to understand them?

Art in China is undoubtedly going to develop; it will be essentially a religious art not easily understood by the uninitiated, and which even specialists in the traditional China will have difficulty in understanding. But whatever form it takes, it will never be a proletarian, international art, even if it celebrates the struggle of Africans and Latin Americans against their oppressors; it will have its roots in the Chinese peasantry, and it will remain Chinese. Trotsky said that if a bean is planted in a flower pot one should not expect to see a flowering tree grow. Russian experience proved him right, and the Stalinist bean did not produce much. What the Maoists are in the process of planting is undoubtedly different, and the earth that fills the pot is completely Chinese. But they are still a bean and a pot, and it would take a miracle for a tree to come up.

THE FOURTH GENERATION AND HOW TO CUT DOWN THE SIZE OF THE FIFTH

The children in the day nursery next to textile factory number eight in Peking are lined up like adults, in rows according to height (from two and a half to three feet), and as we enter the playground they begin to sing:

> We are the fourth generation of the Liberation,
> Heirs of the Revolution.
> Imperialists, have no illusions!
> We shall never be revisionists.
> We shall become true Marxist Leninists!

Our escorts, particularly numerous this morning (six or seven people), are carried away by the song of these miniature Marxists. The female manager of the factory picks up a little girl who has sung particularly well and hugs her tenderly. The other adults follow suit, and we have the feeling that we are taking part in the reunion of a long-separated family. Then a little girl of five, dainty as a doll with her pigtails, her round face, and her smiling little eyes, leaps into my arms and bids the foreign uncle welcome. Immediately the whole class throws itself on me, and I am seized by dozens of tiny arms. I do not know whether this is a prearranged part of the program or whether, simply having overcome their shyness, the representatives of the fourth generation of the Liberation want to have a closer look at my gigantic nose and white face. My guides rescue me and apologize: "What can you expect? They have the luck to live in our epoch and are overflowing with happiness and energy."

Even if they are made to sing songs whose words astound us, it is undeniable that the children of the fourth generation really are privileged, and I cannot do better than quote Robert Guillain's assertion: "When I am asked if the Chinese of today are happier than those of yesterday, there is at least one answer I can give with certainty. That is that the Chinese children have never been as happy as they are today; or as clean, as well dressed, and as well behaved; or as cheering a sight."[16]

Every day nursery and school we were taken to, even in the poorest villages, was a real oasis of happiness and plenty which testified in a moving way to the progress of Chinese society. True, in the U.S.S.R. and the people's democracies they think first of the children, who are particularly pampered. But the Chinese started from much farther down and their country was very much poorer; their child population, already tremendous, is increasing at a rate of twelve to fifteen million a year; they have had to create a prodigious number of day nurseries and schools from scratch.

But there are still not enough of them, and education, which in theory is compulsory, does not seem to be completely universal. In the villages one sees youngsters marching in columns to school; but others stay at home, looked after by their grandparents and sometimes by their mothers, who then have to give up their jobs and their pay. Local and national officials did not attempt to hide from us the fact that Chinese society is not yet in a position to take the responsibility for the whole child population, and they acknowledge that children are a burden on families and especially on women.

The Chinese are firmly anti-Malthusian and deny that their country faces a population problem. The Minister of Agriculture claims that the soil of China can amply feed the expanding population, the industrial planners assert that the problem of employment does not worry them, and the ideologists declare that China's strength lies in numbers. And at the Ministry of Health, officials of the Department of Women and Children tell you that birth control is only necessary because it ensures the liberty of the woman and the balance of the family.

Western specialists on China assert, on the contrary, that the population growth presents a formidable threat to the country. With the lack of statistics it is very difficult to reach a conclusion. One can say, nevertheless, that the Chinese know there is a problem but refuse to admit it in order to avoid contradicting some of their previous proclamations and to escape the reproach that they are abandoning the anti-Malthusian tradition of the workers'

[16] Guillain, Robert, *Dans Trente Ans la Chine,* p. 167.

movement. What really matters is what they are doing, and not their reasons for doing it — and it is obvious that they are making an immense effort to control the birth rate.

The director of the Department of Women and Children told us that the annual rate of increase of the population is about 2 per cent and that the aim is to reduce this by half. To achieve this they are conducting a propaganda campaign urging the use of contraceptives and, in the case of couples who already have two or three children, recommending sterilization. In a big movie theater in Sian we saw a film which very clearly illustrated the director's theories. It told, in a very lively way, the story of a woman over-burdened with children, who at first was very reluctant but ended up seeking advice from the birth-control authorities. There a woman doctor enumerated the methods of avoiding conception: keeping an eye on "the days," using a pessary, and sterilization. The pill was not mentioned, but according to Edgar Snow the Chinese are also interested in this method, which they are now trying to perfect.

In the second part of the film — mildly comic — there was a man whom a doctor proposed to sterilize. The idea revolted the hero, and to the audience's great joy, he protested that although he didn't want to have any more children, he did not want to become a eunuch. The doctor reassured him on this point and even told him that a second operation could make him fertile again.

At the end of the film we were shown the hitherto uneasy male stretched out on the operation table, all smiles.

During our travels we were able to verify that contraceptives are on sale everywhere — and very cheap. But it does not look as if the sterilization propaganda is succeeding in convincing everyone, and it is said that it can affect a woman's health. The director of the Department of Women herself told us that the operation is more successful in the case of men; but the latter, despite all the explanations given to them, remain reluctant. In her view the survival of the old concept of the family is the main obstacle to general acceptance of birth control. Until not so long ago, in the rural areas having children was considered something of an investment, an insurance against old age. Today the state looks after old people, but such deeply ingrained attitudes are not so quickly overcome.

However, in towns the birth rate has dropped considerably in the last few years, and the propaganda campaign is mainly carried out in the rural areas. It is a slow business. "It was much easier to explain to people that it is shameful to be dirty than to get them to accept birth control," concluded the director.

But the state is not discouraged, and it has adopted another method of limiting births — "marriage control." Chinese law permits marriage at eighteen for women and at twenty for men. This is a very high age limit for a country in which, until recently, parents married off quite young children; what is even more, pressure is put on women not to marry before twenty-five and on men not to marry before thirty.

The director explained to me that the intention was to protect women for whom it would be dangerous to have children too soon, and she ended by talking to me about abortion, which is available at no cost when both husband and wife agree, even in districts where hospital facilities are very rudimentary. While perfecting abortion methods, however, the Chinese birth-control specialists plainly advocate contraception and sterilization.

"What do you think of this question in your country? What contraceptive methods do you use? We lack experience and are greatly in need of advice in this field. If you are a friend of our country, tell me frankly everything you do," the director finally asked me, to my extreme embarrassment. I replied as well as I could. Then the conversation became less constrained again, and I asked how unmarried mothers were treated. To be truthful, I wanted to know if women are free to have sexual relations outside marriage. The director replied with great aplomb: "If you know how much we love children in our country, you will fully understand that there is no father who would not marry the mother of his child. We have no problems of that kind, just as we have no abandoned children or even orphans. Yes, children who have lost their parents are always adopted by a family close to them which is given official help."

Finally we got back to the initial question: How many children are there in nurseries and schools and who decides which of them shall be admitted? Reply: Nurseries and schools give priority to children whose parents are working. Naturally, the aim is that they should be open to all, even if only for a few hours a day. This will probably not be achieved for twenty years, and the birth rate will have to drop between then and now.

ON THE "STEEP PATHS OF SCIENCE"

Mr. Hu Cha, director of a department in the Ministry of Higher Education, is very thin and very tall. He has a very intimidating professional tone and manner.

"Let us first look at some figures," he says. "There are in China from 35 to 40 million adults who go to elementary evening classes. There are 5 million who attend secondary courses in the evening, and about 200,000 of these people, who were illiterate before the Liberation, pursue their studies up to the university level without giving up their jobs. We have 100 million children in primary schools and 15 million young people in secondary schools. Compulsory primary education lasts six years. Secondary education consists of the two stages of three years each, punctuated by intermediate examinations. Finally we have about a million students in technical schools who are at a level corresponding to that of the second stage of the secondary school. In the universities we have almost a million full-time students, plus about 500,000 correspondence students who are continuing their studies while working. In all, one Chinese in four is studying today in one way or another."

In no other sphere has China made such spectacular progress as in that of education. In 1948, 85 per cent of the population was illiterate, only 20 per cent of the children went to school, and there were only about 150,000 students at the university. However, Mr. Hu Cha does not seem to be at all inclined to self-satisfaction. As soon as he has dazzled me with his astronomical figures, he moves on to self-criticism and points out the difficulties to me. First of all he states that it will be impossible to wipe out illiteracy completely in China for some time. For one thing, some adult groups in the population are unlikely to be able to master reading and writing and then the decision to standardize the language and impose the Peking dialect throughout the country has made the literacy campaign even more difficult in the outlying regions. How many are still illiterate in China? Mr. Hu Cha tells me that it is difficult to give an exact figure owing to the fact that many adults relapse into illiteracy after taking evening courses, but that even taking this into account, it can be said that no more than 20 per cent are illiterate in the country.

But if the Maoists have resigned themselves to the fact that a certain number of Chinese adults will never learn to read and write, on the other hand the education of all children has been given priority. But in Mr. Hu Cha's view the regime's ambitions are far from being realized because the level of teaching (particularly in the outlying provinces) is still rather low, and this tremendously reduces the number of children capable of taking the secondary curriculum and then going on to the university. Reforms are therefore being worked out, and it is probable that the present system will soon be modified to allow a greater number of young people to undertake higher education.

We now come to university problems, for which, as his title indicates, Mr. Hu Cha is specially responsible. First he tells me about the old China, where the quality of the universities was as derisory as their number. In 1947, the year in which the highest number was reached under the old regime, there were 154,612 students and 16,914 teachers. University teaching was marked by Confucian traditions. The very rare faculties of science did nothing but prepare a few sons of rich families for the entrance examinations of foreign universities — mainly American. No place was given to scientific research, and in accordance with the old mandarin tradition, students were taught the "classics" without being given any modern cultural background; they were turned into perfectly useless literati. Mr. Hu Cha continues:

"A gigantic effort has therefore been undertaken to reform the universities, but the lack of teachers, particularly in the scientific field, has been slowing down progress. We have therefore kept most of the young graduates on in the universities to act as research workers and assistants. Thanks to them it has been possible to set up technical institutes, and today 50 per cent of Chinese students receive a scientific training in 323 specialties, including nuclear physics and electronics. The percentage of teachers in relation to students remains very high — one teacher for eight students — and the average age of our professors ranges from thirty to thirty-five years. As a result of this policy we can look forward with optimism to the future of our scientific institutes. They will provide the country, which needs specialists, with more and more who are better and better qualified."

Mr. Hu Cha takes geology as an example. In the old China there were only 250 geologists, for the most part trained abroad. It was not until 1952 that the Institute of Geology was established in

Peking. At the beginning, 310 students and a few professors were recruited from the university and the Polytechnic Institute in the capital. Today, with 4,000 students and 800 teachers, the Institute is able to supply cadres for the provincial institutes. Mr. Hu Cha, without giving me any details, assures me that in the field of nuclear research even more spectacular progress has been made.

Then he comes to the question of the admission of students. First, a brief recapitulation of the situation under the old regime: at that time the students were all of bourgeois origin and came only from the big cities. The remote provinces often had no university, and as for the children of peasants and workers, they could not even dream of studying. The new regime naturally wanted, at all costs, to enable workers' sons to go to the university and also to help the provinces, until then at a disadvantage, not only by reserving places for them in the universities of Peking and Shanghai but also by creating in every province — even the most distant — institutes and universities which are often "branches" of those in the big cities.

"But," says Mr. Hu Cha, "in the first years after the Liberation students of proletarian origin were rare. In 1952 the percentage of students of working-class or peasant origin was 20.46 per cent; in 1958, 36.42 per cent; in 1962, 42.34 per cent. This year [1965] it is 49.65 per cent. That is still too small. All our young people want to study. I even believe that there are very few countries in the world where the thirst for learning is as great as it is in ours. But we cannot sacrifice quality for quantity by admitting to our universities students who do not meet the standards.

"There is competitive entry at all centers of higher education in China, and, on the average, six candidates apply for every available place. Examinations are held throughout China on the same date (generally in July) and the tests are the same. For the scientific institutes these examinations cover six subjects: mathematics, chemistry, physics, political science, foreign languages, and Chinese language and literature. For the other faculties (with the exception of philosophy and economy) they cover four subjects: history, Chinese language and literature, a foreign language, and political science. Future philosophers and economists take an examination in mathematics. In foreign languages, candidates have the choice of Russian or English, the only two taught today in secondary schools. But teachers of French, a language which will soon be included in the curriculum, are already being trained.

"When there is a tie in marks, the candidate of proletarian origin is given priority. Those who fail the examination are entitled to try again twice in the succeeding years. The age limit for entering the university is twenty-five (twenty-seven for those discharged from the army), but the correspondence courses allow much older workers to continue to study for as long as they wish.

"All students are entitled to a financial grant and living accommodations near the university, but about 20 per cent of the students of nonproletarian origin [Mr. Hu Cha avoids using the word 'bourgeois'] waive these advantages and live at their families' expense. Living-in is obligatory only in teacher-training institutes. The grant is eighteen yuan a month, but food never comes to more than fourteen yuan, and particularly hard-up students get a supplementary allowance to buy clothes. Finally, each student is entitled to free railroad travel to enable him to spend the holidays with his family."

In return for these material advantages do students have to promise to work afterwards for a few years in jobs assigned to them by the state, as is generally the case in other Communist countries? My question surprises Mr. Hu Cha. "This problem doesn't occur in our country. If they have valid reasons for doing so, our graduates can express a wish to work in such and such an enterprise. But as a rule they all want to go where they are most needed, where they can best serve the people. They don't compete with each other to secure the most lucrative jobs or sinecures." Mr. Hu Cha smiles at the idea that such a thought could have occurred to me.

Another problem which "does not arise in China" is that of students who abandon their studies in mid-stream. Mr. Hu Cha even seems not to understand what it could be. "There are perhaps a few students who give up for health reasons, but they are so rare that they are not included in the statistics!" Further, according to Mr. Hu Cha, nearly all students pass the end-of-year examinations. Some are obviously less gifted than the rest, but the professors, who live in close touch with their students, concentrate particularly on such cases, and the student body, which is very well organized and very vigilant, also helps these "weaker comrades."

"As you are no doubt aware, criticism and self-criticism are practiced on a large scale in our country, and that enables us to make sure that everyone has a good education." I ask for details: "Who organizes these self-criticism sessions? Is only education discussed at them or also personal problems? Are they held frequently? Do they take place in the presence of teachers or only of students?" Mr. Hu Cha smiles again.

"Criticism and self-criticism help the student to resolve certain contradictions in his life and work. And these sessions in no way represent group pressure on the individual, as some Europeans think. A student is not mature, either ideologically or professionally. He is a young being who is prey to numerous problems, and he needs to discuss them with his comrades. The professors seldom intervene in these discussions, but obviously they are very interested in them; and if they supervise them, it is merely to prevent some students from being abused too much or to ensure that they don't talk about uninteresting things. You may not like this system, but in our opinion it produces excellent results."

I do not press the point, and Mr. Hu Cha moves on to a less controversial subject.

"Until now we have talked about the general problems of our educational policy, but to understand its real nature you must realize that our aim is not to train pure specialists whose qualifications are limited strictly to one field. What differentiates us from capitalist or revisionist educators is precisely that we reject the idea of the specialist who knows his books and his figures, but nothing else. We want to train complete men, competent of course, but also aware of all the problems of our country and the world, and capable of tackling a wide variety of practical tasks. We do not need an elite that is selfish and cut off from the people, a new kind of scientific mandarin class; we must have worker-intellectuals, living at the same level as the people and helping them in their work."

We have been talking for more than two hours and Chairman Mao's name has not been mentioned once. At the very moment that I notice this omission, and as if he has divined my thoughts, Mr. Hu Cha cites the "Yenan talks."

"From 1942 on, Chairman Mao warned us against purely book knowledge and derided those intellectuals who recite Engels' 'Anti-Dühring' by heart but do not know anything about life."

Once more it is my privilege to hear a summary of the "Yenan talks," which since my arrival in China have become my 'Anti-Dühring' — I could recite them backwards.

Mr. Hu Cha has reached certain conclusions. Much has been done in China to wed theory and practice, science and politics, but the results are still not satisfactory and new reforms are being considered. More time will be devoted to ideological education and practical work. Several institutes have already adopted a system whereby students spend half of their time studying and the other half at manual work. In Shanghai at the big "Institute of Technology for Those at Work" the students attend courses three afternoons a week, studying at home for their end-of-term examinations and working with their hands the rest of the time. According to Mr. Hu Cha, the results are very encouraging, and the theoretical work of these worker-students is as good as that of full-time students. But he is not certain that the system could be generally adopted. Many problems remain to be solved, beginning with that of scientific research, which demands the constant presence of the research workers. One thing has been decided, however; before 1970 Chinese higher education is to be transformed into something more practical, "closer to the people and to life."

"Doesn't this reform risk lengthening the period of study and slowing down the training of scientific cadres?" "Not at all," replies Mr. Hu Cha. "We have a Marxist concept of education, and in our view diversifying the students' activities increases production rather than slowing it down. Karl Marx pointed out in the first volume of *Das Kapital* that from the age of nine a child should devote a third of his day to study, a third to manual work, and a third to leisure. Only such a division of his time can ensure man's harmonious intellectual and physical development. Working with his hands in no way interferes with a student's intellectual work." And Mr. Hu Cha adds: "An adult, of course, does not need leisure as much as a child of nine."

Marx having momentarily eclipsed Mao Tse-tung, Mr. Hu Cha reminds me that Marx advocated the abolition of the differences between manual and intellectual work. I could have replied that as far as children are concerned, they worked ten hours a day in the factories at the time Marx was writing, and that for him the differences between manual and intellectual work were only going to be abolished when technology had practically done away with manual labor. Marx hoped to liberate the "alienated" worker from the manual labor which the Chinese cannot even dream of abolishing today, for obvious material reasons. But they do not like you to insinuate that *their* Marx is a very special one: one day when I dared to say that the Chinese concept of work came from Fourier rather than from Marx, I was roundly snubbed. So this time I refrain, and

Mr. Hu Cha, having told me that neither Chinese teachers nor Chinese students are dismayed by the difficulties, concludes with a quotation from Marx taken from a letter written in March, 1872, to Maurice La Chatre:

"There is no royal road in science, and only they who are not afraid to tire themselves climbing its steep paths will have a chance to reach its gleaming summits."

The events of 1966 have given an added symbolic significance to this last quotation: the Chinese decided to suspend the entrance examinations for the 1966–67 terms until the educational reforms were carried out, and they sent the students who had already been admitted to work in the communes for periods of up to six months or encouraged them to join the Red Guards. The "paths of science" are thus becoming steeper and steeper in China, although it is hardly likely that Marx ever dreamed of this kind of difficulty.

WHEN JENMIN JIH PAO'S PROSE COMPETES WITH TOLSTOY AND BALZAC

The behavior of Chinese students in the Eastern European countries where they studied in large numbers gave rise to a real legend. Their teachers and comrades could not get over their fanatical dedication to work and the extreme austerity of their lives. Games and distractions did not interest them at all, and they apologized for not joining in by saying that they were morally obliged to learn as quickly as possible in order to repay their debt to the people who had given them the chance to study. Even during the period of the East European thaw, after 1956, it was impossible to get them to come out of their shell. They seemed indifferent to the issues which stirred university circles and continued to follow the same hard-working routine as if nothing else mattered. Although their grants were very modest, they managed to economize, and like true Lei Fengs they sent their savings to anti-imperialist organizations or to their families.

As a result of hearing these stories, I built up a mental picture of Chinese students: a very austere breed, permanently buried in their books and living in universities as silent as monasteries. But, in fact, if Chinese universities resemble those of any other country, it is those of the United States. Their campuses are on the edge of town, most often with parks and lawns and plenty of athletic fields, which are nearly always crowded. Students and teachers (they wear badges of different colors to distinguish one from the other) go to and fro, strolling and chatting in an atmosphere that is very relaxed and even exuberant. A deafening uproar marks the end of lectures, and the dining halls and living quarters are thronged with pushing and shoving crowds of smiling students.

The proportion of students in relation to the total population is still low (1 to about 600) but it seems clear that those who have succeeded in getting a place on these pleasant campuses spend the best years of their lives there, with few material worries and plenty of distractions. No luxury, of course. In the dormitories they sleep seven in wooden bunks. On the eighth bed, which serves as a chest of drawers, they pile up the cases — also made of wood — in which they keep all their belongings. A table and a few stools take up what space is left; they work in the libraries. Boys and girls often live on different floors of the same building, but flirtations and affairs are so severely frowned on by the authorities that infringements of this rule can lead to expulsion. Westerners in Peking tell you that students are so strongly encouraged to take part in sports because it uses up their surplus energy.

The universities and institutes almost always have their own clubs which are used for films, performances by amateur theatrical groups, and lectures. The resident students therefore have no need to go into town for amusement, and according to students from France — there are quite a few in Peking — their Chinese colleagues from the provinces seem to have no desire to spend their evenings in the capital. The only part of Peking some of them know after five years' study there is Tien An Men Square, where they go for the big political rallies.

The good humor which pervades the campus made contact easy. The students, who mostly appeared to be very young, flocked around us, although they were rather shy — particularly the girls — and contented themselves with answering our questions, putting few to us in return. But occasionally some of them, ignoring the official guides, discussed a wide variety of subjects with us — everything from how much time the girls wasted braiding their long hair to foreign films they had seen.[17] At the Steel Institute in Peking the fourth-year girl students entertained us in one of their

[17] A French film, *Tamanago,* was a great success in China at the same time as an American film, *The Salt of the Earth,* which had been banned in the U.S.

rooms and told us how they spend their time. Get up at 6:00 A.M. Get dressed. At 7:00 the dining hall opens. From 8:00 to 11:30, classes. Noon, lunch. Sometimes, but not every day, there are additional classes beginning at 2:00 P.M., but these are often optional. Until dinner, served from 5:30 P.M. on, the student's time is her own. From 7:00 to 9:30, entertainment, lectures, or meetings; and at 10:00 P.M., lights out.

In this institute there are 70 professors and 890 assistants for 5,200 students, of whom 900 are girls. There is a very close relationship between teachers and students, and the ties are reinforced by the fact that they all go together twice a year to work in people's communes or factories. The girl students talked gaily about them, as if they were huge picnic outings.

In each university our guides proudly showed us the library, usually situated apart in the large buildings which also contain the teaching staff's study rooms. We were always given permission to inspect the "foreign section," generously stocked by the Soviet government with technical works; discreetly, I did not make too close a check, but I got the impression that 90 per cent of them were in Russian — many Soviet journals and even Russian translations of Western scientific books. As for literature proper, it does not seem as if they have banned either all the works written during the old regime or those by foreign authors. At Wuhan we saw books by D. H. Lawrence and at Kunming those of the arch-imperialist Theodore Roosevelt.

Our guides insisted on showing us the numerous translations of European classics, which are the same as those in the libraries of the U.S.S.R. and the people's democracies; Tolstoy, Gorky, Dickens, Balzac, and Mark Twain occupy the places of honor, but they are encountered less often than Marx, Engels, Lenin, and Stalin, whose works, published in the widest range of editions, are to be found absolutely everywhere. We often found that students reading books in Russian or English in the study rooms were hardly able to speak the language.

In an attempt to gauge roughly the academic level, I asked to attend the French, English, and Russian classes — all languages I speak.

In the fourth-year French class at Nanking, twenty-two students under the direction of a professor in his fifties were discussing the Henri Martin affair.

"Why did Henri Martin enlist as a volunteer in the French

army?" the professor asked a student named Wang. "He wanted to fight the Japanese and free Indochina from their yoke," replied Wang. "But he soon realized that the French imperialists wanted to use him to maintain their colonial rule." Wang spoke correctly but very slowly, searching for the words. The professor asked another student what situation Henri Martin found himself facing in Indochina. "The Vietnamese people to take arms to fight against colonialism." This second student spoke quickly but used scarcely any form of the verb except the infinitive. A third student was asked to continue the recital: "Henri Martin leaves the army and opposes the 'dirty war' in Indochina." Finally, a young girl described his trial and five-year prison sentence. The last two students spoke correctly but with an accent so strong that part of what they said was incomprehensible. The lesson over, the professor dashed up to me and said in an apologetic tone: "What can you expect? They're not very clever." I reassured him politely and asked him if his students had read the book on the Henri Martin case which appeared in France some years ago with a preface by Jean-Paul Sartre, who edited it. "They are not good enough in French to read the whole book — they read summaries of it." "Do they know who Sartre is?" The professor smiled without replying, and my guides tugged at my sleeve — the English lesson for another class was about to begin in a different building.

In the English class there were also twenty students. Their rather young teacher spoke, to my surprise, with a very pronounced American accent. First of all he recounted at length the story of a family from Central Europe which emigrated to America at the end of the last century, and he described, in moving terms, the miserable fate that awaited them there. "The capitalist system is based on the oppression of the poor. That you know." (Everyone nodded his head.) "But between the end of the Civil War and 1900, millions of people, fourteen million people, driven from their homelands by injustice and forced to seek refuge in the United States, suffered unbelievable misery there." Then followed a rather confused report, and then the students, who had taken notes, were invited to reply to such questions as: "What was the fate in America of the refugees from Central Europe at the end of the last century?" They replied by repeating the lecture almost word for word and in an American accent.

I did not stay until the end of the session, as they were waiting for me in the Russian class. Only a dozen first-year students of very low standard. But there, too, everything was politically oriented, and the October Revolution was summarized very briefly. The professor was a woman, a graduate of the Institute of Foreign Languages at Harbin, and she spoke Russian very well.

In Kunming French is not taught, but I attended English and Russian classes and got the same impression as I did in Nanking. In China a foreign language is studied through the medium of political works, hardly bothering with literary classics. As a result, students acquire only a very poor working vocabulary. When I spoke to the teachers, even those at the celebrated institute in Harbin where professors and translators of Russian have been trained since 1946, they seemed a little embarrassed, stressing the necessity of teaching the rudiments quickly, and they assured me that those who went on for a higher degree studied the Russian literary classics very seriously. Unfortunately, French teachers currently working in China told me that this is not exactly true.

Since their quarrel with foreign Communists, the Chinese have been recruiting language teachers from Western Europe without taking political criteria into consideration. It even seems that membership in a Communist party other than the Chinese CP may be a disadvantage. The teachers sign a contract for two years and are very liberally paid. The French, for the most part, are young Sinologists who take advantage of their stay to perfect their Chinese. They never imagined that they would be teaching their language from political articles from *Jenmin Jih Pao,* translated into French with errors that it is often better not to correct. In each faculty there is, in fact, a committee which approves the curriculum and guides the teachers, which, in short, exercises a very strict political control. The Chinese are extremely hospitable and tolerant toward their visiting teachers, doing everything to make their stay agreeable, but they are unapproachable when it comes to the subject matter and methods of teaching.

I must add that my interpreters were always extremely studious, taking advantage of every minute of free time to peruse, dictionary in hand, the Russian or English translation of the Chinese CP Central Committee's nine letters to the Russian Communist Party.

In the universities of Peking, Nanking, and Kunming, several times we met teachers of political science who roughly outlined to us their teaching aims and methods. "We want to teach our pupils internationalism, patriotism, and communist morality," said the Dean of the Faculty at Nanking. And a Kunming professor said:

"We accord special importance to the course on the history of the international workers' movement so that students will understand that since its birth, this movement has been marked by the struggle between revolutionary Marxists and capitulationist opportunists." The textbooks are compiled by the professors "with the help of specialized committees delegated to serve the faculty." And the principal examination subjects are "the works of Chairman Mao, the history of the Chinese CP, the history of the workers' movement, and political economy and logic." On top of this there are regular seminars on political events, domestic and international. And Marxist classics? These are also studied, of course, to throw light on the course of history.

At Kunming I attended one of the classes on a Marxist classic. About a hundred fourth-year students were listening in a big amphitheater to a talk on Lenin's *The State and the Revolution.* The professor was thirty at the most and spoke in a very loud voice which would have been better suited to an open-air meeting than to a university lecture, but which was actually perfectly appropriate to the subject matter, as the professor's intention was to prove that if Lenin were alive he would be the implacable opponent of the "modern revisionists."

"Lenin has shown," asserted the speaker, "that talking about the class struggle is not enough to be revolutionary. To deserve this name one must, above all, accept the principle of the dictatorship of the proletariat." (A few quotations in support and then the following.) "Study as a negative example the program adopted by the twenty-second congress of the Communist Party of the U.S.S.R. which the Soviets wish to present as a contribution to Marxism; you will note that it abandons — that it rejects — the fundamental idea of the dictatorship of the proletariat."

For a whole hour the professor refuted, point by point, the twenty-second congress' program and in the heat of his enthusiasm seemed to me to have slightly forgotten *The State and the Revolution.* The students dutifully took notes, although all their teacher's arguments are printed in one of the innumerable handbooks against modern revisionists which can be bought on every street corner.

This experience was enough for me, and I made no further requests to attend any political science classes but instead asked if I could visit one of the sessions of criticism and self-criticism which, according to my guides, play a key part in molding the students' political consciousness. These sessions usually take place in the evening, after classes, and we were told that they were private. But we insisted, and finally one evening in Harbin our guides, exhausted by our questions and no longer knowing what to do with us, granted our request.

In the large hall of the student union, which was practically full, there were more than 400 students. On the platform, behind a table covered with a red cloth, sat the panel: six stern figures (four professors and two students, to judge from their ages). We were seated in the front row at the very moment that a student began his speech to the panel. He was in his Sunday best, spoke in a solemn voice, and although he read from notes, appeared to be very nervous.

"I entered the Faculty of Foreign Languages because I wanted to become an interpreter. I have always thought that interpreters have an interesting and easy life. They drive about in cars with foreigners and accompany them all around the country. They are also well paid and want for nothing. I therefore envied them their lot. Certainly I have never been opposed to socialism, and I never even realized that my ambition was thoroughly selfish and antisocial. I was simply filled with selfishness and individualism, which prevented me from understanding that to be a true revolutionary I must care about the people's welfare and not only my personal comfort. One day it was announced that only those with the highest grades would become interpreters and that the others would be channeled into teaching. Immediately I redoubled my efforts and became one of the best in my class. But I did all this while thinking of myself and my future, and not in order to be useful and serve the people."

Everyone listened gravely and in a leaden silence. The student gulped a mouthful of water and resumed in a voice which trembled a little.

"It was when reading the letters from our party to the CP of the U.S.S.R. concerning modern revisionism that I began to question myself on my thoughts and conduct. Our party has demonstrated to the Soviets that their cupidity and their taste for the easy life has led them to abandon all Marxist-Leninist principles. And I? I asked myself. Was I not equally preoccupied with my own comfort? I threw myself into the works of Chairman Mao. I reread his article 'Serving the People' and I thought about what he says of Lei Feng. Then I thought, like Lei Feng, I am also the son of poor parents. My father, too, died of hunger. I would never have become a student in the old feudal and capitalist China. Like Lei Feng I owe everything to Chairman Mao and the great Communist Party. How, therefore, can I worry selfishly about my own well-being instead of devoting all my energies to the service of the people?"

At this moment a member of the panel nodded his head with an air of approbation, and the hall broke out in applause. However, the speech was far from finished. The student described at length his life and work *after* this salutary attack of revolutionary con-science, but the atmosphere was now less tense, and it even seemed as if his audience's attention was relaxing. To win them back, the student laced his recital with anecdotes which made the audience laugh once or twice but which, being badly translated, failed to raise a smile from me — it was something to do with methods of studying political books on streetcars.

No discussion followed this confession. It wasn't really a session of criticism and self-criticism but a gathering at which revelations with an educative value were made. My guides explained to me that the student we had heard "is particularly brilliant and knows how to analyze his problems very well," but that "others need criticism and outside help to understand and correct their errors of thought and conduct."

I asked what these interventions and this "outside help" from the group consisted of, and if it did not happen that some students flatly refused it. In vain. My guides confined themselves to answer-ing that everybody in China knows that the sessions of criticism and self-criticism are intended to integrate the individual better into the group, and not to exclude him from it, which is why they are not merely accepted but appreciated by all. The French teachers and students in Peking did not entirely confirm this offi-cial view; on the contrary, it was their impression that sometimes their pupils or colleagues emerged from these sessions in a very dis-turbed state, to say the least. But not even they were able to gather any detailed evidence from the people involved, who never reveal any confidences about the sessions.

While I was trying to understand this "political-moral" aspect of Chinese education, Marc Riboud, who was once an engineer, attempted to assess the laboratories and equipment of the science faculties. He was able to attend some sessions of practical work and photograph research apparatus, which was often "made in

China." But he had the impression that everything he was shown was associated with a rather elementary level of teaching, capable of training technicians quickly but not of teaching scientists.

There are obviously other institutes in China where more advanced research is being pursued and where the equipment is appropriate to the atomic age. The fact that the Chinese have nuclear weapons is sufficient proof; but it seems that such institutes are, as in Russia, attached to the Academy of Sciences, and despite our repeated requests, we were never able to visit one.

However, the Chinese did not attempt to hide from us the existence of these research centers, and they have even published postage stamps showing the prototypes of their nuclear reactors. Eventually, in private conversations we were assured by high officials that the Party never interfered in this field and that China had not committed the Russian error of placing a Lysenko over the scientists or of declaring Einstein's theories "heretical." Without our even raising the question, they made a point of telling us that the "hundred flowers" principle is strictly applied in the scientific sphere. I still do not understand why they consistently refused to let us visit the laboratories of the Academy of Sciences. Without much to go on, I risked the guess that our guides did not want to let us see organizations whose members, in view of the nature of their work, almost inevitably live in privileged conditions. They tried above all to impress us with the tremendous efforts being made in their country to popularize science, to open the universities to students of proletarian background, and to train "intellectuals of a new type, bound to the people." They succeeded on at least one point: it seems certain that in China today an organization exists so that education and culture will spread according to a geometric progression. Without any possible doubt, China will be the first country on the Asian mainland to eliminate illiteracy completely, to provide education for every child, and to have (in terms of absolute value) as many students — and at the same level — as the more developed nations. This prophecy can be made on the basis of the number of teachers being trained and the fact that a sound university base already exists and is being continually reinforced.

But the quality? It is possible that in the scientific sphere quantity automatically ends up by producing quality: the more graduates, the more chance there is of some of them becoming scientists capable of giving a new impetus to research. In a system as dynamic as that of China the development of productive power ensures the development of science and technology. It works otherwise in everything that concerns literature, philosophy, and the social sciences. Here knowledge is nothing unless critical spirit, intellectual curiosity, and a taste for personal experiment and for risks in the realm of thought are added to it; but in Chinese universities the students seem only to learn formulas by heart. Nothing is done to encourage them to think for themselves in an original fashion. For anyone who is familiar with the Soviet precedent, this is disturbing.

During the Stalinist era many specialists perfectly aware of the inadequacies of the educational system, concluded nonetheless that books of any kind confer the taste for knowledge, and that the remarkable increase in the number of students in the U.S.S.R. would by itself guarantee a future political and intellectual maturity. We know what happened. At the time of de-Stalinization, when the old principles were called into question, many political graduates of the previous period were overwhelmed by skepticism or completely sterile cynicism. And there is as yet no sign from Russia of any works of history, economy, or philosophy which might make a really appreciable contribution to world culture by examining the Stalinist epoch.

THE ARMED OCEAN

We never asked to meet any military personnel or to visit any barracks. My Soviet experience taught me always to avoid becoming involved in military questions in the Communist countries. One knows, in fact, that one will merely arouse suspicions by asking questions, which will elicit only halting answers, or no answers at all.

But the men — and the women — who bear arms are so numerous in China that even if you turn your head away as they pass, you cannot avoid them. They are not exactly soldiers, but the "people's militia." On the lawns of Changsha University we came across boys and girls in the "prone firing position" who were watching an invisible enemy and pulling the triggers of their rifles. But they did not even fire blanks — they merely went through the motions of firing. This seemed so odd to us that, forgetting our decision to ignore everything military, we asked to have a closer look. Our guides readily agreed and even seemed to think it was a good idea.

The "section leader" was a second-year student of peasant origin. He was nineteen but looked less, and he suffered from a shyness which was anything but martial. "How did you become section leader?" "I was elected." "Did you take any special courses?" Very embarrassed, the section leader explained that he had the trust of his comrades but knew no more than they about military matters. Then, suddenly eloquent, he launched into a short speech: "Chairman Mao has told us that all China must be like an armed ocean in which every invader would drown. We are all soldiers, and we are learning to bear arms as our fathers did to drive out the Japanese, the Americans, and their Kuomintang lackeys."

The triggers were no longer clicking; the "detachment" was too interested in our conversation to continue the exercise. Under the benevolent gaze of the professors accompanying us, the young leader told me about the militia. As a high school student in Poland before 1939 I also went through military training like these young Chinese. But we wore uniforms, and our officers were regular soldiers who later commanded us full-time when we did our military service. In China the militia is composed of men who have already done their service and young people who perhaps will never wear a uniform. Every man and woman must know how to use arms, but very few citizens serve in the regular army, although in principle the law provides for general conscription. When I asked my student section leader if he would be going to an officer-training school, he appeared completely surprised and replied with a blush: "I do not know if I shall have the honor to be called up by the Liberation Army — only the best are called up."

Later, in Peking, non-Chinese friends told me of the country's paradoxical military situation. If China applied her conscription law to the letter and called up all young people for three and a half years of military service, she would have a permanent army of 25 million men or more. It is obvious that to maintain such an army in peacetime would be as ruinous as it would be useless. So only one Chinese out of every twelve or fifteen does military service. The military training of the others is entrusted to the militia, whose upkeep is not great — they have no uniforms and practically no

Steel mill in Anshan, the Pittsburgh of China.

Anshan.

New steel plant in Wuhan
and a group of young
technicians.

Member of the
managerial staff
of the Peking
coke factory.

Liu Lei-i, "national capitalist," receiving the author in his Shanghai
home.

Poster depicting "socialist rivalry" between different factory teams.

Young worker in the Peking experimental chemical factory. Her husband is in the army.

Assembling diesel engines in the Loyang tractor factory.

Two methods of counting in the accounting department of a Peking factory.

Soldier-hero Lei Feng reads Mao's works.

Demonstration protesting American intervention in the Dominican Republic, May, 1965.

Demonstration in Peking, February 7, 1965, after the first U.S. bombing of North Vietnam.

Workers' militia at the same demonstration.

Gallery of Modern Art in Peking.

The Red Detachment of Women, a new ballet produced in 1965.

"Leaders' Portrait Department" in a big store in Kunming. The leaders in the top row are Mao Tse-tung, Liu Shao-ch'i, Chou En-lai, Chu Teh, Ch'en Yün, Lin Piao.

(*Below left*) Liu Shao-ch'i in the 1920's. The photograph was taken in Mao's house in Changsha. (*Below right*) Liu, Chou, and P'eng Chen at the Peking airport.

Four views of Chou En-lai in the People's Palace during the interview, March, 1965.

Chou Yang during a discussion about politics and culture.

(*Below left*) Ch'en Yi, Vice-Premier and Minister of Foreign Affairs.
(*Below right*) Kuo Mo-jo, President of the Academy of Sciences and
Vice-Chairman of the National People's Congress.

Students in the Petroleum Institute in Peking.

Students in the Polytechnic
Institute in Peking.

Students working on an experimental farm at Wuhan University.

Soldiers building a road near Nanning, Kwangsi-Chuang Autonomous Region.

Sports and games at the Petroleum Institute.

Students' militia training at Changsha University, Hunan.

Girls' dormitory in the Petroleum Institute.

Students of Nanning Medical School building a road.

equipment — and it has the advantage of keeping the country in a permanent atmosphere of general mobilization which stimulates the revolutionary spirit.

Chinese strategists are still affected by their experience during the last war and are convinced that an armed nation can alone make life impossible for an invader, even one a hundred times better equipped than they, as the Japanese were.

There are no longer any military parades in China; it appears that they were banned after the quarrel with the U.S.S.R. The army doesn't leave the barracks on either May 1 or October 1. But the slightest anti-imperialist demonstration — and they occur often — is enough for the streets of Peking (and other cities) to fill with columns of armed civilians whose style of marching would shock the professional soldiers. In the reviewing stands the front rows are always reserved for the crack militiamen, their chests slung with cartridge belts like the marines of Kronstadt. How many militiamen are there in China? According to estimates, from 25 to 100 million — but the question is unimportant. What is plain is that in the event of danger the Chinese army would not lack reserves.

Another thing is obvious — a young peasant called up by the army considers himself, in fact, one of the happy elect. To be housed, fed, clothed, and given a little pocket money is like having a fortune in a country which has learned how to conquer famine but which is still underdeveloped, and in which a man has to work hard to earn his bread. And the Chinese army offers its members more than material security; it looks after their education, their professional and political training, and their health. In short, while giving recruits military training, it also prepares them for civilian life as well as the best schools would.

It is not by chance that Chinese films often portray a demobilized soldier who becomes the head official in his village or the ace worker of his factory. Admittedly, reality is less glamorous, and not all ex-soldiers have brilliant careers. But the fact is I frequently met officials (economic or political) who had been trained by the army. Most of them were trained during the heroic days of the civil war or immediately after, but it remains the declared ambition of the Chinese army to fulfill its role as educator.

This "politico-military secret" was spontaneously revealed to me by Mr. Chen Chun, deputy editor in chief of *Jenmin Jih*

Pao.[18] We had first talked about his newspaper, then moved on to international politics and, of course, tangled over Stalin. I tried to say that the position of the Chinese in their quarrel with the U.S.S.R. would be much stronger if they had not defended Stalin. Mr. Chen Chun retorted, "We have just abolished rank in our army. That's a specific act, more democratic than all those which have been carried out in the U.S.S.R. since their famous twentieth congress. This is a return to Leninism, for Lenin never wanted an army with gilt epaulets, generals covered with medals, and officers paid like bourgeois ministers. Our conception of the people's militia and the people's army comes straight from Lenin and has been wonderfully adapted to Chinese conditions by Chairman Mao. We have won all our battles with this rankless, democratic, and egalitarian army which is supported by the people's militia."

No sooner had the abolition of rank in the Chinese army been announced than the Peking diplomatic community was plunged into speculation about the significance of the measure. The official spokesmen threw very little light on the subject and, as usual, referred questioners to the published text, a very long statement stuffed with Chinese-Stalinist formulas which make its study an arduous exercise. And here I had in front of me one of the country's foremost journalists, who, without my mentioning it, referred to this prickly subject and even dealt with it from an unexpected angle; for although he did not use precise terms, he gave me to understand that the army reform had an anti-Stalinist character. I abandoned my resolution not to broach military problems and bombarded Mr. Chen Chun with questions on the origin and aim of this reorganization.

"Officer ranks were introduced here in 1955," he replied calmly, "and it is probable that Soviet influence had something to do with the adoption of this system which, at the time, also had its advantages. But we never had a strictly hierarchical army in which the soldier became a robot or the officers had unlimited powers. We have always clung to the principle of comradeship in the army,

---

18 *Jenmin Jih Pao* ("The People's Daily"), the main newspaper of the CP in China, is the biggest in the country, with a circulation of 1,500,000; it is printed simultaneously in Peking, Shanghai, Harbin, Canton, Kunming, Wuhan, Urumchi, Chengtu, and Sian. Its fifteen principal editors are appointed by the Central Committee, and its editorials (usually signed "Observer") are mainly written by prominent leaders, sometimes even by Chou En-lai. The price of the paper varies according to the number of pages: one page for one fen.

a tradition of discussion and of discipline by consent rather than imposed discipline. As you know, all our officers were required to serve a period in the ranks, and they spent one month each year as ordinary soldiers. We have always been very vigilant, and we have never allowed epaulets or stripes to confer exceptional privileges on those who wear them, as is the case in certain other countries."

A further allusion to a country with "generals dripping with medals" was very pointed, and it must be admitted that Mr. Chen Chun was right. The Chinese military men we had seen during our travels were much less dazzling sartorially than their Soviet counterparts, and even with their epaulets, the officers were hardly distinguishable from soldiers, sporting neither gleaming jack boots nor custom-made tunics. Both soldiers and officers, with their cloth footgear and their uniforms that were always too big, looked to us as if they had just finished a campaign. I said so to Mr. Chen Chun and added that in our Western eyes the Chinese army appeared to be already so egalitarian that we could not see how it could be even more democratized.

He replied: "In Chairman Mao's famous phrase, an army is only really effective when its relationship to the people is that of a fish to water. But only a profoundly democratic and egalitarian army can stay close to the people, helping them in their labors and living with them. The threat that hangs over our country has increased recently as a result of American aggression in Vietnam and the treason of the modern revisionists. A great debate was therefore organized in our army, and after several months of discussion at all levels the decision was made to strengthen even further the bonds between the army and the people by abolishing rank and giving soldiers an even more intensive political education."

Economic officials had already explained to me that "man means more than machines, since it is he who uses them," and I was therefore not surprised to hear the same formula, adapted to the army, from Mr. Chen Chun's mouth: "The soldier means more than arms," etc. But I wanted to hear more about the "great debate" among the rank and file. Who initiated it? How was it conducted? And how was it that no one outside the army knew that it had taken place? My questions in no way disconcerted Mr. Chen Chun.

"Our party intervenes in all areas, and it pays special attention to the army. Our best soldiers are Communists. I would even say that the more communist they are, the better they are. It was they who initiated the debate and conducted it, in strict accord with the higher authorities of the Party. But everyone took part in the discussion, I repeat, for it was the only way to arrive at solutions."

I asked again why no one knew anything about this debate *before,* since it must have been extremely difficult for millions of soldiers to hold discussions without someone outside getting wind of them. My skepticism seemed to amuse Mr. Chen Chun.

"We didn't want to hold this debate in the market-place, and we congratulate ourselves on the fact that thanks to the discipline and conscientiousness of our soldiers, the secret was very well kept. For you, democracy is bourgeois parliamentarianism. We practice democratic debates of another type, on a much wider scale — and they are effective in a different way."

Mr. Chen Chun then told me that he has been a member of the CP for thirty-eight years and that he could give me other examples of democratic customs practiced in the Party and the army. As Mr. Chen Chun appeared to be forty at the most, I remained speechless; and he began to tell me about his long experience as a militant.

Mr. Chen Chun was not a soldier, but he recruited many of them under the noses of the Kuomintang and the Japanese. This clandestine work taught him the virtues of patience and democracy. For in the "liberated bases" behind the enemy lines everything, absolutely everything, was settled by discussion and persuasion. The Communists did not forcibly enlist peasants in their army or militia; they educated them and did not entrust them with arms until they were sure of their willingness to use them.

Mr. Chen Chun made no sensational revelations to me. Others had already told me of the patient work the Communists had done to awaken the political consciousness and fighting spirit of the peasant masses, who became their striking force. But this historical review, combined with his examination of the recent army reforms, enabled me to understand better the Red Army's very special role in the peasant world. The army has always been a kind of politico-educational laboratory for the Maoists in which they developed the most effective methods of inculcating ideas and of superimposing the revolutionary style of life on the troops before applying them to the population as a whole. All the methods of indoctrination — group study, criticism and self-criticism, the linking of education with production, and the linking of production with military exercises — were first applied in the 8th Route Army.

The soldier trained in this school was, in effect, a politically conscious civilian, capable of bearing arms and, at the same time, of setting an example for others, not only in battle but also at work.

Chiang Kai-shek's ministers and officers (and a number of his American advisers) did not take seriously this Red Army which spent half its time gathering the harvest of organizing meetings, and they looked with scorn on the people's militia, composed of amateurs. Moreover, a Nationalist corporal drew more pay than the Communist Commander in Chief.[19] But when it came to the test, it was Chiang Kai-shek's professional, well-paid, and well-trained army which disintegrated, while the "liberated bases" held fast. Out of this success grew the CP leadership's conviction that the army must devote half of its energy to civilian tasks and remain an integral part of the civilian population, which would be partly militarized itself by the militia. Today, as they sense danger, their first concern is to weld the army and the people even more closely together. This, according to Mr. Chen Chun, is the significance of the recent military reforms. But one can ask oneself why it was necessary to reinforce the bonds between the soldiers and the people. Had integration not been fully carried out? Mr. Chen Chun answered me with the classic theories of the permanent revolution and of the class war which continues during the period of transition leading to the advent of the communist society. It seems, nonetheless, that the real problem may lie elsewhere.

Despite her great economic progress, and although her industry is already very advanced, China is still an underdeveloped and essentially rural country. In this context a soldier, even if he is also a worker, is a privileged member of society — as we have already said — by virtue of the fact that the state looks after his material needs and educates him. The army, which benefits considerably from technical progress, must give a more and more advanced training to its personnel. Despite its attachment to the traditions of Yenan, the Chinese army of today is no longer the army of the epic period, and the Chinese soldier now learns much more than the 800 characters he needs to know to read a simple text.

The lot of the happy elect enlisted in the army is comparable in

[19] Chu Teh was paid five dollars a month. See Forman, Harrison, *Report from Red China.*

many respects to that of a student, who also lives at the state's expense and acquires knowledge that raises him above the average worker. No matter what is said or done, both are privileged people who can look forward to a more promising future than the ordinary citizen. To us Westerners the life led by these students who live seven to a room and receive ridiculous grants and by these poorly clad soldiers who build roads does not seem all that enviable; to the average Chinese it is.

And the same thing happens in every country that tries to overcome its economic backwardness. That is, an agricultural country cannot be transformed overnight into an industrial country. But almost everywhere else except China it is accepted that the growing needs of the middle classes, created by the process of industrialization, should be the first to be satisfied and that the army should have a privileged position (in fact, it often takes over the function of government). So frequently does one observe this new social imbalance in the underdeveloped countries that it seems to be inevitable. China is the exception to the rule and shows an almost obsessive determination to prevent the development of privileged groups, civil or military.

Purely economic measures are not enough, however, to eradicate the causes of social differences during the industrialization period. The disparity in wage levels can be greatly reduced, bonuses for skill can be cut out — and we have seen that this is the case in China — but it is still impossible to pay an engineer less than a laborer or to feed the army poorly. The most effective way to nip the "elitist" mentality in the bud, according to the Chinese, is not economically but ideologically — that is, political education in big doses.

"The soldier must be modest and conscious of his debt to the people and to the Party which entrusted arms to him," Mr. Chen Chun tells me. The debt of one of his commanders (one no longer says "officer") is obviously greater still, and he must therefore be even more modest. Substitute the words "student" and "books" for "soldier" and "arms" and you will have the principle which governs university life and which is also valid for intellectuals and artists, for not even they must ever forget what they owe the people, Chairman Mao, and the Party.

The example of Lei Feng is further proof that it is not enough to be modest, that one must still "serve the people" by daily good deeds. A whole literature built around the works of Mao aims to show that the man of the people is in every respect the best of all, morally the most healthy, and the most necessary to society. As a result of this psychological conditioning, in China the "poor peasant" is prouder than anyone of his origins. Every propaganda technique is used to ensure that everyone absorbs this standard of values. Under such conditions there is no risk that an *esprit de corps* will develop among civilian or military specialists; they would suffer rather from a "militancy" complex.[20]

The Chinese army is unceasingly obsessed by the need to be useful. It must serve the people every day, and in peacetime it can only do this by working. Besides, even in time of war, the Chinese do not have the same idea of heroism as other nations. An ideal example of this is the case of Luo Chang-kiao, who is venerated by the whole nation for his action in the Korean War.

The Chinese volunteers in Korea, it will be recalled, succeeded in pushing the American army back to the 38th parallel and holding it in check for two years. On signing the armistice at Panmunjom, the American General Mark Clark remarked bitterly that he would be ratifying the end of the only war the United States had not won.

The Chinese consider that the victory was theirs in Korea. However, Luo Chang-kiao, son of a poor peasant from Hunan province, is the most famous hero of this war — so famous that in honor of his memory his name has been given to a mountain and a river. What did Luo Chang-kiao do? He may have killed a great number of Americans, since he took part in many murderous battles. If so, it is never mentioned. What won him glory, though, is the fact that he drowned after diving through a hole in the ice in a frozen river to save a Korean child.

"Everybody a soldier!" This Chinese slogan actually means "Let us all be like Lei Feng and Luo Chang-kiao!" It urges people to live in a certain way which is more easily and quickly learned in the army, but which civilians can also acquire. Similarly, the military art, according to the Chinese, is not the perquisite of a professional elite but can be learned by all. Only concentration is needed,

[20] Robert Guillain, in *Le Monde*, September 20–21, 1966, devoted two articles to an exhaustive analysis of the role played by the army in Chinese society since the beginning of the "cultural revolution." His conclusions largely confirmed the impressions I brought from my stay in China and added many new facts which help to explain the rise of Lin Piao, who, like Chu Teh, his predecessor during the Yenan period, became the number two man of the regime.

and the militia is specifically organized to teach this to everyone. From school age on, youngsters learn to handle wooden rifles and, at the same time, to do good deeds in the Lei Feng manner.

In Europe the proclamations and inflammatory articles in *Jenmin Jih Pao* calling for the militarization of the country strike fear in one's heart. One thinks inevitably of the slogans of fascist countries, and the picture that leaps to mind is that of helmeted, jackbooted soldiers, intoxicated with nationalism and possessed by the spirit of conquest. Every year China's enemies lay before the United Nations a fat file of Chinese press cuttings, declaring that a country which indulges in such militaristic propaganda is essentially war-minded and therefore unfit to sit in an assembly sworn to protect world peace.

However, even anti-Communist journalists and professors who visit China, like Professor Hugh Trevor-Roper,[21] admit that the Lei Feng-ized Chinese soldiers in no way resemble those of Mussolini and Hitler. Other anti-Communists even laugh at the Chinese, who in their view are obsessed with the "Yenan complex." Their army, they say, is adapted to battles which would never be fought in the atomic age.

Being neither strategist nor prophet, I do not feel qualified to judge the Chinese army's effectiveness or to predict the form another war might take. I shall go on to discuss the way in which the Chinese look at the international situation and their atomic armament policy. And I repeat that I did not visit any military bases and therefore have no idea what young recruits are taught during their three and a half years of military service. Nevertheless, I feel I can say that the Chinese army is essentially defensive and that, completely integrated into a nation of 650 million inhabitants, all trained to support it as guerillas, it appears to me to be indestructible.

On his return from China about ten years ago, Field Marshal Montgomery gave a private talk to members of the House of Commons. He declared that the first and imperative rule of Western strategy must be: "Never land even a single soldier on the Chinese mainland." Field Marshal Montgomery's political judgments are perhaps a trifle suspect, but one cannot deny him a certain competence in military matters.

[21] See the London *Sunday Times* of November 14, 1965.

CHAPTER FIVE:

China and the World

A SOCIETY OF CHALLENGE

When I left China in 1965 the American military escalation in Southeast Asia was just beginning. But the chain of events which it set in motion continues to grow and today the prospect of a direct confrontation between America and China appears to be nearer than ever. According to commentators as well informed as Edgar Snow, the Chinese-American war has virtually begun.

We do not know to what lengths this confrontation may go. What is certain is that the Chinese anticipated it and accept the American challenge. "The Chinese think that the Americans are logical people," wrote Edgar Snow last summer in the French weekly, *Le Nouvel Observateur*. They know that the United States' aim in Southeast Asia is not to conquer territory but to demonstrate on a global scale that revolutions and wars of liberation are not possible in the world of today because America is powerful enough to crush them. The logic of this policy which sets out to block the expansion of communism by force must lead the Americans to attack China, the only socialist power which today is openly bent on the rapid development of revolutions throughout the world.

"But why don't these Chinese content themselves with peacefully building their communism, which they are doing so well, instead of hurling themselves and their eight million bicycles[1] at giants armed to the teeth like the United States and the Soviet Union?" asked Signor Giorgio della Pira, former mayor of Florence, in 1965. This very Catholic Italian professor is too intelligent to believe that the Chinese are threatening the United States and the U.S.S.R. militarily, but since he has long fought for a *rapprochement* between East and West which would ensure peace, he was irritated in China — as have been many other Europeans of good will — by the daily diatribes against the American "imperialists," the Russian "revisionists," and the new "holy alliance" which, according to the Chinese, unites them.

In fact, despite their verbal extremism, their stereotyped lan-

---

[1] Here Signor Della Pira is paraphrasing Mussolini, who once spoke of "eight million Italian bayonets."

guage, and their tendency to condemn those who do not agree with them, the Chinese have lost nothing of their lucidity in their assessment of the international situation. The events of the last year have shown the Chinese view to be much more accurate than that of their detractors. A year ago many well-meaning people thought that a solution to the Vietnamese war would be found within the framework of co-existence because the pressure of the U.S.S.R., of the pro-Soviet peace movements, and those of the emerging countries would be sufficient to make the Americans withdraw. But it was a vain hope, quickly dashed by the arrogance of American power, and all those who counted on this must ask themselves if their interpretation of American policy was not based on a great illusion. Now it is plain that polite and moderate pressure cannot prevent the growth of escalation and it is difficult to see how it can be stopped in the future. The absence of any decisive anti-American action on the Soviet Union's part amounts, in the Chinese view, to complicity with the aggressor, therefore to treason. Soviet policy is perhaps more complex than that, but the fact remains that Moscow has not given Washington a solemn warning that the violation of the 17th parallel or an attack on China would be regarded by her as a *casus belli*. In the absence of such a warning the Chinese feel that they have been abandoned and that they must be ready to face the American superpower alone. All the recent developments in China have been determined by this prospect.

Why, therefore, does this poor nation, which more than any other needs a long period of peace in which to industrialize herself, accept the burden of a long and exhausting war with an incomparably richer country? We have seen in earlier chapters that China is not experiencing a crisis and that no domestic necessity is driving her into diversionary adventures. But the Chinese are convinced that the United States will not renounce its anti-Communist crusade in Asia as long as it does not get bogged down in an almost impregnable country. They may know America well or otherwise, but their political analysis leads them to the conclusion that this kind of prolonged war will provoke a crisis within the United States and rock the American system of alliances.

Europeans sometimes wonder why, despite this conviction about the inevitability of the anti-imperialist war, the Chinese do not try to gain time, why they do not favor a compromise in Vietnam, which would postpone the trial of strength until later and enable China to perfect her atomic weapons and other military equipment.

But the Chinese believe that no compromise could be reached without inflicting humiliation on the Vietnamese and discouraging all revolutionary bids in the underdeveloped world for years to come. And in the Chinese view the Vietnam war involves more than Vietnam. It is in that country that the Americans want to show that they can crush any revolution. If they succeed, it will be a disaster not only for South Vietnam.

On the other hand, if in their militaristic fury the Americans carry escalation to the point of attacking China, they would at one swoop overturn all the given facts of world politics. The Soviet Union and the Communist movement would be brutally compelled to face their responsibilities: despite the campaign which the U.S.S.R. has been conducting for several months to throw doubt on China's socialist character, as if wishing to create an alibi for an eventual Russian failure to intervene, an American attack on China would be the greatest test for the international workers' movement since 1917. It would seem that the Chinese are not wrong in thinking that the Atlantic alliance, which is already cracking on several sides, would not survive a war on a wider front in Asia, and that inside America herself the opposition which today is still rather embryonic would become a potent force.

To yield to American blackmail in Vietnam or elsewhere, according to the Chinese, would be to compromise all chance of progress for decades. Taking up the American challenge, despite the desperate risks, offers the only possible chance of provoking a deep crisis within the American camp from which the workers' movement has everything to gain. China is the only country to have made such a choice. The Soviet Union and the international Communist movement reject it. But this difference of attitude is not a product of chance; it simply confirms that the Chinese revolution is another communism, a communism which differs more and more from that of the Soviet bloc.

This other communism was not molded in a day, and China did not consciously seek to become what she is. The Chinese proclaim today that they are very satisfied to rely only on their own resources to defend themselves and to industrialize their country. But the fact is that during the last seventeen years their country has suffered severely from pressures of all sorts that have been applied to them first by the Americans and then by the Russians. From 1949 onward, while pointing out in their White Paper that China is permanently on the edge of famine and that she cannot live on her own resources, the Americans have maintained a ruthless blockade against her.

In 1960, at the very moment that China was experiencing particularly grave economic setbacks, the U.S.S.R. recalled her technicians and stopped all deliveries to China, even those that had already been paid for. Today China is the only country in the world with an income of less than $150 a year per capita which receives no foreign aid; worse still, she is not even given any long-term credit for her grain purchases.

These are the facts that cannot be ignored if one wants to understand the Chinese view of the world. If China today attacks the United States and Russia furiously — but only verbally — it is because she has been subjected by both to terrible blows aimed at bringing her to her knees in order to destroy her government or coerce it into compliance.

Admittedly the Americans and the Russians have not joined in a concerted action against the Chinese. They have both tried to help China — the United States aiding Chiang Kai-shek's, the Soviet Union aiding Mao's — but the generosity of their intentions did not prevent them from seeing China simply as a satellite and obedient ally in Asia. From the moment China refused to live under the tutelage of either, her very existence became a challenge to the world.

A challenge, first of all, because China has survived all the ruptures and, to everyone's surprise, proved that she is capable of finding the means and the resources for self-development. Today she takes her place on the world scene as a completely independent and great country, and no one doubts that in a relatively short time she will become one of the important industrial powers. What is more, China, subjected to harsh isolation, has been forced to adopt values radically different from those which govern all other industrial societies, including the socialist societies. She has become a society which challenges the values of the others, and which intends to prove that hers are both better and more effective.

But China is a quarter of humanity. She cannot be looked on as a small peripheral social laboratory, easy to ignore or isolate by a new *cordon sanitaire*. The Chinese society of challenge therefore worries the great powers, and not because it has expansionist ends; the Americans and the Russians know that China adds up to less, and at the same time more, than that. She does not threaten the two great powers militarily, but she brings everything into question because she sets herself up as the model of another form of society.

This model disturbs America, this revolution of the poor, which by its example poses such a threat of inspiring movements of unpredictable potential in every underdeveloped country. This model disturbs the U.S.S.R. no less because it repudiates her own decisions and puts itself forward as an alternative leader of the world Communist movement. Finally, China's mere existence is an embarrassment for the two great powers in the dialogue they have begun and wish very much to continue.

I shall analyze very briefly in this chapter the main stages of the process which has brought about the Chinese society of challenge. I believe, in fact, that China's world perspective is inseparable from the internal structure she has set up, and that the world's attitude to China is determined much more by the fear her Communist dedication inspires than by the threat of the supposed yellow peril.

In August, 1965, a British journalist ended his article in the *Times* with this conclusion: "If China achieved prosperity overnight Mao would be very bored." This is not the paradox it appears to be — China, indeed, is the only country in the world whose final goal is not prosperity as we understand it. According to the Maoists, the Western appetite for consumer goods is not "natural," but is, on the contrary, the manifestation of a serious derangement which causes man to forget that the true source of happiness and freedom is the collective life. Freed of all selfishness and all greed, he who owns nothing can become the happiest of men if, like Lei Feng, he dedicates himself completely to the community.

Certainly the Chinese pursue material progress to improve the collective standard of living. They want more schools, more universities, more theaters, more hospitals. But this improvement must in no way encourage individual appetites which would result in the formation of socially privileged groups. In the Chinese view, the wage differences which still exist in the agricultural and industrial sectors must gradually narrow and eventually disappear. And for them the advent of the truly egalitarian society is quite near; for they do not intend to satisfy all the needs of man (in accordance with communist principles) but only the basic needs which will enable them to subsist during the "period of class war on a world-wide scale."

In short, Mao wants a wealthy China peopled by citizens who are voluntarily austere because they are freed from most material needs. True, this wealth will be relative for a long time to come: China has 650 million mouths to feed. But if one supposes (as did the writer of the article in the *Times*) that as a result of a run of miraculous harvests and extraordinary discoveries the Chinese were suddenly able to advance by giant strides, their surplus production would be devoted to perfecting the social structure as a whole or to helping the poor "sister countries"; the system would block any move toward the ill-fated consumer race to "keep up with the Joneses" which leads to "modern revisionism," source of all disasters.

This attitude is unique. Any comparison between what is happening in China and the Soviet experience would be entirely false because their aims are not the same. The U.S.S.R. has known periods of extreme austerity — during the war, for example — and resorted to political incentives to carry out the first Five-Year Plan; but she has never considered final, and still less as having any value in itself, an organization based on the voluntary and permanent restriction of individual consumption.

It would be equally wrong to question the Chinese model because the wage range still remains rather wide (particularly in the rural sector) and to conclude that in certain respects other countries have been (or are) more egalitarian than China. One would succeed in proving only one thing — that it is easier to control consumption in a rich country than to guarantee a livelihood to all in a poor country. Thus it is perhaps true that in the Britain of Sir Stafford Cripps, immediately after World War II, consumption was rationed in a way that was at least as egalitarian as that in Mao's China. But Britain did not make this consumer equality into a moral principle, and she abandoned it as soon as she was able. In China, on the contrary, the virtues of egalitarianism are preached with unexampled conviction and fervor, and the moral superiority of those who own nothing is proclaimed in the same tone.

However, there remains the question which all foreign observers were discussing during my stay in Peking: will this system run its full term? According to some, the Maoist doctrine was inspired by the experience of the men of Yenan and will disappear with them.

In their austere republic of the Northwest this doctrine proved its extraordinary effectiveness and gave them balance and a kind of puritan happiness. They would like their experience to be perpetuated, but the younger generation has neither the same motivation nor the same vision of the future; and when it comes to power, everything will automatically change.

According to others, the egalitarian ideal is dictated only by the necessity of the moment. China needs all her workers to produce as much as possible, but she cannot pay them; and if she tried to, she would not be able to keep the market supplied, which would result in permanent inflation. The Maoists therefore replace wages and consumer goods with "spiritual nourishment"; but they will no longer have any reason to do this when their country has become richer.

There are others still who stress that the accelerated centralization of the country encourages the proliferation of a hierarchical bureaucracy. In their view the manual labor imposed on cadres, the criticism and self-criticism — all the Maoist customs and rites — are aimed at preventing this new mandarin element from setting itself up as a class which considers itself superior. In vain: in the long run this bureaucratization will distort the Chinese experiment and give rise to serious internal contradictions. On this particular problem, comparisons with the U.S.S.R. which are not entirely false come to mind.

In short, it is too soon to prejudge the future of China's egalitarian society. At the present time, nonetheless, she already represents a development which is virtually without precedent and which is not easy for Europeans to understand, even those with a Marxist background. It is significant that the publications which reach us from Peking often seem to us even more indecipherable than those which used to come from Russia. In fact, Maoism derives only partly from Marxism, from which it has borrowed certain concepts in order to adapt them to a precapitalist situation in an essentially peasant country. The Chinese social system has not much in common with proletarian democracy as conceived by the great revolutionaries of the West; that called for the withering away of the state, while the Chinese are in process of strengthening it by every possible means, including the "cultural revolution." Even the concept of the class struggle, as we have seen, has been adapted in China in a way that profoundly modifies the original Marxist idea. China represents above all, in my opinion, the remarkable incarnation of the egalitarian dream of impoverished peasants. Yet even if this Chinese society does not correspond to the model revolution conceived a century ago by Marxist thinkers, it is no less a revolutionary reality capable of profoundly influencing and affecting the entire workers' movement, including that of the West.

Besides, as Mao Tse-tung said to Edgar Snow, the Chinese model does not consider itself either definitive or eternal. Its premises will necessarily be revised in the light of industrialization, which in China as elsewhere will bring about a transformation of life and values. The worsening of the present international situation and the prospect of armed conflict with the United States obviously does not make this transformation easier. Meanwhile, China's strength and profound significance will lie above all in her nature of total challenge.

It is not by chance that the Chinese never depict themselves so well as when they are attacking Soviet "revisionists" or Western capitalists. While they do not always succeed in demonstrating the moral superiority of austerity, they have no difficulty in denouncing the corruption and lack of progress rife in bourgeois and pseudo-bourgeois societies. Their model values are simplistic, but their denunciation of the consumer society is telling and remains valid. The Chinese experiment is therefore as "shocking" as the Bolshevik Revolution once was. It is even more so in that the world today no longer doubts (as it did in 1917) that a socialist experiment can succeed, even in an underdeveloped country. Furthermore, the Chinese do not merely appeal to the proletariat alone but to all the exploited peoples of the underdeveloped world. Thus they form a huge army of revolt with which they envisage encircling the capitalist fortress, and with which, speeding up history, they will telescope the stages of revolution fixed by the theories of the workers' movements in the advanced countries.

China therefore appears to oppose everything and everyone. Her challenge would perhaps be less dangerous for the United States or for Russia if they proposed solutions for ending "this absolute pauperization" of the underdeveloped countries in relation to the industrialized nations. Every year the United Nations' statistics show in fact that the gulf is growing between the rich nations and those which during the last century have fallen behind in their economic development. The Americans spend more on the packaging of their continually improving consumer goods than the Indians do on their food. Statesmen follow one another to the rostrum in Manhattan to deplore this state of affairs. But no one has discovered a nonrevolutionary method of ensuring the advancement of the emergent countries. So far American aid has not enabled any country to overcome underdevelopment; and in such countries, with their scandalous social inequalities, slogans about democracy and liberty are merely a hypocritical façade in which no one can believe. The onset of awareness in these countries is perhaps slow, but the Chinese success could speed it up considerably. The Americans know this so well that they are not completely wrong in their pharisaic logic of wanting to prevent China from succeeding.

For the U.S.S.R., who also desires the socialist advancement of the emergent countries, China poses a different problem. We know that she is at a point in her social and political evolution where she wants above all to maintain the international balance of power and is therefore anxious to avoid a direct confrontation with the Americans. But in view of her proletarian tradition, any opposition — even tactical — to her policy on the part of the revolutionary movements of the poor countries is a harrowing experience for her. She can neither condemn nor restrain these movements without losing her claim to leadership of the Communist world, but, on the other hand, she does not wish to be led into supporting revolutions which might get out of her control and lead her down a path she cannot risk following.

The Chinese "dissidence" threatens the Soviets in their own country, which has not yet overcome the ideological crisis of de-Stalinization, as well as in their role as head of the international Communist movement. To retain control of the movement, the U.S.S.R. must prove that her policy is not only more realistic but more effective in the long run than China's, and this at the very moment when she wants a period of international calm in which to put her house in order. It is this contradiction which seems to be paralyzing her.

But the Soviet gamble seems more and more chancy and her options less and less tenable. Since the day in 1963 when the U.S.S.R., the United States, and Britain signed the pact banning nuclear testing which was to usher in the era of co-existence, the United States has fomented numerous counter-revolutionary *coups d'état* in Asia, Africa, and Latin America, while the allies and protégés of the U.S.S.R. have neither advanced one step nor gained an inch of territory. The Soviet Union's "moderation" has not been enough to clear the international climate; it has merely allowed the Americans to take the initiative with a great counter-offensive of the right. And if the United States has not succeeded in imposing its "pax Americana" everywhere, it is not so much because of vig-orous resistance from the U.S.S.R. as because force, in certain circumstances, is helpless against a strong revolutionary organiza-tion supported by the people.

My stay in China coincided with the escalation of the war in Vietnam, which provided evidence both of the impotence of the Americans when faced by a revolutionary movement and of the halfheartedness of the Soviet reaction. The U.S.S.R. could not, in the name of world peace, abandon North Vietnam; but to reply to American bombing, she would also have had to engage in a counter-escalation, which she did not wish to do. And the *de facto* independence of the South Vietnamese N.L.F., which would not have agreed to cut down its activities in order to allow the Soviet Union to find common ground for agreement with the U.S., fur-ther reduced her scope of action. The Soviet Union saw clearly that each American raid, at the same time that it destroyed Vietnamese villages, was reducing Russian hopes of peaceful co-existence and *rapprochement* with the United States.

The war in Vietnam demonstrated — and demonstrates — the impossibility of a Russo-American accord on the revolutions of the underdeveloped world, as well as the impossibility of a Sino-Soviet agreement in which opposing ideological principles deeply rooted in either country would not be disputed. Up to the present, China's challenging attitude has seemed to aggravate all political confrontations. It is in this, as we shall see, that the reason for her strength and for her isolation lies.

THE CRUSADE OF THE PHARISEES

The American faith in the virtues of private enterprise and the pursuit of wealth is only equaled by the ardor of the Chinese belief in the virtues of collectivism and the strictest austerity. America in the capitalist bloc and China in the socialist bloc have taken up extreme positions on this front by reason of their histories. It is a fact that the United States has become the most prosperous country in the world within the framework of free enterprise. It is also a fact that China was able to regain her unity and begin to industrialize only through collectivism. To the Americans, their system is a model one whose history proves that it alone is capable of ensuring well-being and liberty. To the Chinese, their experience is proof that only collectivism can emancipate humanity and guarantee true freedom. It is obvious that for two societies so radically opposed the same words cannot have the same meaning; traveling about China, one confirms this at every turn.

In Peking, for example, one of the biggest museums in China displays American press cuttings and official announcements. The curators of the Museum of the Chinese Army of Liberation entertain no fear that the public might be influenced by these texts lauding American democracy. On the contrary, they know that the exhibits will feed the hostility the Chinese feel toward the United States, "the hypocritical defenders of universal injustice."

In any case everything is ingeniously laid out to achieve this effect. At the entrance, in the museum courtyard, are old American planes captured during the civil war and ultra-modern spy planes recently brought down. A guide explained that all these aircraft, in defiance of international law, have been used against China, which for the last twenty-one years has had to contend with underhanded but systematic aggression by the United States. He enumerated in detail for us a whole series of transgressions by the Americans, "who seized the Chinese island of Taiwan, train saboteurs there and land them in China, sail in China's waters, and constantly violate her air space." This is nothing but the truth: the Americans do not even dream of hiding the fact that they indeed are doing all these things "to contain China and defend the national interest."

When this introductory outline was over we asked to visit the museum itself. Our interpreter smiled: "It's very big, you know . . ." In fact, the museum is a skyscraper which dominates the low skyline of Peking.[2] The guide recited: "This military museum of the People's Republic was built in 1959 in 264 days with the help of the population of Peking. It was inaugurated during the celebrations of the tenth anniversary of the Liberation. Nine other enormous buildings were built for the same occasion. This is one of the biggest: 310 feet high, 66,000 square yards of surface. A tour of the eight exhibition halls equals a journey of seven and a half miles."

[2] In imperial Peking it was prohibited to build higher than the Forbidden City (residence of the royal family), which was composed of buildings of only one story. All Peking is therefore made up of little houses huddled together in the "Chinese city" and the "Tartar city."

One needs courage: we visited only one room, the one devoted to the Korean War.

At the entrance, boldly displayed, is President Truman's declaration denouncing the Communist aggression and announcing the dispatching of American troops. I could read it in English . . . America did not seek to conquer any territory, any new riches, but she was resolved, with God's help, to defend the liberty and democracy threatened by Communist subversion and invasion. But I asked for the Chinese version displayed in the museum to be translated so that I could judge how accurately it had been rendered into Chinese. My interpreter and the two officers accompanying me were perfectly at ease. "The imperialists' hypocrisy knows no bounds," said the older officer. "They said the same thing when they fought us in the war of Liberation. They killed millions of our people, but it was for our own benefit."

He shrugged his shoulders and led me to a carefully framed copy of *U.S. News and World Report.* "There is their real war aim," he said and commented on the map which appeared on the cover. Starting from South Korea, a big black arrow cuts through North Korea, Manchuria, Siberia, the Urals, and points toward Moscow. One prong of the arrow points at Peking. North Korea thus appears to be the springboard for an anti-Communist war against the Soviet Union and the Chinese.

Farther on are displayed extracts from *Time* magazine and the *Wall Street Journal,* all fiercely anti-Communist, one of them proclaiming that it is "time to punish the Reds for their aggression and to wipe out finally the threat they represent." I probably read all this at the time but without believing that these warlike declarations really reflected the American leaders' state of mind. But why shouldn't a Chinese take them literally, as well as all those articles displayed here which declare, and even occasionally cry hysterically, that the "Chinese sanctuary" must be bombed, perhaps even with atomic weapons?

We arrived finally at General Clark's book in which he wrote that it was his doubtful honor to be the first senior officer of the American Army to sign the armistice in a war that his country did not win. Beside the General's book is his wife's testimony: Clark wept on his return home. My guides were beaming: "Chairman Mao has always said that men are stronger than any weapon. The imperialists learned that at a cost in Korea, but the lesson didn't sink in and they haven't changed — look what they are doing in Vietnam."

A hundred times I heard the same thing said in China. *Mei-Kuo tsui,* American imperialism (literally, the "imperialism of the Beautiful Land") is not an abstract term to the Chinese: it evokes, very precisely, memories of the civil war and images of planes razing villages. Photographs of bombed Vietnam are displayed everywhere. We in the West have also seen them, but the Chinese can really identify with the Vietnamese: they have the same skin color and the same kind of villages, and their leaders do not hide from them the fact that tomorrow they could, in their turn, be laid waste with bombs by that democratic America which "does not seek to conquer any territory" but does not hesitate to spray with napalm those who do not share her concepts of liberty and justice. The Americans do not deny that the Chinese have good reason to fear them — they even congratulate themselves on this. Without the fear which we inspire in them, they say, the Chinese, these "Asian Hitlerians," would already have invaded the whole of the East. Having thus compared China to Nazi Germany, the Washington militarists are no longer subject to moral scruples, and they thus consider that every action they take against her is justified in the eyes of their country and of the world. Who, indeed, could blame them for nipping the subversion of the Yellow S.S. in the bud?

It is significant that the Americans have chosen this alibi. At first sight it would have been more logical to compare Mao with Stalin rather than with Hitler. But history has proved that the system in the U.S.S.R. could evolve, while Nazism was irrevocably abominable. If, therefore, extreme military methods are envisaged to deal with the Chinese problem, it would be better to prove at once that only such means will be effective and that all compromise would lead to a disastrous Munich. Personally, I am not at all sure that American opinion would readily accept a preventive war against China or that the Pentagon's "big alibi" is completely convincing, but there again I cannot know what I would think if I were Chinese.

The very real and serious threat which hangs over China does not alone explain all her internal and external policies — no more than the encirclement of Russia explained all of Stalin's policies. But it is undeniable that in the Russia of yesterday and in the China of today the constant feeling of insecurity leads to a Manichaean view of the world and therefore to extremism. The immoderateness and violence of China's anti-American propaganda can sometimes make us smile or shock us. The U.S. is accused of historic sins she did not commit: for example, she was not responsible for all the aggression suffered by China during the nineteenth century, and Britain needed no encouragement from Washington to wage the opium war. But it would be profoundly unjust to conclude from these verbal excesses that in the matter of their conflict the Americans and the Chinese are equally guilty. In fact, the history of the conflict is a remarkable illustration of the way the Americans treat all the emancipation movements with Communist leanings.

The Chinese revolution did not triumph after a *coup d'état* cunningly led by a handful of Communist conspirators. It matured for twenty-five years under the very eyes of the Americans, who at that time were the foreigners most substantially represented in China and the best informed as to her situation. Documents published in 1949 by the State Department prove that the Americans were under no illusions about Chiang Kai-shek, that they were well aware of the corruption that reigned in Chungking during the war and in Nanking after Japan's capitulation. Nevertheless, without making any effort to compel their ally to clean up his regime, they continued to provide him with funds and to equip his army.

At the same time, during the war against Japan, they were deeply intrigued (one could even say fascinated) by the Maoist phenomenon. They had their mission in Yenan and were quite well informed about the very special techniques the Communists used against the common enemy. Yet even then they never dared to give them any material aid (as the British gave Tito during the war) or to put pressure on Chiang Kai-shek to lift his blockade of the Northwest. This was undoubtedly to keep on the good side of the Generalissimo, whose China they thought would be a decisive factor in the Asian policy they intended to pursue after the war.

Later General Patrick J. Hurley (famous for having negotiated the Sinclair Oil settlement with President Cárdenas of Mexico in 1939) tried to merge the Communists with Chiang Kai-shek's regime. Convinced that the Maoists were nothing but peasant rebels, he went as far as asking Stalin in person whether or not he considered them true Communists. Stalin replied in a manner vague enough to confirm General Hurley in his belief and assured him that the U.S.S.R. wanted to see in China a democratic regime whose government would be presided over by Chiang Kai-shek. But, of course, the gallant General Hurley's attempts at integration were in vain, on the one hand because the Maoists were true Communists, on the other because Chiang was about as democratic as Franco. The civil war was therefore inevitable; and when it broke out, the Americans found themselves once more on Chiang's side, since they could hardly back the Maoists, who called themselves Communists and whose flag bore slogans that were outrageous even to a liberal American.

After the defeat of the Nationalists, Dean Acheson explained that his country had tried everything to prevent this — but in vain. By doing so he wanted first of all to answer the McCarthyites, who complained that "China was lost to the United States," as if it had ever belonged to her. But having thus admitted, without realizing it, that the Maoist revolution was legitimate in the sense that it was the result of an irresistible popular movement, he declared that the U.S. would not recognize the new regime, which had been established in an undemocratic manner. He even decided to isolate China rigorously in order to hasten the fall of the new regime and the restoration of the old one.

"It has always been difficult for dominant politicians in the United States to understand the social and political reasons for the rise of communism," wrote Aneurin Bevan in August, 1955. "Such an analysis would involve some soul-searching about the 'American way of life' and might lead to conclusions disturbing for American politics. It was more comfortable to believe in a kind of communist demonology with the United States filling the role of demon slayer."[3]

How could the Maoists react to this violently hostile American attitude? And what could they say to the revolutionaries of other countries if not, "The American imperialists will try in every way to defeat you. Be ready to resist them, weapons in hand"? And the Americans seem to be bent on proving them right when they serve notice on the revolutionaries of the whole world that they will crush every revolutionary movement by force, wherever it may appear. Every revolutionary movement of the left, that is. For the Americans are always the first to support — when they have not actually fomented — military coups against democratic governments, as was the case, for example, in Guatemala and in Brazil.

Even worse and more stupid: by trying to strangle China, which has been permanently on the edge of famine, and by threatening her with bombs, America has helped to "harden" the Chinese and

[3] London *Tribune,* August 9, 1955.

make them what they are today. Could Mao have done other than he has to overcome China's underdevelopment with her own resources? Could he have reacted to American atomic threats otherwise than by proclaiming the superiority of the human element in every war, no matter what kind? Could he reassure his people otherwise than by asserting that imperialism would be defeated in the next war? (Which, let it be said in passing, he has never said was desirable, despite the fact that this has been attributed to him a hundred times.) And, finally, could the "apostolic" society of the Chinese live withdrawn into itself while new revolutions breaking out in other countries diminished the American threat and loosened her grip?

For sixteen years the United States refused to recognize the Soviet Union; this did not bring down the Soviet regime. The lesson had no effect. They tried the same thing with China — for almost eighteen years they have refused to recognize her. Having said that, there is a grain of reason in every act of folly: one must admit that the *cordon sanitaire* drawn around the U.S.S.R. has created a great deal of difficulty for her and perhaps reduced her attraction for Western countries, the anti-Soviet propaganda having widely exploited these difficulties and attributed them to the communist system alone. To "decommunize" their workers, the capitalists of the Western countries told them about the very low standard of living of the Russian workers, but they were at the same time compelled to accept numerous social reforms in an attempt to stifle the revolutionary ferment, which they succeeded in doing in some cases, especially in Anglo-Saxon countries.

But what happened with the U.S.S.R. does not seem capable of being repeated in the case of China. The Maoist revolution was not isolated at the beginning — it belonged to an already powerful socialist camp. By overthrowing feudalism, Mao made his country take a leap forward that no other underdeveloped country has achieved; and it is with these underdeveloped countries — and not with the advanced countries — that China wants to vie today and for which she wants to set herself up as a model. The Americans' anti-Chinese propaganda therefore boomerangs on occasion. Pharisaic editorial writers like Joseph Alsop and others periodically announce with contemptible pleasure Chinese famines which exist, fortunately, only in their imaginations; but their editorials are often read in countries with pro-American governments where famine actually rages. Sooner or later truth will out, and it is then doubly unfavorable to the Americans, first because it is disgusting to see the world's most overfed country rejoicing that others — even if they are Communists — are suffering from hunger, and secondly because one discovers that it is not in China but in their own camp — in Central or South America, for example — that people are dying of malnutrition. After the revolution a Russian worker did not eat as well as a Western worker, but today a Kwangtung peasant eats much better than a peasant in Kerala in India — and this is known in Asia.

Furthermore, the development of the underdeveloped countries who benefit from American aid is extremely slow: a few social reforms, a few improvements in the economic system are not enough to speed it up, much less to bring about a redistribution of income which would benefit the less fortunate. American aid benefits, in fact, only a small civil or military aristocracy and does not raise the general standard of living. Admittedly, in certain emergencies, American aid limits the number of famine victims, but it does not resolve any basic problems and never secures the development of productive power, which alone could banish, once and for all, the danger of famine. The result of all this is that the pro-American backward countries are as corrupt and vulnerable as was Chiang Kai-shek's China: the single example of South Vietnam today is enough to prove this point.

I shall mention the Vietnam war only in terms of its repercussions on China. From the Chinese point of view, it provides a powerful demonstration of the justice of their claim that "imperialism has not changed its nature," and it underlines the falseness of the Soviet thesis that profound changes in world equilibrium today prohibit the great powers from resorting to force and encourage hopes of a peaceful changeover to socialism. The famous "balance of terror" has not prevented the Americans from supporting in every way the various governments in Saigon which have no popular base and therefore refused to organize the elections proposed in the Geneva agreements of 1954. It does not prevent them from bombing North Vietnam, an independent country allied with the U.S.S.R. and China and with which they are not at war.

To carry out the war in Vietnam the United States did not even seek a mandate from the U.N., where, thanks largely to the votes of their South American satellites, they could expect to secure a majority. They considered themselves strong enough to break international law without discussion or explanation. They have landed

350,000 soldiers in Vietnam and rain down napalm and vegetation-destroying chemicals on the areas occupied by the Vietcong. The Chinese have only to peruse the Western press to find the evidence that proves their claim: that America, by crushing a small country — one of the poorest in the world — in contempt of all law, is behaving exactly as an imperialist power must inevitably behave.

In Peking's Western colony, and even among the diplomats of countries friendly to the United States, I did not often find anyone who would defend their policy. Some pretended, if not to justify it, at least to explain it by the American fear of losing face and seeing all the countries of Southeast Asia turning against her. "The more unpopular they become, the more they must resort to force to redress the balance and to be able to negotiate an acceptable compromise." But what compromise could end a civil war in which the anti-American Vietnamese (that is to say, the vast majority) are opposed to a handful of officers who have thrown in their lot with the Americans and represent no one but themselves? For the Americans to save face, the South Vietnamese would have to accept a regime which exists only because of the U.S. and against which they are rebelling — in other words, they would have to admit defeat. This is really too much to ask of people who have suffered terribly from this regime and who have been at war for years.

It is always dangerous to draw historical parallels, but it seems, nonetheless, that the situation of the Americans in Vietnam is in some respects the same as that of the French in Algeria at the end of the war. In both cases a large foreign army alienated the population instead of rallying it and thus destroyed all chances of a compromise — assuming that the chances once existed. The "heroes' peace,"[4] self-determination, the call to a "third force," all these attempts at compromise collapsed in Algeria, and the French — although practically masters of the situation from a military point of view — were forced to sign the Evian agreements and transfer power to the N.L.F. The Americans are perhaps in even a worse position in Vietnam, since they do not have a million settlers to support them, and also because, with their bombers killing more Vietnamese civilians than Vietcong, they are even more hated than were the French in Algeria.

[4] In October, 1958, General de Gaulle offered his pardon — the "heroes' peace" — to the Algerian insurgents, who, desiring not compromise but a victory, obviously rejected it.

When I was in China, there was constant discussion of a Vietnam compromise along the lines of the "heroes' peace" proposed by President Johnson. I then questioned the Chinese — even Premier Chou En-lai — without offering my own opinion, and even occasionally playing devil's advocate, which irritated them considerably but did not prevent them from patiently explaining what they thought. Their thesis is simple. If the Americans want to leave Vietnam and negotiate as the French negotiated at Evian, nothing could be easier — they have only to agree to Ho Chi Minh's proposals: the implementation of the Geneva agreements, evacuation of foreign troops, and recognition of the National Liberation Front as the legitimate government of the South. China would support with all her weight any negotiation which would lead to the above, but anything else would be a bonus for aggression and would encourage the Americans to do in other countries what they have done in Vietnam.

Marshal Ch'en Yi pointed out to me the false assessment made by well-intentioned Europeans who, in his opinion, allow themselves to be misled by the American "peace campaign." In his view, if the Americans stay in Vietnam, the Vietnamese people — and tomorrow other peoples — will endure suffering even worse than that of the present war. But how can the Vietnamese David succeed in beating the American Goliath, determined to win, whatever the cost?

The Chinese reply to this question perfectly expresses their view of the world. "The Vietnamese people could hold on for ten years, twenty years, a hundred years if necessary because they are fighting for a just cause. During this period the imperialists will be harassed throughout the world because they are hated by the peoples that wish to free themselves from their oppression. In the long run they will no longer have enough troops or planes to fight on all fronts, and, furthermore, the American people themselves will end up by rebelling against the governing class."

The Santo Domingo affair provided grist for the Chinese mill. In Peking huge posters showed Johnson sitting not only on the Asian volcano but also on a South American cactus; and a vast meeting was organized at the municipal stadium where, in the absence of anyone from the Dominican Republic, a student from Haiti explained to the crowd in French the conditions that exist on the whole island. Patently, the events in Santo Domingo surprised the

Chinese as much as they did the Americans, but they proved that there are revolutionary forces even in places where their existence is not suspected.

To return to the war in Vietnam: the Chinese press gives a vast amount of space to the pacifist demonstrations that take place in the United States. The Peking diplomatic colony finds this amusing. At embassy dinners much fun is made of the profound Chinese ignorance of American society. Some compare the Maoists' naïveté with that of the Russians in Stalin's day, who made a mountain out of the smallest signs of opposition in the United States, seeing them as the forerunners of revolution and periodically predicting a crisis as serious as that of 1929. Others, more forbearing, explain that if the Chinese readily take their desires for reality, it is because they attach great importance to movements led by students, these having played an important role in their own country — which has not at all been the case in the United States.

My guides frequently questioned me about this article by Walter Lippmann or that pacifist declaration by Martin Luther King. One of them even asked me what the reaction of the American people would be if the "militarists" dared to cross the 17th parallel or bomb China. I admit that I kept quiet. If I had replied that the American people would not flinch, I would have been encouraging categorical anti-Americanism. But neither did I want to tell my guides that the American people would rebel, as they liked to think. I tried one day to insinuate very discreetly that Walter Lippmann's articles did not reflect the thinking of the great American public, but plainly no one took the point.

On other occasions the tone changed radically, and the Chinese, fulminating, showed us articles from the Western press accusing them of being responsible for prolonging the war in Vietnam or, on the contrary — as did the *Economist*'s "Confidential Report" — of trying to reach an arrangement with the Americans at the expense of the Vietnamese. "We are as close to the Vietnamese as teeth to lips. Anything that hits them hits us; anything that threatens them threatens us. How could anyone be stupid enough to make such accusations, which do not take into account either politics or geography?" I was asked by one of the directors of the Foreign Affairs Ministry before he explained that China was ready to make any sacrifice that Vietnam asked of them. He then went on to say that if the Americans crossed the 17th parallel, they would find themselves facing the same "Chinese volunteers" who had pushed them back in Korea.

Often I encountered these same private declarations in the official notes from the Ministry of Foreign Affairs which were distributed rather solemnly to us, as if they contained hitherto unpublished revelations. And when the Vietnamese from the N.L.F. held their press conferences, they said nothing new either.

However, all these conversations, notes, and conferences were indicative of the oppressive climate of complete insecurity which prevailed in China that year (1965). On the contrary, no one there wanted another war with the United States, even a localized one as in Korea, but everybody thought that China could do nothing to avert this danger.

Even the most anti-Communist diplomats in Peking acknowledged that China did not want war and that the charge of warmindedness made against her in the West was absolutely unjustified. Whether there will be war or peace in Asia depends solely on America; and the more time passes, the more it is impossible to believe in "the aggression of the Hitlerians of Asia" which the Pentagon uses as its alibi. The only country which in 1965 and 1966 has used force — and the most brutal force — in this underdeveloped continent is the United States, the richest country in the world. It is a fact, and the most twisted anti-Communists cannot deny it.

We left China in a Pakistani plane which was going from Shanghai to Dacca, and as soon as we had taken off, the hostess brought us a bundle of American magazines. We were immediately plunged back into the atmosphere of the Western world. In *Life* one could learn how many megatons were needed to destroy all the Chinese: 30,000 megatons were required, and America had them. It was a very serious scientist who had made this calculation, and several million Americans could read it. And two days later in the Calcutta *Statesman* one could read a letter from an American journalist who reproached the Indians for not helping the Americans in Vietnam, and asked them pointedly: "Do you think that the dollars we give you grow of their own accord on the White House lawns?"

Despite the unbounded pharisaism of some Americans, it is possible to believe, in spite of everything, in the awakening of the other America. And what has been happening for the past few months in the United States appears to indicate that attached as they may be to the values of their society, more and more Americans — and not only students, as Senator Fulbright's speeches show — think that their government is behaving with excessive arrogance and cynicism in wishing to maintain, by force and throughout the whole world, an economic and social *status quo* which benefits only the wealthy nations, and most of all the United States.

But this awakening is still limited to university circles and has not touched America's powerful trade union movement. The American workers seem still to accept with docility the official line that the United States is fighting in Vietnam to halt the Sino-Vietnamese aggression against the very democratic regime of the Saigon generals. And, what is even more serious, by virtue of the constant repetition of the claim that their action in Vietnam is disinterested, the majority of Washington policy-makers — not to mention the military — have come to believe that the other side are in fact the aggressors, that it is the Vietnamese, the Chinese, the Communist conspirators of the whole world who have invaded Vietnam, and not they, the democrats, the Christians, worthy descendants of Jefferson and Lincoln.

This clear conscience on the part of the Americans has frequently been discredited in Europe[5] but it is hardly reassuring for us. The men who believe they are within their rights when they wage an anti-Communist war could hurl the world into unimaginable catastrophe. They are so much more dangerous because they are backed by a country which is experiencing undreamed-of prosperity, and because they feel they have a unique opportunity to destroy communism — having missed a similar "opportunity" after World War II when they had a monopoly of atomic weapons. Afterward, of course, they will be ready to organize a proper world peace and to give generous aid to those who have endured their bombs. Looking at themselves in the mirror, they do not see the faces of crusaders ready for anything but, on the contrary, those of do-gooders; they see themselves as men whose hearts are pure, full of humanitarian intentions. They are even amazed that all Westerners do not appreciate their magnanimity.

I. F. Stone recently noticed on a U.S. Marines' recruiting poster this symbolic phrase: "The *Pax Romana* was the longest period

---

[5] Claude Julien devoted an excellent article to this in *Le Monde*, August 7, 1966.

of peace humanity has ever known. Join the Marines to ensure the *Pax Americana.*" I wonder in what history book the Pentagon recruiting sergeants found this revelation of the benefits of the Roman "peace"; but the comparison is significant. Many Americans believe that their country is so powerful and rich that it can play the role that once belonged in the ancient past to the Romans. And in the American Congress there is no lack of modern Catos to proclaim *Ceterum censeo Carthaginem delendam esse,* Carthage obviously being China today. It seems to me nevertheless that if one wishes to draw a historic parallel between Rome and Washington it would be more accurate to compare the Chinese with the first Christians and not with the Carthaginians.

Admittedly even the ruling circles of the United States do not represent a homogeneous group wedded to a single policy which is leading ineluctably to a wider anti-Communist war in Asia. Reason could still triumph in Washington and it is not impossible that the Johnson Administration may withdraw from the danger such a conflict would involve. But even if we Europeans can nourish such hopes, I am hardly astonished that the Chinese are preparing themselves for the worst.

For they know that not only are there Americans — and not the least important ones — who want to destroy or "atomize" them, but also that the United States supports Chiang Kai-shek's regime in Formosa with a million-strong army and still believes in the old slogan: "Let Asians fight Asians." China will never feel herself secure — and no one can blame her — while such threats and blackmail continue. Even if the best happens and the United States acquires wisdom, peace between China and America will not be an easy thing to bring about. And one would have to be very optimistic to envisage such a development at the present time, for the mechanics of escalation tend to drive the Americans in the opposite direction.

PEKING DURING THE GREAT ROW

The Communist capitals are not as a rule the ideal place for a journalist to discuss the affairs of the bloc: officials are extremely reluctant to talk about "family quarrels" in front of foreigners, who have to fall back on the stories which circulate among the public or on verbal versions of what they have already read in the official press. I was all the more doubtful that I would be able to discuss the Sino-Soviet quarrel with the Chinese because I had arrived in China during a period of truce.

The day after the palace revolution of October 14–15, 1964, which toppled Khrushchev, the U.S.S.R. and China resumed the dialogue. Chou En-lai went to Moscow November 6 for the anniversary of the October Revolution and was warmly applauded at a great reception in the Kremlin. Apparently, negotiations were reopened in private, and in certain Western Communist circles it was even said that an agreement was to have been concluded between Messrs. Chou En-lai, Kosygin, and Brezhnev. Be that as it may, the conference which should have taken place on December 15, 1964, was adjourned *sine die* — the conference to which Khrushchev had invited the Communist parties of twenty-six countries in order to prepare a world Communist congress, to which the Chinese were opposed.

There was certainly no question of a new honeymoon. This became particularly clear when Kosygin arrived in Peking on February 6, 1965. Kosygin was merely passing through Peking on his way to Hanoi and therefore could hardly expect a full-dress reception. But when he disembarked from his plane, one could clearly read the vexation on his normally deadpan face: not a soldier, not a fanfare, not even the most modest ceremony. Chou En-lai, as grim as his guest, waited for him at the foot of the gangway and whisked him off.

The following day, as if to mark Kosygin's arrival in Hanoi, the Americans began to bombard North Vietnam; and on the same evening huge anti-American demonstrations began in Peking and continued for several days, climaxed by an enormous meeting held on February 10 in Tien An Men Square before Mao Tse-tung himself. This meeting had been scheduled for the morning, and Kosygin, on his way back from Hanoi, was due to land at Peking at 2:00 P.M. on the same day; but no one dreamed of postponing the meeting a few hours to enable him to take part.

This time, however, Mao Tse-tung, accompanied by an entourage of leaders, welcomed Kosygin, and five hours later Peking celebrated with tremendous pomp the fifteenth anniversary of the friendship and mutual-aid pact concluded in 1950 between the U.S.S.R. and China. Despite their differences, the two allies were patently seeking grounds for agreement. During this period our guides never said one word about the U.S.S.R.

Then on February 17 we were invited to a banquet given in honor of Julius Nyerere, President of Tanzania. The Chinese had frequently boasted to us of the splendor of the receptions given in the great People's Palace and of the excellence of the cuisine. We were not disappointed: the reception room could comfortably hold 5,000 guests. The atmosphere was cordial, but we were in for some surprises, however.

From the moment cocktails were served, before the arrival of the guests of honor, a number of Soviet diplomats and colleagues, each one smiling more than the other, came over to greet me. My relations with the Soviet officials I had met had always been politely formal and since 1963 had even become downright cold, as they suspected that I was on good terms with several young Moscow intellectuals who were not in favor and even that I had helped one of them, Yevtushenko, to publish his book in France. This cordiality on the part of the Russians in Peking took me by surprise, and so I decided to take advantage of it, asking them bluntly, "On what sort of terms are you with the Chinese?" The reply was every bit as blunt: "Nothing has changed since October, no matter what some people say. Besides, the conference of twenty-six parties will be taking place in Moscow on March 1." And in order to explain the situation to me the Russians invited me to dinner with them two days later.

The second surprise came in the middle of the meal. My Chinese neighbor, a high official in the Foreign Ministry, suddenly stopped talking to me about Chinese cooking and asked, "What do they think in European left-wing circles of the new Soviet leaders?" I replied that they were not well known and that no one really understood what was happening, neither Khrushchev nor his successors having publicly revealed who were against them. Then I asked in my turn, "What do you think of them?" "We don't know them well, either," replied my neighbor and changed the subject.

Two days later I arrived at the Soviet Embassy. It stands in a large garden, formerly that of the Orthodox Church Seminary. The main building is impressively large, in the pompous Stalin style. It is surrounded by a whole series of houses in which the staff and journalists are accommodated. In this little Russian enclave in Peking, with its own schools, swimming pool, and theater, they live as they would in Russia.

At the table Russian wines and brandy quickly warmed up the atmosphere, and over the dessert my neighbor got to the heart of the matter. "We proposed to the Chinese that the controversy should be dropped and that together we should look for points of unity, but they immediately laid down unacceptable conditions. 'Agreed,' Chou En-lai said to us, 'let us be friends; but first of all, carry out the policy we recommend: disavow the Khrushchev of the twentieth congress, rehabilitate Stalin, and seize the Americans by the throat.' Nonsense, as you can see."

"We are 'liudi dielovye,' practical men," says another of my hosts. "We said that we would help Vietnam, and, believe me, she will want for nothing. The only thing the Chinese know how to do is march and shout in the streets of Peking. How does that help the Vietnamese?"

I remarked that Soviet aid was not preventing the Americans from bombing North Vietnam. "Just wait a bit," they answered. "Heavy material cannot be transported like matches."

I replied that the Americans had not bombed for ten days but that their first raid had taken place in August. "That's Khrushchev's fault," replied my neighbor. "Now we have a 'dielovoi' leadership, a team of practical men."

And at that point I noticed that the Russians had changed: for once they were not unanimous, and they began a heated discussion. Two guests held that the responsibility was entirely that of the Chinese, whose attitude was weakening the socialist camp — "If it hadn't been for this controversy, the Americans would never have dared to bomb North Vietnam, either in August or now. Those who are prolonging the quarrel and rejecting common action are responsible." "Do they really reject it?" I asked, incredulous. Everybody jumped on me. "What! Don't you know? What do you think Kosygin talked to them about? And haven't they told you how that old madman Mao treated him?"

I admitted my ignorance and was treated to a violent diatribe against Mao, who, my hosts alleged, is so lazy that he refuses to learn any "civilized" language; does not even know Mandarin; speaks only the Hunan dialect, which no one understands and which prevents him from appearing on television; and thinks he can do anything, as Stalin once did — even insult people.

I asked what Mao had done to Kosygin — promising not to write anything immediately. They explained. Kosygin had proposed that at the conference of the twenty-six parties arranged for March 1 a solemn declaration in support of Vietnam should be made, and he had suggested a whole series of measures to render

Sino-Soviet aid effective. First of all Chou En-lai answered him "with his usual pedantry," violently criticizing the idea of this conference, inherited from Khrushchev and organized :n a way that offended the Chinese CP, and demanding that the U.S.S.R. disown the policy followed since the twentieth congress. Kosygin then insisted that they no longer discuss the past but restrict themselves to studying the conference from the angle of immediate effectiveness. Obstinately, Chou En-lai played his record again: the conference must be canceled to prove to the world that the U.S.S.R. had radically changed its political orientation. Suddenly Mao, who had seemed to be dozing, interrupted Chou En-lai: "You see, Kosygin, our Prime Minister is your friend. He is giving you good advice because he has illusions about you. Not I. I say this: Hold your conference and show the world that you are secessionists of the same breed as Khrushchev."

All my Russians were not in agreement about this last remark of Mao's. Half claimed that Mao had said, "Chou En-lai is your agent," and not "your friend." A long discussion ensued: did this phrase foretell the approaching disgrace of Chou or did the confusion between "agent" and "friend" simply arise from the fact that Mao was speaking Hunanese, which no one knows really well? Be that as it may, everybody agreed with the conclusion that Mao had not wanted to hear about either common aid for Vietnam or a common declaration or any joint move by China and the U.S.S.R. so long as the Soviet leaders had not recanted their errors of the past ten years by condemning them publicly. The matter rested there, and my hosts declared spiritedly that the conference of March 1 would take place.[6a]

On leaving them that evening and all the other times that I met them, I got the impression that the Russians' *amour-propre* was involved and that the mere idea of giving in to the Chinese had become unthinkable. Besides, how could they wish to become reconciled with a country which, in their eyes, was in the fatal grip

[6a] The Chinese subsequently also revealed some details of the Mao Tse-tung–Kosygin meeting. According to them, the Russian Prime Minister tried to persuade them that the Americans are escalating the war in Vietnam to save face but that in fact they want to withdraw. Mao, of course, rejected this explanation and asked what the U.S.S.R. would do if the Americans attacked China. Kosygin, according to the Chinese, refused to reply to this question and refused to commit himself to a unilateral declaration warning the U.S. that an attack on China would be considered by him as an attack on Russia.

of Stalinist madness? Until 1957, until the end of the first Five-Year Plan which had been implemented with the help of the U.S.S.R., China to them was a normal country and even "on the right road." But after that, Mao, seized by megalomania, proclaimed himself the new Stalin and decided to ignore every economic and human law; the appeals to reason addressed to him by the U.S.S.R. and other Communist parties only made him more intractable. Impotent, the U.S.S.R. could only look on at the incredible spectacle of the "Great Leap Forward," the regimentation of the peasants, and the monstrous development of the personality cult. Worse, the megalomania of the Chinese led them into a crushing contempt for the rest of the world and, foolishly, into treating their opponents as "paper tigers" — and therefore into playing with fire. This way of looking at things is debatable, but it is, as closely as possible, the view of all the Russians in Peking, who want no part of reconciliation.

Admittedly, it would be dangerous to assert that the attitude of the small Soviet colony in Peking reflects the opinion of the Soviet Union as a whole. Nonetheless, these diplomats and journalists who have all studied China in Moscow's Oriental institutes, have spent years in China, and speak fluent Chinese, are their country's main informants on Chinese questions. And while for some time now they have been confined to their embassy, they were previously able to travel freely throughout China, accompanying Russian technicians working there, and follow the country's development very closely. All spoke with mistrust if not disgust about the Chinese experiment — the resort to "political incentives," systematic egalitarianism, the imposition of manual work on cadres — all appeared heretical and fruitless to them, not to mention the cult of Mao, which of course reminded them of their own worst memories.

When I got to know them a little better, I asked them in confidence if they considered that the U.S.S.R. had made any mistakes in China, if, for example, she had not been wrong in recalling all her technicians in 1960. These men were not wearing blinders as in Stalin's day. They spoke quite lucidly about their country's recent past, acknowledging that not everything was happening for the best even today; and several even said they missed Malenkov, "the most intelligent man of the post-Stalin era," but they all refused to admit that the U.S.S.R. was in the slightest responsible for the quarrel with China. "The germ of madness," one of them said to me, "was already in Maoist heads during the Yenan period, and no doubt even before that. There was nothing we could do about it, and we can still do nothing to prevent it from being revealed publicly. Saying this, he, like his friends, took the "psychological" point of view without really making allowances for the material conditions in which Maoism was born and which made it what it is. Neither he nor his friends therefore believed in the possibility of any evolution in China, of any change in the Chinese attitude, or of a reconciliation. "Since 1957 our paths have diverged, and they will never cross again. Having said that, it's better not to say any more," they concluded, conforming to Moscow's line of avoiding any aggravation of the controversy.

The Chinese themselves were less scrupulous. Even during the truce, their newspapers reproduced articles by Albanian or Japanese Communists which attacked "Khrushchevism without Khrushchev" and violently criticized the idea of the conference of March 1. Despite the absence of seven of the twenty-six parties invited (the Chinese, Japanese, Vietnamese, Korean, Indonesian, Rumanian, and Albanian) the conference was held in Moscow on the prearranged date. It did not produce very much, and the Italian CP's opposition prevented a clear decision from being made about the main object of the conference, the preparation of a congress of all Communist parties in the world; but it unleashed the fury of the Chinese, whose tongues were loosened, first in private, then in public. Some of them who had said before March 1 that they "knew little about the new Soviet leaders" now talked about them knowingly.

At the beginning of March, on the occasion of the visit of Ayub Khan, the President of Pakistan, big meetings and receptions were held during which our Chinese hosts explained to us at length why "Khrushchevism without Khrushchev" was even more sinister than that "with." The Russians were invited to these festivities. To give an idea of the tone of the conversations between Russians and Chinese, I shall quote a fragment of dialogue I overheard one evening.

"What is the weather like in your country?" a high Chinese official asked the correspondent of a Moscow newspaper.

"My country is very big, and the weather varies from one region to the other. But I believe that, on the whole, it's fine."

"I'm delighted for you," said the Chinese suavely. "That will perhaps save you from having to buy millions of tons of wheat from your American friends."

"No doubt," replied the Russian, even more suavely. "For my part, I hope you have no further need for Australian or Canadian wheat."

From mutual sneering, relations became openly hostile after the demonstration of March 5, 1965, when Asian students marched in front of the American Embassy in Moscow and were driven back by Soviet militiamen with a zeal and vigor that the Chinese considered excessive and politically significant. "Who are your allies? Who are your enemies?" demanded *Jenmin Jih Pao,* which on the following day published two pictures on its front page: one of American policemen clubbing Negro demonstrators, the other of Soviet militiamen clubbing yellow demonstrators — a plain denunciation, without words, of white racism, American or Russian. And on the afternoon of March 6 a demonstration was held in front of the Soviet Embassy in Peking. Only a few hundred people took part, but it was the first time that slogans hostile to the U.S.S.R. were shouted in the Chinese capital.

For ten days the Chinese press devoted columns and columns to the Moscow demonstration and its sequel,[6b] but without going fully into the Sino-Soviet quarrel. So when I went to interview Chou En-lai on March 17,[6c] I strongly doubted that he would agree to talk about it.

I had drawn up and submitted the required written questionnaire a few weeks earlier, during the period of truce, and I had avoided raising this delicate topic. But as the interview ended up taking on a tone that was anything but official, I risked raising the question by asking what significance the conference of March 1 had for the international workers' movement. "Thank you for taking an interest in the international workers' movement," replied Chou En-lai coldly. This was to put me in my place, but I persisted. I said that events of this kind concerned the whole left, which more than ever was questioning itself about the U.S.S.R., while at the same time failing to understand clearly what China wanted. Suddenly Chou En-lai thawed and talked as I had never dared hope he would.

I must say here that Madame Kung P'eng, Deputy Minister of Foreign Affairs, who had arranged the interview, had warned me

---

[6b] The Chinese complained that their students were badly looked after in the Moscow hospitals. The Russians accused the Chinese students of feigning symptoms and expelled several of them for this.

[6c] The full text of this interview will be found in Appendix E.

that Chou En-lai would reply off the record to some of my questions and that I must not publish his replies. An hour after I had left the Prime Minister, she telephoned me at my hotel to remind me of this. Although press messages are not censored in Peking, I nevertheless did not send anything to Paris without first obtaining Foreign Ministry sanction. When I re-read this interview, it seems to me to be couched in a clearly diplomatic style which was not in fact true of Chou En-lai's replies. I still do not intend to publish what I was asked to keep to myself, but I would like to describe the impression I derived from this encounter.

Chou En-lai is a "veteran in Sino-Soviet relations." Long before the Maoist victory, he had been responsible on several occasions for very delicate negotiations with Moscow. When he speaks of the arrogance of the Russians and reproaches them for behaving as "father of the Party" and never treating others as equals, he is no doubt thinking of his experiences at a time when he was in a weak position and unable to slam doors — as he did in 1961 by ostentatiously leaving the twenty-second congress of the Soviet Communist Party in protest against Khrushchev's "excommunication" of the Albanians.

In spite of that, he talked to me about the U.S.S.R. without either bitterness or rancor, and he did not run down the Soviet system. He criticized only the leaders, who instead of improving, grew worse from one generation to the next and seemed to have completely lost sight of the ideal they ought to have been defending. In his opinion, Stalin had been a great revolutionary but a very controversial personality. Stalin often changed his ideas; he had made many blunders and created much havoc, but he had had an excuse: at all costs, he had to defend the country of the Revolution, encircled as it was by the capitalists. Whatever one might think, the mere existence of the U.S.S.R. had helped all revolutionary movements, including the Chinese revolution. After a whole series of victories for communism, one had hoped that whoever succeeded Stalin would be a more flexible and more internationally minded comrade, but it was Khrushchev who appeared on the scene and took over everything that was bad in Stalinist policy, making it even worse. Then came Kosygin and Brezhnev, but the hope that they would be of a different mettle was destroyed in a single meeting at the Kremlin.

First of all, the new Soviet leaders made an analysis of the international situation which in every point resembled that made by their predecessor during the period of his greatest enthusiasm for an entente with the United States. By their account, the Khrushchev co-existence policy was a great success and must be continued whatever the cost. Furthermore, Kosygin and Brezhnev displayed the same ignorance of Chinese problems as Khrushchev, to the point where Chou En-lai must have found it difficult to understand what differentiated them from their former boss. Obviously, they were products of the same school and if their manner was different their doctrine was exactly the same as Khrushchev's.

Certainly, it cannot all come down to a question of personality, and Chou En-lai fully admitted that every society produces the leaders it deserves. Nonetheless, while shocked like other Chinese leaders by the recent evolution of the Soviet system, he seems to believe that if a good team of revolutionary leaders came to power, it could quickly and without difficulty correct these mistakes; he even thinks that if the Soviet masses understood at which point their leaders deviated from the road that leads to communism, they would find the means of changing them — and that this will happen sooner or later, for the rank and file remain as communist as they were in the days of Stalin. All hope is therefore not lost, but one must rely on the people, and not on the leaders. The duty of the revolutionaries of the whole world is thus to help this awakening of the Soviet masses by bluntly denouncing the machinations of Khrushchev's successors; but when the day comes, only the Russians themselves will be able to put their house in order.

That, as I see it, is Chou En-lai's position; in his view, the situation in the U.S.S.R. is not yet irretrievable. He did not talk to me about either the restoration of capitalism or an American-Soviet holy alliance. On the contrary, he told me, and with considerable conviction, that in case of a general conflict in Asia, the Soviet Union would fight alongside the Chinese against the Americans and give President Johnson a sharp and painful shock.

Nevertheless, two days later *Jenmin Jih Pao,* in a leading article on the conference of March 1, attacked the U.S.S.R. in fierce terms that contrasted strangely with the moderation of those Chou En-lai had used to me. In the eyes of the central body of the Chinese CP, the Soviet situation had already been irretrievable from the moment it modeled its economic system on that of its new ally, the United States.

It is obvious that the Chinese position could not have changed radically in two days. Nor do I believe that Chou En-lai revealed to me his personal opinion, an opinion differing from that of his government. I can see only one plausible explanation for these attacks: the Chinese were accusing the Soviets of treason "preventively" in order to incite the Russian rank and file, whom they hope to arouse. I also think that in their usual way they were simplifying and exaggerating excessively to bring the message home to their militants, who understandably might be worried that no common Sino-Soviet front was being formed against American aggression in Vietnam.

Be that as it may, the publication of this article unleashed an anti-Soviet reaction throughout China. We were in Shanghai at that time, and our guides constantly returned to this topic with painful insistence. At first we thought that they were particularly garrulous and sectarian, but afterward, in provincial cities, we were subjected to the same furious diatribes — to the point where I often had to recall remarks made to me by Chou En-lai in order to absolve the U.S.S.R. from charges which seemed absurd to me, without much luck, though, the word of a stranger not carrying much weight in China against an article in *Jenmin Jih Pao*. Besides, in the provinces the official invective did not shock people and hardly even surprised them. During the previous years they had been so stirred up against the Soviet Union that they accepted the most outrageous accusations as gospel. All were convinced, on the strength of innumerable "antirevisionist" documents made available to them, that China had to fight on two fronts — against capitalism and against Khrushchevism.

Faced with my skepticism, people tried to prove that the U.S.S.R. was well on the way to restoring capitalism by bombarding me with quotations from a source difficult to refute — Khrushchev himself.[7a] But Khrushchev never was a theoretician, and it seems a trifle arbitrary to look for a coherent theory of the development of communism in his off-the-cuff talks, stuffed as they were with Ukrainian proverbs. If Khrushchev became popular in the West, it is precisely because he was not like Stalin, an implacable prophet, and because in his jovial extemporizations he humanized his country's image. I followed him on his American tour in 1959.

[7a] The Chinese edition of these works does not contain the famous "secret report" of the twentieth congress. When one remarks on this to the Chinese —who criticize certain passages of it—they retort that neither has it yet been published in the U.S.S.R.

It was an eye-opener to observe how his physical appearance, his "common-man" approach, and his wife's unaffected charm bowled over America's deep-rooted prejudices. And he scored an even greater success in Europe, where anticommunism is less widespread and less rabid. If Khrushchev helped considerably to ease tension and promote peaceful co-existence, it was not because he talked peace — the Soviet leaders have always done that — but because he personally was the symbol of a franker, more tolerant, and less inward-looking Russia.

We knew that serious quarrels had divided the Chinese and Khrushchev, who despite his apparent good humor, had applied ruthless economic sanctions to them. But no commentary recalling his "depravity" accompanies Khrushchev's written works, which are meant to rouse Chinese indignation; it is assumed that just reading them is enough to shock. And, in fact, the Chinese were offended to the depths of their souls by the Khrushchev remarks they constantly quoted to me: "The more one eats, the more democratic one is"; "Socialism is a good thing, but with butter it is even better"; "Everything ripens in its own time, and when the capitalists see how our socialist society is prospering, they will all be converted"; "Those who eat watery soup and share a pair of trousers among five have no right to talk of communism."

The last quotation about "watery soup," was obviously aimed at the Chinese but was in danger of boomeranging because of the U.S.S.R.'s food shortages — and on this point the Chinese suffered from no inferiority complex with regard to the Russians. But they were disgusted by the fact that Khrushchev constantly advocated the growth of individual consumption as the main objective. And in the matter of peaceful co-existence, it was not so much the principle which the Chinese objected to (they even claimed to have proposed it first) but the connotation Khrushchev gave it and the arguments he used to convince Westerners — arguments which tended, according to the Chinese, to prove to the capitalists that the value of a socialist society lies in its capacity to mass-produce consumer goods. "If this is the test for socialism, then the Americans are much further along the road to communism than the Russians, since they are so far ahead in the field of consumer goods," said one of my provincial guides jokingly.

In Europe and in the United States I met people of diverse political shades who smiled at the naïvetés which colored Khrushchev's speeches on the peaceful competition between the two systems. The Chinese themselves did not dwell upon it, for Khrushchev's basic idea seemed to them so *immoral* that it was not even possible to discuss it. And the sincerity of their indignation made one aware of the gulf that separates these members of the society of challenge from the rest of the world. Looking back, I admit that I did not realize to what extent each word, each promise of Khrushchev's could appear heretical, corrupting, and sinister to the Maoists, convinced as they are of the superiority of the altruistic poor man, "the cleanest of all." When Peking declared in March, 1965, that "Khrushchev's successors were even worse and more dangerous than he," they immediately became the incarnation of evil for the militants and therefore readily comparable to the American imperialists.

When, having heard the Russians in Peking, one listened to the provincial Chinese, one became aware of how far apart the two great Communist powers had grown; but afterward one said to oneself that the U.S.S.R. and China were both controlled by a monolithic and all-powerful party, highly capable of enforcing a sudden change of line — all the more easily if it were justified by an external threat. It seemed to me, therefore, that Chou En-lai saw the situation clearly when he declared that in the case of a conflict spreading to all of Asia, the Chinese and the Russians would again find themselves in the same camp. But the Americans seemed determined to continue the escalation and the risk of a general war became greater every day.

Nevertheless, when I returned to Peking in May, Sino-Soviet relations, far from having improved, had grown worse. The Chinese thundered louder than ever against American-Soviet collusion, and Russian attacks on the Chinese became more and more pointed.

"Well? They have said plenty of bad things to you about us?" one of the Russians in Peking asked me. And without waiting for a reply, he explained to me what had happened during my absence. The Chinese had become frankly impossible. They were almost openly sabotaging Soviet aid to Vietnam: they were forbidding flights over their territory by planes carrying Soviet technicians; they were holding up the transportation of heavy matériel; they were inventing all kinds of difficulties and then accusing the Soviet Union of doing nothing. "That is too absurd for us to reply to, and we are continuing to avoid controversy."[7b]

[7b] The Russians abstained from public controversy with the Chinese until August, 1966. It was only after the publication in Peking of the

In fact, all was not serene in the Russian colony. First of all, it was considerably shaken by the news from Vietnam, which proved the ineffectiveness of Soviet military aid: despite the vaunted heavy matériel, the American raids on North Vietnam continued. Although they did not want a total war against the United States at any price, my Russians ardently wanted to see them taught a severe lesson in Vietnam which would remind them of the Soviet Union's military might. This would also be a lesson for the Chinese, to whom it would prove that if the U.S.S.R. does not export revolution, it is capable of preventing the imperialists from exporting counter-revolution — a demonstration that had to be mounted so that peaceful co-existence could be continued and the Chinese discredited in the eyes of all revolutionaries, who would then see Soviet strategy as the only effective solution. In short, the Russians had every reason to want to oppose the Americans firmly in Vietnam, but they realized bitterly that they were not succeeding in doing so.

However, although nothing very spectacular had yet occurred, according to my Russians, the Americans already understood that Soviet aid to Vietnam was dangerous for the U.S. Johnson had begun to talk of unconditional negotiations, while until then he would not even hear of any negotiations. During the whole of May, 1965, proposals for a negotiated settlement of the conflict were put forward, particularly by the neutralist countries. Each time the hopes of the Russian colony were raised only to be dashed as Moscow aligned itself immediately with Hanoi and Peking, which

---

resolution of the CCP Central Committee on the "cultural revolution," which was violently against Soviet revisionism, that Moscow counter-attacked and in her turn questioned the socialist character of Chinese society and its policy. In September, 1966, the Soviet correspondents in Peking cabled violently anti-Chinese reports to the extent that the Tass agency became the main source of Western information about the "misdeeds" of the Red Guards.

Two points must be made on this subject: First, the Soviet journalists are certainly the only foreign correspondents who speak fluent Chinese. This allows them to read all the innumerable posters and leaflets written by the Red Guards much better than their Western colleagues can do. On the other hand, the Russian journalists are even more isolated from the Chinese than their Western counterparts and much of the information they file seems dictated more by their anti-Chinese sentiments than by observable facts.

Finally, it should be repeated that no censorship exists in Peking and no foreign correspondent has been expelled from China. Neither the Chinese nor Western journalists have ever enjoyed the same editorial freedom in Moscow.

both rejected these offers as insincere and declared categorically that negotiations must be based on Ho Chi Minh's four points, which were rejected by the Americans.

My Russians did not condemn these four points, but they all let it be clearly understood that but for Chinese intransigence, negotiations would be possible, and that the Vietnamese had everything to gain from them. Their anger against China grew worse each day: she was sabotaging military aid to Vietnam and she was refusing to take part in any common action because of the risks, while at the same time inciting others to fight, all with the intention of pushing the U.S.S.R. into total war against the United States. "If the Chinese were really supporting the Vietnamese as they claim to be," said the Russians, "they would not reject a pact — even a partial one — with us, and they would put an end to this idiotic quarrel."

High officials of the Chinese Foreign Ministry countered these arguments with others that were no less admissible. According to them, it was in order to disguise their lack of energy in providing matériel that the Russians had invented this charge that the Chinese were obstructing Soviet transportation. "On the contrary, Soviet trains are given absolute priority. It's not our fault, anyhow, if they are few and far between and loaded with old supplies," one of them said to me. And he quoted articles which had appeared in the Western press which "proved irrefutably" that the Russians had intervened in Vietnam only with the aim of inducing her to negotiate under the conditions laid down by Johnson. "They are playing a double game. They are more astute than Khrushchev, but we shall unmask them all the same. The demagogic screen behind which they are hiding is full of holes, and one can already see what they are up to — that is, to dominate the world together with the Americans. They claim they are making war against each other in Asia, but in the rest of the world they embrace one another: diplomatic relations, cultural exchanges, trade, all continue as before. Did the U.S.S.R. have cultural exchanges with Germany during the last world war or with the United States during the Korean War?"

I recalled that during the Korean War Moscow did not sever diplomatic relations with Washington; then, playing devil's advocate, I said that the Russians' Vietnamese policy had changed since Khrushchev's departure: in August, 1964, the latter had not reacted to an American raid on North Vietnam, while today his successors have made their position clear. My companions smiled at my naïveté. "Khrushchev left the Americans to disentangle themselves. The present leaders want to help them. Kosygin has come to tell us that they must be helped to save face. What he wants, indeed, is for the Vietnamese to capitulate without too much loss of face. How can one have discussions with an aggressor who intends to remain by force in a country he has moved into in violation of all law? As Chou En-lai said, the only way for a brigand to save face is to give back what he has stolen."

Two of my host's friends improved on this: "Why doesn't the Soviet Union deny it when the Western press reports that she had promised to induce Vietnam to talk with Johnson? Why doesn't she prevent the Americans from transferring their troops from Europe to Vietnam? Why does she continue to organize what she calls an international Communist conference in opposition to the Chinese CP?"

In short, I was to understand something of which my informants were convinced — that what the Russians want is to help the Americans against the Vietnamese and the Chinese so that afterward they can share the world with the United States.

In the spring of 1965 the political atmosphere in Peking was decidedly odd — baffling: American troops were disembarking en masse in Vietnam; all observers thought that China was being more and more threatened; and the Chinese, almost as violently, attacked America, their powerful opponent, and the U.S.S.R., apparently the only country which could restrain the United States from escalating the war and bombing China. But according to the Chinese, the Americans intended to escalate the war because they were assured of tacit Soviet support.

At the same time, Russian civil and military delegations were passing through Peking on the way to Hanoi, Marshal Chu Teh visited the Soviet Embassy to celebrate the twentieth anniversary of the victory over Hitler, and old Russian films glorifying the Soviet army were being shown in every movie theater in China.

It was a strange mix-up: the Chinese accused the Russians of complicity with the Americans but allowed Soviet supplies to pass through to Vietnam. The United States protested that the delivery of Chinese light weapons to the Vietcong constituted aggression against their Saigon ally but turned a blind eye on the arrival in North Vietnam of Soviet heavy weapons that were being used against their airmen. The Russians did not break with the Chinese, who insulted them daily, nor with the Americans, who bombed one of their allies daily; and at one and the same time they preached peaceful co-existence and the struggle against imperialism.

Rarely has a localized conflict thrown light on such flagrant contradictions between the words and the deeds of the great powers. Thus the Russians and the Chinese were forced to react in the same way against American intervention in Vietnam, but their ideological differences had become so marked that they could not arrive at an agreement to co-ordinate their action. In order for them to be able to work out and apply a common strategy, either China or the Soviet Union would have had to disown the international policy it had followed for years. Neither would agree to do this, thus deepening even more the distrust between them.

But wouldn't the desire to oppose the Americans effectively have justified abandoning the dispute, even temporarily? "No," Marshal Ch'en Yi, Vice-Premier and Foreign Minister, said to me categorically. "On the contrary, this controversy helps the peoples of the entire world to distinguish the true from the false, to determine the difference between the real anti-imperialist struggle and what is merely a counterfeit." But did China believe that in the case of the extension of the war in Vietnam common action would be possible? "Concerted common action," replied the Marshal, "demands, to begin with, a common knowledge of the aggressors and the same determination to fight them. If such an understanding came about, common action would become possible. Otherwise, no."

There was no answer to this, but the Russians had no desire to adopt the Chinese analysis of the Vietnam war in order to prove to them that they "knew" the Americans exactly as the Maoists did. I therefore had the impression, going from the Russians to the Chinese, that I was watching the last act in the great row between the two great Communist powers. In the face of American aggression in Vietnam they should have closed ranks, and one can even say that the instinct of self-preservation alone should have brought them together. But no; the gulf is too great between the Chinese Communists, who extol egalitarian austerity, and the Soviet Communists, in quest of abundance. However, the Americans gave daily proof that they had no intention of establishing a joint hegemony with the Russians but on the contrary wanted to dictate their own terms in Southeast Asia. Admittedly, they treated Russian communism diplomatically because it appears less dangerous to them, but they did not hide the fact that for them the only good Communists are dead Communists. In such a situation all prediction about Russo-American co-existence or a final break between Peking and Moscow is impossible. "War does not always work out according to human wishes," Chou En-lai said to me. God knows what surprises the war in Vietnam may yet bring.

THE SECOND CHINESE BOMB

On the evening of Wednesday, May 14, 1965, the radio, television, and special editions of the Peking newspapers proudly announced the news: a second atomic device had been successfully exploded somewhere in China. Throughout the evening and all the following day the Chinese kept repeating the news. They exulted, visibly bursting to rave about the feat, but holding back in keeping with the Maoist code, which extols modesty and condemns boasting.

The Peking foreign colony was hardly bowled over by the explosion: the American press had predicted it several weeks before; besides, it is a country's first successful nuclear explosion which gets talked about most, and in October, 1964, China's entry into the "atomic club" had evoked considerable discussion. People were already amazed that this underdeveloped country claimed — and was able — to rival the advanced countries. Experts had concluded, after examining the fall-out of the Chinese bomb, that it was undoubtedly more advanced than the French device. Others wondered if the Chinese were on the way to building the rockets necessary to deliver the bomb on American soil. Inquiries were made to find out whether or not the explosion had raised China's prestige in the eyes of the underdeveloped countries, which on the whole are violently anti-atomic.

What could one add to all this in May, 1965? Very little — particularly as everyone in Peking was convinced that this second Chinese nuclear explosion in no way altered the facts of the number one problem, the war in Vietnam. Indeed, for the Chinese bomb to become "deterrent" and really impress the Americans, China would have had to provide proof — by launching a satellite, for example — that she was capable of replying atomically to an atomic attack. But everyone knew that China would have no intercontinental missiles for several years and that her bomb could not therefore worry the United States.

Some even asserted that the fact that she possessed the bomb increased the danger to China; the Americans might indeed be tempted to destroy her atomic installations in order to prevent the establishment between them of the balance of terror which already existed between the U.S. and Russia. "The Chinese must be cautious," a Western military expert said to me in Peking. "The Americans have both the means and the desire to devastate China, while the U.S.S.R. has neither the wish nor very important reasons to defend her rather unbearable allies. Of course, no bombing, no matter how terrifying, could completely destroy China, and by launching such a venture the Americans would be taking enormous risks. The fact remains that they could in a few hours wipe out all the progress China has made in the last sixteen years." The same expert acknowledged, however, that if the Chinese survived the present critical period, winning the race against time which divides them and the Americans and succeeding, before the irrevocable happens, in creating a striking force of real deterrent power, they would draw enormous political dividends from their atomic investment. On that day, indeed, the Americans would be forced to acknowledge the establishment of the Communist regime in China as final. At one blow the political quarantine and the economic embargo of Mao's China and the maintenance of the "spare" regime in Formosa would no longer be justified, even in the eyes of the Americans, who, faithful to their pragmatic tradition, would prefer to see the Chinese take their seat in all the international organizations in place of those who occupy them at present.

"Granted," replied those Peking diplomats more interested in economics than in military matters. "But don't you think that the Chinese could achieve the same result more quickly and at less cost? Atomic weapons are already too costly for the rich countries. To manufacture them, Mao's China must bleed herself and abandon all advance on several essential domestic fronts. Wouldn't it have been more worthwhile for her to hoist the flag of nonviolence and wait calmly for her enemies to recognize her, as have most of the big European countries? And who can assert that the Chinese are merely seeking to ensure their own security when their admitted aim is to reverse the balance between the socialist and capitalist camps by extending their influence to other countries?"

Listening to these discussions rejuvenated me. I had heard the same kind of talk in the late 1940's when the West was wondering to what use the U.S.S.R. would put the atomic arsenal it was in the process of building up. The Soviet example does not enable one to state absolutely that China, once she has atomic weapons, will feel more secure and therefore more moderate and more aware of nuclear dangers; but one could be in the right to think so.

What struck me as paradoxical in Peking was to see the Russians sharing the West's anxieties and wondering if these Chinese fanatics might not risk using their bombs to export their revolution. To be truthful, it was the Russians who even talked with the most apprehension about the "Chinese atomic obsession," which, according to them, was an important factor in the deterioration of Sino-Soviet relations. Besides, on this last point the Chinese could not have contradicted them: in 1963 they themselves declared that the breaking of the contract in 1959 which had bound them to the Russians was the first proof that the latter had betrayed them. To throw light on this, however, it is necessary to go back eighteen years.

In 1948 Stalin admitted to Kardelj, one of Tito's right-hand men, that he had advised the Maoists to disband their army in order to reach an agreement with Chiang Kai-shek and that they had agreed to this in Moscow but afterwards failed to do so. With very untypical modesty, Stalin added that the Maoists were right and he had been wrong. From this unique but not easily refuted evidence, reported by Dedijer[8] in his best-selling book, many have inferred that the Chinese carried out their revolution without Stalin and even despite him.

This is to go a little too fast; the affair is more complex than that. To begin with, Mao's enemies did not believe for a moment that the U.S.S.R. would stay neutral; and if Chiang Kai-shek wanted to prevent the Communists from installing themselves in Manchuria, it was because he was convinced of the opposite. Against the advice of his American advisers he launched his best troops in the Northeast because he believed, with reason, that a Maoist republic established in a rich region and adjoining the Soviet Union would become an impregnable fortress. Chiang Kai-shek fell into the Manchurian trap and lost everything there, but Mao could never have laid the trap had he not known that he could count on the moral — and even the material — support of the U.S.S.R.

After the debacle of his armies in the Northeast, only the Americans could have salvaged the wreck of Nationalist China,

8 Vladimir Dedijer, *Tito Parle* (Paris, Gallimard, 1953).

but this would have meant accepting the risks of direct and massive intervention. If they made no move it was not because they feared a long guerrilla war (they had not yet burnt their fingers, as they have since in Vietnam), but because the great majority of their troops were tied up in Europe, a continent which in their eyes was much more important and much more threatened than Asia.

It is certain that Stalin, by blockading Berlin, initiating the Prague coup, and creating tension throughout Europe by every possible means, wanted first and foremost to defend the interests of the U.S.S.R., and not to divert the Americans from the Far East. Nonetheless, his moves benefited the Chinese Communists — and more than they could have hoped. After his victory, Mao declared: "Without the Soviet Union, without the victory over Hitlerism, without the birth of the European people's democracies, the pressure of the forces of international reaction on us would have been infinitely greater. Could we have been the victors then? Certainly not."[9] Let us admit that he did not completely believe this, that he wished simply to pay homage to the U.S.S.R. and Stalin; but the fact remains that even if the Chinese are convinced that they would have won no matter what the circumstances, they acknowledged then (and acknowledge today) that the Soviet Union made their task much easier.

Stalin's policy benefited them so directly that their fate was bound up with his. They established their regime in the climate of the cold war, and America was hostile to them as much because they were allies of Stalin as because they were Communists. They lived in the same insecurity as the U.S.S.R. because they knew that in the event of war America, with her nuclear monopoly, would very probably extend the conflict to Asia and that that was why she supported Chiang Kai-shek's regime in Formosa. In short, Mao's China had only one friend at the time of its birth — Stalin's Russia.

At the end of December, 1949, Mao therefore went to Moscow. A few weeks later the famous mutual-aid pact was signed by Chou En-lai for China and Vishinsky for the Soviet Union, and the occasion was celebrated with impressive ceremonies and solemn speeches.

Article I of the appendix to this pact was particularly commented on. It concerned economic co-operation and said: "The

[9] *Izvestia,* November 6, 1949.

Government of the Soviet Union grants the Government of the People's Republic of China a loan of 300 million American dollars at the value rate of thirty-five dollars to one ounce of pure gold. Bearing in mind the exceptional devastation caused in China by the military actions that have taken place on her territory, this loan is granted at the special interest rate of 1 per cent a year." Another article laid down that China was to repay the loan by the end of 1963.

Admittedly, the Russians accorded the Chinese other material advantages — they contracted to restore to them the Manchurian railroad and the ports of Dairen and Port Arthur. But this did not obscure the point that in view of China's crying needs, a loan of 300 million dollars was derisory. Some members of the British Labor government (which recognized the Mao regime on January 5, 1950) therefore thought that China would seek additional credit elsewhere and that the intelligent political attitude toward the new revolution would be to help it to overcome its difficulties, not to try to strangle it. This was in particular the view of Aneurin Bevan, who never ceased defending it, even during the worst phase of the cold war. Unfortunately, Britain was no longer the world's banker in 1950 and was not in a position to help China. Further, not all members of the Labor Party had Bevan's independence of mind and farsightedness; many wanted to avoid any clash with the United States.

Rare Americans, like Edgar Snow, explained to their compatriots that China had no wish to be Russia's satellite and that she could not become one; but they did not have enough influence to affect Washington policy, and the McCarthyite fury threatened those bold spirits who dared to talk of "Chinese Titoism." Things grew still worse until in June, 1950, the Korean War broke out, and in November of the same year G.I.'s and Chinese "volunteers" faced each other to the north of the 38th parallel. The Americans' attitude hardened: they included Formosa in their "national perimeter of defense" (in fact, according to the Chinese, they annexed it), and their 7th Fleet was given the task of defending Chiang Kai-shek whatever the cost.

Little is known about the secret history of the Korean War. But given the political climate which prevailed in the U.S. at that time, it broke out so opportunely that the possibility of an American provocation cannot be ruled out without examination. This theory has been advanced in particular by the non-Communist American journalist I. F. Stone.[10] According to him, the North Koreans fell into a trap set for them by the South Koreans with American aid. It goes without saying that this version of the events is contested. Many think that Mao was the instigator of this war: on the one hand, Korea belonged traditionally to the Chinese sphere of influence, and on the other, Mao wanted to reinforce the defenses of his Manchurian border. According to others, the war was decided on jointly by Stalin and Mao during their historic meeting in Moscow; Mao was paying his political debt to the Soviet Union by pinning down the Americans in the Far East and thereby reducing American pressure in Europe. Still others, including Edgar Snow, did not exclude the possibility that Stalin alone had unleashed the war to bring about a confrontation between the Chinese and the Americans which would eliminate any chance of Chinese Titoism and make agreement between the two countries absolutely impossible.

Once again, this is entirely a matter of guesswork. Never in their bitterest exchanges have either the Russians or the Chinese accused the other side of starting the war, and the files are still secret.

Nonetheless, one thing is certain: in June, 1950, the Chinese, who were in the process of bringing their civil war to an end, were not in North Korea; while the Russians were. The Chinese press did not announce the outbreak of the war until two weeks later, while the Moscow papers were boasting about North Korean victories immediately after fighting began. Logically, American reprisals should have been directed against the U.S.S.R. rather than against China, yet today the Americans still declare China to be an "aggressive power" unfit to sit in the U.N. because of the Korean War while choosing to forget the part played in it by the Russians. If the Americans apply double standards it is not because they regard the Maoists as more "guilty" than the Russians but rather because they consider the Soviet regime firmly established and not to be unseated, while Mao's could yet be overthrown.

Paradoxically, the Chinese do not complain about the American attitude, which seems to them to be normal for an imperialist power, but they are beginning to reveal that the Soviet Union behaved badly in the Korean affair. I was given to understand in Peking that when the war was over, the Russians presented their

[10] Stone, I. F., *The Hidden History of the Korean War* (New York, Monthly Review Press, 1952).

bill as if they were armaments dealers rather than allies in a common cause. Even the living and travel expenses of their Korean War correspondents were included in the Russian invoice; and as the final charges had been calculated after Stalin's death, the Chinese charged his successors with this act of sordid cupidity.

It would appear, however, that the Korean War had already caused their relations with Stalin to deteriorate seriously. There again the record is not available and details are lacking, but there is an important piece of evidence — Khrushchev's — and one event confirms it: the brusque change in the Chinese attitude during the peace talks four days after Stalin's death. In a private talk with Polish CP leaders Khrushchev alleged that Stalin, in his last days, had provoked dangerous Sino-Soviet tensions.[11a] And the fact is that after Stalin's death, Chou En-lai put forward a peace plan for Korea very similar to the Indian one which the Chinese until then had always rejected. From that day on, the Panmunjom negotiations moved rapidly to the successful conclusion which Mao had wanted for some time, for in 1953 he faced formidable tasks in China and had no desire to get bogged down in Korea.

It was in 1953 that the Chinese started to implement their first Five-Year Plan, which the Russians in Peking talked about to me much more than did the Maoists. According to them, the plan was conceived and carried out thanks almost entirely to Soviet help, and whatever China has today is due to the capital built up during those five years. The figures they give seem to be hard to gainsay. Westerners also admit that China made great progress during this period. And in the Northeast in particular it is obvious that the Russians set up huge enterprises and provided capital goods in quantity. The Chinese, nonetheless, talk of Russian aid with bitterly ironic "ingratitude."

"The Russians never gave us anything for nothing. And if you would like to see the bills, you will see that we paid more for machines than they were worth," I was repeatedly told. It was a figure of speech. I am quite incapable of assessing the price of machinery, and besides they never showed me any bill. But I had already heard Yugoslavs and Poles complain of the Russians' toughness in business matters. And in a more general way I had noticed that the Communist countries (with the Soviet Union in

[11a] The New York Times, June 4, 1956. Cited according to A. Doak Barnett, Communist China and Asia.

the vanguard) enthusiastically tried to take commercial advantage of each other and shared at least one firm conviction — namely, that "the others" were trying to exploit them.

The man responsible for this state of affairs was obviously Stalin, who in his thirty years as master of the Communist world introduced these selfish usages and customs so alien to the doctrine of proletarian internationalism. In such conditions it was impossible to invent a system for the economic integration of the socialist countries.

It was this (and not a few commercial anomalies) which hit the Chinese — as it had hit the Russians after the death of Stalin. The Russians had made greater efforts to enable China to carry out her first plan, but at the same time they modified their policy in regard to the underdeveloped countries and began to grant credit to non-Communist countries — all without consulting anyone. On the other hand, the Chinese declared that they were not receiving enough aid, that the methods advocated by the Russian experts were not applicable to their country, and that their economy was developing at too slow a pace to satisfy the necessities created by industrialization *à la russe*. But neither in Moscow nor in Peking was there an organization or an assembly of the Communist countries at which such problems could be discussed. Furthermore, the struggle that was taking place in the Soviet Union over the succession to Stalin had repercussions throughout the Communist world. And the Chinese — like the others — frequently found themselves faced with *faits accomplis* they in no way approved of.

For instance, when Khrushchev hurried to Belgrade to see Tito in May, 1955, they were given no warning of the visit, nor were they informed of his famous "secret report" on Stalin to the twentieth congress, in February, 1956.

Preoccupied above all with the internal situation of the U.S.S.R., Khrushchev wanted to get things done quickly, without taking into account the reactions of foreign comrades. He was not aware that he was affecting the common heritage of the world's Communists; he never thought that he was involuntarily provoking crises in every country in the Eastern bloc. When these came to a head, as in Poland and Hungary in the autumn of 1956, he hesitated, improvised, and occasionally aggravated the situation dangerously by useless displays of force (as in Poland, for example) or by making promises he could not fulfill. In Hungary he had agreed not to intervene militarily and to withdraw his troops.

Instead of calming the rebels, this encouraged them, and four days later Khrushchev launched his tanks on Budapest.

A "very highly placed" Chinese said to me in Peking one day: "I cannot believe that a politician unleashes crises of the gravest kind without first having weighed the consequences and without having prepared a long-term strategy. Looking at Khrushchev, one got the impression he didn't know where he was going. For example, he denounced Stalin and Stalinism in his blustering way without putting forward any plan for reform or any substitute doctrine. Today we know that he simply wanted to destroy in order to set up his own regime and introduce the revisionist policy, but at the time we did not know what he was up to."

Personally, I do not think Khrushchev entertained such base ambitions. But it is true that the more dogmatic and farsighted Chinese were often baffled by Khrushchev and that Mao himself had to make prodigious speeches in order to interpret for his countrymen the unexpected and often contradictory declarations of the Soviet leader.

This was the climate in which the Chinese had to make decisions affecting their second Five-Year Plan and their policy within the bloc. They decided to "turn left" in the matter of domestic affairs, which led to the "Great Leap Forward"; and they decided that their attitude within the Communist camp would be one of "militant monolithism."

Within a few months the Chinese leaders underwent a radical transformation. Until then they had been admired in all the Eastern countries for the caution and adroitness with which they had carried out collectivization. Their much-quoted formula had been: "To run a co-operative you must choose the most patient and well-trained man"; and now, suddenly, they were setting up people's communes with unprecedented haste and making militancy a cardinal virtue. While Europe was still talking of the almost Fabian moderation with which the Chinese were socializing the urban sector, they were already hurling themselves headlong into industrialization and banning material incentives for the workers. The Poles still remembered how in Peking in 1956 they had been urged to fight for the democratization of the bloc, and yet in October, 1957, Mao declared to them categorically that the bloc must remain united under one leader alone, the U.S.S.R. In short, if the Chinese had not gone mad, they had become totally incomprehensible to their partners.

However, there was an explanation for the Chinese "madness."

The experience of the "hundred flowers" had taught them that it is not enough to invite criticism in order to find new ideas for the creation of a franker and more effective socialism. They had also learned that industrialization *à la russe,* even when adapted to their country, produced mediocre results in the political field as well as in the social field, and that if they continued along this path without making allowance for popular discontent, they would run the risk of being forced to resort to terror and of seeing a repetition of the Stalinist tragedy.[11b] But although he may have defended — and still defends — Stalin, Mao does not approve of his methods and has never wanted to see them applied in China. Unable either to "liberalize" or to operate as he did during the first Five-Year Plan, Mao, who had to find some other way out, resorted to the methods which had succeeded in the Yenan days and undertook to transform all China into a vast egalitarian community.

No one in Peking explained the great turn to the left of 1957 to me in such terms, but it seems that this may be the explanation, judging from all the available evidence with regard to the situation in all sectors of economic and social life at that time.

This is not to say that the Chinese decision was historically necessary, that it was impossible for them to make another, and that all the errors that resulted from it may be justified. There were undoubtedly other acceptable solutions. But given the inadequacy of Soviet aid, given international tension, and given the experience of the Maoists and their intellectual training, it was logical that they should have turned to the left.

The corollary of this change of direction in China's internal policy was the radicalization of her foreign policy. Organizing the "permanent revolution" in China only made sense if one envisaged a world-wide revolutionary movement. As he had done in the past to the veterans of Yenan, Mao had to explain to his activists that they were fighting in a limited sector of an immense world-wide front on which the exploited opposed the exploiters and the poor

---

11b The Chinese do not deny that their economy made considerable progress during the first Five-Year Plan and that the U.S.S.R. helped them to build at least 166 big industrial enterprises. But they claim that the Soviet planners insisted that the Chinese adopt the Russian system of paying workers and that this policy provoked serious social imbalances that were extremely dangerous for the coherence of Chinese society. The competition for production bonuses was responsible for the lowering of the political and moral standards of Chinese workers. According to this theory, the unrest in the social field was responsible for the bitter criticism which exploded in 1957 during the "hundred flowers" period.

fought the rich. A doctrine capable of taking the place of material incentives had to be universalist and exalting. One can say in a sense that Mao, by rejecting the Stalinist pattern, took over a considerable number of Trotskyite ideas. He was perhaps not aware of this, and in any event he was not eager to announce it publicly. Quite the opposite: to protect his rear, Mao needed the Communist bloc to stay monolithic, the guarantor of his security and the sole group prepared to help him. One can suppose that the Chinese would have agreed to the international Communist family's reorganizing and democratizing itself and centering itself less on Moscow, but only if this was going to reinforce its unity and fighting spirit. But in view of what was happening in their countries at that time, neither Khrushchev nor the rebels of the people's democracies envisaged anything of the kind; de-Stalinization had unleashed centrifugal forces in the Communist world, and each national party was more intent on regaining its independence than on developing a new democratized internationalism. Faced with this situation, it appears that Mao chose to retain the old system: a monolithic bloc with the U.S.S.R. at its head.

And here we come back to the bomb, for Mao only agreed to Soviet leadership for want of anything better, and he had taken out some insurance. At the conference of all the parties held in Moscow in November, 1957, he defended the Soviet CP eloquently as the guiding party, but on the fifteenth of the preceding October he had concluded a pact with the U.S.S.R. under which she was to help technically and materially in the construction of a Chinese atomic arsenal. It quickly became plain that this was an illusory deal and that this "atomic" agreement, far from improving Chinese-Soviet relations, led instead to their deterioration. It is therefore interesting to know how and why it was concluded, and particularly why Mao attached such importance to it.

It should be noted for a start that the Soviet press never reported either the signing or the breaking of this pact and that the Russian leaders have never mentioned it during their quarrel with the Chinese. The Chinese themselves talk freely about it, but their story is hardly convincing. They cite Lenin, who in *Left-Wing Communism: An Infantile Disorder* wrote that the Red Army would be committing an error and even a crime if it did not try to acquire all the weapons available to the enemy. The People's China, from its birth in open conflict with the United States, an atomic power, had therefore a duty to secure the bomb. This appears logical, but one may ask all the same why China did not feel adequately protected by the atomic power of the Soviet Union, which in the autumn of 1957 had launched the first Sputnik and thus demonstrated to the whole world that she possessed the means of replying to any aggression against the Eastern camp.

But it is precisely there that one comes to the heart of the problem. In 1957 Mao already had no more confidence in the Soviet leaders. This is confirmed by all the Communist leaders who often visited him at that time and complained about Moscow themselves. China therefore had to have her own striking force. But two allied atomic powers must work out a common strategy, since each would automatically be involved in a conflict concerning the other. They must march shoulder to shoulder militarily and politically; they must sign pacts binding them closely together — pacts which can only be concluded in a climate of confidence in which reciprocal criticism is possible.

On the other hand, perhaps Mao already feared that the fact that they shared a monopoly of atomic weapons might lead to a *rapprochement* between the Russians and the Americans and even, possibly, to a partnership. This is the theory advanced by Mao's admirers, who congratulate him on having, in 1957, foreseen the installation of the "hot line" which today links the White House and the Kremlin. If this theory is accurate, one can assume that already at that moment, Mao wanted to prevent the installation of this special direct line.

Be that as it may, Mao could allow himself to extol the leadership of the U.S.S.R. in the socialist camp without misgiving, convinced that after the signing of their atomic pact the Soviet Union and China would be united for better or worse, and that of the two, only China had a stable policy and doctrine. He told himself that in fact there would be two heads of the international Communist movement: the official one, the Soviet Union; and the doctrinal one, China.

In the same year, 1957, Mao made two speeches in Moscow: the first to the conference of Communist parties, the second at the university. The tenor of these was not revealed until 1963 and 1964, when the Russians and the Chinese began to argue; as we know, either his opponents discovered in these speeches the proof of his irresponsibility or his friends the proof of his genius. In Soviet eyes, Mao displayed in his speeches a crass ignorance of what atomic weapons really are and a dangerous propensity to play with fire. In them he revived the expression, first used by him in 1946, that imperialism was a "paper tiger," plainly forgetting that the tiger had atomic teeth. He asserted that humanity would survive an atomic war and would continue, even if half of it were to perish, to march toward communism. And he ended with a meteorological metaphor, "The wind from the East is prevailing over the wind from the West," which Mikhail Suslov, the Kremlin ideologist, declared to be "totally devoid of class significance."

The Chinese interpret their Chairman's speeches in a totally different way. Although armed to the teeth and "fierce as a tiger," imperialism is nonetheless a doomed force, a remnant of history destined to be swept away. It will not dare unloose a world war which would inevitably finish it. Besides, what could American bombs achieve against China? They did not even permit America to win against small countries like Korea and Vietnam. The fact that the bombs may be atomic today in no way changes the mechanics of the class struggle and ought not to discourage revolutionary movements. Imperialism is in crisis, and the revolutionary wind blows strongest where the contradictions are most flagrant — in the underdeveloped countries.

The final resolution of the 1957 conference was couched in terms vague enough for Chou En-lai still to be able today to claim that it contained "a good number of revolutionary principles" and for the Russians to regard it as conforming to the principles laid down at the twentieth congress. With the exception of Yugoslavia, all the parties in power signed it; but this document, so much disputed afterward, was flawed by an internal contradiction: it said, in effect, that each Communist country was free to carry on its own internal policies but had to join in a common anti-imperialist strategy, to be conducted under the aegis of the Soviet Union.

But it is obvious that China, with its "Great Leap Forward" and its people's communes; the U.S.S.R., with its Seven-Year Plan for prosperity; Poland, with its partial collectivization; and all the other Communist countries, with their own particular problems to solve, could not possibly share the same point of view on international matters. And despite the proclaimed freedom of each country to conduct its internal policy as it wanted, the "comrades" were not sparing in their criticism of each other. Khrushchev severely criticized the system of the people's communes, and Mao was sarcastic about the Russian economic innovations. Nevertheless, this took place in private, the 1957 convention formally forbidding all public criticism of the domestic affairs of others. But they made up for it in the sphere of international politics. Although at this time the Russians and the Chinese did not have specific "crimes" to accuse each other of, neither lacked opportunities for denouncing as inconsistent with the promises made in 1957 what the other said about the actions of the imperialists.

In principle a difference of accent between Moscow, which was conducting a dialogue with the West, and Peking, which was addressing itself to the underdeveloped world, could have made the implementation of a common strategy easier. But for this division of labor to be effective there would have had to be complete agreement on the fundamentals. As there was none, the two Communist giants constantly irritated each other. Khrushchev thought that Chinese propaganda was preventing him from overcoming American suspicions and persuading the Americans that he sincerely sought peaceful co-existence. In the Chinese view, the Soviet Union's overconciliatory attitude was the reason why their appeals to revolutionaries were having no effect.

We do not know what specific incident Khrushchev used as his pretext to break the Chinese-Soviet atomic pact unilaterally on June 20, 1959.[11c] The Chinese claim today that Khrushchev only made this decision in order to boast about it to Eisenhower when he met him at Camp David three months later. If that was so, "well-informed circles" would certainly have learned about it, for the Eisenhower administration was never a model of discretion; yet all the Western specialists were unaware of the existence of this Chinese-Soviet atomic pact, and furthermore, it appears highly unlikely that the Chinese would have waited four years to denounce this "treason" if they had had proof of it.

The fact remains that the logic of the Russo-American *rapprochement* demanded that the brake be applied to Chinese ambitions. Khrushchev needed the promises he had made in the name of the socialist camp to be kept willy-nilly by all those who belonged to it, and for further safety he broke the Chinese-Soviet atomic pact.

[11c] Many analysts consider that the crisis in the Straits of Formosa in August, 1958, forced Khrushchev to stop atomic supplies to China. It was then that the Soviet leader became aware that the Chinese would use atomic weapons to satisfy their territorial claims and first of all to liberate Formosa. There is no doubt that Sino-Soviet relations were greatly strained during that crisis. However, the Russians broke the pact with Peking nearly one year later and it is legitimate to suppose that Khrushchev had more immediate reasons for his decision.

By thus facing the Chinese with a *fait accompli* he achieved exactly the opposite of what he had expected. China did not give up manufacturing the bomb, and she concluded from the breaking of the agreement that her partner had deserted her and that therefore she no longer had any obligation toward Russia. From that day on, the Chinese began to mount their great offensive against the Soviet Union, discreetly at first, then with increasing violence.

It must not be assumed, however, that the Russians and the Chinese split purely on the atomic question; their divorce was simply the proof that an atomic alliance is not enough to bind together indissolubly two countries which are evolving internally in opposite directions and which have different meanings for the same words. It proved equally that anti-imperialism alone does not determine the shape of a society and that under its banner two countries with different systems and needs could follow two very different foreign policies.

Mao's visit to Moscow in 1957 would have produced completely different results if the Soviet Union and China, bearing in mind the fact that they were at different stages of development, had concentrated on a common strategy adapted to the needs of both. To achieve this, they would have had to abandon the principles which until then had governed relations among Communists. The Soviet Union would certainly have had to give up her leadership, while China would have been compelled to admit the existence of a new movement in countries faced with problems altogether different from her own.

Monolithism was still spoken of, but in fact there was no longer either internationalism or a common concept of world revolution. To revive these it would have been necessary to reopen the file and rewrite the history of world communism, which neither the Chinese nor the Russians wanted to do at any price, as the verbal excesses of Khrushchev's "secret report" against Stalin showed. The realities, the systems, and the needs of each country remained. And what also remained was the fact that China, by the vastness of her experiment alone, and without having to say so, was putting herself forward as a candidate for the leadership, until then held by the Soviet Union.

These problems were not broached. They contented themselves with generalities about anti-imperialist solidarity, and agreement on an atomic pact seemed easy. It was nevertheless illusory and paradoxical for the two great Communist powers to want to found their alliance on a pact of this nature.

I revealed this viewpoint to one of my Russians in Peking — the one who regretted Malenkov's departure and who most readily acknowledged some of his country's mistakes. We talked a whole morning in the Temple of Heaven, in the center of a circular wall which produces curious acoustical effects but where we were surer of not being overheard than in the Soviet Embassy or the Hsin Chiao Hotel. Even under these conditions my Russian was unwilling to admit that both sides were responsible for this business and that in 1957 Mao, like Khrushchev, had helped to bring about the conditions for the future divorce. According to him, the Chinese at that time could have obtained plenty from Russia, where they enjoyed enormous prestige and popularity. They had even been the great moral beneficiaries of the twentieth congress, for in denouncing Stalin's crimes and follies Khrushchev had implicitly paid homage to their wisdom; and he had implicitly congratulated them on successfully collectivizing the land and starting industrialization without recourse to Stalinist excesses. Mao was then considered in the Soviet Union to be a great man. Moscow students studied his writings on the "mass line" and agreed that if Stalin had listened to the voice of the rank and file in past days as the Chinese were doing, the Soviet Union would not have had to live through years of hell. "If Mao had known how to exploit his moral credit," said my Russian, "and if he had simply come to ask us for help, he would have found enough volunteers in Russia to build a dozen Magnitogorsks in China. But he was the victim of heady atomic ambitions and thought only of his bomb. Besides, he sorely disappointed his young admirers at the university. I listened to his speech; it was not a man who spoke but a god who deigned to reveal a few truths to simple mortals. The following day *Jenmin Jih Pao* reported the meeting in such terms that our newspapers did not reproduce them in order not to harm Mao. Among other things, the article said: 'While he spoke a few specks of dust fell from the sleeve of his tunic, and henceforth this rostrum at the University of Moscow will be cherished by all humanity.' Even in the worst period of the cult of personality at home no one ever spoke like that about Stalin."

THE BIRTH OF A HERESY

In a Chinese plane the stewardess does not ask you if you are thirsty or want to read; she gives everyone tea and political pamphlets, translated into every language, even Russian. These pamphlets, which all deal with the Chinese-Soviet differences, are to be found at airports, in hotels, everywhere foreigners gather.

Their titles are enticing: *Where Do the Divergences Spring From? Why Has Khrushchev Left the Political Scene?* Everyone would like to know the answers to these burning questions, but the unwary reader is diappointed. Most of the pamphlets are composed of sermons given to the Russian CP, and of its replies to the sermons, always published as an appendix. Usually summaries of them have been published in the Western press, and the complete text adds nothing other than a certain obscurity born of the unrelenting repetition of the same denunciations of "modern revisionism" and dogmatism.

The Western reader remains incredulous and thinks, "They don't publish everything. They must have told each other off privately and much more clearly." I am not sure that he is right. Communists talk among themselves in the same way as they do in public, and the messages exchanged between the Soviet and Chinese CP's give a very accurate idea of the tone of the doctrinal debates between leaders of different parties. On this point it is my belief that when future historians gain access to the Communist archives, they will find few revealing documents. Theories published by Communist parties are couched in a language that is quasi-liturgical, for the initiated; and because they deal with the symptoms of a crisis rather than with its fundamental causes, they never elucidate the problems they are concerned with. Reality never enters into it.

This becomes particularly clear if one examines the official versions put out by the Russians and the Chinese of the two events from which the "Chinese heresy" has grown: the meeting of Khrushchev and Eisenhower at Camp David in September, 1959, and the recall of the Soviet technicians from China in July, 1960.

Today the Chinese untiringly declare that the Camp David meeting marked a turning point in the Soviet Union's policy and that since then it has ceased to be communist in order to become openly revisionist. It was at Camp David that Khrushchev and Eisenhower agreed, if not to divide the world between them, at least to maintain the *status quo*. Driven by "great power chauvinism," the U.S.S.R. abandoned the revolutionaries of the world to the Americans in return for a few advantages granted her by the United States. Indeed, what was sealed at Camp David was a veritable Russo-American holy alliance.

Soon afterward, say my guides, "Khrushchev was heedless enough to praise Eisenhower, chief of the American pirates, in front of Mao himself while he was in Peking for the tenth anniversary of the People's Republic of China." Mr. Kuo Mo-jo, a vice-chairman of the People's Congress, still trembled with indignation as he told me about this scene, which he had witnessed. "It took place on September 30, 1959, at the inaugural banquet held for 5,000 guests in the People's Palace. Khrushchev rose and made a whole speech explaining that the President of the American imperialists had recently become transformed into a genial Buddha and that we must be blind not to see this."

Mr. Kuo Mo-jo assured me that these remarks had scandalized him and everybody else.[12] However, no one answered Khrushchev until three months later, in January, 1960, when *Jenmin Jih Pao* studied the "Eisenhower case." The author of the article did not breathe one word about Russian "treason" nor about the conclusion of a holy alliance. He contented himself with saying, in very moderate terms, that Eisenhower had not accepted the principle of peaceful co-existence and that he had simply wanted to gain time to close the missile gap caused by Russian rocket superiority. This "friendly warning" to the Russians, who ran the risk of being tricked by the United States, was supported by quotations from the American press itself. That was all, and nothing in this article enabled one to guess how profound Chinese indignation was or to conclude that they already considered Khrushchev a traitor.

One can wonder further if they really thought so. Work went on at the Palaces of Sino-Soviet Friendship being built in Peking and in Shanghai, hotels (at Sian, for example) designed to cater to Soviet technicians were enlarged, and Russian was still the favorite foreign language in higher-education centers. I never found any explanation of this bizarre situation in any pamphlet. Sometimes

---

[12] In fact, it was not at this banquet but on October 6, at Vladivostok, that Khrushchev spoke so warmly of Eisenhower. "We have had a frank conversation with the President of the United States on the means of guaranteeing peace. I must say that I was very pleased: Eisenhower is intelligent and understands the gravity of the international situation. . . . If he states that I'm afraid of war and if I answer that he's the one who's afraid, that won't lead to anything. We'll stay facing each other like two cocks ready to fight. I told him this and he replied, 'I'm a soldier and I confess that I dread war very much. . . .' Then I said, 'If we both understand how much human suffering war can cause, why don't we agree to act together to preserve peace.' He replied, 'Let's agree.' " *Confrontations* (Moscow, Ed. Langues Etrangères, 1960), pp. 492–493.

— rarely and in private — Chinese friends risked one: "Our differences with Khrushchev concerned only the two parties, and we did not want it to have repercussions on the relations between states." But it is hardly possible to dissociate state from Party in countries where the Party is all-powerful and where as a rule the same men occupy key posts in both Party and government. Discussions between CP's therefore degenerate inevitably into more or less "hot" disputes between states. This is so true that within the world Communist movement the CP's which are not in power in their respective countries tend, when opposed to each other, to talk as if they were. We saw this, for example, during the talks between the French and Italian CP's after the twentieth congress. In short, among themselves the CP's readily employ the language of a Pharaonic diplomacy; this is also part of their Stalinist heritage.

As for the relations between a Communist government and the Western countries, they are always in contradiction to the revolutionary leanings of the CP, and its unity of principle with the opposition forces in these countries. This problem arose at the formation of the Soviet Republic, which was obliged to establish diplomatic relations with governments against which it was urging the local CP's to fight.

The Camp David affair posed a similar if not identical problem. "We want to live in peace and friendship with you," declared Khrushchev on his arrival in America. Nothing could be more normal: as a country, the U.S.S.R. is not in direct conflict with the American government. But the United States proclaims that she is opposed to all revolutionary change in the world; she guarantees the security (a euphemism for internal stability) of forty-two countries in every continent, and she is even ready to intervene to defend certain so-called "pro-Western neutralists." But a good number of these countries "guaranteed" by America are ruled by dictatorships and feudal or capitalist oligarchies, which create social conflicts that breed revolutionary movements denied all peaceful development. The Soviet CP believes that the revolutionary struggle carried on in these countries is a just one and that they cannot ask their Communist comrades to give it up: if they did, they would not always be heeded; for revolutions do not necessarily break out "on order from Moscow," and they are not always easily restrained.

From their own point of view, then, the Americans were justified in replying to Khrushchev: "You cannot become our friend as long as you are supporting those who oppose governments which are our friends. Give us a token of your good will: use your influence to end the revolutions, and we shall reach all the agreements with you that you want concerning peaceful co-existence."

There was nothing new in this; at Yalta in 1945 Stalin, Roosevelt, and Churchill had signed a pact in which reciprocal guarantees of this kind were implicitly given.[13] This pact remained practically a dead letter, and above all, it created the rancor and mistrust which poisoned the postwar political atmosphere. However, Khrushchev saw no other way of putting an end to the cold war than again concluding an agreement of this type with the United States.

In trying to bring this about, he in no way revised the traditional doctrine and tactics of the Soviet Union; on the contrary, he followed Stalin and, like him, considered that the Soviet Union's interests came before those of all the CP's in the world, the future of world revolution depending much more on the Soviet Union's victory than on any other victories.

But Stalin was a veritable Pope in the Communist church, and his tactics were almost never contested by any militant.[14] He could sign any kind of accord with the West (or even with Hitler) without being regarded as a "modern revisionist." Khrushchev did

[13] In February, 1945, at Yalta, Stalin, Roosevelt, and Churchill tried to foresee the future of Europe after the war. Each of them felt that his own country had vital interests to defend. In order to avoid conflicts just at the moment of victory, each decided to admit that the interests of the two others were legitimate. So Stalin obtained the right to install "friendly governments" in the countries bordering on Russia, but, in exchange, he agreed that in certain Western countries in which the Communists were very strong they would not oppose the reestablishment of parliamentary democracy. Certain other countries, Yugoslavia, for example, were to be shared equally. It has since been seen how the different interpretations given to the pact by the signatories and the push of national forces made the treaty's application practically impossible. The example of Yugoslavia is typical: having taken power by themselves, Tito and his partisans had no intention of sharing it with the pro-Western parties. In other countries — Poland, for example — there were anti-Communist movements: the West protested that a "friendly government" did not necessarily mean, as the Russians wished it to mean, a "Communist government." Finally, the political and social struggles of France and Italy indicated that Stalin was not "containing," as he was supposed to be doing, the Communists of these countries, even though, according to certain historians, he seriously put the brakes on them. Even today we still do not know who the winner was in this endeavor to change the evolution of Europe by secret treaty.

[14] Nevertheless, his orders were not carried out after the war, either in Yugoslavia or in China.

not have such great power over the foreign Communists who were already in power in twelve countries and whose deep distrust had been aroused by the "Stalin revelations." To speak in the name of the U.S.S.R. and of world communism, Khrushchev would have had to receive a mandate after having worked out a common strategy with the representatives of the Communist countries. No organization existed which would have enabled this to happen, and besides, Khrushchev did not want to set one up any more than Mao did.

After his famous talk on Eisenhower, Khrushchev left Peking without signing a joint declaration with Mao, but one can imagine the position of the latter. "Negotiate as you want with Eisenhower," he must have said to Khrushchev in effect, "but if the agreements that you sign do not suit us, we shall not recognize them and we shall advise foreign comrades to do the same." No one would ever have used such language to Stalin, and it is the relative weakness of Khrushchev's position which explains the drama that followed ten months after this meeting.

Who was wrong in this Camp David incident? One can answer that everyone was right. Khrushchev was right to say that Russo-American tension risked unleashing a cataclysmic atomic war. The Chinese were right to say that Moscow and Washington had no right to order the world about or to end by decree the struggle for freedom of oppressed peoples. Mao pointed out that the United States continued to intervene militarily against revolutionary movements, that their interests demanded the maintenance of the *status quo* throughout the world, and that they refused to recognize four Communist countries, including China, and had not given up hope of "recovering" them one day. "How can you be friends with such a country?" the Chinese demanded of Khrushchev. "And aren't you running the risk of demobilizing the militants by advocating peace and friendship with America?"

Khrushchev considered the atomic danger greater than all others and thought that it was necessary first to find a way to avert this and to organize disarmament; only then would it be possible to establish rules for co-existence which would modify the *status quo,* at present unfavorable to revolutionary movements. He also thought that the Americans were in no hurry to reach even a limited agreement — whether from pathological anticommunism or from the conviction that the U.S.S.R. was being hurt more than they by the cold war. He therefore could not admit that the

Chinese were conducting a furious revolutionary campaign or that they were exploiting, against his interests (in his own party and in the foreign parties), every setback he encountered.

But this is precisely what they set about doing. In June, 1959, after the breaking of the atomic pact, the Chinese made no fuss: this was an "affair between states." Nor did they make a fuss after the Camp David meeting; the only specific complaint they had against Khrushchev was his praise for Eisenhower. But in the spring of 1960, when Soviet-American relations bogged down, they immediately opened a "second front" on Khrushchev's flanks. They did this without regrets, and even with a clear conscience, convinced that they were rendering a service not only to the world Communist movement but even to the U.S.S.R., which Khrushchev was leading to disaster.

On May 1, 1960, an American U-2 spy plane was brought down in the Sverdlovsk region, in the heart of Russia. This plane was certainly not the first to fly over Soviet territory, but this time the pilot was their prisoner and ready to admit everything. Astutely, Khrushchev allowed the American military to tie themselves up in confused and lying explanations. His aim was to exploit the affair at the expense of "the American militarists who support the cold war," while at the same time refraining from implicating Eisenhower. He was convinced that the latter, to get out of a nasty situation, would seize the proffered opportunity, declare that the Air Force generals had acted without his knowledge, and condemn them publicly. Thus he would be in full agreement with Khrushchev, whose leitmotiv since the Camp David meeting had been the following: "Certain American circles want to continue the cold war, but Eisenhower is against them."

Unfortunately, Eisenhower reacted in a completely different way — almost as if, on the contrary, he wanted to side with Mao. He declared that he was responsible for the U-2 flight, refused to apologize to the Soviet Union, and even added that the violation of the Eastern European countries' air space was necessary to ensure the protection of the "national interests of the United States."

The result of this affair was the cancellation of the summit meeting which was to have taken place in Paris between the Soviet Union, the United States, Britain, and France; and the Chinese had the satisfaction of being able to say that they had predicted this defeat. Their triumph was not complete, however; Khrushchev did not lose control of his own party, and he announced that he would go to New York in September to continue his peace campaign at the U.N.

This time the Maoists decided to act. During the meeting of the General Council of the World Federation of Trade Unions in Peking in June, 1960, they opposed the Soviet resolution, which they considered too "co-existentialist." Then they invited the foreign Communist trade unionists to a private meeting and, for the first time, told them what they really felt and accused Khrushchev of sacrificing the revolutionary movements of the underdeveloped countries and of being a "modern revisionist." Their accusation came like a thunderclap out of a clear sky. The foreign Communists knew very well that all was not going smoothly between Peking and Moscow; but they had no idea how grave the quarrel was, and they had not expected that they would be asked to take sides. This was also the first time in thirty years that Communists had been heard accusing the glorious Soviet CP of betraying Marxist orthodoxy.

The Soviet delegate, Grichin, ostentatiously left the room; the others remained in stony silence. Then when a European delegate, having regained the use of speech, tried to say that it was perhaps a question of misunderstanding, the Chinese answered him with a question: "Why do you hate the revolutionaries of the underdeveloped countries so much?"[15]

The Russians were not long in countering this blow. At the end of the same month, June, 1960, a congress of the Rumanian CP was held in Bucharest. Communist leaders from all countries were invited; before them, at a private session, Khrushchev in person put Chinese dogmatism on trial, reproaching the Chinese for their nostalgia for Stalinism and their unspeakable conduct in the border

[15] Here is the Chinese version of the event (extract from *D'où proviennent les divergences* [Lausanne, Editions de la Cité, 1963], p. 16): "In May 1960, after the flight over the U.S.S.R. of the American U-2 on a spying mission, the Four-Power summit conference, which was to have been held in Paris, was canceled. We had then hoped that the comrades who had so warmly approved of the supposed 'Camp David spirit' would draw a lesson from this experience and reinforce the unity of the brotherly parties and countries for a battle against imperialist America's policy of war and aggression. Our hopes were deceived: in June 1960, in the general meeting of the World Federation of Unions, comrades of certain brotherly parties refused to condemn Eisenhower, propagated erroneous ideas, and even fought the right ideas of the Chinese comrades."

dispute with India. All the foreign delegates rallied to Khrushchev, with the exception of Albania and, of course, the Chinese delegate, P'eng Chen,[16] who remained intractable.

But Khrushchev had nothing to gain from an intensification of the dispute. The important thing, for him, was to silence the Chinese and to make them acknowledge his authority to negotiate freely with the West. An appeal to the other parties to put pressure on the Chinese would not have been effective. Khrushchev therefore decided to act on his own — and without scruples.

At the beginning of July, 1960, he summoned the Central Committee of the Soviet CP and during a three-day session revealed his anti-Chinese plan. The final communiqué announced laconically: "The Central Committee has approved its First Secretary's conduct in Bucharest and his general policy."

That was all. There was no question of publicly announcing that an economic war was going to be launched against the People's Republic of China. It was, however; all Soviet experts and technicians working in China received the order to leave without delay. They were to bring back with them all the plans of enterprises under construction and were in no way to facilitate the task of their Chinese successors. Furthermore, all deliveries to China of raw materials, manufactured goods, and spare parts were suspended.

The Chinese, as we have seen, talk a lot today about this "Russian calamity" of 1960 and assert that their industry was more seriously damaged by it than it would have been by armed invasion. There were only 1,720 Russian experts in China at that time, but they occupied all the key posts.[17] The great steelworks at Wuhan, which had been equipped by the Russians, was almost completely paralyzed for two months after the departure of six

---

[16] This did not stop Khrushchev, October 1, 1960, at the United Nations, from eulogizing P'eng Chen. "The representative of the United States has made a statement here about Comrade P'eng Chen. I know P'eng Chen well and if you could see him you would understand that he isn't like what he was presented to be here. He's an honest man, held in high esteem in his own country. The representative of the United States has cited some of Comrade P'eng Chen's phrases in which he calls America an imperialist power. But is this something new, gentlemen? The birds sing that song from the rooftops."

[17] 10,800 Russian experts worked in China in the period 1953–1960; their number had already declined by 1959 and the final break occurred during the summer of 1960 when many of the Russians still working in China were on vacation.

engineers. In the truck factories at Changchun there had been no Russian technicians, but the lack of supplies slowed production down dramatically. A hundred other examples could be cited.

Economic sanction is the weapon to which one resorts to overthrow a country's regime without attacking it militarily; one understands why the Americans use it against China, but what advantage did Khrushchev hope to gain by bringing China to her knees? The collapse of Communism in China would have been a defeat for every Communist in the world, and, moreover, it would have compromised the security of the U.S.S.R. as a state.

It was not the first time that the Soviet Union had acted ruthlessly against another Communist country. Twelve years earlier, in 1948, Stalin had mounted an embargo against Yugoslavia; but before making this decision, he had had Tito excommunicated by the Cominform, a kind of international Communist tribunal on which the representatives of the nine biggest European CP's sat. The sanctions applied by Stalin, therefore, did not hurt comrades but "traitors," and the collapse of Tito's regime would have strengthened Stalin's church — at the modest cost to the Eastern camp of a small territorial loss.

Stalin failed, as we know. Tito did not fall but continued his socialist experiment, and Stalin's successors are still paying for this defeat: it permanently weakened the U.S.S.R.'s authority over foreign CP's. It is difficult to understand why Khrushchev, after having harshly condemned Stalin for the "great error of 1948," made the same mistake on a monumental scale. China is, whatever one may think, a thousand times more important to the socialist camp than Yugoslavia ever was; moreover, she has never been excommunicated by the (now defunct) Cominform nor even simply by the Soviet Union, and her loss could in no way strengthen Communist unity — quite the opposite.

What is the explanation? The evidence is that Khrushchev could not have desired the collapse of the Maoists; he only hoped that his economic big stick would compel them to capitulate politically. With his country heading for disaster for lack of Soviet economic aid, Mao would make a Canossa-type pilgrimage to Moscow, renounce his doctrinal pretensions, and the U.S.S.R. would recover all its authority.

None of this happened, and Khrushchev simply lost what little control he had over China. One can understand, nevertheless, why he thought he could easily bring Mao to heel. The Russians are still convinced today that China has progressed only because of the help they gave her during her first Five-Year Plan and that, at the time, the Maoists' doctrinal interventions were slowing down rather than speeding up economic development.

Khrushchev himself did not conceal his scorn for the system of the people's communes or his skepticism about the efficacy of political incentives; he must have been absolutely convinced that China owed him everything and would realize this as soon as she was deprived of his help. But his poker game yielded nothing precisely because the Chinese system had its own dynamics and a capacity for adaptation great enough to enable it to survive the "Russian calamity."

The workers of the industrial Northeast, where the factories temporarily closed their doors, went back to the country, where the people's communes, after much fumbling and much reorganization, were now functioning well enough to take them in. In this country which at last has eliminated the famine which haunted it for centuries, they are now much better able to deal with transient problems, even grave ones.

Possibly, in 1957, when China turned to the left, Mao already wanted to be able to do without all foreign aid and to become a more attractive and more easily copied model for the underdeveloped countries than the Soviet Union. It is probable that if the "Great Leap Forward" (held back by the difficulties described earlier) had produced the expected results, China herself would have demanded the withdrawal of Russian technicians within a few years. Their presence was doubly offensive. First of all, from the point of view of education, it was difficult to explain to activists why the "Soviet comrades" had to live in luxury hotels and be paid huge salaries, while according to Mao, Communist man ought to work for an ideal and scorn comfort. Second, because as long as the Russians were there the Chinese system was unable to prove itself, and any successes could be attributed to Soviet aid.

In 1960 China still needed Russian help and therefore had nothing to gain from exacerbating the controversy with Khrushchev; it was he who forced the break on China and who, like the sorcerer's apprentice, brought about the rise of the Chinese heresy, even conferring on it a heroic aura. Abandoned to their own devices in such dramatic circumstances, the Maoists had to become even more extremist. With their resources diminishing, they had to resort more than ever to political incentives to persuade the workers to work more for less material reward. They had to indoctrinate the people even more, conduct more and more rigorous anti-imperialist and antirevisionist campaigns. But with the triumph of the Chinese system and the freeing of the country from its obligations to the U.S.S.R., China could at last set herself up as a model for underdeveloped countries.

"We are the only ones able to industrialize an underdeveloped country without external aid and without creating new privileged social groups in the process. We have solved the land problem by setting up people's communes in which our peasants feel they are working for the community and at the same time for themselves." That is what the Chinese are saying today to the countries of Asia, Africa, and Latin America which face the same problems. And one senses in the slightest remark by the Chinese a critical attitude toward the Russians, who have *nouveaux riches* and who conceived a kolkhoz system in such a way that with two and a half times as much tillable land as the Chinese, they have not succeeded in feeding a population three times smaller. Mr. Kuo Mo-jo ended his diatribe against Khrushchev with this vengeful phrase: "The Russian's soil is like his skull — nothing grows there."

That said, Khrushchev is not solely responsible for the Chinese heterodoxy — he inherited it from Stalinism; but with his "error of calculation" in 1960 he turned it into a real heresy, firmly enshrined in the heart of the Communist church. In a bid to ward off the danger it threatened, he tried to excommunicate the Chinese in 1964, but this attempt cost him his power without settling the dogma question.

It is generally considered that Chinese opposition to the signature of a nuclear test ban treaty between the U.S.S.R., the United States, and Britain in August, 1963, was the straw which broke Khrushchev's patience. It is a fact that during the spring and summer of 1963 Sino-Soviet relations became particularly strained and it was at that time that the Chinese published their 25-point proposal to challenge the whole U.S.S.R. line.

For me, however, the decisive moment in the dispute between Peking and Moscow happened in the summer of 1960. Since that time the Chinese have no longer been integrated in the bloc; they have no direct links with it and represent a separate entity. When he decided to sign his test ban treaty with the Americans and the British, Khrushchev simply proved that he did not care to maintain a façade of unity which did not in any case exist. He believed that once free from the Chinese "mortgage" he would have a better chance to defend the U.S.S.R.'s interests in dealings with the United States. Possibly it was also a mistake, for he deprived his diplomacy of an important element of flexibility: he no longer could threaten the West that if it did not make concessions he would adopt the tough line recommended by Peking.

It seems that his temperament was driving Khrushchev into intransigence toward the Chinese. As it happens, this kind of policy had least chance of succeeding. For the Chinese had too long and bitter an experience of foreign dictation to be willing to accept *faits accomplis* or bullying from anyone.

THE BORDERS OF THE MIDDLE KINGDOM

Each time that I raised the subject of their technicians' withdrawal from China with Russians I was reminded of my discussions with Kennedy supporters a few years earlier in Washington about their Cuban fiasco in the Bay of Pigs. In both cases defeat had been admitted; it was, in fact, too glaring to be denied. But that was all. The principle of the economic embargo of a friendly nation did not shock the Russians any more than an attempt to overthrow the regime of a neighboring country by force appeared morally reprehensible to the Americans. "Something went wrong," both acknowledged, but the "something" referred only to the execution.

To have such a clear conscience one must obviously be absolutely convinced that the enemy deserves only "the punishment that fits his crime." And the Americans were absolutely convinced. They rejected our "European naïveté" which tended to make us believe that United States policy with regard to Castro — the refusal to buy his sugar, the gasoline reprisals, the Bay of Pigs landing — drove the Cuban revolution toward communism and helped to bring into existence the first people's democracy in the Caribbean. "We have proof," declared the Americans, "that Castro has always been a party-line Communist and that he only hid his hand to deceive his people as well as the United States."

Historically and morally, therefore, America considered herself absolved from all blame in any action she might have taken against this "cheat who betrayed the Cuban revolution."

The Russians in Peking were no less shocked by European criticisms of the 1960 affair — and particularly those contained in Togliatti's famous will, which appeared, moreover, in *Pravda* in the autumn of 1964 and in which the secretary of the Italian CP reproached Khrushchev for his economic reprisals against China. "How could it come about that a man as intelligent as Togliatti did not understand the true nature of Chinese dissidence?" they asked me with a pained air. "Didn't he know that in September, 1960, we offered to normalize our economic relations with the Chinese and that it was they who refused?" And for want of being able to convince the late Togliatti, they explained to me at great length the nature of the "Maoist plot," which closely resembled — apart from its political shade — the "Castro plot" whose "victims" had been the "poor Americans."

For, according to my Russian contacts, Mao Tse-tung has always been first and foremost a Chinese nationalist, eager to restore the ancient Middle Kingdom in all its splendor. But he had obviously been obliged to disguise his intentions from the Russians in order to secure their aid in particularly difficult times. It was only after his accession to power that he threw off this pseudo-Communist mask and acted almost openly like the heir to the ancient empire. This "Maoist madness," according to my Russians, must have germinated in Mao's mind well before the Yenan days, well before even the foundation of the Chinese CP. "He is convinced," they assured me, "that China's 4,000 years of history confer on him a crushing superiority over all other countries. To Mao we are all barbarians, you as much as I. And for us Russians this superiority complex is a serious subject for thought. For it is hardly enviable to have the longest border in the world — as in our case, unfortunately — with a country as 'superior' as China."

Certainly Stalin could have been blamed for his lack of foresight at a time when there were still ways of "saving the Chinese Party" by preventing Mao from taking over the leadership. But Khrushchev, like Kennedy with Cuba, had inherited a prickly, not to say ineluctable, situation, and could only salvage the wreckage by doing his best to counter Chinese megalomania — first by warnings, then, as they had no effect, by more radical measures. Is it not unjust to reproach him for these measures, forgetting the perfidy of his opponent? Can one lose sight of the fact that at that time the Chinese had already begun to contest not only the policy but also the borders of the U.S.S.R.? The Russians only complained in private of our "European bias"; officially they were not supposed to talk about the territorial conflict between the two "sister countries." But a number of them assured me confidentially that this border affair was the aspect of the Chinese-Soviet dispute they were most concerned about. And I was not the only one to be told such confidences. All the foreigners in Peking knew that the Russians were anxious, above all, to ensure the security of Siberia and of their Asian republics threatened by China.

The diplomats were a little too prone to take the private recriminations of their Soviet colleagues literally. Seen in the classic context of rivalry between nations, the dispute between the U.S.S.R. and China suddenly became much more comprehensible to them. There was considerable discussion in foreign circles in Peking, therefore, of the famous map of Asia published in 1964 by the Chinese which "incorporated" into their country a certain number of territories legally part of the Soviet Union. They discussed Mao's declaration to the Japanese socialists that Russia had always benefited from unjust treaties that had been imposed on China in the past. They ended up by calculating the advantages that an overpopulated China could derive from the annexation of a Siberia which was three-quarters empty and still had unexploited resources.

Everybody in Peking, therefore, was talking about this "gigantic common border" — everybody except the Chinese. None of those I met ever raised the question. Not once did I hear them say that the Soviet revisionists, guilty of so many other sins, had illegally occupied part of China. When they denounced Soviet "chauvinism" to me, the Chinese were referring only to the way in which the Russians treated the other countries of the Communist camp or foreign Communist parties; and this chauvinism, according to them, manifested itself basically in the U.S.S.R.'s desire to impose on the international workers' movement directives which were solely dictated by its selfish interests as a great power. But at no time, I repeat, did any of the Chinese I met refer to the problem of the celebrated Chinese-Soviet border.[18]

Let us admit for the sake of argument that I met only particularly discreet Chinese and that it is tricky to base one's judgment

[18] True, in the notes and documents exchanged by Moscow and Peking during their violent controversy of 1963–1964, the two parties mentioned frontier incidents in the region of Sinkiang and accused each other of taking over more or less nomadic populations by force. But my Chinese contacts in 1965 did not consider this question important enough to discuss it. Their silence appeared to me all the more significant.

on such limited experience. We all know, nevertheless, what it is like in a country imbued with the heady taste for power and which also has border problems. We knew countries in Europe which had the same problems not so long ago. Even today it is enough to put one's foot inside the Federal Republic of Germany to see, at every street corner, maps which show slices of territory "occupied" by the Russians (East Germany) or the Poles (on the other side of the Oder-Neisse line) and which bear the word *Niemals!* ("Never!") Similarly in China there are maps displayed in public places, but these show Formosa and bear legends denouncing the American occupation of the island. Nowhere in China did I see the famous map of 1964 claiming the annexation of Soviet territory. I had Chinese newspapers translated for me daily, in Peking as well as in the provinces; never did I see the slightest hint of a border dispute with the U.S.S.R.

I attended dozens of meetings, large and small, and no speaker ever raised the problem. Must one therefore believe that Mao is still concealing his "game" from his own country? Or is nationalism so deeply rooted in the Chinese mind that — like Déroulède's famous "Let us always think about it, never speak of it" — they are so familiar with all their complaints against the Russians that there is no need to mention them?

Having said that, it is obvious that the Russians fear Chinese power in Asia, but not so much because of its nationalist character as because of their own difficulties in solving the problems of the nationalities within the Soviet Union itself. The Maoists have never needed to resort to ruses or camouflage to conceal the fact that their revolutionary struggle had its "national element." China was once a great empire; but when Mao and his troops came on the scene, she was no longer anything but a colony humiliated and pillaged by European powers who had taken advantage of the almost complete absence of national sentiment among the population. The Chinese civilization is 4,000 years old, as everyone is aware, but it enveloped the individual within the framework of the family without giving him the slightest idea of national solidarity. It offered stability to a peasant society protected by the Great Wall, but it did not enable him to resist the highly developed nations which invaded China in the nineteenth century. Mao, perfectly aware of all this, proclaimed quite openly that the Chinese CP had to mobilize the masses for both the anti-imperialist struggle and for the revolution. These two postulates have always been inscribed on the Party banners, and that is why in China the word "revolution" is a synonym for "liberation." There was no contradiction between revolutionary aims and national aspirations. No Chinese Communist has ever suffered an attack of conscience because he was obliged to play the role of the Piedmontese, the role of unifier of his country.

It was quite otherwise in Russia at the time of the 1917 revolution. Indeed, the empire of the czars oppressed dozens of nationalities assembled under the crown, sowing Byzantine discords in order to divide them, using Great Russian nationalism to slow down their emancipation and to consolidate its own power. In such a climate communism and nationalism could only oppose each other, and well before 1917 the revolutionaries were forced to base their propaganda on the opposition of class solidarity to a false national solidarity. But with the October victory came the problems and discords. By proclaiming the right of peoples to self-determination, Lenin meant to arouse feelings throughout the world in places which had never envisaged such a possibility. This was the case in China, as we have seen. But in the former czarist empire such a move ran the risk of unleashing the anti-Russian feelings of oppressed nationalities and leading to the partial disintegration of the country. Rosa Luxemburg, who was by no means a "totalitarian revolutionary," severely criticized Lenin for his self-determination policy: "Instead of defending the territory of the Russian Empire tooth and nail as the Land of the Revolution, instead of making the cohesion and the inseparable union of the proletarians of all nationalities within the territory of the Russian revolution the supreme law of their policy, the Bolsheviks, on the contrary, by their phraseology on 'the right of free determination to the point of the separation of states,' provided the bourgeoisie of the neighboring countries with the most specious and most sought-after pretexts for its counter-revolutionary plots."

In fact, the Bolsheviks did everything to keep most of the nations of the old czarist empire within the Soviet republics. Mass education and the new way of life, according to them, would abolish the old prejudices, and they insisted on the fact that "the land of the revolution" no longer had anything to do with the former Russian empire; by laying bare its history they hoped to reassure the former victims of the czars and lay the foundations of a common fellowship among all the citizens of the U.S.S.R. Admittedly, the right to secession of the republics included in the

Soviet federation quickly developed into a fiction, but the will to combat all discrimination that favored the Russians was always real. For many years any pejorative illusion with respect to a national minority, any expression of racist views, was severely punished by law in the U.S.S.R.

But twenty years of this policy was not enough to transform radically the mentality of the nations incorporated in the Soviet Union. Perhaps because Stalin always relied more on repression than on persuasion and because his actions often contrasted with his proclaimed aims, in 1941 he made a sudden appeal to Russian (rather than Soviet) patriotism, and he began to exalt the merits of czarist generals like Suvorov or Kutuzov. He was admitting implicitly that in the face of the German invasion, Russian nationalism was, in his eyes, more profitable than proletarian internationalism. This total switch posed problems of conscience for Russian and foreign Communists, and it was fraught with consequences for the future. For even after the victory, Stalin did not consider it useful to return to the former theories. His celebrated toast at the Kremlin banquet in May, 1945, drunk to "the health and glory of the great *Russian people*" (and not the Soviet people), was the first shot in a new campaign of glorification of the military and cultural merits of Russia, which hardly pleased the national minorities within the U.S.S.R. or its allies, the people's democracies. It was really too much to ask the Poles, for instance, to join in the adulation of Suvorov, who had been the "hangman of Warsaw."

This strange Stalinist nationalism reached its climax with the revival of quasi-official anti-Semitism in the last years of the Soviet dictator's life.

True, de-Stalinization partly rectified these mistakes and excesses; one of the first acts of Stalin's successors was to show that the so-called plot of the "White Smocks," a pure and simple anti-Semitic maneuver, had never existed. But the problem of the integration of the different peoples within the U.S.S.R., like that of her relations with the people's democracies on the national level, is far from being resolved. The anti-Russian sentiments in certain Asian republics like Kazakhstan or Uzbekistan can easily become explosive if another "fatherland of communism" in Asia offers them a wider prospect of autonomous development at the same time as ethnic and cultural affinities very much closer than those which link them with Moscow. The growth of China and the attraction

she could have tomorrow if she offered more enticing solutions for
the problems of the minorities therefore represent a real threat to
the Russians; it is not surprising to see the U.S.S.R. already accusing China of playing the game of Asian solidarity against the
"whites" and of spreading the "same race, same culture" line of
propaganda to attract and win over her neighbors. Yet, once again,
I never encountered the slightest trace of a comparable campaign
in China.

It is true that Chinese propaganda lays particular stress on its
solidarity with the underdeveloped continents, which are largely
inhabited by nonwhite races. It is only a step from this to the
conclusion that the whites are less virtuous, less worthy of the
friendship of the revolutionary masses; however, it does not seem
to me that the Maoists have taken that step. On the contrary, they
seem to be doing everything to prevent any demonstrations of antiwhite xenophobia or any spirit of revenge. Yet such a danger did
exist in China, not due to any superiority complex arising from its
4,000 years of history but to the sufferings it endured during a
century of "white colonization."

Robert Guillain was right to raise these pertinent questions in
his preface to Roger Pelissier's book[19] on the recent history of
China.

"Did you really know how the West treated China and the
Chinese for more than a century? Did you really know this from
direct experience? Doesn't the basic explanation of China's present
anger, her suspicious and rebellious moods, lie in more than a
century of Western cruelty and rapacity? I do not know if a yellow
peril exists, but ask the Chinese what they think of the white
peril."

Millions of Chinese who knew those evil days are still alive
today; and when the curator of the "Shantytown Museum" in
Shanghai tells you that she was a beggar before the Liberation, one
can readily enough understand why she has no love for the white
former masters of her home town. It was lucky for all the powers
that once occupied China — and there are quite a few! — that she
regained her independence under the leadership of resolutely antiracist and antixenophobic men. In the four volumes of Mao's
Selected Works, which the Chinese study with such application,
they learn among other things that what divides men is not the

[19] Pelissier, Roger, *La Chine entre en scène.*

difference in the color of their skins or the difference in nationality, but class differences which pit the poor against the rich and the exploited against the exploiters throughout the world.

Nevertheless, foreign diplomats declared to me that there had been numerous demonstrations of xenophobia against the whites all over China, especially after the departure of the Soviet technicians in 1960. One can believe them, for during this painful episode, many Chinese were struck by the simple fact that a white nation, Russia, was once again attacking their country. This merely proves the strength of the long pent-up feeling which Maoist indoctrination has not yet succeeded in exorcising completely. But none of our guides ever insinuated to me that Khrushchev could have had "racist motives," just as no diplomat ever claimed that the Chinese CP had tried to present the affair in this light.

Everywhere in China they even explained to me that Khrushchev's "wickedness," was entirely due to his "modern revisionism" and that the Soviet experts were all "good comrades" who had left with tears in their eyes, swearing to come back to China. This account might seem to have been a trifle embellished, although it is confirmed in large part by the West's only existing evidence on the subject, that of the Soviet chemist Mikhail Klotchko, who is now a refugee in Canada. "My professional conscience," he wrote, "rebelled against the directives of our embassy urging us to sabotage the work we had begun by a withdrawal as precipitate as it was incomprehensible."

On the day after the Asian students' demonstration in Moscow in March, 1965, *Jenmin Jih Pao* hinted at the racism of the Soviet militiamen. On my return to Europe I talked with Westerners present that day in Moscow who assured me that the Russian gendarmes had hardly bothered to abuse the "yellow rabble." The Chinese therefore showed themselves to be rather moderate by not referring openly to what they were rebelling against, no doubt to avoid playing on their compatriots' antiwhite feelings.

Two years ago China asked one of the European people's democracies to recall from Peking her ambassador, who had made anti-Semitic remarks when he was slightly drunk at a banquet. A small point, no doubt, but one that proves that the Chinese are more "Communist integrationists" than racists. I could — but it would be too tedious — give many more anecdotes and examples of this kind.

The paradox of China's position seems to me to reside in the fact that she is compelled to repeat the experiment of "socialism in a single country" — comparable to that of Russia under Stalin — and at the same time retains a revolutionary spirit which makes one think of certain of Trotsky's postulates rather than those of the former Soviet dictator. China's present isolation, her feeling of insecurity, her conviction that she can succeed, her socialist experiment of "relying on her own strength" strangely recalls the political climate of the U.S.S.R. when, encircled by the *cordon sanitaire* of hostile European powers, she fought alone. The Chinese, however, do not appear to believe that the success of their experiment will suffice to change the world. Their faith in the imminent revolutions of the underdeveloped countries, in the fellowship of all oppressed peoples, leads them to think that there can be neither security nor any long-term prospect for their own country until there is a vast anti-imperialist revolution which would radically alter the face of the globe.

If China was simply anxious about her own national interests she would have had no valid reasons either for refusing to allow the return of Soviet technicians when Khrushchev made this offer or for intensifying her present dispute with the U.S.S.R. She would have gained on the economic front as well as in terms of her international security. But the Chinese do not resign themselves to the idea of seeing communism turn bourgeois, of compromising in the anti-imperialist struggle and by the same token delaying the advent of the new order they hope to establish throughout the world. Their tenacity is neither imperialist nor racist — it springs from a "Messianic communism" that is unique.

This view of the world explains the "patience" of the Chinese in their dealings with the underdeveloped countries they are trying to win to their cause at the same time that they prove themselves intractable with foreign Communists who show themselves to lack fighting spirit by failing to agree 100 per cent with Peking. During my stay, President Nyerere of Tanzania was feted and cheered everywhere although he had frankly declared that he wanted to have friends in the West as well as in the East. In contrast, the Italian CP delegation on its way to Hanoi to show its solidarity with Vietnam got only two lines in *Jenmin Jih Pao,* which merely reported that it had been greeted by the Secretary-General of the Chinese Party, Teng Hsiao-p'ing.

But the patience and good intentions of the Chinese are apparently not enough to convince the leaders of the undeveloped world to rebel against the United States or to refuse aid from the Soviet "revisionists." China has not won any new allies in Asia, Africa, or Latin America despite her promises and anti-imperialist appeals. Her failures have certainly helped to aggravate China's domestic climate for they reinforce her isolation and demonstrate how vain are certain of her hopes. It is in the light of these problems and not in terms of her nationalism that Chinese policy has prompted the greatest doubt.

BETWEEN NEHRU, AYUB KHAN, AND AIDIT

The Russians are not the only neighbors of China to be anxious about their borders. The Indians are too, and at first glance they have rather stronger reasons, having already experienced two armed conflicts with the Chinese in the Himalayan regions — a modest one in 1959 and a much more significant one in 1962 which resembled a real war. One remembers, indeed, that the Chinese army then inflicted severe defeats on the Indians; and if she had wanted to or been able to exploit her successes, she could rapidly have occupied India's vital centers. The United States quickly changed the facts of the situation with their spectacular airlift from Frankfurt to New Delhi, and the Chinese wisely turned back and proposed, after having returned to the Indians prisoners and war supplies abandoned during the retreat, that the dispute should be settled by negotiation.

In a war of this kind the loser always tries to explain his defeat by the enemy's treachery — troops secretly massed, surprise attacks, etc. The Indians did not fail to present their border conflict with China in this way; and in view of the intensity of American propaganda about Mao's warlike attitude, they did not have much trouble in convincing Western opinion that they had been the victims of studied aggression. Even the European Communists allowed themselves to accept the Indian version; and although they avoided branding their Chinese comrades openly, they could not refrain from showing their disapproval. Togliatti was the first to express publicly his serious reservations about the Chinese attitude in the Himalayas — at the tenth congress of the Italian Party in December, 1962.

The Chinese answered him sharply, refusing to plead guilty,

claiming that it was in fact India which began the hostilities, and complaining indignantly about this "sister Party" which was unable to recognize the real aggressor. With several colleagues I personally attended a showing of documentary films on the 1962 Chinese-Indian war, during the visit to Peking of President Ayub Khan of Pakistan. For once we did not need interpreters, for the films had French commentaries; they were plainly intended for export, but although four years have passed since then, the Chinese have not yet succeeded in placing them on the European market.

Obviously it would be presumptuous to reach a definitive judgment on the Chinese-Indian conflict on the mere evidence of films that were necessarily partisan. Nevertheless, I found in them a number of unrevealed facts which did not corroborate — far from it — the Indian version of events rather too hastily accepted in Europe. On the Himalayan border between India and China there are two distinct stretches which were rather arbitrarily fixed in 1914 by the British diplomat McMahon (it is in fact known as the "McMahon Line") and obviously to the advantage of what was then a colony of His Gracious Majesty. In fact, no Chinese government has recognized the validity of this division which, particularly in the eastern stretch, annexed the best arable land in the region to India. The conflict did not, however, break out over this issue.

The western sector, the cause of the dispute, which runs along the inaccessible Karakoram Mountain chain is important to the Chinese because of the caravans traveling from Tibet to Sinkiang. The Chinese, having re-established their sovereignty over Tibet without being challenged, soon felt the need for better access to Lhasa and decided to transform the rude caravan trails into a wide motor road. It took several years of work and a considerable amount of money to realize the project. The Sinkiang-Tibet highway was opened in 1957, to the great pride of the Chinese, who considered it a "gigantic piece of engineering." The Indians, who knew of its existence only from photographs published in the Peking press, immediately declared that the Aksai Chin plateau which it crossed was part of their national territory. "How could we have carried out such a huge operation in territory belonging to India without the Indians noticing it?" the commentator of the Chinese film demanded ironically. But not only did the Indians not know exactly what was going on in this stretch of no man's land —

which, according to the Chinese, was in any case situated to the north of the "illegal McMahon Line" — but access to it was particularly difficult for them. After they had learned of the existence of the Chinese operations, it took them more than a year to clear a route across the sheer mountains and establish military posts there. Reaching the area of the Aksai Chin plateau in 1959, the Indians demanded the withdrawal of the Chinese, whose presence, they said, constituted "studied aggression against our country." The border dispute now broke out in broad daylight. It also coincided with a distinct chill in Chinese-Indian relations, due largely to China's repression of a religious revolt in Tibet.

The Chinese made repeated offers to negotiate, and in April, 1960, Chou En-lai even went to New Delhi to put before Nehru a compromise which practically acknowledged the *status quo:* China would accept as final the eastern stretch of the border although the line was clearly in India's favor; but the latter, in exchange, would have to abandon her claims in the western sector. "We have settled our disputes with Pakistan, Nepal, and Burma in this same spirit of conciliation and mutual concession," said the commentator of one of the Chinese films. "These borders were imposed on us by the imperialists whose victims we all were, and it was our duty to eliminate these remnants of former colonization."

But the Indians refused to negotiate, or more exactly, they demanded that China first accept their claims, after which they could begin discussions. In the meantime they had continued to reinforce their points of access, with the intention of recovering their "territory which had been violated militarily." Reproductions of Chinese newspapers in one of the films we saw underlined the warnings given by Peking to New Delhi on the dangers of tension and incidents, as well as the proposals for simultaneous withdrawal of Chinese and Indian troops to a distance of twelve miles on each side of the "border" to avoid the worst. But the Indians would not hear tell of this and — shots of Indian newsreels to support this were shown to us — they "redoubled their warlike anti-Chinese campaign."

Finally, on October 14, 1962, a week before the outbreak of hostilities, *Jenmin Jih Pao* launched a new and solemn appeal to India: "We want at all costs to avoid exchanging fire with you. . . . Let us settle the dispute by peaceful means. . . . Give up your aggressive plans and do not interpret our peaceful offers as a sign of weakness. . . . Do not embark on a futile venture. . . ."

But the Indian Minister of Defense, Krishna Menon, replied the following day in a statement at Bangalore: "We shall fight to the last man, to the last weapon, to drive the Chinese from the sacred Indian soil they have illegally occupied."

"On October 20," said the commentator of one film gravely, "the Indian troops started a vast offensive and inflicted very heavy losses on the Liberation Army's border guards." But the shots which follow show us a rapid reversal of the situation — the Chinese counter-attack and the Indian army's great retreat. Impressive quantities of American arms are abandoned by the Indians and whole regiments capitulate — in short, collapse. The Chinese did not take advantage of this to annex territory which they did not claim anyway but re-established the former *status quo*. One of the films that I saw was entirely devoted to the restoration to India of prisoners and of all the weapons "made in U.S.A.," previously and carefully cleaned by the Chinese. The commentary proudly stressed that such restitution was without precedent in the history of war.

The Chinese, moreover, have probably not yet told all. As the films were made before 1963, that is to say, before their controversy with Moscow became public, they slide discreetly over the Indians' Soviet arms, while later the Chinese accused the U.S.S.R. of having supplied arms in great quantity to the "Indian aggressors against People's China." But these films were essentially designed to destroy the Indian claim that the Chinese had made a surprise attack, and from this point of view they are rather convincing. One can, in fact, ask oneself why *Jenmin Jih Pao* should have launched warnings about the dangers of war on the very eve of the aggression, thus putting the Indians on their guard. These enormous quantities of American supplies must also have already been in place in the future operational area, otherwise the Chinese would not have been able to seize them so quickly before they could be used. For another thing, the shots could not have been faked; we were not only shown general shots of stocks of arms with the inscription "U.S." but the ceremony in which they were handed back to India, with the higher officers on both sides attentively examining rifles, guns, and other weapons. The Chinese would hardly have indulged in the luxury of making a present to the Indians of all those American arms (supposing they had bought them on the black market in Singapore) merely for the purpose of making a propaganda film, nor would the Indians have been likely to lend themselves to such a comedy.

We know that India has since continued to refuse a negotiated settlement of the dispute and has gradually alienated the sympathies of a great number of countries which were clearly on her side in 1962. It is difficult to grasp the reasons for this obstinacy on the part of New Delhi which has done considerable harm to India's prestige among the underdeveloped countries and increased her dependence on the United States, thus weakening the "neutralist" character of her policy. The foundation for Indian claims in the Himalayas appears highly doubtful to Western experts as well as to experts in Indian affairs, and it is hard to find any reason why New Delhi is so determined to recover these mountainous and desert-like plateaux which can have neither economic nor strategic importance for her (although this is not so in her neighbor's case).

But, one can ask oneself, is China not equally the loser in this affair? Would it not have been better for her to have ceded the disputed region, despite the investments she had made in it, as the price of preserving India's friendship, so valuable to her during the preceding years? This was the opinion of the Russians, who from the start of the dispute thought that the Chinese should have shown themselves less intransigent even if their case was basically right. They recalled in this connection the Russo-Finnish precedent, when Lenin, following the revolution, "sacrificed" certain border and geographically hybrid regions in order not to make his relations with the Finnish republic worse. But the controversy between Peking and Moscow has rapidly mushroomed from this straightforward problem of the Chinese-Indian border into a demonstration of the difference between the two capitals' views on the relations that the Communist bloc ought to have with the underdeveloped countries.

The Russians remain attached to the old theory once advanced by Lenin[20] and erected into a dogma by Stalin: revolution in former

[20] In fact, the controversy in 1920 between Lenin and M. N. Roy, then a member of the Indian Communist Party, concerned the attitude toward the "national bourgeoisie" during the period of the anticolonialist struggle and not the relations between the socialist countries and the newly independent countries in Asia, Africa, and Latin America. The references to Leninism which the present leaders of the U.S.S.R. are constantly making would seem to be rather arbitrary. It should also be noted that Stalin often invoked his theory of "revolution by stages" to put a brake on CP's and avoid explosions he feared would be dangerous for his Soviet fortress. After World War II he showed very little eagerness to help the newly independent states, preferring to keep his resources for the development of the U.S.S.R. Only after his death did the Kremlin start to show interest in the neutralist countries of the emergent world.

colonies must first pass through a bourgeois stage. In societies where the proletariat virtually does not exist, it is obviously impossible to have a proletarian revolution; whereas the bourgeoisie, anxious to liberate itself from the tutelage of the imperialists, already represents an important and, in a certain sense, progressive force. The Communists ought therefore to help this bourgeoisie to arouse its anti-imperialist feelings and enable it to modernize its country and create suitable conditions there for future and more profound changes. Moreover, this help is even profitable on a short-term basis, for it weakens the Western camp's position; not being the only supplier, such a capitalist country cannot dictate political conditions to its former colonies in exchange for credit or technical assistance. The existence of a socialist alternative has already enabled Nasser, for example, to resist in 1956 the blackmail of the West, which would only agree to finance the building of the Aswan Dam if he renounced nationalization of the Suez Canal. If Egypt had not been able to rely on other help, she would have had to yield. Thanks to the U.S.S.R., she was able both to nationalize the canal and to build the dam.

In Russian eyes, India is a perfect example of the effectiveness of their line on aid to bourgeois regimes. Although the Congress Party may be a bourgeois party par excellence, Nehru succeeded in giving it a certain socialist flavor; and India's policy infuriated the West during the cold war to the point where John Foster Dulles considered her "immoral." India's economic needs are such that Nehru would not have been able to continue for any length of time if he had had to depend only on Western aid, which could easily have been withdrawn. But since he was also benefiting from the disinterested assistance of the Eastern bloc, the West did not dare to put pressure on him because of the risk of alienating Indian friendship. The U.S.S.R. thus afforded a wide margin for political maneuvering to all those countries which by natural inclination, due largely to their past, tried justifiably to escape neo-colonialism and development methods favored by the capitalist powers. The revolutionaries inside these countries also benefit from this policy, thanks to the popularity of the Soviet Union, which increases their audience among the masses and is already preparing the first step toward socialism.

But the Chinese, on the contrary, consider the theoretical premises of this whole policy false; proletarian revolutions, in their view, can take place just as well in predominantly rural underdeveloped countries. China is proof of this. Only uprisings involving masses can represent a force that is at the same time both revolutionary and national and that is capable of guaranteeing the independence of colonized countries or those recently freed. Bourgeois regimes are therefore neither effective nor necessary, and this stage on the road to socialism can be eliminated. Besides, popular insurrections need not necessarily be communist at the beginning. It is enough for them to be revolutionary and resolutely anti-imperialist; the hostility of the opposing camp will, in any case, force them to move to the extreme left and evolve rapidly in the direction of Marxist Leninism. Cuba must be considered a conclusive example of this.

The Communists' duty is, therefore — according to the Chinese — to help the true revolutionaries who spring from the people and not to be the dupe of the socialist-sounding or pseudo-nationalist phraseology of bourgeois politicians who, sooner or later, end up in the arms of the imperialists. To the Chinese, the Indian phenomenon is a living illustration of their thesis. Nehru had been one of the first heads of state to go to Peking in 1954, and it was on this occasion that Chou En-lai drew up his five principles of "peaceful co-existence," based on noninterference in each other's internal affairs. The following year, during the Afro-Asian Conference in Bandung in Indonesia, all those taking part wildly acclaimed Nehru and Chou En-lai and promised to conclude agreements on this basis.

But Nehru's party, the Congress Party, is no more than an Indian variation of the Kuomintang. When the people's movements began to increase their pressure in India, the Congress Party, immediately sought an anti-Communist counter. The sudden "discovery" of "the Chinese aggression on the Aksai Chin plateau" marked the political turning point of the Indian bourgeoisie, which wanted to distract the masses from their social struggle and at the same time to secure a "guarantee of stability" from the United States. Nehru's policy was therefore no longer neutralist; it was "subjectively, militarily, and economically" bound to the imperialist camp. That is why the Chinese CP proposed in Moscow in 1960 — and the conference of eighty-one Communist parties accepted it — this final resolution: "The Communists denounce the attempts of the reactionary wing of the bourgeoisie to pass off its selfish class interests as the interests of the whole nation; they denounce the demagogic use for the same end of socialist slogans by these bourgeois politicians." After having signed these declarations, say the Chinese, the U.S.S.R. ought never to have continued to help India, just as China would have been acting with great fickleness if she had yielded to Nehru's claims.

The Chinese do not say that they do not wish to have anything in common with regimes which are not 100 per cent proletarian. The only criterion which, in their eyes, must guide Communists in their attitude toward the underdeveloped countries is the anti-imperialism of these countries. The bourgeoisie always has a progressive wing which, rejecting its class selfishness, opposes its former oppressors and thus plays an important and worthy historic role. It must, therefore, be helped, and the revolutionary forces inside the country will gain from this. But if the reactionary wing succeeds in supplanting the progressive wing, this help must immediately cease. It is plainly absurd to help your own enemies. In fact, the Chinese draw these generalizations from their own experience in the Kuomintang days. When Sun Yat-sen was at the head of the Kuomintang, the party was primarily anti-imperialist, and the CCP was perfectly right to support it. But when Chiang Kai-shek replaced Sun Yat-sen as leader, the CCP was wrong to continue to collaborate with him. Now Nehru, who had been in a position similar to that of Sun Yat-sen, had been transformed into a Chiang Kai-shek by the pressure of events.

Nehru "unmasked himself," they say in Peking, when he attacked China, and his metamorphosis is easy to understand and analyze. But how is one to know if Nasser, for example, is about to change in the same way. Can the Chinese Communists condition their aid to and their relations with a country on the basis of its adherence to an anti-imperialist political line so clearly defined that each deviation from it would be easily noted? And, besides, doesn't China co-operate with countries that maintain good relations with the United States and even benefit from American help?

The contradictions of Chinese policy in relation to the underdeveloped countries and the difficulty of applying their own criteria have become particularly noticeable since the Maoists began "to fly with their own wings" and were no longer able to blame their ambiguities on the treatment meted out to them by the European Communist bloc.

Although they deny any desire to found a new International, since 1963 the Maoists have not hesitated to organize, wherever they can, "Marxist-Leninist" parties independent of already existing CP's. On June 14, 1963, they launched their twenty-five-point manifesto constituting the charter of these new revolutionary movements opposed to the conciliatory revisionism of the Soviet Union. The moment was well chosen by the Chinese, as the U.S.S.R.'s prestige had seriously declined in the Communist world after the Cuban crisis the previous autumn. The militants who had at first manifested their indignation at the American accusation that there were Russian rockets in Cuba were compelled a few days later not only to admit the facts but, into the bargain, to swallow the wise but humiliating Russian "climb-down." This did not put them in a particularly good mood. In Latin America the Chinese line made headway, while in Asia almost all the CP's visibly aligned themselves with China.

Despite the dynamism of their militant members, not all these movements succeeded in creating partisans, or *maquis,* of the former Chinese type (except in Venezuela and Guatemala, where, in any case, they had already existed). The Chinese claim they were not particularly surprised, for they know from their own experience that popular uprisings call for years of preparation. What was most important for them was that these movements should get off to a good start, beginning by infiltrating the population, and that they should toughen themselves for the struggle. Their aim should be to force the United States, the "international gendarme," to disperse its forces. Only such a policy of harassment, say the Chinese, can prevent American counter-revolutionary intervention and reduce the danger of a new world war.

But experience has proved that the pro-Chinese Marxist-Leninist groups are compelled to expend more energy in fighting the rival groups faithful to the U.S.S.R. than in harassing the class enemy. The politically trained nucleus in the emergent countries, being extremely small, and the masses rather unwilling to respond to the call to arms, the American "gendarme" often has not needed to intervene with his troops: the forces of the local oligarchy have proved themselves strong enough to deal with those embryonic revolts. The Chinese obstinately believe — or pretend to believe — that the victories of the right are essentially ephemeral and that revolution will inevitably explode everywhere tomorrow. In the meantime, they try to find allies, even among the regimes which can hardly pretend to be revolutionary, claiming that they stimulate their anti-imperialist feelings. This policy, since it is eminently pragmatic, does not differ much from that of the U.S.S.R., at least to a nondoctrinaire observer.

These questions often come to mind, particularly when one reflects on the way in which the Chinese put their policy of "alliance with all anti-imperialist forces" into practice. I had the opportunity of observing this rather closely during my stay, especially when I attended numerous receptions in honor of Ayub Khan, President of the Moslem Republic of Pakistan. The Pakistan International Airways American Boeing 707 which brought him to Peking was in itself symbolic of the Pakistanis' well-known ties with the United States. But the most noteworthy aspect of these singular V.I.P. guests of People's China was the extraordinary sartorial splendor of the President and the members of his suite. They were really the perfect embodiment, almost to the point of caricature, of the semifeudal and bourgeois regime which rules Pakistan. And almost as if they wanted to show that neo-colonial links had not yet disappeared, they were accompanied by several British military advisers, themselves a study, with officers' sticks under their arms and their Colonel Blimp mustaches. The Chinese children who were lined up in a guard of honor in the streets of the capital must have been dumbfounded at the sight of this astonishing procession of the kind of notables they had never laid eyes on before — the kind their textbooks usually describe in the most pejorative terms.

No one can blame the Chinese for wanting to detach the Pakistanis from their SEATO allies and to have one less "explosive neighbor." But Ayub Khan was not converted politically by Liu Shao-ch'i's beautiful eyes. The Chinese-Pakistani flirtation developed parallel with and proportionally to the deterioration of relations between Peking and New Delhi. The Pakistanis had come to Peking in search of an ally to support their claims to Indian-occupied Kashmir. At one swoop the Chinese agreed to be involved in a dispute between the heirs to the former British colony, a conflict heavy with religious, racial, and national passions but lacking in the slightest class significance. For, even admitting the accuracy of China's view of political evolution in India, it is hard for us to believe that the Indian middle classes are more reactionary and more closely linked with the imperialists than the Pakistani middle classes.

The tenor of the speeches I heard at several banquets given in Ayub Khan's honor seemed rather unusual to me. True, no one expected to hear the Chinese criticize their guests' regime or to bring up the fate of their comrades in Pakistan, where the CP is banned and its leaders in prison. But it seemed to me, all the same, that the Chinese, without offending anyone, could have touched on the differences of concept which separate them from this Moslem republic. But all the toasts were drunk either to undying and immutable Chinese-Pakistani friendship or to the doom of the reactionary Indians. I was not surprised, therefore, when, a few months later, China formally supported Pakistan in the new armed conflict over Kashmir and was even on the point of involving herself directly.

The train of events was completely logical: China could not allow herself to "lose" both India and Pakistan, and she knew that a defeat for Pakistan in Kashmir could be fatal for Ayub Khan. But by promising to protect their ally whatever the cost, weren't the Chinese undertaking to guarantee a regime which can hardly be described as the "progressive wing of the bourgeoisie"?

Hardly had fighting stopped in Kashmir than another Southeast Asian country was thrown into violent and bloody strife — Indonesia. In October, 1965, the Indonesian army, largely equipped by the U.S.S.R., seized power and began a massacre of Communists that has few precedents in history. President Sukarno, a great friend of the Chinese, was relegated to a purely honorary role and could not prevent either the unloosing of an anti-Communist campaign or the sudden switch in the nation's policy. The events in Indonesia were a complete disaster for the Chinese in both political and human terms: not only their comrades but also their nationals (the Chinese colony in Indonesia is a very big one) were the victims of a virtual genocide which the Maoists were powerless to prevent. The Indonesian tragedy calls for some explanation.

Admittedly, the Maoists could not have the same guilty feelings as Stalin when Chiang Kai-shek became a turncoat and massacred the Shanghai Communists in 1927. The Chinese had no direct control over the Indonesian CP, as Stalin had over foreign parties at the time of the Comintern. Further, their "friend" Sukarno had not double-crossed them, since the Indonesian army had acted against him as well as against the Communists (although he came out of it better). Peking did not have a clear conscience, however.

The Indonesian Communist Party had, in fact, become more Chinese than the CCP, and its leader, Aidit, more Maoist than Mao. Having embraced Peking's political theories without reservation, Aidit advocated them in his newspapers with a violence that surpassed that of *Jenmin Jih Pao* itself. The leaders of the Italian CP, who were known to have differing views, paid a courtesy visit to Djakarta in May, 1965, and found themselves forced to speak at a meeting under a larger-than-life portrait of Mao and banners that pilloried all "revisionists." All of which indicates that Peking was not without a certain influence on the Indonesian Communist Party, the most important in the world outside the Communist bloc.

The people I met in China did not conceal their pride in having Aidit and his party in their camp; and when I asked them what the situation in Indonesia was, they invariably replied with delight: "It is so good that Indonesia may perhaps provide the proof that a peaceful transition to socialism is now possible; and although we have always believed the opposite, we shall not complain if events prove us wrong in this particular case." Their smiles at the very thought were wide and frank — but they were sadly misplaced. Four months later the Indonesian military chiefs wiped out the foremost militants of the CP, including its leader.

If the coup succeeded with disarming ease it was only because the military leaders were the only ones to plan to seize power; the sole aim of Aidit and his friends was to push Sukarno's coalition in an anti-imperialist direction. Super-Maoist when it came to words, they never dreamed of applying the Maoist tactic in their own country, and they were quite unprepared for an armed struggle. But perhaps their confidence in the Sukarno regime could be explained by their desire not to create any trouble within Indonesia, which already represented a precious trump card for China.

The then Mayor of Peking, P'eng Chen, attended the forty-fifth congress of the Indonesian CP in Djakarta a few weeks before the military coup. His speech was so violently anti-Soviet that Moscow, while in theory refraining from controversy, felt itself obliged to deny his allegations about Russo-American collusion. The whole of P'eng Chen's peroration was devoted to the denunciation of the "new holy alliance" between Russia and the United States and the priority that must be given to combating the alliance. Not once did the Chinese leader think it necessary to remind the Indonesian militants of Mao's basic precept that each Communist party must first concentrate on the political situation in its own country and analyze it as accurately as possible. Yet this was the moment, if any, to have done so.

P'eng Chen fell into disgrace soon after his return from Djakarta, and it is permissible to assume that his "bad advice" to the Indonesian comrades was one of many reasons for his dismissal. Peking's smiling Mayor was the last Chinese Communist official to have visited Indonesia and address the hard core of Aidit's party. For several years he had been actively engaged on the problem of the CCP's relations with other parties abroad, and he had taken part in the Party congresses in Italy in 1956, in Rumania in 1960, in the Soviet Union in 1961, and finally in Indonesia in 1965. The disaster which followed shortly after the Indonesian congress logically called into question his direction of the international section of the CCP. But it is obvious that Peking could not reproach him openly without implicitly admitting his responsibility for the fiasco of the Indonesian Communists.

While it must be admitted that the search for a scapegoat after a political disaster is common to all parties, proletarian or otherwise, it is equally obvious that P'eng Chen himself had not worked out Chinese policy with regard to the underdeveloped countries. And it was precisely this policy that was seriously impugned by the events in Indonesia.

The Chinese have good reason for believing in the instability of regimes set up in recently decolonized countries and for decrying their inability to develop with the aid they get from the Western powers, tied as they are to neo-colonial strings. Chinese refusal to believe that it is possible for the great powers to divide the world into spheres of influence also seems to be confirmed by events. But while their accurate assessments have been confirmed by all statistics on the increasing backwardness of underdeveloped countries compared with industrialized societies, the Chinese have not been any more successful than anyone else in explaining the mechanisms which govern the evolution of former colonies. Their concepts of the "progressive bourgeoisie" and the "reactionary bourgeoisie" are really too simplistic.

To understand the reasons for the Chinese failures one must, in my view, come back to the basic problems of the Communist policy since the birth of the Third International. A party which succeeded in making a victorious revolution in its country is not necessarily the best adviser for those comrades who are struggling in other countries and in other parts of the world. It has inevitably a tendency to recommend the formulas which were successful in its own case, and its prestige is such that those formulas are uncritically accepted as if they were infallible weapons. But revolutions neither lend themselves to export nor to imitation: they are "children of necessity" and the necessities are different in each country.

Moreover, the leaders of a victorious revolution always have their eyes fixed on their own country and they use the language and the arguments which their own people are most likely to understand. The Chinese publications are a case in point. Whatever the merits of the "cultural revolution," it is obvious that it has a particular Chinese character and the parties abroad are unlikely to arouse great enthusiasm by promising their compatriots to wage a similar revolution when they finally come to power. The cultural and political traditions abroad are too different from the Chinese, and Peking's appeal finds little echo. Last but not least, the revolutionary movements in opposition have suffered so much in the past from their comrades already in power that they fear today to become once more an instrument in the hands of a big and prestigious party which governs the new "land of the revolution." The Maoist intentions are no doubt much purer than Stalin's: the mere fact that they did not interfere in the internal affairs of the Korean Party, which they saved in the 1950's and which is completely independent today, proves that their methods are very different from those of the former Soviet dictator. Nevertheless, the suspicion engendered by the memories of Stalinism weighs heavily on the whole Communist family and the Chinese are perhaps suffering more from this than all the other parties.

COMMUNISM'S "UNHAPPY CONSCIOUSNESS"

Shortly before our departure from Peking the officials of the Ministry of Foreign Affairs' press service organized a farewell dinner in our honor. For us this was obviously not the long-awaited moment to express opinions on the crisis in the Communist movement which would risk upsetting our hosts. But the Chinese custom demands, as a sign of friendship, that you should offer your criticisms on the eve of departure. Our dinner companions insisted that we give vent to ours, assuring us that they respected those who frankly expressed their opinions on Chinese policy, no matter how critical they might be.

I then tried to explain what in my opinion was the weakest point of the Chinese CP's position: its inability to make plain to the world the guiding lines of Maoist policy, an inability which is due to a superficial but stubborn attachment to Stalinist mythology.

"The paradox of China," I said, "is that she is a living contradiction of Stalinism but she refuses to admit it, and even gives the impression that she wants the workers' movement to return to the supposed 'good old days' of former years. What you are doing in China would have been condemned by Stalin and you yourselves know it. What you are denouncing in present-day Soviet policy one could have denounced in Stalinist policy. After all, Khrushchev did not fall from the sky into his seat in the Kremlin: he was the product of Stalinist society and the continuator of a tradition founded by the former dictator, which laid down that Soviet interests took precedence over all others within the workers' movement. If you want this state of affairs to change, why do you not combat the heritage of the previous era instead of defending it?"

Our hosts interrupted me: "Khrushchev was a flatterer who advanced himself in the Soviet hierarchy by shamelessly singing Stalin's praises. The first two volumes of his complete works that we published are entirely composed of his dithyrambic speeches. He thus succeeded in outwitting the vigilance of the Russian Communists and installing in power a clique of his own that was revisionist and ready to do anything to protect its privileges. We know that there were errors in Stalin's time, but the U.S.S.R. in those days was a different place from what it is today and communist internationalism was vastly different from that advocated today by the revisionists. That's why we defend Stalin and we believe that the rank and file in the Soviet Union and elsewhere understand our point of view better than you do."

"Then how do you explain that this 'healthy' rank and file of the Soviet CP could allow a vile flatterer to seize power and retain it for ten years in a great country like the Soviet Union? Don't you think rather that the Russians judge the nature and quality of Stalin's 'errors' quite differently than you do? Don't you think that the Soviet system which prevents activists from expressing themselves was created by Stalin, who stifled all opportunity for discussion in the U.S.S.R. and any check on the government by the people? Admitting that your hypotheses about Khrushchev and his successors may be justified, don't you think that the path of possible change passes through the democratization of Russia and therefore through de-Stalinization?"

There was momentary consternation. When it had died down

my hosts contented themselves by replying with a lecture on the limitations of parliamentary democracy of the British type and on the fact that the workers' movement had nothing in common with bourgeois concepts of this kind.

"Invent another kind of democracy, then, but admit that a system in which any adventurer (since that is what you call Khrushchev) can stay in power for ten years at the head of a party of fourteen million members and of a country of 200 million inhabitants, is not a proletarian system worthy of the name."

My hosts agreed that democracy functions in a "very special" way in the U.S.S.R. and they assured me that in China steps have been taken to ensure that the masses take part in politics and that there is real discussion within the Party. It is therefore not the Party's monolithic structure which must be denounced, in their view, but the form which the Russians have given it and above all their deliberate refusal to maintain correct relations with the masses. Then, to my great satisfaction, they acknowledged that all these anomalies dated from the days of Stalin and must be considered serious mistakes. But after conceding that the problem of democratization was important for the workers' movement, they clung to the old theme: the most important thing is to recover the communist fighting spirit that existed before de-Stalinization.

Obviously these arguments did not convince me, but neither did mine succeed in shaking the certitude of my hosts. We parted amicably, promising to resume the discussion in a few years.

This final conversation struck me forcibly, although I had discussed this theme very often during my four months' stay in China. I had tried a hundred times to recall for the Chinese my exact memories of my long stay in Stalin's Russia in order to show that the ideological façade of the Russia of that period merely served to hide a reality which was hardly brilliant. No one treated me as a liar, and some even supported my evidence with examples of their own experiences in Russia. However, at the end of these discussions, as during the farewell dinner, my Chinese always sighed: "Yes, but even so the Soviet people had a fighting spirit at that time, a communist internationalism existed, and the revisionists have destroyed all that." This strange nostalgia deserves to be explained.

Following World War II and particularly after the victory of the Chinese revolution in 1949 the Communist camp appeared to be in the course of full expansion. America had a more powerful atomic arsenal than the U.S.S.R., but that did not prevent Stalin from ruling an "empire" such as history had hardly known before, committed to a total and coherent doctrine, endowed with an undeniable economic dynamism, and guaranteeing its stability by basic and irreversible social reforms. Its strength resided in its capacity to organize a planned economy and, as its supporters claimed, in the "scientific" character of the analyses and political foresight of Stalin and other Communist leaders. This was the era of the great lay orthodoxy, with its millions of faithful adherents, to whom the kingdom of earth was promised. The power of this orthodoxy was so great that many men who lived inside the "empire" accepted it, while knowing that the deeds which it announced daily in no way agreed with the reality of experience.

After the dictator's death there was a period of wavering and anxiety, but the emergence of a new leadership in the U.S.S.R. soon restored confidence to the faithful. In February, 1956, from the platform of the twentieth congress of the Soviet CP, Khrushchev announced an ambitious prospectus for the Communist camp. He asserted that the world was henceforth divided into two systems, one socialist, the other imperialist, and the former yielded nothing to the latter either in power or productive capacity. All the conditions of the class struggle on an international scale were thus turned upside down: the socialist system felt itself capable of defeating its rival in economic competition and of guaranteeing every country the chance to achieve independence and socialism without fear of military blackmail or repression by imperialist forces.

Over ten years have passed since the day this solemn proclamation was made and the socialist system no longer exists as a coherent unity. It is true that capitalism has not been restored in any country of Eastern Europe and that more than a thousand million people today live under Communist regimes. But the orthodoxy which acted as the cement of the socialist world has crumbled.

It is not so much the imperialist camp but the Communist camp which has split under the pressure of events. Suddenly the victory of progressive regimes in the underdeveloped world, which seemed already to have been consolidated, is revealed to be fragile. The great schism has spared no revolutionary movement and the right has profited from this everywhere. The Western Communist parties mark time while in the people's democracies of Eastern Europe the revival of nationalist sentiment seems to be leading to a slow breakup of their regimes.

How are these changes of the last ten years to be explained? Can one attribute them, as the Chinese do, to Khrushchev's personal "crimes"? Are they the result of the "irresponsibility" of the Maoists, as the Russians allege? Should not the real reasons for the crisis be sought in the defects of the doctrine and structure of the bloc — that is to say, in the features which, although they did not come into the open, were already below the surface during the period of great Communist optimism?

It was the extension of the Soviet system to other countries after 1945 that produced the germs of dissension which undermined both the orthodoxy and the monolithism. So long as the U.S.S.R. was the only socialist country, and therefore the sole bulwark of the international Communist movement, its own concept of the revolution and of the world retained a validity that was uncontested by all the other parties. This concept was certainly an "ideology" founded on unprovable dogmas, but at the same time it had an actual base in the world's first socialist state, which had to face difficult internal and international problems. Only the unsuccessful revolutions in Europe and China had occasionally demonstrated the Comintern leaders' lack of foresight and their inability to direct the Communist movement effectively on a world scale. But the defeats of parties which were not in power were not enough to shake the certitude of an organized society like the U.S.S.R. The Soviet Union was endowed with a "false conscience," but nevertheless it was this country, which, by its very existence, had ensured the expansion of the Communist system. The unconditional loyalty to the U.S.S.R. that Stalin demanded from Communists was sometimes a difficult choice for them, but they always accepted it. It is true that Stalin often abused the loyalty of foreign comrades, involving them in battles which did not serve their own cause. But that did not prevent Communists from feeling that they belonged to a united family and, in making sacrifices for the U.S.S.R., from manifesting this proletarian internationalism the Chinese continually evoke.

After 1945, however, the U.S.S.R. was no longer the only socialist country. The people's democracies of Eastern Europe came into being thanks to the Red Army, but this did not prevent each of them from being an individual society, with its own material problems to resolve. From that moment on, it became evident that the Soviet dogma had its limitations, for Stalin was unable to create an appropriate framework for this new entity, and he wanted to model it simply on the facts of the Soviet situation. He believed he could direct the whole bloc in the same way that he governed the U.S.S.R. The orthodox line had to be respected everywhere, even where it did not square with the facts in existing societies. Now, the Communist parties of the people's democracies, instead of being the interpreters and promoters of new social experiments, turned into spokesmen of the Soviet model, cutting themselves off more and more every day from their own peoples. Such a policy was bound sooner or later to provoke a reaction, and almost immediately after Stalin's death the cracks appeared in the edifice of his empire.

However, at the time of the twentieth congress in 1956, the Russians still believed that their system was so firmly entrenched that they could denounce certain of the Party's mistakes in the past without risk of shaking it. But when de-Stalinization revealed the existence of centrifugal forces which led to the "Polish October" and the Budapest uprising, the Soviet leaders cautiously retreated, contenting themselves with putting Stalin on trial, not Stalinism. Admittedly they eventually realized that the too-rigid protectorate the U.S.S.R. exercised over its partners could no longer be maintained, and they tried to make it more flexible. But they dared not change the entire system because they could not with impunity impose a democratic structure on the Communist movement and promote free discussion while retaining inside the U.S.S.R. a system based on a monolithic party which is the sole repository of a sacrosanct doctrine. So they rejected a real process of democratization within the Soviet Union: that would have risked setting off a chain reaction which might get out of control and transform the very nature of the power they exercised.

Of course Khrushchev revised certain governmental methods inherited from Stalin, but the hope that the Soviet CP might be able to renovate Communist theory by eliminating the gulf between the dogmas of the old era and the new reality was shown to be unfounded. Unable to find principles adapted to diversified movements and capable of investing them with a real dynamism, the Communist parties fell back on a formal defense of a monolithism which no longer had any substance. Behind its façade the differing situations continued to develop in flagrant contrast to the stereotyped and generalized definitions of the common official literature. The gulf between reality and theory led most parties into an attitude of complete contempt for the ideology, into empiricism pure and simple, and into a lowering of moral standards and the abandonment of the internationalist feeling that once had been a bond among Communists. Thus it is that the Stalinist epoch has become retrospectively for many Communists the epoch of major mistakes and even of atrocities, but also the epoch of the revolutionary faith which nothing has since replaced.

Because it has been unable either to carry out a real de-Stalinization or to evolve a new theory of the workers' movement, the socialist camp since 1956 has floundered between the complete absence of principles on the one hand and Stalinist nostalgia on the other. Following the twentieth congress the only European Communist leader who foresaw this crisis, Palmiro Togliatti, called for a real and profound revision of the system. Unfortunately he was sharply rebuked by Moscow and received very little support from his own comrades.[21]

Nonetheless the Communists knew very well that all was not for the best in the best of all possible Soviet worlds. But each of the parties of the people's democracies tried to defend its own interests as best it could and to rally the masses by stressing the national aspects of their programs, which had been neglected from Stalin's day. Thus they all became rather unpredictable allies of the U.S.S.R., but the logic of their reconversion to nationalism drove them into parochial attitudes rather than into the discovery of original ideas that might have benefited the debate between Communists. None of these parties carried great enough weight to contest Soviet leadership and demand a new organization for the bloc.

One country alone was powerful enough to denounce the Soviet Union's "false conscience." That country was China. The Maoists, as we have seen, spoke out against many of the anomalies which existed within the socialist camp, but without succeeding in explaining them; and instead of insisting that the Soviet leaders abandon their doctrinal immobility they attacked them fiercely because, in their view, they were moving away from Stalinism. In doing this they further destroyed the monolithism of the previous regime and gave all parties — even tiny Albania's — an opportunity to contest Moscow's political line. But in this affair the question was not

[21] After the twentieth congress of the Soviet CP, Togliatti declared in *Nuovi Argumenti* that Stalin alone could not be responsible for all the distortions of the "personality cult" period and that a discussion of the structural faults of Soviet society was necessary. He also put forward a concept of "polycentrism" to replace the unstable monolithism of the Communist movement.

simply one of guaranteeing the independence of small parties. The crisis was not limited to the nature of the formal relations among the former members of the Comintern; it lay in large part in the grave shortcomings of the doctrine and thought of the workers' movement.

Therefore, by rending the veil of monolithism China resolved nothing. But it can be said that the Maoist heresy transformed the former "good conscience" of the Communist movement into what Hegel called an "unhappy consciousness," or alienated soul. It is thanks to the Chinese challenge that the Communists have been compelled to face up to the fact that their vision of the world was sharply contradicted by the march of events. Yet their old methods of analysis have not enabled them to explain this outbreak of unforeseeable elements. Neither Moscow nor Peking has been able to produce a new system to confirm their theories and interpret their society. Russia and China have preferred to set themselves up respectively as the only authentic guardian of Communism, and for several years now we have been witnessing not a rational debate but a festival of "beautiful souls." Such a controversy could not make mutual understanding easier; rather does it risk causing the communist ideology to vanish "as a shapeless vapor dissolving into thin air" in accordance with the poetic image of the great Prussian philosopher.[22]

Certainly, the crisis does not exist only at the level of conscience. The lack of understanding between China and Russia resulted — as I have said earlier — from the real and profound contradictions which divide these two countries. The Soviet Union has only outwardly revised the former concept of Communism's world strategy. Despite all the speeches about the independence of every Communist party, in Moscow's eyes the future of the workers' movement is always identified with the U.S.S.R.'s power. A stronger Russia would be able to guarantee the peaceful development of socialism. A richer Russia would be able to help the underdeveloped countries. A more prosperous Russia with a higher standard of living would be the great socialist model. A Russia that succeeded in developing fully its productive capacity would demonstrate the inferiority of capitalism. The setbacks of the last ten years, the Chinese breakaway, and the wave of nationalism among the people's democracies have not shaken the Russians' old con-

[22] All the quotations are from Hegel's *La Phénoménologie de l'esprit*, Vol. I (Paris, Aubier), pp. 176ff.

victions; on September 7, 1966, *Pravda* once more explained that all the problems of the Communist world boil down to loyalty to the Soviet Union's aims, to the acceptance of *its* tactics and *its* international strategy.[23] And, since it happens that at the present time the U.S.S.R. needs not only a period of calm but also an agreement with the United States, it is trying to force all the other parties to show themselves reasonable and patient.

This tactic is not new, and it is because of it that the Chinese-Soviet conflict has become so explosive. Since the Camp David meeting the Chinese have angrily opposed the Soviet view of relations with the United States. From that day onward Peking declared that the Americans were seeking to gain time in order to counterattack and that they would never countenance the tilting of the balance in favor of communism in Asia and Latin America. Two visions of communism have resulted from this: China has become the symbol of revolutionary haste, even at the cost of greater sacrifices; the Soviet Union's image is one of peaceful construction, even at the cost of compromise and the restraining of revolutionary movements. All the problems which arise on the international scene have therefore been interpreted by Moscow and Peking in diametrically opposite ways.

Such a difference of opinion, aggravated by the internal evolution of the two societies, did not take long to bring about a split in every sphere, and its result has been the birth of two concepts of socialism, of two different communisms. Yet this was the outcome the two adversaries most feared. In Communist eyes there cannot be *several* revolutions in place of *the* revolution unless the totality of the Marxist vision, the great revolutionary Messianism, is to disintegrate. If communism ceases to be a unique concept of history, a human truth, if it is replaced by several "scientific visions," one contradicting the other, it ceases by the same token to be the "great truth" and becomes merely one of the political utopias of our time.

The road to secession is therefore long. For six years or thereabouts the Russians and the Chinese have been accusing each other of being secessionists while at the same time swearing by all their gods that they want to maintain the unity of the Communist movement at any cost. Apparently they made several attempts between 1960 and 1963 to reach a semblance of agreement. In No-

[23] See the important theoretical study by Yuri Arbatov in *Pravda*, September 7, 1966.

vember, 1960, they even called the most important conference ever held by the Communist movement, known as the Conference of the Eighty-One Parties. Although it opened barely four months after the recall of the Soviet technicians from China and while the two parties were at loggerheads, they nevertheless managed to publish a common declaration, which, however, did not conceal the magnitude of their dispute from the outside world.

The final resolution of this strange Chinese-Soviet "treaty of ideological peace" was sufficiently vague for both Peking and Moscow to be able to interpret it according to their own lights. Even today the two parties tear each other to pieces and accuse each other of heinous crimes while protesting their undying loyalty to the joint declaration of 1960.

The Chinese, nonetheless, had good reason for being satisfied with this conference which had demonstrated that Moscow was no longer able to excommunicate them. Indeed, it was the Russians' last chance to get the whole Communist movement to condemn China. The vast majority of delegates came from the old Stalinist school of loyalty to the U.S.S.R., and they were ready to follow Khrushchev despite all the revelations of Soviet mistakes in previous years. De-Stalinization, which had caused many crises of conscience among Communists, had not brought about many changes in the leadership of the various parties. For these veterans of the Comintern the idea of rebelling against the U.S.S.R. was morally unthinkable.

But in a religious sect excommunication can only be carried out in the name of a strict orthodoxy. On what grounds, however, could the U.S.S.R. accuse China in order to show that she had betrayed the Communist doctrine to the point where she should be excluded from the international workers' movement? Could the Russians say that the abolition of material incentives and the egalitarianism of the Chinese put them outside the pale of socialism? They could certainly have attacked the monolithic structure of the Chinese Party and the schematic nature of its ideology. But what Communist party is prepared to throw the first stone in this matter? All that the Russians could claim was that these terrible Chinese were showing too much impatience in their revolutionary ardor, but such criticism would have risked creating a situation in which the Chinese would gain the sympathy of some of the militants whose parties were not yet in power.

After numerous accusations and counter-accusations "in private," the controversy came out into the open, and Khrushchev came to the conclusion that he would rather have the Chinese outside the movement than in it (whatever the motives for the verdict of excommunication). He therefore tried at the beginning of 1964 to convene a new conference which would ratify China's expulsion. But he was too late. Certain European CP's — even those traditionally anti-Chinese, like the Italian Party, for example — refused to follow his lead, and — what was much more serious, from his point of view — his own party failed to back the idea. His fall was due to a combination of complex events, but his clashes with the Chinese were a prime factor.

Khrushchev's successors decided to suspend the dispute in the hope that in time they would succeed in isolating China or else reach a *modus vivendi* with her. But events in Asia have not given the U.S.S.R. the time needed to implement her plan. By starting to bomb North Vietnam systematically in February, 1965, the Americans brought the Soviet Union and China face to face with the crucial problem that has always been fundamental to their discussions: What is America's policy in Southeast Asia and what strategy should be used to combat it?

From the Chinese point of view, there could be no hesitation. By attacking North Vietnam, the Americans had attacked the whole bloc. The war in South Vietnam could, in a strict sense, be regarded as a local civil war, but from the moment that the Americans moved against a country of the Eastern camp, a trial of strength between the two systems was under way. The U.S.S.R. must therefore regard herself as much the victim of aggression as North Vietnam or China, and she must act accordingly. For her as for China the overriding aim must be to drive the Americans out of Vietnam by winning the war they had unleashed, whatever the cost.

The Soviet leaders rejected this analysis. They have not cut their links with the United States. In their eyes, the Vietnam affair is not a global confrontation between the two camps, but rather an unfortunate exploit by the "reactionary elements in the Pentagon" which must be countered, certainly, but without increasing the stakes and risking a wider conflict. According to Moscow, the Vietnam war remains a local incident which must be de-fused to prevent the danger spreading. Although angry with the Americans, the Russians in no way appreciate the intransigence of the Chinese, fearing that because of them the Vietnam war might become a struggle between the two extremisms. While aiding the North Vietnamese, the U.S.S.R. therefore continues to reject the Chinese line on the class struggle at the international level as too "schematic."

The political and ideological consequences of this attitude have not been slow in making themselves felt. Although she sends arms to North Vietnam, Russia gets a good press in the United States. Almost everywhere she is discovered to be a responsible power, attached to peace, preaching a respectable, realistic socialism, without ideological or moral passion, capable of taking its time, favoring mediation; in short, the exemplar of a wiser communism which even anti-Communists of the old school can accept without too much trepidation. In Europe this undreamed-of popularity of the Soviet Union's has facilitated the campaigns against the Vietnam war and — who can tell? — in the long run the Soviet decision may be shown to be effective, for the gulf between the American "crusaders" and world opinion grows wider every day. Tomorrow the pressure on Washington could become so great that America will be forced to halt the war in Asia. It all depends, however, how much time the operation in Vietnam will give Soviet policy a chance to succeed.

But, as one could expect, China has seen in the U.S.S.R.'s cautious tactics merely the proof of Soviet connivance with imperialism. She has therefore refused to join with the Russians in concerted aid for North Vietnam, calculating that even the mildest joint statements would provide an alibi for the Russians when they have to be indicted before the militants of the world for the double game they are playing.

For the time being this intransigence has led China into isolation, for foreign Communists understand neither her anti-Soviet rancor nor her refusal to co-operate with the Russians against the common enemy. For more than a year the Soviet leaders refused to reply to the Chinese attacks and they even declared during the twenty-third congress of the Russian CP that they always hoped for a reconciliation with the "Chinese comrades." They only took up the counteroffensive in August, 1966, linking their propaganda to a single theme: "It is you who are betraying the common cause by rejecting the unity we offer you." And since the Red Guards appeared on the Chinese political horizon at almost the same moment, the Tass news agency became the great purveyor of news about the disorders, the slaughter, and the insults to the Party, to culture, and to socialism that were taking place in China. Almost every Communist party was shaken by all this and each in turn hurled accusations at the Chinese which were immediately reproduced without comment in *Pravda*. The schism seems complete.

In fact, according to the Russians, there is no occasion for talking about a schism since China is alone and, by shutting herself off from the world Communist family, she no longer threatens to win over the several parties which until recently sympathized with Peking. Many observers accept this thesis and believe that Chinese intransigence has refashioned the unity of the international Communist movement around the U.S.S.R. once more.

It seems to me, however, that this is a fallacious view. In this new trial of strength the U.S.S.R. has won only Pyrrhic victories. For a start, the dispute with Mao, even though conducted with more prudent arguments than in Khrushchev's day, has contributed still more to the disintegration of what remained of the internationalist cement that once held Communists together and bound them to the U.S.S.R. The parties which have drawn away from China are not drawing any closer to Moscow. They are opting for complete independence rather than for any sort of realignment within the Communist bloc. The appeal for unconditional loyalty to the U.S.S.R. evokes barely an echo.

Furthermore, the Chinese criticisms have influenced the rank and file of the various parties much more than the pro-Soviet attitude of their leaders would allow them to admit. Communist activists, even if they do not understand the Chinese intransigence, nevertheless ask themselves many questions about the Soviet position and policy. They feel that the moderate attitude of the U.S.S.R. may one day yield diplomatic successes, but in the meantime this policy calls for such cautious behavior on the part of the rank and file that it will lead to a decline in political consciousness and the deepest disheartenment.

One must yield to the evidence: the unity of the Communist movement no longer exists, and Russia alone will never again be able to rebuild it around her. Isolated as she is, China remains the real protagonist of the controversy between Communists, and no excommunication will prevent her from representing a very stable reality with its own dynamism and its own aims. China is the other Communism and, whether we like it or not, this other Communism is destined to play an important role in the history of our time.

It does not behoove me to make prophecies, but in this autumn of 1966 events in Asia threaten to come to a head. If the United

States decides to attack China, the Soviet Union will not be able to deny this time that it is a question of global conflict between the two systems. The Soviet Union will be forced to define her position in relation to it, and that in itself will mark a decisive moment in history. If, on the contrary, the Americans resign themselves to withdrawing from Vietnam, the victory of the Vietnamese revolution will inevitably result in the spread of communism in Asia, and China's role will be more important than ever. No matter from which angle one envisages the immediate future, this fundamental fact must be faced: China is at the center of world politics and too many things depend on her for one to be content to condemn or ignore her. Rather is it time to understand her.

Appendixes

APPENDIX A

A Brief Chronology of China Since 1915

1915

Sept. 15. Ch'en Tu-hsiu, nonconformist professor and future Secretary-General of the CP, founds the review *Youth* (later *New Youth*). Mao Tse-tung later contributes to it under a pseudonym.

1917

Bolshevik Revolution in Russia.

1918

Ch'en Tu-hsiu and Li Ta-chao, two eminent intellectuals, come out in favor of the Soviet Revolution and organize Marxist study groups. Mao Tse-tung, twenty-five years old, becomes assistant librarian at Peking University where Li Ta-chao is chief librarian.

1919

Four hundred Chinese students leave for France; among them are Chou En-lai, Li Li-san, and Teng Hsiao-p'ing, who form the Chinese Communist section in Paris in December, 1920.

Apr. 30. At Versailles the victors of World War I decide to transfer the former German concessions in Shantung province to the Japanese.

May 4. Mass demonstration by Peking students in the legation quarter against the Versailles decision. Start of the May Fourth Movement, which calls on all Chinese to fight imperialism.

June 14. Mao Tse-tung organizes a study group at Changsha which later became Marxist.

June 28. The Chinese delegation refuses to sign the Treaty of Versailles.

1920

Nov. 29. Sun Yat-sen, founder and leader of the Kuomintang, returns to Canton and, under the protection of General Ch'en Chiung-ming, forms an independent regime there.

1921

Apr. 7. Sun Yat-sen, elected in Canton to the Presidency of the Southern Chinese Republic, announces his determination to put an end to war-lordism and to unify China.

July 1.   In Shanghai twelve representatives of the Marxist circles found the Chinese CP. Ch'en Tu-hsiu, who did not take part in the meeting, is elected Secretary-General of the CP.

1922

Jan. 12–Mar. 5.   Mass strike of seamen and dock workers at Hong Kong.

May 1–6.   First congress of the All-China Labor Federation at Canton.

June 16.   General Ch'en Chiung-ming seizes power in Canton. Sun Yat-sen flees to Shanghai.

July.   Second congress of the CCP at Canton.

1923

Jan. 26.   Sun Yat-sen signs an agreement in Shanghai with Adolf Joffe, a representative of the Soviet government. Object: U.S.S.R. aid to the Kuomintang and future co-operation between the latter and the Communists.

Feb. 7.   Strike of Peking-Hankow railroad workers and shooting of strikers by soldiers.

Feb. 21.   Sun Yat-sen returns to Canton, which becomes his capital.

June.   The third congress of the CCP accepts the co-operation with the Kuomintang advocated by the Comintern.

1924

Jan. 20–Feb. 1.   First congress of the new Kuomintang at Canton. The Communists join the controlling bodies and Mao Tse-tung is elected an alternate member of the Central Executive Committee of this party.

May 5.   Foundation of the Whampoa Military Academy, directed by Chiang Kai-shek, with Chou En-lai as political commissar and the future marshal Vasili Blücher as principal Soviet adviser.

Nov.   Sun Yat-sen departs for Peking to negotiate with the northern war lords the peaceful unification of the country.

1925

Jan.   Fourth congress of the CCP at Canton.

Mar. 12.   Death of Sun Yat-sen in Peking.

Apr.   Strikes in the Japanese-owned textile mills in China.

May 30.   The Anglo-American police in Shanghai fire on anti-Japanese demonstrators parading on the Nanking Lu, killing twelve Chinese students and workers.

June 1.   General strike in Shanghai.

June 11.   British sailors fire on Chinese demonstrators in Hankow.

June 23.   British and French soldiers machine-gun Chinese demonstrators in Canton.

June 19.   Strike in Hong Kong and boycott of British goods in Canton, lasting until October, 1926.

Aug. 20.   Liao Chung-k'ai, leader of the left wing of the Kuomintang, assassinated in Canton.

1926

Jan. 4–19.   Second national congress of the Kuomintang in Canton.
Mar. 20.   Putsch by Chiang Kai-shek in Canton. The future Nationalist generalissimo gains control of the Kuomintang and imposes Draconian conditions on the Communists regarding their continued participation in the "united bloc."
Mar.   Mao Tse-tung writes his first important essay, "Analysis of the Classes in Chinese Society."
July.   The Nationalist army, commanded by Chiang Kai-shek, begins its Northern Expedition to free China from the war lords.
July 12.   The Nationalist army occupies Changsha.
Oct. 10.   The Nationalist army occupies Wuhan.

1927

Jan. 1.   Wuhan is proclaimed capital of China. Wang Ching-wei forms a national government and entrusts two ministries to the Communists.
Feb. 19.   General strike in Shanghai.
Feb. 22.   Attempt at insurrection by Shanghai workers.
Mar. 21.   New insurrection by Shanghai workers succeeds.
Mar. 22.   Nationalist troops enter Shanghai, already liberated by Communist insurgents.
Mar.   Mao Tse-tung's "Report on an Investigation into the Peasant Movement in Hunan" appears.
Mar. 24.   The Nationalist army enters Nanking. Western warships shell the city.
Apr. 6.   Police of the war lord Chang Tso-lin raid the U.S.S.R. legation in Peking. Li Ta-chao and nineteen other Communists arrested; executed three weeks later.
Apr. 12.   Anti-Communist putsch by Chiang Kai-shek in Shanghai.
Apr. 17.   The Wuhan government condemns Chiang Kai-shek and appeals for continued co-operation between the Kuomintang and the Communists.
Apr. 18.   Chiang Kai-shek forms a separate government at Nanking.
Apr. 27–May 2.   The fifth congress of the CCP at Wuhan declares for the maintenance of the common front with the Kuomintang left wing.
July.   The Wuhan leaders of the Kuomintang rally to Chiang Kai-shek and break with the Communists.
Aug. 1.   Detachments led by Ho Lung and Yeh T'ing take Nanchang and form the Red Army of China. Start of the Chinese Communists' armed struggle for power.
Aug. 7.   Ch'ü Ch'iu-pai replaces Ch'en Tu-hsiu as Secretary-General of the CCP.
Sept. 5–18.   Peasant insurrection in Hunan province, organized by

Mao Tse-tung and known as the "autumn harvest uprising."

Nov. Ch'ü Ch'iu-pai presents his report to the Central Committee on the need to intensify the armed struggle in town and country.

Dec. 11–14. The Canton commune is bloodily crushed after three days' fighting.

1928

Jan.–May. Mao Tse-tung and Chu Teh reassemble the remnants of their troops, lead them to Ching-kan-shan and organize there the first "revolutionary base."

July–Sept. Sixth congress of the CCP, in Moscow: Ch'ü Ch'iu-pai relinquishes secretary-generalship to Hsiang Chung-fa. Li Li-san becomes the "strong man" of the new leadership of the Party.

Oct. 5. Mao Tse-tung publishes his essay, "Why Can China's Red Political Power Exist?"

1929

Jan. The Red Army of Mao and Chu Teh comes down from the mountains of Ching-kan-shan and occupies part of the province of Kiangsi.

1930

June. Li Li-san orders a Red Army offensive against urban centers.

July 27. The Red Army led by P'eng Teh-huai captures Changsha but has to evacuate it a few days later. The troops of Mao and Chu Teh hurry to their aid and begin the siege of the city.

Sept. 13. Mao, Chu Teh, and P'eng Teh-huai decide to disobey the Central Committee by lifting their siege of Changsha.

Sept. 30. The Central Committee of the CCP declares the "dissidents" correct and mildly rebukes Li Li-san for his "left-wing deviation."

Nov. 16. The Comintern writes a letter to the Central Committee of the CCP blaming Li Li-san for errors committed. The end of Li Li-san's power.

1931

June 21. Hsiang Chung-fa, Secretary-General of the CP, executed by Kuomintang in Shanghai. Wang Ming and Po Ku become the supreme leaders of the Party.

Sept. 18. Japanese invasion of Manchuria. Chiang Kai-shek's government decides to address League of Nations at Geneva, but not to resist militarily.

Nov. 7. First All-China Congress of the Soviets of China at Juichin. Mao is elected Chairman of the Chinese Soviet Republic.

1932

Jan. 28. The Japanese besiege Shanghai. The Chinese 19th Route Army of General Ts'ai T'ing-k'ai puts up a resistance as unexpected as it is heroic.

Mar. 3. General Ts'ai T'ing-k'ai evacuates Shanghai and retreats with his army into Fukien province.

June–Mar., 1933. Failure of a new offensive by Chiang Kai-shek against the "Red bases" of Kiangsi.

Dec. 12. The U.S.S.R. establishes diplomatic relations with the Chiang Kai-shek regime in Nanking.

1933

Nov. 20. Chiang Kai-shek liquidates the "dissident" army under Ts'ai T'ing-k'ai at Fukien, without the Communists going to its aid.

1934

Jan. New general offensive by Chiang Kai-shek against the "Soviet Republic of Kiangsi."

Oct. Start of the Long March.

1935

Jan. 6. Mao Tse-tung is elected Chairman of the Central Committee and of the Politburo of the CP after an extended session of the Politburo held at Tsunyi, in Kweichow province.

Aug.–Nov. Mao's troops reach the Northwest and end the Long March.

Dec. 16. Mass demonstration against the Japanese by the students of Peking.

1936

May 5. The Central Committee of the CCP proposes to Chiang Kai-shek that hostilities should cease and a common front be made against the Japanese.

Dec. 9. Chiang Kai-shek arrives in Sian to launch a new anti-Communist attack.

Dec. 12. Chiang Kai-shek arrested at Lintung by his subordinates and transferred to Sian, where Chou En-lai negotiates with him a cessation of the civil war and the establishment of a common front against the Japanese.

1937

July 7. The Japanese attack the Marco Polo Bridge, near Peking. Start of the war between Japan and China.

Aug. The Red Army becomes the 8th Route Army, which remains independent but fights at the side of Chiang Kai-shek's Nationalist army.

Sept. 22. The Kuomintang and the CCP appeal to the nation to fight against the Japanese.

Dec. 13. The Japanese occupy Nanking. The Chinese government withdraws to Wuhan.

1938

Oct. 25. The Japanese occupy Wuhan. The Chinese government withdraws to Chungking.

Dec. 18. Wang Ching-wei, number two man of the Kuomintang, goes over to the Japanese. Less than two years later he will form a pro-Japanese puppet government in Nanking.

1939
Sept. 1. The Germans attack Poland. Start of World War II.

1940
Sept. 27. The tripartite pact between Germany, Italy, and Japan signed in Berlin.

1941
Jan. 5. Kuomintang troops attack the Communist New 4th Army in Anhwei province.

June 22. Germany attacks the Soviet Union.

Dec. 7. The Japanese air force attacks the United States fleet in Pearl Harbor.

Dec. 22–24. Anglo-American-Chinese military conference in Chungking.

1942
May 23. "Talks at the Yenan Forum on Art and Literature" given by Mao Tse-tung.

1943
Jan. 11. At Chungking Britain and the United States sign new treaties with Chiang Kai-shek abolishing foreign extraterritorial rights in China after victory has been achieved.

Nov. 22–26. Meeting between Roosevelt, Churchill, and Chiang Kai-shek in Cairo.

1944
Apr.–May. New Japanese offensive in China.

June 18. The Japanese occupy Changsha.

1945
Feb. 7–12. Yalta conference between Roosevelt, Churchill, and Stalin. The U.S.S.R. promises to enter the war against Japan three months after the end of hostilities in Europe.

Apr. 23–June 11. Seventh congress of the CCP in Yenan. Mao demands a coalition government in order to avoid a new civil war.

May 7. Germany surrenders unconditionally.

Aug. 6. The United States drops the atomic bomb on Hiroshima.

Aug. 8. The U.S.S.R. enters the war against Japan.

Aug. 28. The American Ambassador Hurley escorts Mao Tse-tung to Chungking to negotiate with Chiang Kai-shek.

Sept. 2. Japan surrenders unconditionally.

Oct. 11. Communiqué on the negotiations between the Kuomintang and the CCP.

Dec. 16–27.   Anglo-American-Soviet conference in Moscow advocates a peaceful solution to the Chinese problem.

1946

May 4.   The Communist Party decides to go ahead with land reform in the regions it controls. The estates of big landowners will be confiscated and distributed to the poor peasants.

June.   Start of the civil war.

June 23.   The CCP protests against American aid to Chiang Kai-shek and calls its own army the "Army of National Liberation."

1947

Mar. 19.   Kuomintang troops occupy Yenan.

1948

Sept.   Great Communist counteroffensive in Manchuria.

Oct. 17.   The Nationalist garrison of Changchun surrenders.

Apr. 22.   The Maoists reoccupy Yenan.

Nov. 2.   The Nationalists surrender at Shenyang.

1949

Jan. 31.   The Communists enter Peking.

Apr. 20.   The Communists cross the Yangtze Kiang.

Apr. 23.   Fall of Nanking.

Oct. 1.   Mao Tse-tung proclaims the People's Republic of China in Peking.

1950

Jan. 5.   Great Britain recognizes the Peking government.

Jan.   Mao Tse-tung and Chou En-lai pay official visit to Moscow.

Feb. 14.   Chinese-Soviet pact of friendship and aid signed in Moscow.

Apr. 30.   Marriage law enacted authorizing divorce and forbidding the sale of children.

June 25.   Start of the Korean War.

June 30.   Decree on land reform throughout China.

Nov. 26.   The Chinese "volunteers" enter Korea.

1951

Feb. 21.   Law enacted for the "suppression of counter-revolutionary activities."

May 23.   Agreement on the peaceful "liberation" of Tibet.

July 10.   Korean armistice negotiations begin.

1952

Jan.   Campaigns of the "Three Anti's" (against corruption, waste, and bureaucracy) and the "Five Anti's" (corruption of civil servants, fiscal fraud, commercial fraud, misappropriation of public property, and extortion of economic information to the prejudice of the state), begun after Chinese entrance into Korean War, go into full swing.

Sept. 16. The U.S.S.R. agrees to return the Changchun railroad to China and dissolves the joint companies.

1953–1957
China's first Five-Year-Plan. Increase in Soviet aid to China.

1953
Feb. 15. The Central Committee of the CP calls on the peasants to group themselves in co-operatives.
Mar. 5. Death of Stalin.
July 27. Korean armistice signed.

1954
Feb. 6. Plenary session of the Central Committee, which posthumously condemns Kao Kang, one of the country's principal leaders, who committed suicide in Shenyang because his administration had been criticized.
Apr. 26–July 21. The Geneva conference ends the war in Indochina and decides on the temporary division of Vietnam into two states (North Vietnam, capital Hanoi; South Vietnam, capital Saigon).
Sept. 15–28. First session of the National People's Congress, which approves and promulgates the New Constitution of the People's Republic.

1955
Apr. 18–27. Conference of Asian and African countries at Bandung in Indonesia.
Apr. 27. The U.S.S.R. pledges to help Chinese science in all research, including nuclear research.
May 24. The U.S.S.R. hands over Port Arthur and Dairen to the Chinese.
July 31. Mao Tse-tung makes a report on "The Question of Agricultural Co-operation."

1956
Jan. At a Central Committee conference on intellectuals Mao Tse-tung talks of the "hundred flowers" for the first time.
Feb. 14–25. Twentieth congress of the CP of the U.S.S.R. In his famous "secret report" Khrushchev violently attacks Stalin.
Sept. 15–27. Eighth congress of the CCP in Peking.
Oct. 19. Opening of the eighth session of the Central Committee of the United Workers' Party of Poland instigates an unexpected visit by Khrushchev and several other Soviet leaders anxious to prevent Gomulka's election to the leadership of the Polish party.
Oct. 20. Gomulka is elected despite Soviet opposition. Anti-Stalinist wave in Poland.
Oct. 23. Pro-Polish demonstration in Budapest gives the signal for the Hungarian uprising.

Oct. 30. Solemn declaration by the Soviet government on the new conditions governing co-operation and friendship between the U.S.S.R. and the other socialist countries. The U.S.S.R. pledges to withdraw her troops from those people's democracies which request this action.

Nov. 2. The Chinese government publicly approves the Soviet declaration of October 30.

Nov. 4. Soviet troops intervene against the Hungarian insurgents in Budapest.

Dec. 29. *Jenmin Jih Pao* publishes the editorial "More on the Historical Experience of the Dictatorship of the Proletariat."

1957

Jan. Chou En-lai visits Poland and Hungary, and talks with leaders of East Germany in Moscow.

Feb. 27. Mao Tse-tung addresses the Supreme State Conference and invites the Chinese to work out constructive criticisms to help in the building of socialism. Start of the "hundred flowers" period.

June 8. Editorial in *Jenmin Jih Pao* attacking the "right-wingers and bourgeois who, under pretext of criticizing, have preached counter-revolution." End of the "hundred flowers" period. The commissions of forty deputies of the National Congress are canceled. Many intellectuals, including Ting Ling, the most famous woman writer in the country, are severely censured and make their self-criticisms.

Oct. 15. A secret Chinese-Soviet agreement concerning the manufacture of atomic weapons in China is signed in Moscow.

Nov. 6–20. Moscow conference of all the Communist parties in power. Talk by Mao on Communist unity under Soviet leadership. It is at this meeting he declares, "The wind from the East is prevailing over the wind from the West."

1958

China undertakes her second Five-Year Plan and begins the "Great Leap Forward."

Aug. 29. A special session of the Central Committee at Peitaiho launches the people's communes.

Dec. 10. A new resolution of the Central Committee, meeting at Wuhan, tends to "moderate" the commune movement.

Dec. Mao resigns as Chairman of the People's Republic.

1959

Mar. 17. Dalai Lama flees from Lhasa after the Chinese army crushes the revolt in Tibet.

Apr. 27. Liu Shao-chi elected Chairman of the Republic.

June 20. The U.S.S.R. repudiates its atomic pact with China.

Aug. 26. The Central Committee admits that its statistics are over-optimistic and reduces the objectives of the Five-Year Plan.

Sept. 15–27. Khrushchev visits the United States and meets President Eisenhower at Camp David.

Sept. 30. Khrushchev attends the tenth-anniversary celebrations of the Chinese People's Republic.

1960

May 1. An American U-2 spy plane is shot down in the Sverdlovsk region of the U.S.S.R.

June. Chinese-Soviet dispute in Peking, at the congress of the World Federation of Trade Unions, and in Bucharest, on the fringes of the fifth congress of the Rumanian CP.

July. The U.S.S.R. recalls her technicians from China and cancels all commercial contracts with the latter.

Nov. Moscow conference of eighty-one Communist parties from all over the world. It ends with a compromise resolution.

1961

Apr. 17. American bid to overthrow regime of Fidel Castro in Cuba; Bay of Pigs defeat.

Oct. 17–31. During the twenty-second congress of the CP of the U.S.S.R. Chou En-lai ostentatiously leaves the room as a protest against Khrushchev's attacks on Albania.

1962

Oct. New Russo-American trial of strength in the Caribbean. The U.S.S.R. agrees to withdraw the rockets she had installed in Cuba. Peking accuses Moscow of following a policy "both adventurist and capitulationist."

Oct. 20. Skirmishes on the Chinese-Indian frontier take on the aspect of a minor war. The Chinese drive back the Indian troops, then withdraw, returning their prisoners and even their war material to the Indians.

1963

June 14. The CCP publishes its proposals concerning the general line of the international Communist movement, set out in twenty-five points.

July 5–20. The meeting of the Russian and Chinese parties in Moscow produces no results.

1964

Feb. 7. The Central Committee of the Soviet CP approves the anti-Chinese report by Suslov and proposes the convening of a new international Communist conference. China refuses to take part, as well as most Asian CP's.

Apr. 23. The Central Committee of the Italian CP also declares against the idea of a conference.

July 30. Khrushchev convokes for December 15, 1964, a meeting of twenty-six parties, charged with the task of preparing a world conference of CP's.

Aug. 21.   Palmiro Togliatti dies at Yalta and leaves his "memorandum to Khrushchev," which is highly critical of Soviet policy.

Oct. 14–15.   The Central Committee of the Soviet CP removes Khrushchev from office and appoints Brezhnev Secretary-General of the Party and Kosygin Chairman of the Council of Ministers (Prime Minister).

Oct. 16.   China explodes her first atomic bomb.

Nov. 6.   Chou En-lai arrives in Moscow for the forty-seventh anniversary of the October Revolution.

1965

Feb. 7.   The Americans begin systematically to bomb North Vietnam coinciding with Kosygin's visit to Hanoi.

Feb. 10.   The meeting between Mao Tse-tung and Kosygin in Peking ends without any agreement on joint Chinese-Soviet aid for North Vietnam.

Mar. 1–5.   Nineteen parties instead of the envisaged twenty-six meet in Moscow, despite the opposition of the Chinese CP. Although no decision is taken in Moscow on the hypothetical world conference of Communist parties, Peking launches a great campaign against the "secessionism of the modern revisionists."

May 14.   Explosion of China's second atomic bomb announced.

Oct. 1.   Military *coup d'état* in Djakarta and massacre of Indonesian Communists.

1966

China begins her third Five-Year Plan, but does not reveal its objectives.

Apr.   Start of "cultural revolution" in China. Mayor of Peking, P'eng Chen, dismissed and several cultural officials, including Chou Yang, removed from office.

May 10.   Explosion of China's third nuclear bomb.

APPENDIX B

The Institutions and Leaders of the
People's Republic of China

By virtue of the Constitution adopted on September 20, 1954, the National People's Congress is "trustee of the sovereignty of the Chinese people." Members of this congress are elected by universal suffrage (eighteen being the minimum voting age) for a period of four years.

The Congress appoints the Chairman of the Republic and his two Vice-Chairmen. The first chairman thus elected was Mao Tse-tung, but in December, 1958, he asked to be freed from this responsibility in order to be able to devote more time to his theoretical work. On April 27, 1959, the National People's Congress elected, and on December 30, 1964, re-elected, Liu Shao-ch'i Chairman of the People's Republic of China.

The two Vice-Chairmen are: Tung Pi-wu (born 1886), one of the founders of the CCP, and Madame Soong Ch'ing-ling (born 1890), widow of Dr. Sun Yat-sen. The Chairman and Vice-Chairmen are elected for the same period as members of the Congress, four years. The next elections are due to take place in 1968.

The National People's Congress, composed of 1,226 members, meets for a few weeks only once a year, except in case of emergency. During this session it appoints the Premier and examines the administration of his government. Since 1949 the Premier has always been the same: Chou En-lai (born 1896). His government, known as the State Council, consists of sixteen vice-premiers and thirty ministers.

Most of the vice-premiers are responsible for the most important ministries. For example:

Lin Piao (born 1907) is Vice-Premier and Minister of National Defense.

Ch'en Yi (born 1901) is Vice-Premier and Minister of Foreign Affairs.

Li Hsien-nien (born 1905) is Vice-Premier and Minister of Finance.

Po I-po (born 1907) is Vice-Premier and Chairman of the State Economic Commission.

In the absence of Chou En-lai, the Acting Premier is usually Teng Hsiao-p'ing (born 1904), who is a Vice-Premier without portfolio and also Secretary-General of the Party.

440

The National People's Congress delegates its powers between sessions to a limited committee responsible for supervising the activities of the government and expressing the views of the Congress on everything within its competence. This Standing Committee of the National People's Congress is presided over by Marshal Chu Teh (born 1886), aided by eighteen vice-chairmen (including Kuo Mo-jo and several non-Communist personalities). It is composed of about sixty-five members. Its titular Secretary-General is P'eng Chen (born 1899), who is now in disgrace and rumored to be under arrest.

Two other institutions are provided for by the Constitution, the National Defense Council and the People's Political Consultative Conference, but their functions are not very clearly defined.

The National Defense Council is presided over by the Chairman of the Republic and is composed of about a hundred members of the armed forces, including several former Kuomintang generals who rallied to the Communist regime. It is permissible to think, therefore, that the main decisions relating to national defense are taken by the Military Committee of the CP, presided over by Mao Tse-tung or Defense Minister Lin Piao, assisted by the army general staff.

The People's Political Consultative Conference is not elected and it embodies the "National Front." Most of its members are non-Communist personalities.

In addition, the Chairman of the Republic is empowered to convene periodically a Supreme State Conference in which all the members of the highest bodies previously referred to take part. It was at such a Supreme State Conference that Mao Tse-tung made his famous "hundred flowers" speech on February 27, 1957. The Constitution does not lay down, however, how often the Supreme State Conference must meet.

China consists of twenty-two provinces, five autonomous regions (Inner Mongolia, Sinkiang-Uighur, Tibet, Kwangsi-Chuang, and Ningsia-Hui) and two cities invested with a special status, Peking and Shanghai. Each administrative area has its own provincial congress or its municipal council, elected by universal suffrage for a period of four years (or occasionally only two years), which appoints and supervises the executive bodies. The provincial administration functions in principle according to the same rules as the national administration.

Elections are therefore frequent in China and they are the occasion of innumerable meetings, processions, and other popular demonstrations. But the Chinese electoral system is comparable to that of the U.S.S.R.: the electors are required to vote for a single list, drawn up by the Communist Party, although a certain number of the candidates on it either have no party or belong to minority parties (such as the Revolutionary Kuomintang or the Democratic League).

But the ties between the administration and the CP are even closer than in Russia. In China the mayor of a big city or the governor of a province is almost always the Party secretary for the city or province, while in the Soviet Union these two functions are considered incompatible. For example, Marshal Ch'en Yi was for a long time Mayor of Shanghai and secretary of the Party for the city. He relinquished his post to K'o Ch'ing-shih (died 1965), who also assumed both titles. In Peking, P'eng Chen was Mayor and secretary of the CP at the same time until, in May, 1966, he was relieved of the latter appointment. It is not known if he remains Mayor.

The real power is therefore wielded by the CP even more directly than in the other Communist countries. The title that really counts in China is a Party title.

The CCP is similar in structure to the other parties of this type, based on the principle of "democratic centralism." The Party Congress represents the supreme example of this. The Congress elects the Central Committee (composed of ninety-six members and ninety-four alternate members), which in turn appoints the Politburo (composed of eighteen members and seven alternate members). In fact the CCP rarely holds a congress (between the sixth and seventh congresses there was a gap of seventeen years, between the seventh and eighth—held in 1956—a gap of eleven years; and the ninth congress has not yet been announced). Real power belongs to the Politburo, backed by the Central Committee.

The Politburo is headed by a Standing Committee of seven members who are now the seven top leaders of China. They are:

Mao Tse-tung	Chairman of the Chinese Communist Party
Liu Shao-ch'i	
Chou En-lai	
Chu Teh	Vice-Chairmen of the Party
Ch'en Yün	
Lin Piao	
Teng Hsiao-p'ing	Secretary-General

Other members of the Politburo are: Tung Pi-wu, Liu Po-ch'eng, P'eng Chen, Ho Lung, Li Hsien-nien, Ch'en Yi, Li Fu-ch'un, T'an Chen-lin, Po I-po, P'eng Teh-huai, Li Ching-chüan.

Alternate members are: Ch'en Po-ta, Ulanfu, K'ang Sheng, Teng Tzu-hui.

This list is no doubt susceptible to change, for the Central Committee has published no communiqué indicating the replacement of members who have died, such as Lo Jung-huan and K'o Ch'ing-shih, or those who have been dismissed. For example, Marshal P'eng Teh-huai has been relieved of his post as Defense Minister since 1959 and K'ang Sheng has been promoted and is now a member of the Standing Committee of Politburo.

After the session of the Central Committee in August, 1966, the Communist leaders appeared in public in the following order: Mao Tse-tung, Lin Piao, Chou En-lai, Tao Chu (who replaced Lu Ting-i as Minister of Culture), Ch'en Po-ta, K'ang-sheng, Li Fu-Ch'un, Liu Shao-ch'i, Teng Hsia-p'ing, Ch'en Yün. Although no official communiqué on the reorganization was published, this new order of precedence no doubt corresponded to the change in the hierarchy.

APPENDIX C

NAME	SIZE	POPULATION	BRI-GADES
Chi Tsi Tchin ("Green All Year") Near Peking Founded August, 1958	2,660 hectares^2	36,000 (8,100 families)	12
"October" Near Nanking Founded September 1, 1958	723 hectares	10,546 (1,857 families)	7
Huang Tu 15 miles from Shanghai Founded September, 1958	2,116 hectares	19,650 (3,942 families)	16
Lon Chan ("Dragon Spring") Near Kunming	1,200 hectares	22,000 (5,123 families)	20
Lin Kuo-po ("Gateway to the Forest") Near Kunming Sanyis national minority	300 hectares	1,556 (359 families)	7
Shao-shan (Mao's birthplace) Near Changsha Founded August, 1958	800 hectares cultivated	10,720 (2,412 families)	11
Ma Tchi-tse Near Sian Founded August, 1958	1,660 hectares	9,865 (1,700 families)	19
State Farm 6 miles from Nanning Founded in 1952	5,320 hectares (2,000 culti-vated—25% rice, 25% pineapples)	2,210 Workers and cadre members	

[1] 1964 figures.
[2] hectare: 2.47 acres.

444

Some Facts[1] About Communes Visited by the Author

TEAMS	EQUIPMENT	PRODUCTION	ANNUAL INCOME PER HEAD
125	19 tractors, 41 electrified wells, 498 electric sprinklers, 10 semi-mechanized tools, 6 miles of irrigation canals	115,000 metric tons of vegetables 2,430 metric tons of fruit, wheat	600 yuan
89	8 tractors, 8 reservoirs, glassworks, cement works	5,250 kilograms of wheat per hectare	200–220 yuan
134	5 tractors, 2 trucks, 3 boats, 13 irrigation stations, 62 pumps	6,705 kilograms of rice per hectare	500 yuan
192	15 tractors, 1 truck, some planting machines, livestock	rice	196 yuan
17	livestock	corn, rice, sweet potatoes, sunflowers	50 yuan plus rice
137	2 tractors, 91 diesel pumps, 19 electric pumps	4,750 kilograms of rice per hectare	160 yuan
70	55 miles of canals, 3 hydraulic stations, 51 ploughs	3,000 kilograms of wheat per hectare, vegetables, fruit 2,00 kilograms of rice per hectare 2,000 metric tons of pineapples	420 yuan

			yuan
		director:	1,152
		CP sec.:	1,320
		agri-culturist:	900
		Workers:	324–540 plus bonus

APPENDIX D

Wages in Chinese Industry

In Chinese industry the wage variation is not wide. The relationship of the highest pay to the lowest is in the proportion of three to one. In enterprises in the same sector and under the same ministry there can be slight differences. Here, by way of example, are the monthly wage scales in three heavy machine tool factories we visited.

	Wuhan	*Kunming*	*Shenyang*
Minimum Pay	32.5 yuan	30 yuan	37.5 yuan
Average Pay	50 "	52 "	74 "
Maximum Pay	104 "	104 "	112 "

In Shanghai, maximum monthly pay at the diesel engine factory: 123 yuan; at the Wou-chin chemical fertilizer factory, maximum pay: 128 yuan; at radio factory number four, maximum pay: 123 yuan. But in clothing factory number two in the same city the maximum pay was only 78 yuan (double the minimum pay of 39 yuan), and in the textile printing factory in Sian the maximum pay was only 80 yuan.

All the factory managers we met earned more than the highest-paid workers, but their salaries were not always identical. Here are a few examples:

Mr. Tchin, manager of Wou-chin fertilizer factory (Shanghai) 181 yuan
Mr. Liu, manager of radio factory number four (Shanghai)   128   "
Mr. Fan, manager of heavy machine tool factory (Kunming)   165   "
Mr. Chen, manager of optical instrument factory (Shanghai)   140   "
Mr. Yan, manager of light truck factory (Shanghai)   154   "
Mr. Kang, manager of boiler factory (Harbin)   190   "

Technicians are grouped in twenty-four categories and are paid accordingly. A beginning engineer receives a lower salary than the worker's average wage, but the chief engineer of a factory gets more than the manager. Three times we met chief engineers who earned more than 200 yuan a month. Mr. Tsou Pei-chin of the Ming Hang factory in Shanghai earned 210 yuan. The chief engineer of the Harbin boiler factory earned 205 yuan, as did the chief engineer of the machine tool factory at Kunming.

Factory apprenticeship lasts three years, and what the apprentice earns is more a grant than a salary: eighteen to twenty yuan a month

—about the amount a student gets. There are an enormous number of apprentices, and if one adds to these the students, who do a stint of at least one month a year in the factories, the total adds up to a very large but low-paid labor force.

Women receive the same pay as men for the same work. In the case of pregnancy they work reduced hours for seventy days and receive fifty-six days' leave upon the birth of their child. The family allowance is four yuan a month for the first child, eight for the second, but only two for the third (to check the birth rate). Retirement age is fifty-five for women and sixty for men. Maximum pension is 70 per cent of pay, and only 50 per cent if the worker has less than fifteen years' service— which, in view of the "youth" of Chinese industry, is most often the case.

APPENDIX E

Interview with Chou En-lai

It was 10 P.M. last Tuesday when Marc Riboud, the photographer, and I entered a large salon in the Palace of the People in Peking. There we found Chou En-lai, the Prime Minister, Mrs. K'ung Peng, the Assistant Minister of Foreign Affairs, and Mr. Chin, the Information Director. Despite the hour, Chou appeared relaxed and unhurried. Confident in his charm and his ability to handle questions of any kind, he quickly turned our interview into a discussion with no holds barred. I spoke English, which Chou knows well enough to get the drift of my questions; occasionally he replied directly in English.

After a few words about our earlier meeting in Algiers in December, 1963, we plunged straight into the Vietnam problem and the possibility of a new peace conference at Geneva. I pointed out that Mr. Gromyko's visit to London gave Britain and the Soviet Union, as cochairmen, the opportunity to summon a new conference.

"It is true," replied Chou, "that Britain and the Soviet Union are cochairmen of the Geneva Conference. If they wish to do their duty, they should first of all oblige the United States to cease its violations of the 1954 Geneva Agreements. This is also the view of the South Vietnamese National Liberation Front. They demand that the U.S. withdraw all her armed forces and military installations from South Vietnam, and so allow the South Vietnamese people to settle their problems themselves. The Democratic Republic of Vietnam has made the same demand. As one of the guarantors of the Geneva Agreements, the government of the Chinese People's Republic backs this joint demand of the N.L.F. and the D.R.V. without reserve. The U.S. is in the process of extending its aggression. It is sending marines to South Vietnam and in a single month it has bombed the D.R.V. six times. But the American government will never force the South Vietnamese people and the D.R.V. into talks by intensifying the war."

Was the American object in stepping up their operations, I asked, to save face before beginning the negotiations they really wanted? "Saving face?" asked Chou, half astonished, half indignant. "A brigand who has committed an armed robbery—can he save face by committing

---

This interview was originally printed in the *New Statesman* (London), March 26, 1965.

a second or a third? How many crimes are required before America's face is, as you put it, saved? In my view, the best way this bandit can save his face is by giving back the property he has stolen. The best way the Americans can save face is by withdrawing their forces from South Vietnam and by renouncing the right they claim to carry the war into the north."

But in the meantime, I remarked, the D.R.V. suffers from these raids, against which she can't defend herself alone. "In the first place," said Chou, "she can defend herself. Next, the American aggression against the D.R.V. is an aggression against the socialist camp in its entirety. This being so, all of us have the duty to help the N.L.F. of South Vietnam and the D.R.V., in accordance with the international engagements we have undertaken. We cannot look at the question in any other way. The menace of the U.S. concerns not only the D.R.V. and the other countries of Indochina, Laos and Cambodia, but also the Chinese People's Republic. Our position is perfectly clear. You have certainly read the declaration our government made on March 12, which needs no further explanation. Let the Americans act as seems good to them, and we will act as we mean to act. In any case, the war will develop not in accordance with human wishes, still less the wishes of American imperialism."

For the second time I tried to put the case for negotiations, by reminding Chou that in both Indochina and Algeria France had intensified her military efforts during the periods immediately preceding the peace talks. But Chou rejected this comparison. "France has learned the lessons of the colonial wars," he said. "She knows that they can't be won. That is why, each time I meet my French friends, I ask them: 'Why can't you persuade your American allies to learn from your experience?' and each time I speak to my American friends I ask: 'Why aren't you capable of producing a de Gaulle?'"

In order to broach the subject of Sino-Soviet relations, I said to Chou that many European commentators believed that America's recent actions in Southeast Asia would draw Russia and China together. But in fact the opposite seemed to have happened. Chou replied: "To talk of drawing nearer or farther apart is only a way of putting it. More important is to look at the roots of the question. If the Americans confine themselves to frightening people, some will allow themselves to be frightened, others not. This will produce disagreement, very great disagreement, between the first group, who fear imperialism, and the others, who are determined to stand up to it. But if the Americans are not content with threatening gestures and really want to provoke a wider conflict, then the Chinese and Russian people will close ranks. That is the truth. Remember that and you will see that history will bear it out. That is why Johnson, who is dancing on the tightrope of war, and doesn't know how to turn about, is risking some surprises." Chou emphasized the last phrase to such a degree that it seemed to me pointless to ask him exactly what he meant by it.

Chou agreed that the disputes within the Communist movement were not confined to international policies, and I asked him how they could be resolved, since China refused to attend international Communist meetings, such as the March 1 conference in Moscow. He replied calmly: "We have repeatedly said that conditions were not yet ripe for summoning a conference, and that therefore we must not rush things. If we do, the result will be the opposite to what we hope for. It is therefore better to organize bilateral or multilateral talks instead of such a meeting. It doesn't matter if we can't all meet together for the moment. In any case, an international conference will not necessarily play a decisive role. When Khrushchev was in power, two such conferences took place. President Mao Tse-tung himself took part in the first, at Moscow in 1957, and Chairman Liu Shao-ch'i in the second in 1960. The declarations published at the end of these two conferences were not at all bad. They included a great number of revolutionary principles. But this did not prevent Khrushchev from going on in his old way and treating the declarations with contempt. The peoples of the world who want to carry through the revolution will do so without any need for international conferences."

THE SINO-SOVIET SPLIT

"However," said Chou, "let us get back to the March 1 conference. This is exactly the same meeting summoned on July 30, 1964, by Khrushchev for December 15, 1964, which was simply postponed until a late date. It is the same meeting of secessionists. We put our hopes in the new Soviet leaders, after they came to power. I myself went to Moscow last year for the anniversary of the October Revolution, on our own initiative. The Chinese Party sent a delegation and proposed that other socialist countries should do the same. I advised the Soviet leaders not to hold the December 15 meeting, on the grounds that this would be a gathering of secessionists. Khrushchev having fallen, wouldn't it be a simple matter for them to cancel it? But here the question of saving face, as you put it, arose: they were determined to harvest the legacy of Khrushchev and they therefore had their March 1 meeting." Chou then cited several examples to show that the meeting did harm to the Communist movement, dwelling particularly on the case of the Indian Communist Party and its pro-Soviet leader Dange. "Dange is a renegade," he said. "The Indian people have no confidence in him. The Indian Communists have denounced him. Most of the leaders have left his party. A great number of these Indian revolutionary Communists have now been imprisoned by the Indian government, while Dange himself has become its favorite. The results of the Kerala elections are, nonetheless, very instructive. Of Dange's eighty candidates, only two were elected. But of the seventy-odd candidates put up by the Revolutionary Communist Party, forty-three were elected. Most of them are at the moment in prison.

This is an exceptional phenomenon in the history of the Indian workers' movement. Yet the Soviet Party insisted on inviting Dange to the March 1 meeting. Who then is sabotaging the workers' movement?" Chou evidently regards the March 1 meeting as of great importance, with grave consequences for the Communist bloc.

THE AFRO-ASIAN WORLD

No doubt Chou had a good deal more to say on this point, but I was anxious to widen our discussion and remarked that I had been struck, during my visit to China, by the extent to which the problems of Asia, Africa, and Latin America were given absolute priority by China. "Don't you feel," I asked, "that socialism in Europe is at least as important as, for example, socialism in Mali—without wishing to underrate the importance of this country?"

Chou replied: "You are confusing two different problems. If the working class in Europe succeeds in carrying through its revolution, this would naturally be very important. If the revolution succeeded in the U.S., this would be even more important—of world importance. This was what Marx and Engels dreamed of. Being Marxist Leninists, I have no need to tell you that we attach the greatest weight to the diffusion of revolutionary ideas within the workers' movement. But which are the first regions to experience a revolutionary situation? Because a revolutionary situation must exist before the revolution can break out. Objectively, a revolutionary situation is produced above all in the backward regions. Marx and Engels did not foresee that the proletarian revolution would triumph in backward Russia. Lenin took a different view. From his experience, he calculated that in all probability the revolution would break out first in the backward East. Hence, although the workers' movement in Europe and North America is very important, an objective revolutionary situation does not yet exist in these continents. While in Asia, Africa, and Latin America, especially Asia and Africa, there are regions where an objective revolutionary situation exists, due to the frenzied oppression of imperialism and the troubles which it creates everywhere. This state of things will certainly hasten still more the advent of further revolutions. This is why such regions must secure our main attention. But this does not mean to say that we underestimate the role of the workers' movement in Europe."

After finishing this phrase Mr. Chou En-lai looked discreetly at his watch, indicating no doubt that we could not resolve the problems of Europe that evening. I was even afraid that his gesture meant that the interview was over, although we had not touched on any internal Chinese problem. So, without waiting, I tried to frame in general terms a question often debated in Europe: Does China use Stalinist methods? "You often speak," I said, "of the continuation if not the intensification of the class war in China. But wasn't it Stalin who later formulated a similar theory to justify massive repressive acts in the Soviet Union?"

"Stalin's appraisals of the Russian internal situation were often varied," replied Chou En-lai, pushing aside this question. But he did not refuse to discuss Chinese views in this field: "The Chinese revolution did not make the social classes disappear with a wave of the magic wand. They always exist and where there are classes the class struggle continues. We have taken the means of exploitation from those who used their property to exploit, but we haven't physically liquidated them or deported them to distant virgin lands. Former landlords and rich peasants, who represent about 7 per cent of the population, are still in their villages and work like the rest. Now, fifteen years after, a certain number of them have been re-educated and have become workers. But there are still a good number who, clinging to their belief in exploitation, are still motivated by hostile feelings. The situation is a little different in the case of the bourgeoisie, who number about a million. Dissatisfied with Chiang Kai-shek, the middle classes took part in the revolution or demonstrated their sympathy for it by not opposing it. After the liberation, elements of the middle classes enjoyed full civil rights. In the socialist phase the government's policy with regard to the latter was to take over their factories, paying them an annual interest of 5 per cent. It is a fact, therefore, that former landowners and middle-class elements exist. The influence of the practices of the old society remains alive enough. Even among those who have done well in the new society there are some who submit to this influence and take part in illegal speculation. It is this which gives birth to new middle-class elements. Marxists must not ignore these facts if they do not want such people to commit sabotage and corrupt others. There are also outside enemies who try to create trouble. American imperialism and its lackey, Chiang Kai-shek, send large numbers of their agents here. For all these reasons we remember ceaselessly that the classes and the class struggle continue to exist and we alert the people to revolutionary vigilance.

"The exploiters, when they were able to defend their privileges with arms, did not hesitate to use even the most extreme methods against us. Now that the power is in our hands we rely above all on education. We tell our ex-exploiters that they can be re-educated if they want to serve the motherland. This is how we apply our policy: in the case of sabotage we resort as little as possible to imprisonment and even less to capital punishment. Repressive measures are only used in the case of grave breaches of the law, when the life of others is involved."

REFORMING THE U.N.

When the interpreter finished translating this long passage it was no longer necessary to look at our watches to know that it was time to end the conversation—it was already after midnight. I put my last question: "What do you think of General de Gaulle's proposal that the five great powers should meet to discuss the reform of the United Nations?"

"But China has nothing to do with the U.N.," replied Chou En-lai. "It is true that China is not at all interested in the U.N. For fifteen years this organization, manipulated by the U.S., frustrated China's legitimate rights. Why cannot China envisage entering it at all? Why cannot one envisage founding another U.N. that might be revolutionary? That is what I said recently in Peking at a banquet for Mr. Subandrio, Indonesia's foreign minister. Elsewhere China has put forward a positive formula—that is, that the U.N. rectify its mistakes and submit to a radical reorganization. This proposal was supported by numerous Asian and African countries."

In his statement, Chou added, General de Gaulle also criticized the misdeeds of the U.N. under American control. That was a good thing. "Is it the moment to convene a meeting of the five great powers?" he said. "In my opinion this is not the moment. How could it be managed—particularly with the U.S.? The talks between the Chinese and American ambassadors have been going on for ten years. They have already met 125 times in Warsaw. Do you know what they are talking about? You don't know?" he asked, very amused. "Our ambassador proposed an agreement on principle on two points to the American ambassador. First of all, on peaceful co-existence. Revisionists pretend that China is opposed to peaceful co-existence, the U.S. repeats this loudly and the Indian government echoes it. Yet we have been proposing peaceful co-existence to the Americans for ten years. But obviously peaceful co-existence must be based on certain principles and there is no question of establishing it without principle. To ask China to co-exist peacefully with the U.S. while the latter maintains military bases around China and occupies the Chinese territory of Formosa—that is impossible."

Obviously caught up in his subject, Mr. Chou En-lai continued spontaneously: "China is ready to practice peaceful co-existence according to the five principles with all countries. Let us take France as an example. General de Gaulle is a bourgeois statesman and his ideas are very different from ours. Between China and France there is neither a dispute nor a direct conflict of interest at the moment. Certainly China sympathizes with the French working-class movement, but if the two countries accept reciprocal noninterference in each other's internal affairs—as is the actual case—they will be able to co-exist peacefully very well and even co-operate in many fields."

It was on this relaxed and optimistic note that our conversation ended. True to the great Chinese tradition of courtesy, Mr. Chou En-lai accompanied us to our car. It was exactly half an hour past midnight. The interview had lasted two and a half hours.

APPENDIX F

Interview with Marshal Ch'en Yi

It is easy everywhere in China to confirm the existence of a strong anti-American feeling and a deep distrust of the Soviet Union. It is much more difficult to find out how China sees the outcome of the war in Vietnam or why she is stepping up the controversy with Moscow. That is why I put several direct questions to the Vice-Premier, Marshal Ch'en Yi. His written replies constitute a record of thoughts and views on Chinese foreign policy that do not require a commentary.

Do you believe that the National Liberation Front can by its military action force the United States to withdraw her troops from Vietnam? If not, how would you envisage negotiations that would bring about this result?

Ch'en Yi: "I think that the Vietnamese people are perfectly capable, with their own forces, of driving the American aggressors from their territory. The war that they are now conducting is a just war, a war against aggression and in defense of their mother country, a people's war. It is precisely for this reason that American imperialism is exhausting itself in its war of aggression against Vietnam while the Vietnamese people are developing a growing power as a result of their struggle. Four fifths of the territory of the 10 million South Vietnamese people is already liberated. American imperialism is fighting furiously. However, the heroic Vietnamese people are determined to drive out the American aggressors and are ready to fight until the next generation if necessary. The power of the people is inexhaustible. I am firmly convinced that the United States will not be able to escape their fate, that is to say their final defeat, whatever their maneuvers. The negotiations you have just spoken of are tied to your supposition that the Vietnamese people would not be strong enough to resist their aggressors, yet today such a belief is without basis. In our opinion the present situation is extremely favorable to the Vietnamese people and extremely unfavorable to American imperialism. Victory will go to the Vietnamese people and not to American imperialism, engaged as it is in 'escalation.' Now it is American imperialism and its lackeys which need negotiations to get their breath back and withdraw from the

---

This interview was originally printed in the *New Statesman* (London), May 28, 1965.

deadlock, and not the Vietnamese people. To look at it as a whole, we are by no means against talks. But, like the Vietnamese people, we are resolutely against the 'unconditional negotiations' of the Johnson administration and the trickery which it has embarked on under cover of negotiating peace.

"We firmly support the conditions drawn up by the government of the Democratic Republic of Vietnam and the National Liberation Front of South Vietnam: the Geneva Agreements of 1954 must be revived, the United States must withdraw her troops from South Vietnam, the National Liberation Front of South Vietnam is the only legal representative of the South Vietnamese people, the internal affairs of South Vietnam must be controlled by the South Vietnamese people, and the peaceful reunification of Vietnam is exclusively the affair of the Vietnamese people.

"What the United States understands by 'unconditional negotiations' means in reality that the American troops obstinately refuse to leave South Vietnam, that the United States persists in not recognizing the National Liberation Front as the sole legal representative of the Vietnamese people, that she wishes to repudiate from top to bottom the Geneva Agreements of 1954 and the reunification of Vietnam, transforming South Vietnam into a puppet state under American control. In other words, they want to continue their aggression against Vietnam to their last breath. The peace talks concocted by them are aimed solely at gaining at the conference table what they have not been able to get on the battlefield. It is obvious that such peace negotiations would profit only the aggressor. Certain well-meaning friends want to see a quick end to the Vietnam war and sanction peace talks. This wish is perfectly understandable, but all the same I would like to put them on their guard. If peace talks were not opened on the basis of conditions drawn up by the government of the Democratic Republic of Vietnam and the National Liberation Front of South Vietnam, they would not solve any problem and would serve only to prolong the suffering which the South Vietnamese people endure under American imperialism and impose heavier sacrifices on them."

Do you not think that your dispute with the Soviet Union diverts world opinion from the Vietnamese problem and thus plays a negative role?

Ch'en Yi: "That is not my opinion. You can see the obvious opposition of world opinion to American imperialism's aggression against Vietnam and that which it has recently committed against the Dominican Republic. It is true that certain elements, for unrevealed motives, try to create confusion among the ill informed. That is not because of the controversy you speak about. The controversy itself embraces above all a series of important questions of principle, one of which is to know if one can or cannot resolutely combat American imperialism and firmly support the armed struggle of the peoples of oppressed nations. This controversy helps the peoples of the world to distinguish the true from the false, to draw a sharp distinction between the real anti-imperialistic struggle and the counterfeit anti-imperialistic struggle, between real support and counterfeit support. It contributes to the struggle of the peoples of the world against American aggression and allows them to see through the political plots of the United States. Consequently, it is not negative but positive. It contributes in large measure to the mobilization of peoples everywhere so that they are even more firmly on the side of the Vietnamese people and fight against the aggression of American imperialism."

In the event of the stepping-up of the Vietnam war, do you envisage the possibility of common and concerted action with the Soviet Union to help the N.L.F. and the Democratic Republic of Vietnam?

Ch'en Yi: "The Vietnamese people are engaged in a just war against American imperialist aggression. Even before any stepping-up of the war all socialist countries ought to unite firmly and support the Vietnamese people with all their strength. If not, they would no longer be socialist countries. All common and concerted action must be founded on a common understanding of the aggressors and on the common determination to combat them. If this basis were laid, common action would be possible. Otherwise it would be impossible."

The Chinese government has repeatedly said that it is ready to co-exist with all other countries that accept the five principles set out by Premier Chou En-lai in 1954. But the Chinese Communist Party has promised unconditional support for all the revolutionary movements of the world. Do you not think that one day there could be a conflict between these two positions?

Ch'en Yi: "The general line of China's foreign policy has three aspects: to develop, on the principle of proletarian internationalism, relations of friendship, of mutual aid and co-operation between the countries of the socialist camp, to struggle for peaceful co-existence between countries of different social systems on the basis of the five principles and against political aggression and imperialist war, and to support the revolutionary struggle of all oppressed peoples. Far from being contradictory, these three aspects are linked to each other. Over the fifteen years since the foundation of the Chinese People's Republic, the Chinese government has established friendly relations and developed economic and cultural exchanges with a great number of countries with different social systems but all of which conform to the five principles of peaceful co-existence.

"These relations have never been in conflict with our position of support for the revolutionary struggle of the peoples of the world. They will be no more so in the future, because our policy of peaceful co-existence is founded on principles indissolubly linked with the struggle against the policy of aggression and imperialist war. Intervention and aggression are in the nature of imperialism. We shall never stop supporting the revolutionary struggle of oppressed peoples and nations to oblige imperialism. On the contrary, we shall consider that only firm support for this struggle and resolute opposition to the imperialist policy of aggression and war can keep the latter in check."

Index

458 INDEX

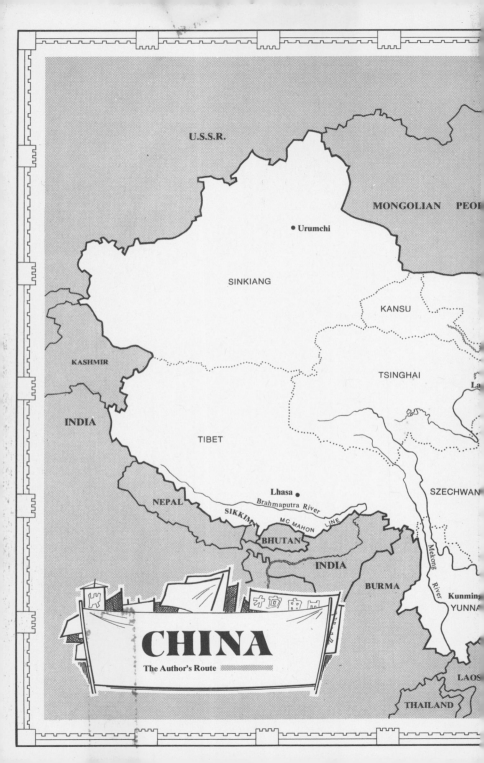

U.S.S.R.

MONGOLIAN PEOP

• Urumchi

SINKIANG

KANSU

KASHMIR

TSINGHAI

La

INDIA

TIBET

Lhasa •

NEPAL

Brahmaputra River

SIKKIM

SZECHWAN

MC MAHON   LINE

BHUTAN

INDIA

Mekong River

BURMA

Kunmin

YUNNA

CHINA

The Author's Route

LAOS

THAILAND